STONE HOUSES AND EARTH LORDS

MESOAMERICAN WORLDS

From the Olmecs to the Danzantes

GENERAL EDITORS: DAVÍD CARRASCO AND EDUARDO MATOS MOCTEZUMA

Ancient Tollan: Tula and the Toltec Heartland,
Alba Guadalupe Mastache, Robert H. Cobean, and Dan M. Healan

Eating Landscape: Aztec and European Occupation of Tlalocan,
Philip P. Arnold

Empires of Time: Calendars, Clocks, and Cultures, Revised Edition,
Anthony Aveni

In the Realm of Nachan Kan: Postclassic Maya Archaeology at Laguna de On, Belize,
Marilyn A. Masson

Life and Death in the Templo Mayor,
Eduardo Matos Moctezuma

The Madrid Codex: New Approaches to Understanding an Ancient Maya Manuscript,
Gabrielle Vail and Anthony Aveni, editors

Mesoamerica's Classic Heritage: Teotihuacan to the Aztecs,
Davíd Carrasco, Lindsay Jones, and Scott Sessions

Mockeries and Metamorphoses of an Aztec God: Tezcatlipoca, "Lord of the Smoking Mirror,"
Guilhem Olivier, translated by Michel Besson

Representing Aztec Ritual: Performance, Text, and Image in the Work of Sahagún,
Eloise Quiñones Keber, editor

Stone Houses and Earth Lords: Maya Religion in the Cave Context,
Keith M. Prufer and James E. Brady, editors

Tamoanchan, Tlalocan: Places of Mist,
Alfredo López Austin

Thunder Doesn't Live Here Anymore: Self-Deprecation and the Theory of Otherness Among the Teenek Indians of Mexico,
Anath Ariel de Vidas

Topiltzin Quetzalcoatl: The Once and Future Lord of the Toltecs,
H. B. Nicholson

The World Below: Body and Cosmos in Otomi Indian Ritual,
Jacques Galinier

STONE HOUSES AND EARTH LORDS

MAYA RELIGION IN THE CAVE CONTEXT

EDITED BY KEITH M. PRUFER AND JAMES E. BRADY

UNIVERSITY PRESS OF COLORADO

Published by the University Press of Colorado
245 Century Circle, Suite 202
Louisville, Colorado 80027

First paperback edition 2021
Printed in the United States of America

ASSOCIATION of UNIVERSITY PRESSES The University Press of Colorado is a proud member of the Association of University Presses.

The University Press of Colorado is a cooperative publishing enterprise supported, in part, by Adams State University, Colorado State University, Fort Lewis College, Metropolitan State University of Denver, Regis University, University of Colorado, University of Northern Colorado, University of Wyoming, Utah State University, and Western Colorado University.

∞ This paper meets the requirements of the ANSI/NISO Z39.48–1992 (Permanence of Paper).

Library of Congress Cataloging-in-Publication Data

Stone houses and earth lords : Maya religion in the cave context / edited by Keith M. Prufer and James E. Brady.
p. cm. — (Mesoamerican worlds)
Includes bibliographical references and index.
ISBN 0-87081-808-2 (hardcover : alk. paper) — ISBN 978-1-64642-185-5 (pbk. : alk. paper) — ISBN 978-1-64642-186-2 (ebook)
1. Mayas—Religion. 2. Maya cosmology. 3. Mayas—Anthropometry. 4. Caves—Religious aspects—Mexico. 5. Caves—Religious aspects—Belize. 6. Sacred space—Mexico. 7. Sacred space—Belize. 8. Human remains (Archaeology)—Mexico. 9. Human remains (Archaeology)—Belize. 10. Mexico Antiquities. 11. Belize—Antiquities. I. Prufer, Keith M. (Keith Malcolm), 1960– II. Brady, James Edward, 1948– III. Series.
F1435.3.R3S76 2005
972.81'016—dc22

2005019239

This book is dedicated to a group of field archaeologists whose work in the decades following World War II set the high standards for cave investigation on which this generation has built:

E. Wyllys Andrews IV
Carlos Navarrete
David Pendergast
Robert E. Smith

Contents

Illustrations

Tables

CONTRIBUTORS

Juan Luis Bonor Villarejo
James E. Brady
Robert Burnett
Allan B. Cobb
Pierre R. Colas
Cesar Espinosa
Sergio Garza
David M. Glassman
Christina T. Halperin
Amalia Kenward
Andrew Kindon
Patricia A. McAnany
Christopher T. Morehart
Holley Moyes
Vanessa A. Owen
Shankari Patel
Polly A. Peterson
Keith M. Prufer
Timothy W. Pugh
Frank P. Saul
Julie Mather Saul
Ann M. Scott
Andrea Stone
Vera Tiesler

STONE HOUSES AND EARTH LORDS

Chapter One

Introduction

by Keith M. Prufer
James E. Brady

Religion and Role of Caves in Lowland Maya Archaeology

> Archaeological practice, like that of any other science, is conditioned by the problem-interest of its practitioners.
> —William Sears (1961: 224)

This book represents the first volume dedicated exclusively to cave archaeology in the Maya Lowlands. As such it provides an indication of the exciting research currently being conducted in caves. More important, this volume demonstrates that cave research, a peripheral subject just fifteen years ago, is now a component of mainstream Maya archaeology. The idea for this book grew out of a large session held at the 2002 meetings of the Society for American Archaeology in Denver, Colorado. It has evolved since then, although the title and content reflect our original intent for that gathering: to illuminate the breadth and quality of caves studies currently being undertaken across the Maya Lowlands.

In the past decade archaeological investigations of caves have grown to become some of the most progressive in Maya studies. Concurrent with major interpretive advances in discussions of social and political organization, ceremonialism, economics, and linguistic modes of elite interaction, we now frequently see references to an underlying worldview that incorporates the physical and conceptual multilayered earth into political, social, and ideological reconstructions. Many archaeologists now recognize that Maya caves functioned as arenas for religious rituals, with all the social and political baggage that ritual implies. Since archaeological remains found in caves unequivocally represent the remains of ritualized actions of a religious nature, caves represent the single best context for the archaeological investigation of Maya religion (Brady and Prufer 2005). The mainstream acknowledgment of the importance of caves as features in the social landscape owes much to those investigators who have focused their research on subterranean spaces.

The acceptance of caves as vital arenas for religious practices is a recent development. As a result, during the period of rapid growth in Maya archaeology in the 1960s and 1970s, cave studies were not considered part of mainstream archaeology. Furthermore, the dominant theoretical position did not acknowledge that ceremonial spaces could contribute to important topical issues such as political interactions and social organization. Although the lack of investigations may be, in part, a result of the inhospitable nature of cave environments (dark, claustrophobic, and bat-filled), we are more concerned that the neglect is a direct result of their association with religious activity.

In most archaeological reporting before the 1990s caves were either not mentioned or were treated as disassociated from surface contexts, and only a few attempts were made to link caves with surface sites (e.g., Andrews 1971; Millon 1981; J.E.S. Thompson 1959). We find the general paucity of information on caves puzzling, since caves tend to be present in large numbers across the karstic landscape, and most show clear evidence of human use in the archaeological past. Because caves were ignored, archaeologists had little idea of how caves functioned in Maya society. The state of the field's thinking at that time was summed up by Norman Hammond's (1981: 177) frank admission: "Whether residence in caves was permanent, periodic or sporadic, regular or only for ritual and refuge, we do not yet know." Given this lack of clear understanding of how caves functioned, general texts on the Maya tended to avoid the topic, so the indices of books published between 1960 and 1990 rarely contain references to caves. We see this shortcoming as linked to a general distrust of contexts deemed "religious" and an outgrowth of trends in American archaeology to marginalize discussions of religion or ideology in favor of more economic or technological interpretations of sites and contexts.

ANTHROPOLOGY, PROCESSUAL ARCHAEOLOGY, AND RELIGION

Beginning in the 1960s archaeologists debated the relevance of studies not grounded in ecomaterialist or evolutionary theory (Wylie 2002: 15–18), and one of the areas of inquiry most directly affected was the study of religion. Mayanists interested in religion have, like other students of American archaeology, faced an uphill battle for recognition that the study of material culture could be reconciled with religion as a productive area of inquiry. Although not completely ignored in American archaeology, religion was often treated as a residual factor in, or by-product of, technology, the economy, or the environment in adaptive evolutionary scenarios and hence of little concern in archaeological understandings of the past. The general philosophical rejection of religion influenced the training of several generations of archaeologists to the point where we cannot think of a single dirt archaeologist working in the Maya Lowlands who specializes in the archaeology of religion.

Although the merits of the New or Processual Archaeology have been debated at length (Hodder 2002; Patterson 1989; Willey and Sabloff 1980; Wylie 2002), few have ventured to make statements regarding the status of religion in prehistory. Here, we will briefly review the history of and current thinking on the archaeology of religion while keeping in mind that contentions in the archaeological community mirrored similar debates in anthropology and the social sciences in general.

Although the stated goals of the New Archaeology were to make research more anthropological (Willey and Phillips 1958: 2), they were also part of a general trend to "harden the social sciences" (Gibbon 1989: 139–140) to bolster the credibility of social research through positivist and empirical experiments. With an emphasis on quantitative methods and "the rhetoric of logical empiricism," New Archaeologists quickly saw a means to reaffirm the credibility of their discipline as a scientific enterprise (Wylie 2002: 78). This movement in archaeology was influenced by changes in American anthropology, where general theories of cultural evolution, dominated by the writings of Leslie White and Julian Steward, became an explicit framework for the New Anthropology. In White's version of techno-economic-dominated cultural determinism all aspects of ideology (therefore, religion) were limited by the technological sphere and therefore epiphenomenal, and they were at best by-products of the more powerful forces driving directional change (White 1947, 1959). Steward's injection of the environment into his multilineal evolutionism was less reductionist, and he considered religion to be part of a "culture core" of determinist elements (Steward 1955: 37), although he clearly viewed religion as having a peripheral role in culture change. There is no doubt that White's cultural determinism and the Stewardian ecological approach produced a vocal set of followers (Harris 1964, 1969, 1979; Vayda 1976) and varying degrees of acceptance by others (Carneiro 1973; Ember and Ember 1971; Rappaport 1979; Vayda and Rappaport 1968). However, it is debatable whether American anthropology ever unified behind this, or any, field of intellectual inquiry (Asad 1979: 608; Kelly and Kaplan 1990: 120).

Religion remains an uneasy topic in social research. Anthropology (and archaeology) have been criticized for tending to treat tribal and other non-Western religions not as complete systems but as composed of atomistic "phenomena" such as myth, witchcraft, and magic while at the same time treating world religions "as discrete and distinct entities, such as 'Buddhism' or 'Islam'" (Insoll 2001: 4; also see Morris 1987: 2–3). Critics link this essentialization of religion to the discipline's conceptual roots in nineteenth-century social evolutionism, specifically Weberian distinctions between magic and religion (Giddons 1971: 214–215), but they also see problems in the application of European categories of religion to native systems (Schneider 1984: 181–185). Talal Asad (1983: 237) considers that anthropological definitions of religion derive from "privatized forms of religion so characteristic of modern (Christian) society in which knowledge and power are no longer significantly generated by religious institutions." Recently, there have been methodological criticisms that an overreliance on the domain of "ritual" tends to reduce studies of religious behavior to belief systems, in turn making the study of ritual activity the same as the study of symbolic instead of instrumental action (Asad 1979, 1993: 126).

In American archaeology of the 1960s and 1970s the discussion of religion did not even progress to the level of methodology. Proponents of the New Archaeology, most notably Lewis Binford (1962, 1968; also see Binford and Binford 1968), embraced a neo-evolutionary perspective and argued for the primacy of ecological-materialist forces driving all cultural change across time, with artifacts providing the empirical testing ground. The reconstruction of history was replaced by the search for nomothetic generalizations (Binford 1965). Under the guise of "archaeological theory," Binford proposed what were primarily methodological "prescriptions for investigating and thinking" (Cowgill 1993: 552) that never revolutionized archaeology or created new paradigms (Wylie 2002: 25–41). Very important, however, they did effectively stifle discussions of religion, an area of interest as late as 1961 (Sears 1961). Critics of the New Archaeology point out that the approach has "not paid sufficient attention to its object of inquiry, to the implications of its theoretical and methodological foundations, or to the context in which archaeological research was carried out" (Patterson 1989, 1990: 191) and that New Archaeology's primary failing is its "overemphasis on validation and efforts to be objective" (Redman 1991: 300). To be considered a by-product of techno-environmental evolutionary processes, religion had to be reduced to teleological behaviors that are little more than responses to adaptive pressures.

Although the relationship between religion and archaeology has always been an uneasy one (Demarest 1987: 372), in the New Archaeology the fate of religion was a foregone conclusion. Limited to discussions of ecology and technology and denied the context of history, archaeologists could elicit only the most "generic characteristics of religion and ideology from archaeological residues" (Pauketat 2001: 78). The generalizing search for nomothetic laws reduced specificity and constrained archaeologists from exploring the "causal processes, structures, and relations of dependence responsible for prehistoric cultural forms and their archaeological record" (Wylie 2002: 224–225). The use of processualism's reductive explanatory models masks the broader impacts of religion on power relations, historic change, and political and social organization.

Since the 1990s there has been considerable interest in history, agency, and the reconciliation of many fractious debates that characterized preceding decades (e.g.,

Patterson 1990; Pauketat 2001). However, religion is still an area that has been inadequately addressed. It has been suggested that archaeological approaches to ideological aspects of past cultures would directly benefit from a more structural analysis of social phenomena (Leach 1973, 1977; Wylie 2002: 130–135; contra Conrad and Demarest 1984: 228n57[1]). Among those who actively write on the archaeology of religion, three issues emerge: the distinction between belief and ritual action (Walker 1995), the need to recognize just how imbedded religion is in other social formations (Renfrew 1994), and the use of historic analogs to understand archaeological contexts (Marcus and Flannery 1994; Wylie 2002).

The contrast between belief and ritual is an important one. Although it may be possible to discuss the implications of belief systems or to analyze iconographic, textual, or other symbolic media for understanding prehistoric beliefs, it is not possible to archaeologically investigate a belief system. Also, the study of subjective and emic symbols of meaning and belief will not usually inform us about the often stressful and chaotic actions of religious rituals. All too frequently, descriptions of religion deal effectively with identifying iconographic symbols of beliefs but then refer to amorphous "rituals" conducted by prehistoric peoples who shared suspected beliefs. We suggest that the identification and analysis of ritual contexts can provide us with windows into the activities and actors involved in religious systems, linking belief to other complex systems of social meaning, including political and economic systems. We caution, though, that conflating the study of religious ritual with ideology creates both methodological and interpretive issues that mirror anthropology's problems with belief-based approaches of the 1970s (discussed previously). For archaeology, that "intrinsic contradiction between thought and action has forced researchers to emphasize the decoding of particular ritual attitudes or belief systems" instead of investigating religion as a "disciplined and skillful behavioral practice" that leaves material residues (Walker 1995: 67–70).

Religion permeates all levels of societies and is often reflected in domestic and public contexts across the spectrum of social actors. Whereas elite interaction and religious suzerainty are favored topics, the material remains of religious actions can be found in even the most mundane contexts (Prufer 2002). Methodologically, an archaeology of religion requires finding archaeological indicators of ritual activity (Renfrew and Bahn 1991: 359–360), as well as analysis of religious architecture and "contextual analysis of religious paraphernalia" (Marcus and Flannery 1994: 55). The use of analogy, discussed in more detail later, can be an important and powerful tool for archaeologists to understand prehistoric religion. We will not reiterate the long debate on the use of analogy (see Lyman and O'Brien 2001; Wylie 2002: 136–153). The hostility toward analogy (Binford 1968: 14) is characteristic of Processual Archaeology's excessively reductive approach during the 1960s and 1970s. Most would now agree that careful scrutiny of source and subject can inform the extent and relevance of similarity (Wylie 2002: 149). Suffice it to say there must be, of course, limits to the kinds of information analogy can supply. Some cultures, time periods, and contexts are more amenable to some types of analogy than others (e.g., Yellen 1977: 4). Archaeological studies of religious rituals, because they are related to belief systems, can benefit from direct historic analogies when it is possible to reconstruct both the activities undertaken and their emic relevance. In the Maya area in particular, perceived continuities between past and present forms of indigenous religion are supported by vast bodies of ethnographic, historic, and pre-Columbian texts, making analogy an important heuristic tool.

The systematic investigation of the remains of ritual activities leads to a more informed and holistic perspective of the societies archaeologists study. Although calls made in the early 1960s for the development of methodological and theoretical perspectives on religion (Sears 1961) were greeted enthusiastically (Fairbanks 1961; Mayer-Oaks 1961; Sturtevant 1961), the topic was never developed in any coherent way. Today, we recognize the inadequacy of how we deal with interpreting the material remains of religious activity and call for renewed efforts to understand the broad impacts of religion in archaeological societies. Using all the tools in our anthropological-archaeological tool kit will help us decipher more particulars. On the other hand, reducing religion to just another adaptive strategy of secondary importance in social complexity completely fails to acknowledge its causative efficacy.

MAYA ARCHAEOLOGY, RELIGION, AND CAVES

Despite assertions that the impacts of the New Archaeology in the Maya area were not as severe as elsewhere (Sabloff and Henderson 1993: 2), it is nevertheless apparent that throughout the 1960s and 1970s and into the 1980s mainstream Maya archaeology, like its counterparts in North America, encouraged strictly eco-materialist models to explain social and political change (e.g., Sanders and Price 1968; also see Sabloff 1990). Major syntheses of Classic period settlement (Ashmore 1981), architecture (Becker 1982), political dynamics (Culbert 1973), demography (Culbert and Rice 1990), economics (Sabloff and Rathje 1975[2]), and subsistence (Flannery 1982) largely ignored manifestations of religion. Although these were not the only perspectives of the time (Becker 1979; M. Coe 1977; Marcus 1981; Puleston 1977; Sabloff and Willey 1967) and some spoke out against the marginalizing of religion[3] (Flannery 1972: 400; Willey 1976), ecological-materialism was a dominant approach in field archaeology as reflected in literature spanning a twenty-year period. Indeed, it is instructive to recall that Gordon Willey (1982: 10), referring posthumously to Dennis Puleston's interest in iconography and religion (including caves; see Harrison and Messenger 1980), describes him as a man with the "qualities of a mystic" for his interest in the "spiritually allegorical or symbolical." Willey goes on to point out that Puleston's interest in ideological explorations of the Maya collapse was enough to "set a good materialist's teeth on edge" (1982: 12).

Although archaeologists in general agreed that religion permeated Maya life (M. Coe 1966: chapter 8; Willey 1971), the observation was usually based on iconography or "art" (Sanders and Price 1968: 142). The occasional description of religion as an important system for facilitating "communication necessary for cultural development" (Adams and Culbert 1977: 20) was rarely followed by serious discussion of how religion interplays with social and political organization. Field archaeologists from the 1960s through the mid-1980s were more likely to consider religion secondary to other concerns in modeling societal complexity, although paradoxically the theocratic nature of Maya civilization was seen as leaving it vulnerable to collapse (Webb 1973). Most publications of the time that dealt specifically with religion in Maya prehistory were based on iconography (M. Coe 1977; León-Portilla 1973; Robicsek 1978; J.E.S. Thompson 1970), published in obscure sources (Kampen 1981; J.E.S. Thompson 1959), or both (Dütting 1976). Publications purporting to deal with both archaeology and religion were often quite general and comparative (Marcus 1978; Price 1974). The few that dealt directly with archaeological data remain fairly informative (Becker 1979; W. Coe 1965; Leventhal 1983).

When archaeological investigations in caves began producing a body of literature in the late 1980s, they immediately contributed to our knowledge of Maya religion, because the investigators recognized that they were dealing with the material remains of religious rituals. Given the intellectual climate, however, it is not surprising that most archaeologists were slow to appreciate the relevance of these studies. We see both the lateness and reticence as directly attributable to the earlier influence of Processual Archaeology. It certainly was not the result of a lack of descriptive data from caves. It would appear that Mayanists simply ignored a large body of evidence, archaeological and documentary, pointing to caves as ritual spaces that could inform the study of pre-Columbian Maya religion (Brady 1996).

Although we have reviewed the history of cave investigations in Mesoamerica elsewhere (Brady 1989: 10–31; Brady and Prufer 2005; Prufer 2002: 117–161), it is informative to look briefly at the academic development of the field in the Maya area. Discussions of cave use date back to the late nineteenth century, with a number of excellent reports produced during the 1890s. In 1896, Edward Thompson (1938: 27) discovered a ceremonial cave directly below the center of an impressive pyramid in the core area of Chichén Itzá, and his interest extended to speculation on the function of Loltun, a massive cave located in Yucatán, Mexico (1897). During this period, Henry Mercer (original 1896, 1975) published the first survey of caves in the Maya area, George Gordon (1898) described the caves surrounding the ruins of Copan in Honduras, and Eduard Seler (1901) reported his investigation of caves in Highland Guatemala.

Following this early interest in caves, they were largely ignored by the institutional projects that dominated Maya archaeology through World War II. A notable exception was the British Museum's Pusilha project (Gruning 1930; Joyce 1929; Joyce et al. 1928), which devoted lengthy sections of several publications to cave studies. In the decades immediately following the war there were only a few attempts to link the caves archaeologists encountered with the sites they studied. The best effort was the Carnegie Institution's Mayapán project, which noted that architecture appeared to have been built in direct relation to the site's many *cenotes,* but, interestingly, the project did not advance explanations of why this should be (Chowning 1955; Proskouriakoff 1962; A. L. Smith 1962: 210–211; P. Smith 1954, 1955). Following the Carnegie project the situation deteriorated, and more recent projects have tended to ignore caves altogether. For example, Dennis Puleston (1974: 119, 121) recorded a number of caves during the Tikal Transect project, but these do not appear to have been investigated and did not warrant discussion in any of the project summaries. The only caves mentioned by the Barton Ramie project are the Black Rock Caves listed in Gifford's ceramic inventory sheets (Willey et al. 1965: Ceramic Evaluation Chart 36), but the excavations were never described and the site does not appear on the project map. Finally, the Seibal project does not report on any caves at all. We find the general paucity of information on caves puzzling, since caves are natural features present in unbelievable quantities across the Maya Lowlands, and most show clear evidence of human use in the archaeological past.

It was not until 1959, with the publication of J.E.S. Thompson's "The Role of Caves in Maya Culture," that the first comparative synthetic statement on the religious function of caves appeared. Within the context of its time, Thompson's statement was significant. He linked the use of caves to both Maya ritual and religion, discussed the relationship of caves to architecture, and proposed that they were repositories of objects used in religious rituals. Unfortunately, this rather obscure publication failed to inspire serious scholarship. Throughout the 1960s and 1970s cave archaeology in the Maya area languished. In Central Mexico a series of publications were aimed at focusing attention on the religious use of caves (Heyden 1973, 1975, 1981), but the response of the archaeological community appears to have been tepid.

In the Maya area there were a number of noteworthy publications, although these were largely descriptive (Andrews 1961, 1965, 1970; Lee 1967, 1969; Pendergast 1962, 1964, 1966, 1968, 1969, 1970, 1971, 1974; Schmidt 1977) and none attempted to explain why caves appeared so heavily utilized. Perhaps more important, they failed to draw on comparative data from the growing body of cave excavations to create a picture of how widely caves were used or to note remarkable similarities among different archaeological contexts. A 1975 revision of J.E.S. Thompson's original (1959) synthesis, as well as MacLeod and Puleston's 1978 article based on actual fieldwork, became the only synthetic discussions for the next decade. Beginning in the mid-1980s prehistorians began to seriously address the growing body of descriptive cave data. In 1983 John and Mary Pohl suggested that the ritual events of royal succession were linked to caves. In 1989 two synthetic publications, Brady's dissertation and Juan Luis Bonor Villarejo's *Las Cuevas Mayas: Simbolismo y Ritual,* combined archaeological investigations with rich ethnographic descriptions of cave use in an effort to stimulate interest in cave investigations. Beginning in the mid-1990s cave studies began to appear in refereed publications, signaling their gradual acceptance by mainstream archaeology.

Earlier we asserted that caves offer the single best context for the archaeological study of religion. Methodologically, the study of religion in archaeology necessitates identifying artifacts or contexts that can be unequivocally associated with ritual activity (Renfrew and Bahn 1991: 359–360). This is very much in keeping with the traditional view of the archaeological enterprise, in which function is determined by the analysis of artifacts recovered from features, areas, or sites. Although at first blush this may sound very straightforward, in actual fact it is quite complex. We know from ethnoarchaeological studies that "artifacts rarely function in the utilitarian, social, or ideological domain to the exclusion of the others" (Hayden and Cannon 1984: 96). In fact, any artifact could be considered religious if it was used in a ritual context. A number of years ago Brady observed a Day of the Dead ceremony in a tropical area of Mexico. As a component of the celebration, the vegetation in the cemetery was cut, cleared, and burned and the aboveground cement crypts were painted during the week before the holy day. While observing the actual ceremonies, Brady also noted a piece of a machete blade that had been broken on a stone and a used paintbrush discarded next to a newly painted grave. Although machetes and paintbrushes would normally be considered utilitarian "tools," they had clearly been employed in a religious ritual in this case.

If our interpretation of a context is based on the artifacts recovered but if we must first understand the context to apply the correct interpretation to artifacts, we have an untenable situation. If a context entertained multiple activities, how does one decide which function an artifact was associated with? To complicate this issue further, the use-function of many artifacts at the time of deposition may have differed from the initial function at the time of manufacture (see Brown 2000; Walker 1995). The solution for surface archaeologists looking at religion is to analyze those artifacts that are so specialized that they are assumed to have functioned only in the religious domain. Thus, archaeologists have looked at the distribution of figurines and formal *incensarios*[4] to discuss Maya religion. In caves, however, these items generally make up less than 1 percent of the ceramic assemblage, the bulk of which is composed of the same types of unslipped, unslipped striated, and monochrome slipped vessels found at surface sites. In caves, however, it has been shown that the vessels were often used to burn incense (Escobedo Ayala 1993). There is every reason to believe such unassuming vessels were also used in household rituals at surface sites, but archaeologists are simply unable to recognize the religious function. Thus, studies relying only on limited classes of artifacts tell us less about Maya religion and more about the shortcomings of ignoring 99 percent of the evidence.

Cave archaeology has developed a different approach, perhaps because of the uniqueness of the context. Cave sites are first examined to show that they were associated with religious activity rather than habitation or some other economic or utilitarian function. This same approach has been used in a more limited fashion by surface archaeologists when they have analyzed caches and burials for insights into Maya religion. We note that surface site deposits are produced by rather specialized ceremonies and generally do not supply large amounts of material evidence. Cave assemblages, by comparison, are often enormous and tend to provide a much more representative collection of ritual artifacts.[5]

Clearly, in any archaeology of religion it is the determination that the contexts under investigation are actually the result of activity related to religion that is critical to assigning the artifacts to a behavior related to a belief system. We base our assessment of the ritual function of caves in part on the voluminous body of documentary sources indicating that the use of caves excluded secular activity. As mentioned previously, many of these sources date to the dawn of Western imperialism in the New World. We can also add a number of pre-Columbian documentary sources (Vogt and Stuart 2005). However, the establishment of caves as religious rather than habitational space is based first and foremost on a much more intimate appreciation of cave environments. Most introductory archaeology texts are very explicit about the fact that, for the most part, humans have never, in either the Old or the New World, lived in caves. Nearly fifty years ago, Miles Burkitt (1956: 7) stated the case well:

> The expression "cave man" is somewhat misleading; our prehistoric forerunners never lived in the depths of their caves. For one thing caves are very damp and rheumatism seems to have been rife then as it is now; furthermore, they would have required perpetual artificial light.

It is generally agreed that rockshelters rather than caves were utilized for shelter (Chard 1975: 171). Caves can be advantageous dwellings in very cold areas (Straus 1990: 260), but it is difficult to see the attraction in the tropical lowlands. Deep caves presented severe problems of providing a constant light source. The burden of gathering required fuel would have negated any advantage caves could offer. Further, the implications of having a fire in a cave are rarely considered. In modern cave rituals, the candles and burning associated with copal incense rapidly turn tunnels into stifling, oppressive, choking, hellish environments. The archaeologists who recorded the ceremony at Balankanche, Mexico, had to work in shifts because they were able to stand the conditions in the inner chamber only for short periods (Andrews 1971: 260–262). Whereas humans have been known to endure such conditions for finite periods in the name of religion, it is inconceivable that they would choose to live in this environment. Finally, we simply do not see evidence of habitation. Fire associated with habitation would produce deposits of charcoal several meters deep in just a few years of even seasonal occupation.

The dampness Burkitt mentions is another problem that has received too little attention. The relative humidity was monitored in the cave of Naj Tunich, Guatemala, for several years, and it never fell below 90 percent. Organic material left in the cave by the project developed mold within days. Although recognizing some variation in caves, we suggest in general that archaeologists who assert that supposedly "dry" caves may have been used for storage of foodstuffs are displaying a woeful lack of familiarity with actual conditions.[6]

On these scores alone, any proposal of cave, as opposed to rockshelter, habitation should be greeted skeptically. If the entrance to the cave requires a difficult or dangerous climb, this should also be seen as evidence that habitation was unlikely. Habitational sites often develop a characteristic midden in front of the entrance where garbage has been thrown. The lack of such a feature tends to suggest that the utilization was not habitational. Our extensive surveys of caves in the Maya Lowlands has failed to turn up a single example of what could be called cave habitation.

Often, even the light and twilight zones near cave entrances provide only marginal shelter. Most archaeological work in the lowlands is conducted in the dry season, so there is little opportunity to observe the site in other seasons. Cave environments can change dramatically during rains. A large chamber in Naj Tunich that was dry in March held a lake 5–7 m deep in August. Similarly, access to caves located on steep slopes or with steep entrances becomes perilous during the rainy season. Cave archaeologists have become sophisticated in noting evidence of the movement of water in cave contexts that may indicate that the site was uninhabitable during the season when shelter is most necessary.

When all the evidence is considered, it is clear that cave contexts are religious. With caves established as singularly unambiguous religious contexts, all of the artifacts and paraphernalia found within the caves can be interpreted within a framework of religious ritual. Cave studies in the Maya area inform religion in concrete ways epigraphic and iconographic studies alone cannot by examining the material expressions of Maya religion, which are the remains of ritual behaviors. Analysis of these residues allows us to potentially reconstruct both the actual activities as well as the socioeconomic and political status of a range of actors. Combined with our knowledge from epigraphy and symbolic studies of iconography, cave archaeology is a powerful tool in the reconstruction of Maya society.

ORGANIZATION OF THIS VOLUME

The following chapters present an opportunity to explore the most recent data on the use of caves by the pre-Columbian Maya. They enjoin the reader to see caves as more than just holes in the earth used for offerings or feared dark and mysterious places. The authors of these chapters demonstrate how caves were, and are, integrated into the most fundamental aspects of any peoples' worldview: concepts of creation and the origins of social life, reproduction and fertility, and the human life cycle—including the triad of birth, personhood, and death. They demonstrate that archaeological cave contexts represent the material remains of rituals conducted in the past and that it was through these rituals that the Maya marked life cycles, made appeals for health and prosperity, and reified social hierarchies and the status of individuals and communities.

This volume is arranged around three central topics of archaeological interest: settlements, ritual action, and mortuary behavior. The first section, "Sacred Landscape and Artificial Caves," examines the role of ritual space in the built environment as a symbolic microcosm of the landscape features considered sacred. The idea that landscape features are replicated in Maya ceremonial architecture is not new (Carlson 1981). Temples were built to replicate sacred mountains, and interior rooms and tomb chambers are metaphoric caves (Benson 1985: 184). Sites are frequently constructed in direct relationship to caves (Brady 1997), or architectural features may contain artificial or even natural caves (Brady and Veni 1992). The chapters in this section explore several overlapping themes related to caves in the constructed environment. Chapters by Prufer and Kindon and Pugh demonstrate that caves are powerful features, and their presence on ceremonial architectural groups reaffirms the inherent social power of elites. These chapters also discuss that natural and artificial caves are critical places in Maya creation events, and hence their presence in the built environment reflects their cosmological importance. The remaining chapters in this section, by Halperin and Patel, discuss the role of caves as fundamental features in Maya cosmology and explore how they are implicated in other important social arenas, primarily those involved in the construction of status and the exploitation of sacred landscapes through pilgrimage.

The second section of this book, "Reconstructing Ritual and Cosmology," addresses several ways the earth-focused worldview of the Maya manifested itself in behaviors and choices detectable in the archaeological and pre-Hispanic historic record. Working under the premise that caves were central to cosmology in Maya society, the authors of these chapters examine the ways specific implements, actions, and resources reflect cave-focused ideologies. Epigraphic data, presented by Brady and Colas, illustrate the likelihood that caves may have been desecrated as parts of warfare events, examining both texts and material evidence that caves sites were sacked and burned. Stone examines the roles of actual scribes and how they have been involved with communicating the concept of caves and in actual cave ritual. She concludes that scribal visits to caves may have reaffirmed the supernatural ties they so often reflect in images and text. In Chapter 6, Brady explores several aspects of how cave pilgrimages may have created or fed into local ritual economies, spurred by a demand for implements for the successful completion of cave-focused activities. Moyes examines a specific cave that appears to have functioned in part as a sweatbath. She demonstrates that both caves and sweatbaths are strongly associated with aspects of fertility, earth deities, creation, and renewal. Several chapters focus on artifact classes found in caves. Morehart examines the types and uses of botanical materials recovered from cave sites, primarily in and around the Belize Valley. His discussion illustrates the remarkable preservation in caves of materials rarely recovered from surface sites. Three chapters look at specific classes of artifacts, some natural resources occurring in caves and others brought into caves. Chapters 11 and 12 by Brady, Cobb, Garza, Espinosa, and Burnett and by Peterson, McAnany, and Cobb, respectively, look at how cave formations, or speleothems, became important cave resources, exploited for use both in caves and at surface sites. Cave formations are also central to the chapter by Kenward, which explores several unique cave structures in central Belize.

The third section of this volume, "Interpretations of Human Skeletal Material in Caves," clarifies one of the more interesting and least reported areas of Maya cave utilization. Although caves were fundamentally important features in the landscape and intimately associated with life, death, and the otherworld, they were not the preferred location for the Maya to inter the dead. Hence, the presence of human remains has intrigued archaeologists for over a century. Scott and Brady review the history of investigations of these contexts, as well as changes in interpretation over time. They conclude that early studies provided few data on contexts, so interpretations were weak. They note that the quality of recent work on mortuary contexts in caves has improved markedly, and, as a result, the complexity of the questions being asked of the data has increased. Examples of this complexity can be found in chapters by Saul, Prufer, and Saul and by Glassman and Bonor Villarejo. Based on excavations in rockshelters in Belize, these chapters examine contexts of recovery and osteological markers from the skeletons to offer interpretations based on the actual individuals who were interred. Tiesler looks at skeletal populations from a very specific context—waterlogged *cenotes* in the Yucatán—examining the effects of submersion on human remains and the demographics of those found in such watery environs. Looking at human remains from another perspective, Owen examines the possibility that some remains might be from activities related to ritual murder or sacrifice.

For dirt archaeologists working in the Maya area, caves represent the optimal laboratories in which to reconstruct aspects of Earth-focused Maya religion. Although belief systems are ambiguous from archaeological data, discussion of ritual behavior and actions related to belief is quite possible. Since caves are contexts where religious ritual activities are known to have taken place, they offer the opportunity to explore and reconstruct Maya cosmology from the ground up.

NOTES

1. Conrad and Demarest's criticism may be accurate in that some structural analyses can emphasize pan- or cross-cultural explanations of cultural change to the detriment of processes that are unique and culture specific. However, as Wylie (2002: 135) points out, "[A] structuralist approach offers archaeologists a compelling way to conceptualize archaeological data as cultural material when there is reason to think that this material is meaning-structured and meaning-bearing. Although a structuralist archaeology is often understood to raise the specter of a paralyzing epistemic dilemma, there is nothing in the commitment to explore the cognitive dimensions of the cultural past that renders it categorically unscientific. Inasmuch as structuralist archaeologists engage a process of reaching beyond observables, formulating and testing models of the conditions and processes responsible for the archaeological record, their work is well within the scope of practice that characterizes science at its best and most successful."

2. See Petel, this volume, for a critique and reevaluation of their trade model.

3. The comments of Flannery and Willey were not insignificant. Willey (1976: 205) noted that archaeologists have been reluctant to recognize that the ideological "provided controls for and gave distinctive forms to . . . culture" throughout time and was not just limited to "complex societies." Flannery (1972: 399–400) described the "limited success of so-called ecological approaches" and specifically called for a holistic approach that recognized the integral role of religion.

4. By *incensario* we are referring to elaborate vessels specifically produced for this single function (e.g., *Miseria appliqué*).

5. Indeed, much of the original context of cave assemblages may have been organic materials, now difficult to discern in the archaeological record (see Morehart, this volume).

6. For an appreciation of the problem, see Puleston's (1971) experiments with storage in chultunes.

REFERENCES CITED

Adams, Rechard E.W., and Patrick T. Culbert

1977 The Origins of Civilization in the Maya Lowlands. In *The Origins of Civilization in the Maya Lowlands,* ed. Richard E.W. Adams. University of New Mexico Press, Albuquerque.

Andrews, E. Wyllys IV

1961 Excavations at the Gruta de Balankanche, 1959. Appendix to *Preliminary Report to the 1959–60 Field Season, National Geographic Society–Tulane University Dzibilchultun Program,* Miscellaneous Series, No. 11:28–40. Tulane University Middle American Research Institute, New Orleans.

1965 *Explorations in the Gruta de Chac,* Publication 31:1–21. Middle American Research Institute, New Orleans.

1970 *Balankanche, Throne of the Tiger Priest,* Publication 32. Middle American Research Institute, New Orleans.

1971 Balankanche—Throne of the Tiger Priest. *Explorers Journal* 49(4):254–262.

Asad, Talal

1979 Anthropology and the Analysis of Ideology. *Man n.s.* 14(4):607–627.

1983 Anthropological Conceptions of Religion: Reflections on Geertz. *Man n.s.* 18(2):237–259.

1993 *Genealogies of Religion: Discipline and Reasons of Power in Christianity and Islam.* Johns Hopkins University Press, Baltimore.

Ashmore, Wendy

1981 *Lowland Maya Settlement Patterns,* ed. Wendy Ashmore. University of New Mexico Press, Albuquerque.

Becker, Marshall J.

1979 Theories of Ancient Maya Social Structure; Priests, Peasants, and Ceremonial Centers in Historical Perspective. In *Occasional Publications in Mesoamerican Anthropology,* 12. University of Northern Colorado, Museum of Anthropology, Greeley.

1982 Ancient Maya Houses and Their Identification: An Evaluation of Architectural Groups at Tikal and Inferences Regarding Their Functions. *Revista Española de Antropología Americana* 12:111–129.

Benson, Elizabeth P.

1985 Architecture as Metaphor. In *Fifth Palenque Round Table,* 1983, ed. Virginia M. Fields, 183–188. Palenque Round Table (5 session 1983), Pre-Columbian Art Research Institute, San Francisco.

Binford, Lewis R.

1962 Archaeology as Anthropology. In *Contemporary Archaeology: A Guide to Theory and Contributions,* ed. Mark P. Leone, 93–101. University of Southern Illinois, Carbondale.

1965 Archaeological Systematics and the Study of Culture Process. *American Antiquity* 31:203–210.

1968 Archeological Perspectives. In *New Perspectives in Archeology,* eds. Sally R. Binford and Lewis R. Binford, 5–32. Aldine Press, Chicago.

Binford, Sally R., and Lewis R. Binford

1968. *New Perspectives in Archaeology.* Aldine Press, Chicago.

Bonor Villarejo, Juan Luis

1989 *Las Cuevas Mayas: Simbolismo y Ritual.* Universidad Compultense de Madrid, Madrid.

Brady, James E.

1989 An Investigation of Maya Ritual Cave Use With Special Reference to Naj Tunich, Peten, Guatemala. Archaeology Program, Ph.D. Dissertation. University of California, Los Angeles.

1996 *Sources for the Study of Mesoamerican Ritual Cave Use.* Studies in Mesoamerican Cave Use, Publication 1. George Washington University, Washington, D.C.

1997 Settlement Configuration and Cosmology: The Role of Caves at Dos Pilas. *American Anthropologist* 99(3):602–618.

Brady, James E., and Keith M. Prufer

2005 Introduction: A History of Mesoamerican Cave Interpretation. In *In the Maw of the Earth Monster: Mesoamerican Ritual Cave Use,* eds. James E. Brady and Keith M. Prufer, 1–18. University of Texas Press, Austin.

Brady, James E., and George Veni

1992 Man-Made and Pseudo-Karst Caves: The Implications of Subsurface Features Within Maya Centers. *Geoarchaeology* 7(2):149–167.

Brown, Linda A.

2000 From Discard to Divination: Demarcating the Sacred Through the Collection and Curation of Discarded Objects. *Latin American Antiquity* 11:319–333.

Burkitt, Miles

1956 *The Old Stone Age.* New York University Press, New York.

Carlson, John B.

1981 A Geomantic Model for the Interpretation of Mesoamerican Sites: An Essay in Cross-cultural Comparison. In *Mesocamerican Sites and World-Views,* ed. Elizabeth P. Benson, 143–216. Dumbarton Oaks Research Library and Collection, Washington, D.C.

Carneiro, R.

1973 Structure, Function, and Equilibrium in the Evolutionism of Herbert Spencer. *Journal of Anthropological Research* 29:77–95.

Chard, Chester S.
1975 *Man in Prehistory*, 2nd ed. McGraw-Hill Book, New York.

Chowning, Ann
1955 Excavations in the Itzmal Ch'en Ceremonial Group at Mayapan. *Carnegie Institution of Washington Year Book* 54:280–283.

Coe, Michael D.
1966 *The Maya*. Praeger, New York.
1977 Supernatural Patrons of Maya Scribes and Artists. In *Social Process in Maya Prehistory: Studies in Honor of Sir Eric Thompson,* ed. Norman Hammond, 327–347. Academic Press, New York.

Coe, William R.
1965 Caches and Offertory Practices of the Maya Lowlands. In *Archaeology of Southern Mesoamerica,* Handbook of Middle American Indians, 2, ed. Gordon R. Willey, 462–468. University of Texas Press, Austin.

Conrad, Geoffrey W., and Arthur A. Demarest
1984 *Religion and Empire: The Dynamics of Aztec and Inca Expansionism.* Cambridge University Press, Cambridge.

Cowgill, George L.
1993 Distinguished Lecture in Archaeology: Beyond Criticizing New Archaeology. *American Anthropologist* 95(3):551–573.

Culbert, T. Patrick
1973 *The Classic Maya Collapse,* ed. T. Patrick Culbert. University of New Mexico Press, Albuquerque.

Culbert, T. Patrick, and Don S. Rice
1990 *Pre-Columbian Population History in the Maya Lowlands,* eds. T. Patrick Culbert and Don S. Rice. University of New Mexico Press, Albuquerque.

Demarest, Arthur A.
1987 Archaeology and Religion. In *Encyclopedia of Religion,* vol. I, ed. Mircea Eliade, 372–379. Macmillan, London.

Dütting, Dieter
1976 Great Goddess in Classic Maya Religious Belief. *Zeitschrift für Ethnologie Braunschweig* 101(1):41–146.

Ember, M., and C. Ember
1971 The Conditions Favoring Matrilocal Versus Patrilocal Residence. *American Anthropologist* 73:571–594.

Escobedo Ayala, Héctor Leonel
1993 Resultados preliminares del análisis de la cerámica de Naj Tunich, Petén. In *Tercer simposio de arqueología Guatemalteca*, eds. Juan Pedro Laporte, Héctor L. Escobedo, and Sandra Villagrán, 151–162. Ministerio de Cultura y Deportes, Instituto de Antropología e Historia, Asociación Tikal, Guatemala.

Fairbanks, Charles H.
1961 Comments on the Study of Social and Religious Systems in North American Archaeology. *Current Anthropology* 2(3):237–238.

Flannery, Kent V.
1972 The Cultural Evolution of Civilizations. *Annual Review of Ecology and Systematics* 3:399–426.

1982 *Maya Subsistence: Studies in Memory of Dennis E. Puleston,* ed. Kent Flannery. Academic Press, New York.

Gibbon, Guy
1989 *Explanation in Archaeology.* Blackwell Press, Oxford.

Giddons, Anthony
1971 *Capitalism and Modern Social Theory: An Analysis of the Writings of Marx, Durkheim, and Weber.* Cambridge University Press, Cambridge.

Gordon, George Byron
1898 *Caverns of Copan, Honduras.* Memoirs, 1:137–148, Harvard University, Peabody Museum of American Archaeology and Ethnology, Cambridge, MA.

Gruning, E. L.
1930 Report on the British Museum Expedition to British Honduras, 1930. *Journal of the Royal Anthropological Institute* 60:477–483.

Hammond, Norman
1981 Settlement Patterns in Belize. In *Lowland Maya Settlement Patterns,* ed. Wendy Ashmore, 157–186. University of New Mexico Press, Albuquerque.

Harris, Marvin
1964 *The Nature of Cultural Things.* Random House, New York.
1969 *The Rise of Anthropological Theory: A History of Theories of Culture.* Routledge and Kegan Paul, London.
1979 *Cultural Materialism: The Struggle for a Science of Culture.* Random House, New York.

Harrison, Peter D., and Phyllis E. Messenger
1980 Dennis Edward Puleston, 1940–1978. *American Antiquity* 45:272–276.

Hayden, Brian, and Aubrey Cannon
1984 *Structure of Material Systems: Ethnoarchaeology in the Maya Highlands.* Society for American Archaeology, Washington, D.C.

Henderson, John S., and Jeremy A. Sabloff
1993 Reconceptualizing the Maya Cultural Tradition: Programmatic Comments. In *Lowland Maya Civilization in the Eighth Century A.D.,* eds. Jeremy A. Sabloff and John S. Henderson, 445–468. Dumbarton Oaks Research Library and Collection, Washington, D.C.

Heyden, Doris
1973 ¿Un Chicomostoc en Teotihuacan? La cueva bajo la Pirámide del Sol. *Boletín del Instituto Nacional de Antropología e Historia,* Época II, No. 6:3–18.
1975 An Interpretation of the Cave Underneath the Pyramid of the Sun in Teotihuacan, Mexico. *American Antiquity* 40:131–147.
1981 Caves, Gods and Myths: World-View and Planning in Teotihuacan. In *Mesoamerican Sites and World-Views,* ed. Elizabeth P. Benson, 1–39. Dumbarton Oaks Research Library and Collection, Washington, D.C.

Hodder, Ian
2002 *Archaeological Theory Today,* ed. Ian Hodder. Polity Press, Cambridge.

Insoll, Timothy
2001 Introduction: The Archaeology of World Religions. In *Archaeology and World Religion,* ed. Timothy Insoll, 1–32. Routledge, New York.

Joyce, T. A.

1929 Report on the British Museum Expedition to British Honduras, 1929. *Journal of the Royal Anthropological Institute* 59:439–459.

Joyce, T. A., T. Gann, E. L. Gruning, and R.C.E. Long

1928 Report on the British Museum Expedition to British Honduras, 1928. *Journal of the Royal Anthropological Society* 58:323–349.

Kampen, Michael E.

1981 *The Religion of the Maya.* Brill, Leiden.

Kelly, J., and M. Kaplan

1990 History, Structure and Ritual. *Annual Review of Anthropology*19:119–150.

Leach, Edmund

1973 Concluding Address. In *The Explanation of Cultural Change: Models in Prehistory; Proceedings,* ed. Colin Renfrew, 761–771. Duckview, London.

1977 A View From the Bridge. In *Archaeology and Anthropology: Areas of Mutual Interest,* ed. Matthew Spriggs, 161–171. B.A.R. Supplementary Series, no. 19. British Archaeological Reports, Oxford.

Lee, Thomas A., Jr.

1967 Excavation of a Rock Shelter in Chiapas. *Katunob* 6(3):4.

1969 Cuevas secas del Río La Venta, Chiapas: Informe Preliminar. *Antropología e historia de Guatemala* 21(1–2):23–37.

León-Portilla, Miguel

1973 *Time and Reality in the Thought of the Maya.* Beacon Press, Boston.

Leventhal, Richard M.

1983 Household Groups and Classic Maya Religion. In *Prehistoric Settlement Patterns: Essays in Honor of Gordon R. Willey,* eds. Evon Z. Vogt and Richard M. Leventhal, 55–76. University of New Mexico Press, Albuquerque.

Lyman, R. Lee, and Michael J. O'Brien

2001 The Direct Historical Approach, Analogical Reasoning, and Theory in Americanist Archaeology. *Journal of Archaeological Method and Theory* 8(4):303–342.

MacLeod, Barbara, and Dennis E. Puleston

1978 Pathways Into Darkness: The Search for the Road to Xibalbá. *Tercera Mesa Redonda de Palenque,* Vol. 4, eds. Merle Greene Robertson and Donnan Call Jeffers, 71–77. Hearld Peters, Monterey.

Marcus, Joyce

1978 Archaeology and Religion: A Comparison of the Zapotec and Maya. *World Archaeology* 10(2):172–191.

1981 Archaeology and Religion: A Comparison of the Zapotec and Maya. In *Ancient Mesoamerica: Selected Readings,* ed. John A. Graham, 297–314. Peek Publications, Palo Alto.

Marcus, Joyce, and Kent V. Flannery

1994 Ancient Zapotec Ritual and Religion: An Application of the Direct Historical Approach. In *The Ancient Mind: Elements of Cognitive Archaeology,* eds. Colin Renfrew and Ezra B.W. Zubrow, 55–74. Cambridge University Press, Cambridge.

Mayer-Oaks, William J.

1961 Comments on the Study of Social and Religious Systems in North American Archaeology. *Current Anthropology* 2(3): 238–239.

Mercer, Henry C.

1975 *The Hill-Caves of Yucatan.* University of Oklahoma Press, Norman (original 1896).

Millon, René F.

1981 Teotihuacan: City, State, and Civilization. In *Archaeology,* ed. Jeremy A. Sabloff, 198–243. Handbook of Middle American Indians, Supplement, 1, University of Texas Press, Austin.

Morris, Brian

1987 *Anthropological Studies of Religion.* Cambridge University Press, Cambridge.

Patterson, Thomas C.

1989 History and the Post-Processual Archaeologies. *Man* 24:555–566.

1990 Some Theoretical Tensions Within and Between the Processual and Postprocessual Archaeologies. *Journal of Anthropological Archaeology* 9:189–200.

Pauketat, Timothy

2001 Practice and History in Archaeology: An Emerging Paradigm. *Anthropological Theory* 1:73–98.

Pendergast, David M.

1962 Breve reconocimento arqueológico en Honduras Britanica. *Estudios de cultura Maya* 2:197–203.

1964 Excavaciones en la Cueva Eduardo Quiroz, Distrito Cayo, Honduras Britanica. *Estudios de Cultura Maya* 4:119–139.

1966 The Actun Balam Vase. *Archaeology* 19(3):154–161.

1968 Four Maya Pottery Vessels From British Honduras. *American Antiquity* 29:379–382.

1969 *The Prehistory of Actun Balam, British Honduras.* Art and Archaeology Occasional Paper No. 16. Royal Ontario Museum, Toronto.

1970 *A. H. Anderson's Excavations at Rio Frio Cave E, British Honduras (Belize).* Art and Archaeology Occasional Paper No. 20. Royal Ontario Museum, Toronto.

1971 *Excavations at Eduardo Quiroz Cave, British Honduras (Belize).* Art and Archaeology Occasional Paper No. 21. Royal Ontario Museum, Toronto.

1974 *Excavations at Actun Polbilche, Belize.* Royal Ontario Museum Monograph 1, Toronto.

Pohl, Mary, and John Pohl

1983 Ancient Maya Cave Ritual. *Archaeology* 36(3):28–51.

Price, Barbara J.

1974 Burden of the Cargo; Ethnographic Models and Archaeological Inference. In *Mesoamerican Archaeology: New Approaches,* ed. Norman Hammond, 445–465. University of Texas Press, Austin.

Proskouriakoff, Tatiana

1962 Civic and Religious Structures at Mayapan. In *Mayapan, Yucatan, Mexico,* eds. H.E.D. Pollock, Ralph L. Roys, T. Proskouriakoff, and A. Ledyard Smith, 87–164. Carnegie Institution of Washington Publication 619, Washington, D.C.

Prufer, Keith M.

2002 Cave, Communities, and Ritual Specialists: A Study of Sacred Space in the Maya Mountains of Southern Belize. Ph.D. Dissertation. Department of Anthropology, Southern Illinois University, Carbondale.

Puleston, Dennis Edward

1971 An Experimental Approach to the Function of Maya Chultunes. *American Antiquity* 36:322–335.

1974 Ancient Maya Settlement Patterns and Environment at Tikal, Guatemala: Implications for Subsistence Model. Ph.D. Dissertation. Department of Anthropology, University of Pennsylvania, Philadelphia.

1977 Art and Archaeology of Hydraulic Agriculture in the Maya Lowlands. In *Social Process in Maya Prehistory: Studies in Honor of Sir Eric Thompson,* ed. Norman Hammond, 449–467. Academic Press, New York.

Rappaport, R. A.

1979 *Ecology, Meaning, and Religion*. North Atlantic Books, Berkeley, CA.

Redman, Charles L.

1991 Distinguished Lecture in Archaeology: In Defense of the Seventies—The Adolescence of New Archaeology. *American Anthropologist* 93(2):295–307.

Renfrew, Colin

1994 The Archaeology of Religion. In *The Ancient Mind: Elements of Cognitive Archaeology,* eds. Colin Renfrew and Ezra B.W. Zubrow, 47–54. Cambridge University Press, Cambridge.

Renfrew, Colin, and Paul Bahn

1991 *Archaeology, Theories, Method, and Practice*. Thames and Hudson, London.

Robicsek, Francis

1978 *Smoking Gods: Tobacco in Maya Art, History and Religion.* University of Oklahoma Press, Norman.

Sabloff, Jeremy A.

1990 *New Archaeology and the Ancient Maya*, Scientific American Library, 30. W. H. Freeman, New York.

Sabloff, Jeremy A., and John Henderson

1993 Introduction. In *Lowland Maya Civilization in the Eighth Century AD,* eds. J. Sabloff and J. Henderson, 1–10. Dumbarton Oaks Research Library, Washington, D.C.

Sabloff, Jeremy A., and William L. Rathje

1975 *Study of the Changing Pre-Columbian Commercial Systems: The 1972–1973 Seasons at Cozumel, Mexico: A Preliminary Report,* Monographs, 3, eds. Jeremy A. Sabloff and William L. Rathje. Harvard University, Peabody Museum of Archaeology and Ethnology, Cambridge, MA.

Sabloff, Jeremy A., and Gordon R. Willey

1967 Collapse of Maya Civilization in the Southern Lowlands: A Consideration of History and Process. *Southwestern Journal of Anthropology* 23(4):311–336.

Sanders, William T., and Barbara Price

1968 *Mesoamerica: The Evolution of a Civilization.* Random House, New York.

Schmidt, Peter J.

1977 Post Classic Finds in the Cayo District, Belize. *Estudios de cultura Maya* 10:103–114.

Schneider, David M.

1984 *A Critique of the Study of Kinship*. University of Michigan Press, Ann Arbor.

Sears, William H.

1961 The Study of Social and Religious Systems in North American Archaeology. *Current Anthropology* 2(3):223–231.

Seler, Eduard

1901 *Die Alten Ansiedlungen von Chaculá, im Distrikte Nentón des Departments Huehuetenango der Republik Guatemala*. Dietrich Reiner Verlag, Berlin.

Smith, A. Ledyard

1962 Residential and Associated Structures at Mayapan. In *Mayapan, Yucatan, Mexico,* eds. H.E.D. Pollock, Ralph L. Roys, T. Proskouriakoff, and A. Ledyard Smith, 165–319. Carnegie Institution of Washington Publication 619. Washington, D.C.

Smith, Philip E.

1954 Excavation in Ceremonial Structures at Mayapan. *Carnegie Institution of Washington Year Book* 53:273–276.

1955 Excavations in Three Ceremonial Structures at Mayapan. Department of Archaeology, *Current Reports,* No. 21. Carnegie Institution of Washington, Washington, D.C.

Steward, Julian H.

1955 *Theory of Cultural Change*. University of Illinois Press, Urbana.

Straus, Guy Lawrence

1990 Underground Archaeology: Perspectives on Caves and Rockshelters. In *Archaeological Method and Theory, Volume 2,* ed. Michael B. Schiffer, 255–304. University of Arizona Press, Tucson.

Sturtevant, William C.

1961 Comments on the Study of Social and Religious Systems in North American Archaeology. *Current Anthropology* 2(3):243–244.

Thompson, Edward H.

1897 *Cave of Loltun, Yucatan: Report of Explorations for the Museum, 1888–89 and 1890–91,* Memoirs, 1(2), Harvard University, Peabody Museum of American Archaeology and Ethnology, Cambridge, MA.

1938 *The High Priest's Grave, Chichen Itza, Yucatan, Mexico*. Prepared for publication, with notes and introduction by J. Eric Thompson. Field Museum of Natural History, Anthropology Series 27, No. 1.

Thompson, J. Eric S.

1959 The Role of Caves in Maya Culture. *Mitteilungen aus dem Museum für Völkerkunde in Hamburg* 25:122–129.

1970 *Maya History and Religion*. Civilizations of the American Indian Series, 99. University of Oklahoma Press, Norman.

1975 Introduction to the Reprint Edition. In *The Hill-Caves of Yucatan*, by Henry C. Mercer, vii–xliv. University of Oklahoma Press, Norman.

Vayda, Andrew P.

1976 On the "New Ecology" Paradigm. *American Anthropologist* 78:645–646.

Vayda, Andrew P., and Roy A. Rappaport

1968 Ecology, Cultural and Non-Cultural. In *Introduction to Cultural Anthropology: Essays in the Scope and Methods of Man,* ed. James A. Clifton, 477–497. Houghton Mifflin, Boston.

Vogt, Evon Z., and David Stuart

2005 Some Notes on Ritual Caves Among the Ancient and Modern Maya. In *In the Maw of the Earth Monster: Mesoamerican Cave Use,* eds. James E. Brady and Keith M. Prufer, 155–185. University of Texas Press, Austin.

Walker, William H.

1995 Ceremonial Trash? In *Expanding Archaeology,* eds. James M. Skibo, William H. Walker, and Axel E. Nielsen, 67–74. University of Utah Press, Salt Lake City.

Webb, Malcolm C.

1973 Peten Maya Decline Viewed in the Perspective of State Formation. In *The Classic Maya Collapse,* ed. T. Patrick Culbert, 367–404. University of New Mexico Press, Albuquerque.

White, Leslie A.

1947 Evolutionary Stages, Progress, and the Evolution of Cultures. *Southwestern Journal of Anthropology* 3:165–192.

1959 *The Evolution of Culture*. McGraw-Hill, New York.

Willey, Gordon R.

1971 An Archaeological Frame of Reference for Maya Cultural History. In *Desarrollo Cultural de los Mayas,* eds. Evon Z. Vogt and Alberto Ruz Lhuillier. Universidad Nacional Autónomade México, Mexico.

1976 Mesoamerican Civilization and the Idea of Transcendence. *Antiquity* 50:205–215.

1982 Dennis Edward Puleston (1940–1978): Maya Archaeologist. In *Maya Subsistence: Studies in Memory of Dennis E. Puleston,* ed. Kent V. Flannery, 1–18. Academic Press, New York.

Willey, Gordon R., William R. Bullard Jr., John B. Glass, and James C. Gifford

1965 *Prehistoric Maya Settlements in the Belize Valley*. Papers of the Peabody Museum of Archaeology and Ethnology, Vol. 54. Harvard University, Cambridge.

Willey, Gordon R., and Philip Phillips

1958 *Method and Theory in American Archaeology.* University of Chicago Press, Chicago.

Willey, Gordon R., and Jeremy A. Sabloff

1980 *A History of American Archaeology,* Second Edition. Freeman, San Francisco.

Wylie, Alison

2002 *Thinking From Things: Essays in the Philosophy of Archaeology.* University of California Press, Berkeley.

Yellen, John

1977 *Archaeological Approaches to the Present.* Academic Press, New York.

I

Sacred Landscape and Artificial Caves

Chapter Two

Replicating the Sacred Landscape

The Chen at Muklebal Tzul

by Keith M. Prufer
Andrew Kindon

Today, it is recognized that pre-Columbian Mesoamerican people replicated elements of landscape in the built environment. The initial observations were based on the perceived similarity of mountains to pyramids (Vogt 1964: 194). That structural relationship has become generally accepted with the reading of the *witz* glyph (Stuart 1987). Over the past few decades the analogy was expanded to include the presence of natural springs, tunnels, and chambers associated with architecture (Benson 1985: 184; Gendrop 1980, 1985; Rivera Dorado 1987: 29; Rivera Dorado and Amador Naranjo 1993; Schavelzon 1980). The presence of such features in the built environment underscores the frequency with which ceremonial architecture appears to have been built based on a model of the natural world. David Stuart and Stephen Houston (1994: 86) note that "the idiom for referring to human construction is often a metaphor for hill. The geography of the Classic Maya apparently involved a conceit in which there existed substantial overlap between natural and artificial categories."

Given the reality that landscape features are frequently focal points in the indigenous worldview throughout Mesoamerica, it should come as no surprise that linguistic terms designating toponyms sometimes also refer to human communities. In Nahuatl the term for community, *altepetl,* literally translates as "water filled mountain" (Broda 1996: 460); and the Maya used a similar expression, *chan-ch'een*, "sky-cave" (Martin 2001: 178), to describe some communities. More recently, decipherment of the Maya glyph *ch'een* has been debated, and it now appears to refer to both caves and, in certain contexts, named population centers (Martin 2001: 178; Vogt and Stuart 2005). We suspect there were frequent and deliberate attempts to recreate important natural features linked to fertility, ancestral deities, and creation myths within the social and built environment. Angel García-Zambrano (1994: 218) states that settlement location was selected based on resemblance to the primordial landscape at the moment of creation. The most important feature was "a natural cave [that] had to contain water or be surrounded by it. Many times, the grotto was manually excavated to approximate its shape to that of the mythological cave with internal niches." The feature was not simply a religious or mythological symbol but a profoundly political one as well. García-Zambrano (1994: 218) continued: "These cavities, when ritually dedicated to the divinities, become the pulsating heart of the new town, providing the cosmogonic referents that legitimized the settlers' rights for occupying that space and the ruler's authority over that site."

In 1999 we investigated an artificial tunnel containing a functioning spring or well in the ceremonial precinct of the Late Classic site Muklebal Tzul in the Maya Mountains of southern Belize. Located in a restricted plaza atop a large platform, the 13-m passage has many features commonly associated with natural caves: a dark zone, an underground stream, and a twilight activity area. However, the volume of water it produces, combined with its location under a large platform that houses a stelae complex, argues that the water from the well was used for ceremonial or other restricted activities.

Artificial water caves are fairly rare, or at least underreported, in the southern Maya Lowlands. However, they have been consistently described from the Maya Highlands, Central Mexico, and Oaxaca, indicating that they may be an important component of the pan-Mesoamerican idea that the built environment is a reflection of the natural world. For the Yucatek Maya, caves, springs, wells, and *cenote'ob* all fall into a loosely defined category of *ch'eenob*. Here, we discuss the symbolic value of water and caves in political ideology, review other examples of artificial water-mountains across Mesoamerica, and explore the implications of the *ch'een* at Muklebal Tzul for understanding these types of features.

THE POWER OF WATER

Discussions of the significance of water in Mesoamerican societies, in particular the management of water resources, have been ongoing for at least forty years

(Sanders 1957, 1968). The majority of the discussions revolve around the functional harnessing of water resources and the relationship between controlling these resources and societal complexity, as well as how humans adapt to variable access to water resources in different environmental regions (Doolittle 1995; Lucero 1999; Rice 1997; Scarborough 1996). Only recently have religious thought and worldview entered into these discussions as archaeologists have begun to suggest that water management was a highly ideological affair (Scarborough 1998).

Three lines of evidence can be drawn on to support the idea that considerable ideological significance was assigned to water in Maya statecraft. First is the presence of reservoirs and other large-scale water management projects in or directly adjacent to ceremonial precincts of Maya cities, especially in locations like Tikal where water resources are scarce (Scarborough 1996). Proximity to centers of religion combined with behaviors in the form of "water rituals" are thought to have legitimated elite authority through the manipulation of symbols related to important resources (Scarborough 1998: 146).

Second is the significance of water in contemporary indigenous religions across Mesoamerica. For example, the Tzoltzil consider springs important sources of water that also have clear associations with Earth Lords, who often manifest themselves at sources of water (Vogt 1976: 16–17). This belief is actualized through lineage- and other community-based ceremonial activities conducted at water holes and springs (Vogt 1976: 99). For the K'iche', public shrines are equated with both water and mountains (Tedlock 1992: 262n12). In the northern lowlands water specifically from *cenotes* is collected by *h'men* (Yucatec shamans) for use in rain-making ceremonies (Redfield and Villa Rojas 1934: 139), and access to underground water resources is sometimes restricted to religious specialists (Barrera Vásquez 1970). Elsewhere, in the Sierra Ñähñu the goddess of fresh water, Maka Xumpo, resides in the local lake and pilgrimages are regularly made to her (Dow 2001: 73). The Nahua believe water ties the world together, in that it links the sky, the earth, and the underworld (Sandstom 1991: 247, 249).[1]

The third indicator that ideological processes were involved in water management is iconographic representation of water-related imagery in elite contexts (Rands 1953, 1955). The Maya underworld has been depicted as a watery place complete with aquatic plants, fish, turtles, and frogs—suggesting that clear and clean water is one of the main features of the interiors of mountains, which are accessible by means of a cave. All common media of political discourse include elements related to water, including codices (Pincemin Deliberos and Rosas Kifuri 2000), carved monuments (Schele and Miller 1986: 267–269), and ceramics (Hellmuth 1987; Reents-Budet 1994). Most water-related elements depict or imply a transition point between the terrestrial world and the underworld marked by a reflective watery interface. The implication for political ideology is that since these elements appear in elite contexts, they likely represent the specific positioning of rulers at this important point of control over the critical juncture between humans and the forces that animate the universe.

In his review of the role of water in Maya statecraft, Vernon Scarborough (1998) touches on the more significant political aspect of water ideology: the quadratic relationship between the built environment and water, caves, and mountains. Embedded in this relationship is a fundamental aspect of Mesoamerican belief systems: the linking of water to fertility and the belief that mountains are the source of both flowing water and rainfall[2] and that these resources emanate from mountains through caves. This belief is reflected in some of the earliest known iconographic examples of political complexity in Mesoamerica, including Long-Lipped Earth Monsters from Izapa (Parsons 1973) and the well-known Olmec throne-sculptures depicting rulers poised at the entrances to caves (Grove 1973). The pervasiveness of pre-Columbian elite water iconography and the importance of water in a range of contemporary Mesoamerican religious expression argue for the deep, unrecorded antiquity of water as a fundamental aspect of regional belief systems. During the development of urban landscapes and concomitant elite political ideologies, the appropriation of water symbolism as a legitimizing mechanism would have been a potent symbol of rulers' links to creative forces seen as responsible for human genesis, survival, and social reproduction.

The proposal that pyramidal structures were constructed as architectural mountains and that tombs represent metaphoric caves is still an area of interest (Benson 1985: 184; also see Hohmann-Vogrin 2001; Stuart 1997). It has been well documented that caves, both natural and artificial, are directly linked to ceremonial architecture. Ball courts replicate gorges, which, like caves, are entrances to the interior of mountains (Colas and Voss 2001: 191). Site planning may have involved a consideration of juxtaposition or proximity of buildings to caves, and when caves were not present they were sometimes constructed (Brady 1997). What has been less clearly discussed, however, is the importance of the conflated symbolism of the water-filled mountain and its cave opening in site planning, although the relationships between water, mountains, and caves are an integral part of Mesoamerican religious thought. The importance of water in political ideology is perhaps most clearly represented in those cases where architectural features incorporate both artificial caves and natural springs to replicate the archetypal water-mountain.

CAVES, SPRINGS, AND ARCHITECTURE

Central Mexican historic records indicate that the placement of ceremonial architecture over a spring, where water flows from the base of the structure, is the "ideal type," reflecting replication of scenes from mythic creation and migration events that explain and give meaning to human existence and legitimate ancestral ties to the place. This is articulated clearly in legends surrounding the construction of the Aztec Templo Mayor over a spring that symbolizes the water-mountain as a creative "naval of the universe" (Sahagún 1950–1982: vol. 6, 19). The mythic-historic migration of the Aztec is recorded as a search for a place identical to their homeland, Aztlan, which led to a spring in a reed-grass field where Tenochtitlan was later constructed (López Luján 1994: 81–83). The Templo Mayor contained shrines dedicated to Tlaloc, a deity of rain and a resident of the watery underworld (Broda 1982). Another chronicle, the West Mexican Mixteca-Puebla *Crónica Mexicáyotl,* also depicts a pyramid with water flowing from its base (Alvarado Tezozomoc 1975: 63), further reflecting the ideal ceremonial structure as one that replicates the water-mountain.

The antiquity of this complex in Central Mexico has been demonstrated in excavations conducted by Bodo Spranz (1967) near Totimehuacan, Puebla. There, a pyramidal building contained a hollow interior area accessible by a walkway leading to a 3- by 2-m basal basin surrounded by frog motifs. A series of drains appears to channel rainfall into the basin. Spranz dates artifacts from the basin to approximately 200 B.C. Similarly, René Millon (1981) proposed that water drained from the surface into the artificial cave under the Pyramid of the Sun at Teotihuacan. This water would have been carried into the cave during rainfall via a series of U-shaped channels and then could have been observed gushing out of the cave entrance (Millon 1981: 234). The Great Pyramid at Cholula provides a dramatic example of architecture actually constructed over a flowing spring. There, "[S]treams of water emerge from a cave at the base of the mound" (McCafferty 1996: 3), and the same pyramid is depicted in the *Historia Tolteca-Chichimeca* (Kirchhoff, Odena Guemes, and Reyes 1976: 7v) with water flowing from a cave at the base and frogs on the summit.

In the Maya area we do not have such a detailed historic and architectural corpus of artificial water-caves. However, there is still a compelling body of data suggesting that artificial water-caves and similar types of architectural features were constructed as powerful symbols reflecting political appropriation of elements of the natural landscape, which legitimated elite ideologies. Whereas this chapter is concerned with those artificial caves that carried water and the water-carrying feature must have been significant, it is important to bear in mind that in nature caves vary greatly in morphology and hydrology. Although we do not yet fully understand the significance of distinctions between different types of caves, both cave form and proximity to settlement likely played a role in determining how they were utilized (Prufer 2002). We suggest that artificial caves may have also had a range of recognized types, and those bearing water were particularly significant because of their conflation of multiple elements of the sacred landscape.

In the highlands, dry artificial caves associated with architecture have been documented at Zaculeu, Ixmiche Viejo (Brady and Veni 1992), La Lagunita (Ichon and Arnauld 1985), Xabaj (Smith 1955: 43), and San Sebastian Lemoa (Ximénez 1967: 144). Two caves, one at Mixco Viejo (Brady and Veni 1992: 151) and another at Llano Largo (Brady 2004), were constructed around natural springs. The one at Llano Largo is interesting in that it was constructed along a natural fault line to capture water dripping from the ceiling and channel it toward an artificial basin at the entrance.

These artificial caves are significant in that natural caves are rare in the volcanic highlands. Their presence likely reflects the participation of highland people in what is clearly a pan-Mesoamerican phenomenon of artificial cave construction (Brady 2004). Like their Central Mexican counterparts, the lack of natural caves may have made their replication all the more compelling for the promotion of political ideologies. With archetypal mountain-caves implicated in creation, fertility, and links to ancestral deities, creating such potent features may have been a preferred mechanism in many communities to promote authoritative links between elites and the sources of divine legitimacy.[3]

Although sites in the Maya Lowlands also participated in the reproduction of sacred landscapes at ceremonial centers, they present different sets of circumstances. There, examples of artificial caves, as sources of water or otherwise, are neither common nor well documented from surface sites. This may be attributable in part to the vast number of natural caves found in the limestone that makes up the Yucatán Peninsula and Petén.

In the northern lowlands water-caves and *cenotes* were heavily utilized as sources of potable water. Tulum, Cozumel, and San Lorian all had well-like features incorporated into their site cores. Numerous sites, including Chichén Itzá and Mayapán, were built to incorporate these sacred features into their urban landscape (Brown 2005).

In the southern lowlands caves are frequently a source of water. J. Eric Thompson (1959: 124ff) proposed that, for the Maya, cave water was considered sacred and distinct from water found on the ground. Wells are rare in the Petén; the only known example of a stone-lined vertical well comes from Ixcanrio, in the northeast (Ball 1972). In the Pasion region, architecture and natural caves are closely linked, and it has been suggested that site-planning decisions incorporated the presence of caves, at least some of them water bearing. At Dos Pilas, several acropoli were oriented around water-bearing caves and a large upwelling spring (Brady 1997; Brady and Rodas 1992), and there are hieroglyphic toponyms associated with the acropoli based on the word *ha,* or water (Vogt and Stuart 2005).

Along the Raspaculo River in the northern Maya Mountains of Belize we observed a small, eroded platform that had been constructed over a perennial spring. A small stone-lined channel funneled water away from the structure toward a small cliff where it cascaded into the river. This site is located less than 50 m from the river, making the management of the spring more a luxury than a necessity (Prufer 2001).

In the Maya area the most dramatic example of architecture associated with a modified spring comes from Palenque, known to the pre-Columbian Maya as *Lakam Ha*, or Great Water. There, within the site core, fifty-six individual springs have been documented, with twelve springs directly below or adjacent to the architecture, rendering many buildings watery mountains (French 2002: 13–16). Although the number and complexity of water management projects at Palenque do indicate that they may have had functional or secular uses, several clearly fit within the model of artificial caves and thus likely had ideological significance. More than one spring was housed in an arched building. One in particular, a 50-m-long walled tunnel, or aqueduct, channels water through an artificial underground river; when the water emerges into the open there is a 3.4-m stone alligator effigy that would have appeared to have floated in the water (French 2002: 54).

These few examples make clear that the Maya shared with their Central Mexican neighbors a proclivity for replicating elements of sacred and mythic geography in the built environment. Later we discuss a recently discovered example of an artificial water-cave from the Maya Mountains of southern Belize. This *ch'een* adds to a growing body of data relating site planning, religious belief, and elite ideology to larger pan-Mesoamerican conceptions of an animate and living earth as a source of social and political power.

THE *CH'EEN* AT MUKLEBAL TZUL

Muklebal Tzul is the largest site in the southern Maya Mountains and one of the largest sites in southern Belize. It is located in the uppermost of the major valleys on the Bladen Branch of the Monkey River (Figure 2.1). Of all the valleys in the region, the one containing Muklebal Tzul is the least incised. It is not an alluvial bottomland but consists of ridges and rolling hills of extremely fertile soils derived from limestone and volcanic materials. The valley measures 4.5 km by 2 km, with elevations between 300 and 450 m ASL (Figure 2.2). Its primary geographic feature is a highly dissected transverse ridge on top of which the site's ceremonial core was built, as well as numerous smaller ridges with narrow spines located to the west, all of which are separated by small intermittent drainages and many of which were settled. To date, 204 structures have been mapped in eleven ridgetop settlement groups (Figure 2.3). Although quantifiable comparative data for other sites do not exist, we feel confident that Muklebal Tzul is the largest site in southern Belize, eclipsing Lubaantun, Nim Li Punit, Uxbenká, and Pusilhá in both size and complexity (Prufer 2005).

The main ceremonial core of the site contains an exceptional example of an artificial cave that also functioned as a well. The feature is located in the western corner of a large artificial platform that is the focal point of the site (Figure 2.4). This massive earthen platform, measuring 109 m (E/W) by 43 m, was apparently constructed by cutting away the earth from the slope of a natural ridge and then leveling the surface to create a large flat area. It is bounded by a steep terrace on the downhill southwest side and a high wall on the northeast, or uphill, side. We conservatively estimate the volume of earth moved to construct the platform at approximately 6,770 cubic meters, based on half of the entire platform volume, since the construction clearly made use of a natural slope, reducing the amount of earth and rock that needed to be moved. Access to and from the platform was made via a 37-m-long, 12-m-wide parapeted causeway, leading from the southeast corner of the platform up the slope of the ridge to the southwest corner of a series of complex civic and residential plazas that make up another complex of civic-ceremonial architecture at the summit, including what were likely residences of the local elites.

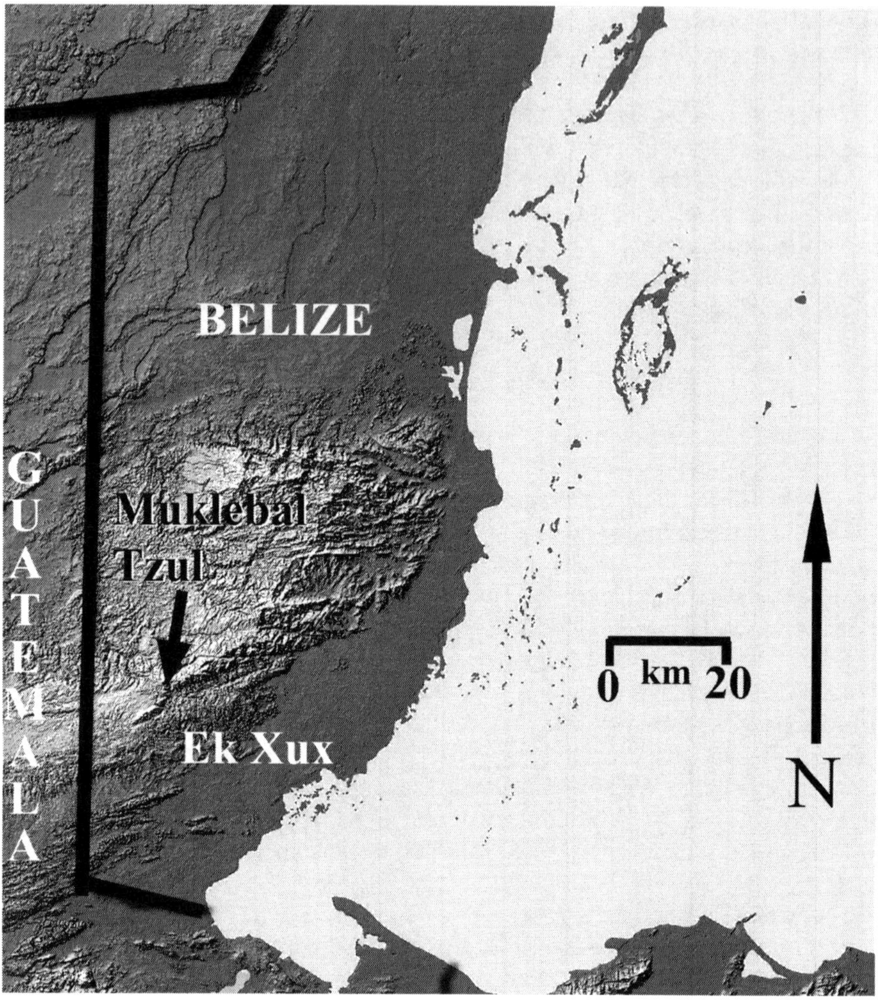

FIGURE 2.1. *Radar relief map of southern Belize with the location of Muklebal Tzul (courtesy of NASA/JPL).*

The artificial cave, or well, is a constructed tunnel located at the northwestern corner of this primary ceremonial platform (Figure 2.5). It is accessed by descending a three-step stairway that leads to a small plaster-lined basin or pool. The spring that feeds the basin is located 13 m into the tunnel, in a dark zone, and is not visible from the entrance. The tunnel is quite narrow, being 1 m wide at its entrance and tapering to slightly less than 30 cm wide where the spring emerges from the ground (Figure 2.6).

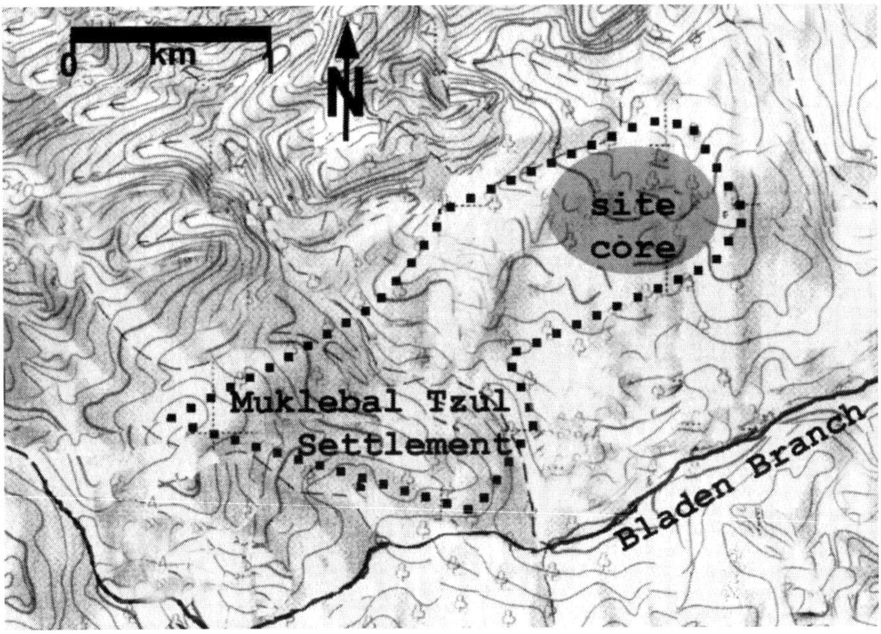

FIGURE 2.2. *Topographic map with the location of Muklebal Tzul and delineating primary settlement area (modified after DGMS 1993).*

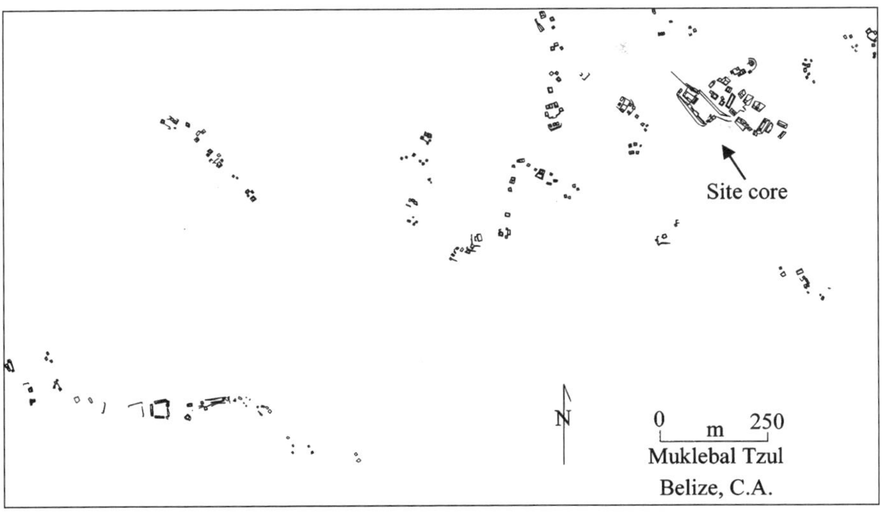

FIGURE 2.3. *The site core and settlement at Muklebal Tzul.*

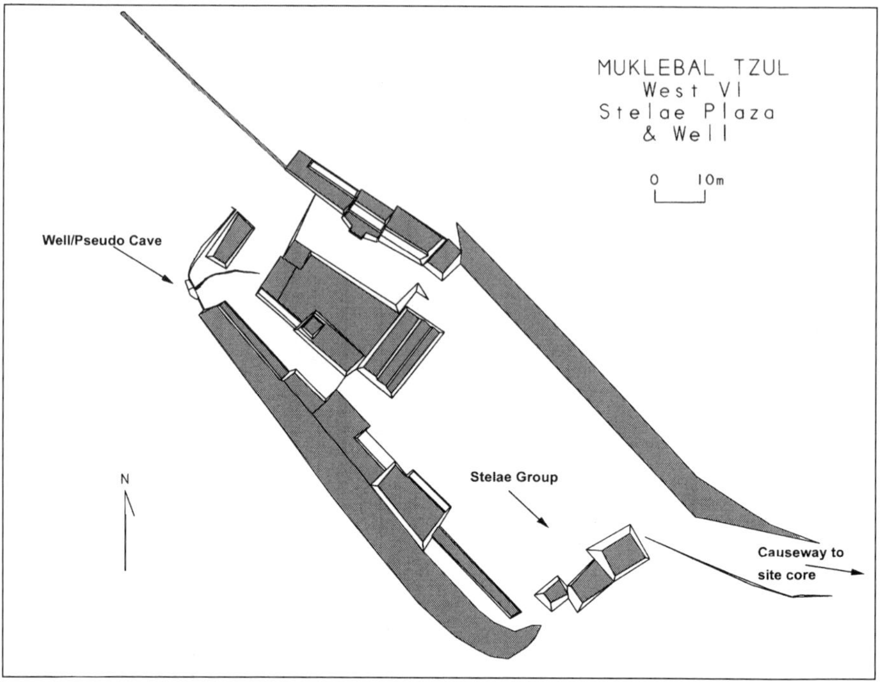

FIGURE 2.4. *The main platform at the site core at Muklebal Tzul. The platform is over 100 m long. Note the location of the well in the southwest corner.*

In 2000 the well was cleaned and partially excavated to confirm the presence of the water-collection basin at its opening, to look for any diagnostic ceramics to date its use, to ascertain the extent of plaster flooring in the spillway, and to better understand how the feature was constructed in relation to the platform. The plaster-lined basin was uncovered in the entrance under approximately 70 cm of collapsed debris and silt (Figure 2.7). A total of three sherds were recovered from the basin, leading to speculation that the feature was regularly maintained and kept clean when used by residents of the site. All three sherds are from nondiagnostic jar forms, which may emphasize the use of the well for water collection.[4]

The water emerges from a small spring at the rear of the passage, approximately 2 m beneath the platform surface. The actual spring is a small fist-sized fissure in the bedrock. The area around the spring had been plastered, and water was channeled through the tunnel into the basin. There is a small, 10-cm artificial waterfall where the water drops from the passage into the basin. The basin itself was designed to hold approximately 26 liters, or 7 gallons, of water.

The plaster-floored spillway that runs the full length of the tunnel is largely intact and still functional (Figure 2.8). The flooring extends underneath the walls of the feature, indicating that it was installed before the construction of the masonry

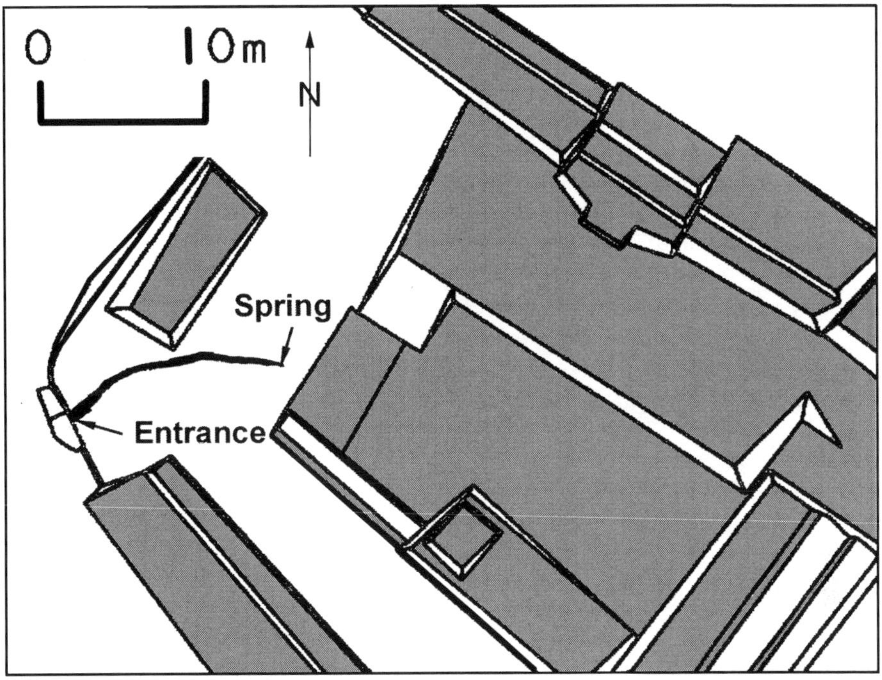

FIGURE 2.5. *Close-up of the area of the platform containing the well.*

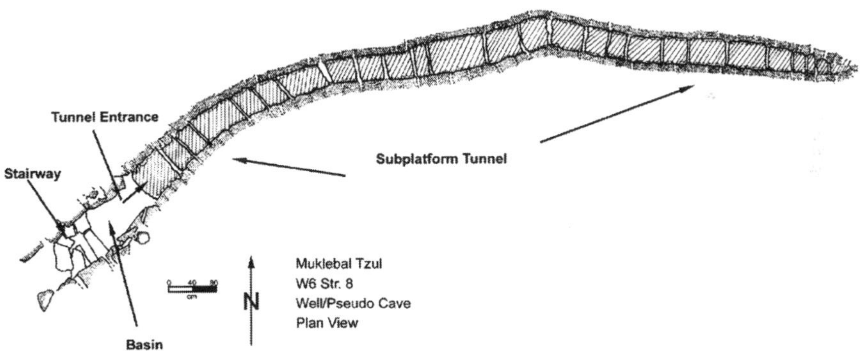

FIGURE 2.6. *Plan view of the well tunnel showing the tunnel, basin, and stairway.*

tunnel and likely at the same time as or before the platform itself. The walls of the tunnel are cut stone and were at one time plastered. The roof of the tunnel is constructed of twenty-four large capstone blocks that lie below the debris fill and flagging stones that form the surface of the platform.

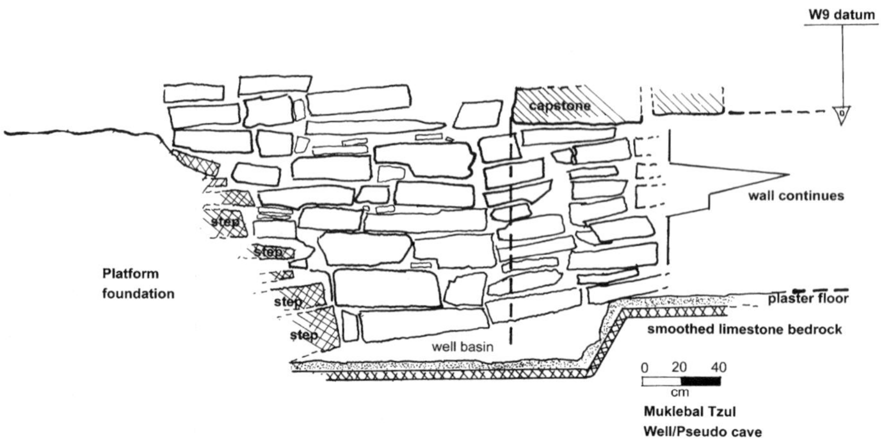

FIGURE 2.7. *Profile of the basin and tunnel entrance.*

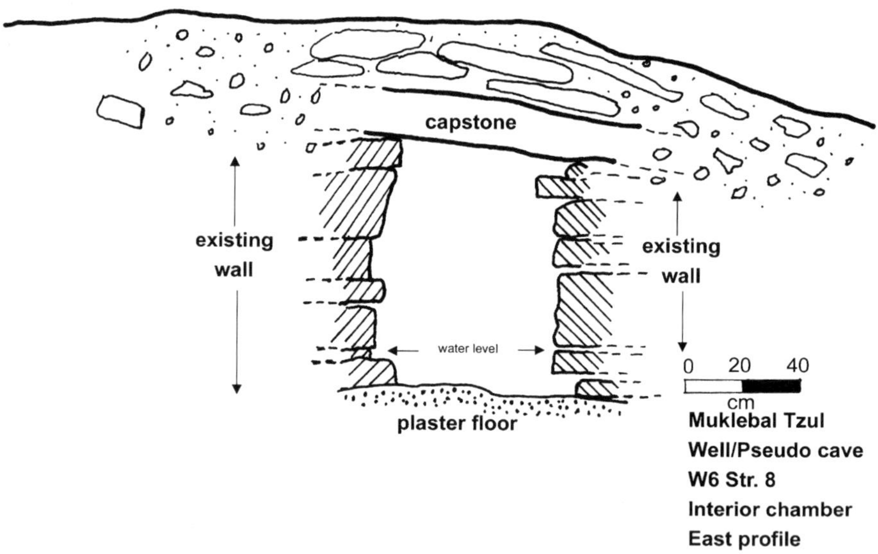

FIGURE 2.8. *Cross section of the well tunnel showing the plaster floor extending under the walls of the platform.*

Following excavation of the basin at the entrance to the tunnel, the passage was cleared of debris and silt. Remarkably, at this point water began to flow through the passage and to fill the basin. Before this, water had been obstructed by silt and debris and was likely draining through the walls of the tunnel where the plaster had eroded away. We estimated the dry season flow to be approximately 2.6 liters per minute, hardly a massive volume of water but sufficient to fill the basin in a little over 10 minutes. We observed overflow from the basin draining behind the stairs and dissipating below the platform. To the residents of the site, the source of the water would not have been visible. They would have seen a small stream flowing out of the tunnel, down a small "waterfall" and into the basin, and then mysteriously disappearing as it drained into the bedrock. This is very similar to the visible processes seen at numerous natural caves in the area, where water emerging from the earth quickly drains back into the porous limestone.

CONSTRUCTING CEREMONIAL SPACES AT MUKLEBAL TZUL

The previous description clearly indicates that the *ch'een* replicates a natural cave, and incorporating the spring into the construction of the ceremonial core indicates its significance as a source of political power. However, the substantial platform that was constructed around the well is also critical to understanding the significance of the *ch'een* in the larger context of the site.

The summit of the platform is divided into two distinct plaza areas. The larger of the two plazas is a massive open space that occupies the southeastern two-thirds of the platform. This plaza measures 50 m (E/W) by 35 m (N/S). It is bounded on the northeast by the upslope wall of the ridge and by low structures on the northwest, southwest, and southeast. Directly in front of Structure 12, the easternmost and tallest structure in the plaza, a total of six stelae and what may be one hemispherical altar were found. All of the stelae were broken, and only three of the six stelae bodies remain, although all of the bases appear to have retained their original placements. Like elsewhere in the southern Maya Mountains, none of the exposed faces of the stelae shows any signs of carving or other adornment. It may be that these monuments were once plastered, painted, or both, but no traces of such treatments are visible. To the north of the stelae lies the causeway linking the platform to the three large civic/residential groups on the summit of the ridge, several of which have large intact tombs. Individuals passing between the ceremonial platform and these latter groups would have had to pass directly in front of the stelae and Structure 12. This would have reinforced the ideological and political importance of the ceremonial platform, including the artificial cave that was clearly an important part of it, to the residents of the site.

The secondary plaza where the well is located is smaller but far more architecturally complex than the stelae plaza, and a narrow wall separates the two, suggesting a very intentional demarcation of space and most likely of function as well. Whereas the stelae plaza is a large open space unobstructed by construction or features, the well plaza is crowded with structures and architectural features. It measures 33 m (E/W) by 29 m (N/S), is completely bounded by a series of platform mounds and range structures, and has several low constructions built in the center that effectively bisect the plaza into two separate spaces: a smaller interior plaza surrounded by a much larger open walkway. This division of space is very interesting in that it suggests the restriction of access to activities carried out in this area, an idea lent further support by the presence of the wall separating the well plaza from the larger, more public stelae plaza and restricting movement between the two spaces. The only access to the well plaza is through a small ramp connecting a corner of the well plaza to a corner of the stelae plaza.

The only portion of the well plaza not bounded by terraces or structures slopes steeply, indicating that access to the well plaza was primarily from the stelae plaza. At the same time, the only access to the stelae plaza is via either the ramp from the well plaza or the parapeted causeway descending from the ridgetop and the series of civic/residential plazas situated there. Hence, access to both plazas appears to have been relatively restricted. However, it seems clear from the layout and nature of these two conjoined plazas that there was a significant difference between them: the stelae plaza almost certainly functioned as an important ceremonial focus for the community and as such was probably at least periodically open to public displays. The wide causeway leading from this plaza into the civic/residential area of the site core would have facilitated the movement of relatively large numbers of people, and the broad, open space of the plaza itself could have accommodated a substantial congregation of people. The well plaza, on the other hand, was extremely restricted and may have been space reserved for religious or other specialists and those whose duties related directly to the maintenance and use of the well.

Interestingly, the most prominent structure in the well plaza (Structure 2) has a finely crafted cut-block staircase ascending the front and a large bench on the summit of the platform. From the vantage point of Structure 2's frontal terrace, an observer could have seen all activities being carried out, not only in the well plaza but also in the stelae plaza, making it possible to monitor activities in both plazas.

ACCESS TO THE *CH'EEN* AND CENTERS OF POWER

The center of power at the site included both the expansive elite residential area on the ridgetop and the two ceremonial spaces on the large platform. However, Muklebal Tzul is a large and complex site, at least by regional standards. Settlement is spread out over 3 km^2 and across a series of modified ridgetops. At least 20 percent of all the residential buildings at the site contain substructural chambers, many of which were used as tombs (Figure 2.9). These chambers were all constructed at the same time as the buildings that house them. They are finely built from dressed stone; many contain stairways, and several are round or oval in shape. Elsewhere, we have argued that some of these were in fact artificial caves, built at the "household level" (Kindon 2002; Prufer 2002). The site also boasts a second stelae plaza, located in an outlying settlement group. Many of the residential groups in the hinterlands are as well built and complex as those located in the site core, although perhaps smaller and not as prominent; the combined well/stelae platforms and the three plazas overlooking them occupy the highest point in the valley and no doubt were the

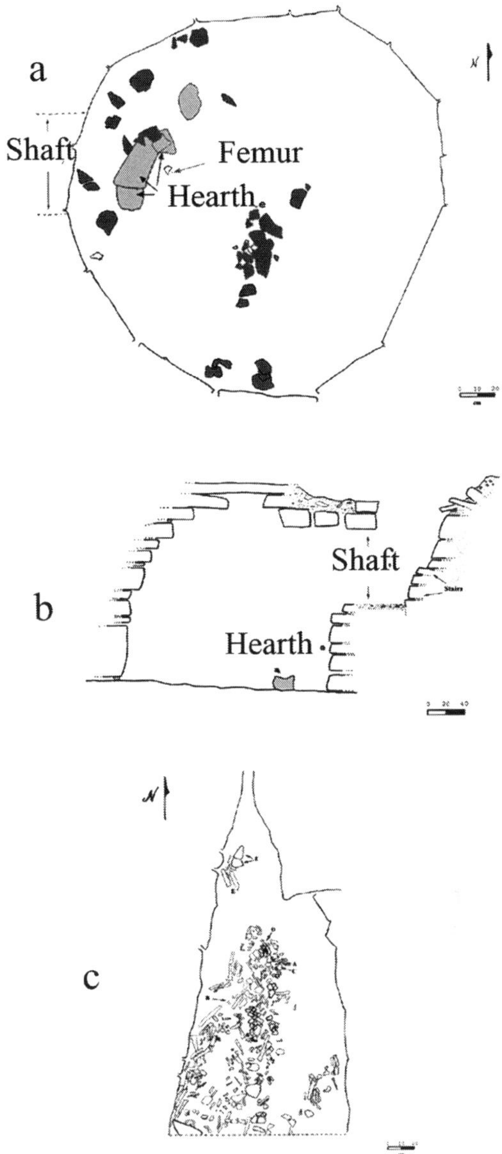

FIGURE 2.9. *Views of two subsurface chambers at Muklebal Tzul. A. and B. are a circular chamber under Structure 38. It was accessed by a shaft entrance and did not contain evidence of burials (with the exception of a single well-preserved femur shaft). C. is a substructural chamber that is a modified natural crevice under Structure 36. It contained the remains of at least three individuals and associated grave goods.*

centers of political and ceremonial activity.

Clearly, we cannot know how or if residents of other precincts of the site would have accessed the site core. On one hand, the sheer size of the open stelae plaza could argue that it was, at least on occasion, open to the public. On the other hand, the well plaza was likely far less accessible, separated from the stelae plaza by a wall and then further bisected into different areas, with the well hidden from view. At the very least, residents of the site would have been aware of the *ch'een* and its importance to the ceremonial center.

Despite its obvious importance, it is curious that the well itself is such an understated feature in the site architecture. Its entrance lies in the extreme western corner of the well plaza, and no large buildings or monuments are associated with it. Although the construction of the well entrance and tunnel shaft is excellent, its external appearance is relatively humble, with no existing surface indications aside from the descending stairway. In fact, when the survey team originally discovered the well, it was thought to be simply another collapsed tomb with a stairway entrance, like so many of the ones that dot the settlement. The fact that the source of the water for the well is actually located *underneath* the plaza could only have added to the significance and importance of this area.

There is also considerable evidence that the well did not serve as a large-scale source of water for the site at large. This needs to be considered in light of the fact that there is no other apparent source of year-round water at the site. The nearest permanent water source is a small creek located roughly 1 km north and over 100 m below the site core. There are some indications that several small drainages in the site settlement area that flow only during the rainy season may have been dammed to collect water, but this has not been thoroughly investigated and remains speculative. As for the well, its location in a restricted plaza argues that access was limited. Had this been a source of water for the larger population, we would have expected it to appear in a more accessible location. We would also expect it to have had a larger entrance that could have facilitated use by more than one person at a time. In addition, the small collection basin does not indicate large-scale use. Finally, the volume of water we observed flowing from the well would have been insufficient to support the needs of even a fraction of the local population (estimated at roughly 1,200 people).

The Classic period residents of Muklebal Tzul were heavily involved in the use of caves. Over thirty cave sites have been investigated within 3 km of the site, including a substantial sinkhole located less than 150 m from the site core and twelve caves located at the base of the ridge the site sits on. One of the most stunning caves in the area is the source of the Bladen Branch of the Monkey River, located less than 2 km from the site core, where the river emerges from a cavernous opening. It seems probable that the artificial well at Muklebal Tzul was intended to reproduce a water-bearing cave on a miniature scale. If so, it would have allowed the residents of the site to, in effect, center their community over a feature with both mythical and sacred qualities. Although the spring itself might have been sufficient to fulfill these qualities, it was certainly enhanced by the construction of the tunnel as a cave leading under the massive platform, which in turn is a metaphor for the all-important and centering sacred hill. The feature is thus part of a larger Mesoamerican tradition of replicating elements of the sacred landscape in civic ceremonial architecture to enhance the political-religious status of rulers and religious specialists and undoubtedly to contribute to the prestige of public and private ceremonial activities. At the least, such an arrangement would have had considerable local importance in the Maya Mountains, an area already replete with hills and caves.

NOTES

1. The Nahua believe water comes from the sea and is carried inland by the *pilhuehuentsitsij,* old male dwarves who dress in black and are metaphors for the clouds. Once inland, water is controlled and given to people by *apanchanej,* a female water spirit who dwells in a cave at the top of the mountain Postectli. The cave is seen as the source of fertility, since life-giving water comes to humans and their crops from caves (Sandstrom 2005).

2. Ceremonies related to rainfall and fertility are common across Mesoamerica. In Yucatán rain prayers are officiated by community specialists (Bartolomé 1978: 78; Hanks 1990). Chaak, the rain gods, live in caves called the "trunk of heaven" and appear with the first thunder at the beginning of the rainy season through a hole in the clouds (Redfield and Villa Rojas 1934: 116, 333). The Lacandon believe mountains that contain water-filled caves are the source of all rain and clouds (Tozzer 1907: 81), a perspecitve shared by the K'iche' (Tedlock 1992: 128). The Lacandon god of rain, Mensäbäk, lives in a cave and makes it rain by burning copal, the smoke of which turns into rain clouds (Toor 1947: 473). The Chol also believe the gods that control wind and rain reside in caves and mountains, both of which have a sacred character (Villa Rojas 1969: 236). Tzoltzil Earth Lords control clouds, rain, lightning, and thunder (Gossen 1974: 21).

3. Brady (2004) has noted that numerous other, less secure reports of artificial caves exist in the highlands and that the actual number may be in the hundreds or thousands.

4. Tzoltzil kin and political groups regularly participate in cleaning communal wells and springs (Vogt 1976: 99).

REFERENCES CITED

Alvarado Tezozomoc, Fernando
1975 *Crónica Mexicana,* Second Edition. Biblioteca Porrua, 61, Editorial Purrua, Mexico.

Ball, Hall C.
1972 A Maya Well in Northern Guatemala. *Muse News* 3(3):398–401, 419.

Barrera Vásquez, Alfredo
1970 Ceremonial of Tsikul T'an Ti' Yuntsiloob at Balankanche: Description of Ceremony. In *Balankanche, Throne of the Tiger Priest,* 72–78, Publication, 32. Tulane University, Middle American Research Institute, New Orleans.

Bartolomé, Miguel A.
1978 Medicine Men Speak: Stories of Mayan Shamans of Yucatan. *Latin American Indian Literatures Journal* 2(2):78–84.

Benson, Elizabeth P.
1985 Architecture as Metaphor. In *Fifth Palenque Round Table, 1983,* ed. Virginia M. Fields, 183–188. Palenque Round Table, 1988, Pre-Columbian Art Research Institute, San Francisco.

Brady, James E.
1997 Settlement Configuration and Cosmology: The Role of Caves at Dos Pilas. *American Anthropologist* 99(3):602–618.
2004 Constructed Landscapes: Exploring the Meaning and Significance of Recent Discoveries of Artificial Caves. *Ketzalcalli* 1:2–17.

Brady, James E., and Irma Rodas
1992 Hallazgos recientes y nuevas interpretaciones de la Cueva de El Duende. In *Simposio de investigaciones arqueológicas en Guatemala* (5 session 1991), 185–194. Ministerio de Cultura y Deportes, Instituto de Antropología e Historia, Asociación Tikal, Guatemala.

Brady, James E., and George Veni
1992 Man-Made and Pseudo-Karst Caves: The Implications of Subsurface Features Within Maya Centers. *Geoarchaeology* 7(2):149–167.

Broda, Johanna

1982 El culto mexica de los cerros y el agua. *Multidisciplina* 7:45–56.

1996 Calendarios, Cosmovisión y Observación de la Naturaleza. In *Temas Mesoamericanos,* coordinated by Sonia Lombardo and Enrique Nalda, 427–469. Instituto Nacional de Antropología e Historia, Mexico.

Brown, Clifford T.

2005 Caves, Karst, and Settlement at Mayapan, Yucatan. In *In the Maw of the Earth Monster: Mesoamerican Ritual Cave Use,* eds. James E. Brady and Keith M. Prufer, 373–402. University of Texas Press, Austin.

Colas, Pierre R., and Alexander Voss

2001 A Game of Life and Death, the Maya Ball Game. In *Maya: Divine Kings of the Rainforest,* ed. Nikolai Grube, 186–193. Könemann Verlagsgesellschaft, Cologne.

DGMS

1993 1:50,000 Topographic Map of Belize (Series E 775-MIL Edition 5-GSGS). Director General of the Military Survey, Surrey, UK.

Doolittle, William E.

1995 Indigenous Development of Mesoamerican Irrigation. *Geographical Review* 85(3):301–323.

Dow, James E.

2001 Central and North Mexican Shamans. In *Mesoamerican Healers,* eds. Brad R. Huber and Alan R. Sandstrom, 66–94. University of Texas Press, Austin.

French, Kirk D.

2002 Creating Space Through Water Management at the Classic Maya Site of Palenque, Chiapas, Mexico. MA thesis. Department of Anthropology, University of Cincinnati, Cincinnati.

García-Zambrano, Angel J.

1994 Early Colonial Evidence of Pre-Columbian Rituals of Foundation. In *Seventh Palenque Round Table, 1989,* eds. Merle Greene Robertson and Virginia Field, 217–227. Pre-Columbian Art Research Institute, San Francisco.

Gendrop, Paul

1980 Dragon-Mouth Entrances: Zoomorphic Portals in the Architecture of Central Yucatan. In *Third Palenque Round Table, 1978, Part 2,* ed. Merle Greene Robertson, 138–150. University of Texas Press, Austin.

1985 Portadas zoomorfas y mascarones asociados en la arquitectura de la región Río Bec: un análisis descriptivo. *Cuadernos de arquitectura Mesoamericana* 3(6):47–50. Mexico.

Gossen, Gary H.

1974 *Chamulas in the World of the Sun: Time and Space in a Maya Oral Tradition.* Harvard University Press, Cambridge, MA.

Grove, David

1973 Olmec Altars and Myths. *Archaeology* 26(2):128–135.

Hanks, William F.

1990 *Referential Practice: Language and Lived Space Among the Maya.* University of Chicago Press, Chicago.

Hellmuth, Nicholas

1987 *Surface of the Underwater World: Iconography of the Gods of Early Classic Maya Art in Petén, Guatemala.* Foundation for Latin American Anthropological Research, Culver City.

Hohmann-Vogrin, Annegrete

2001 Unity in Space and Time, the Maya Architecture. In *Maya: Divine Kings of the Rainforest,* ed. Nikolai Grube, 194–215. Könemann Verlagsgesellschaft, Cologne.

Ichon, Alain, and Marie C. Arnauld

1985 Le Protoclassique á la Lagunita, El Quiché, Guatemala, Centre National de la Recherche Scientifique, Paris.

Kindon, Andrew W.

2002 Classic Maya Sociopolitical Organization and Settlement Patterns in the Maya Mountains of Southern Belize. Ph.D. Dissertation. Department of Anthropology, University of California, Los Angeles.

Kirchhoff, Paul, Lina Odena Guemes, and Luis Reyes

1976 *Historia Tolteca-Chichimeca.* Fondo de Cultura Economica, Mexico.

López Luján, Leonardo

1994 *Offerings of the Templo Mayor of Tenochtitlan.* University Press of Colorado, Niwot.

Lucero, Lisa J.

1999 Water Control and Maya Politics in the Southern Maya Lowlands. In *Complex Polities in the Ancient Tropical World,* eds. Elisabeth A. Bacus and Lisa J. Lucero, 35–50. Archaeological Papers, 9. American Anthropological Association, Washington, D.C.

2002 The Collapse of the Classic Maya: A Case for the Role of Water Control. *American Anthropologist* 104(3):814–826.

Martin, Simon

2001 Under a Deadly Star—Warfare Among the Classic Maya. In *Maya: Divine Kings of the Rain Forest,* ed. Nikolai Grube, 174–185. Könemann, Cologne.

McCafferty, Geoffrey

1996 Reinterpreting the Great Pyramid of Cholula. *Ancient Mesoamerica* 7:1–17.

Millon, René F.

1981 Teotihuacan: City, State, and Civilization. In *Archaeology,* ed. Jeremy A. Sabloff, 198–243. Handbook of Middle American Indians, Supplement, 1, University of Texas Press, Austin.

Parsons, Lee

1973 Iconographic Notes on a New Izapan Stela From Abaj Takalik, Guatemala. In *Proceedings of the International Congress of Americanists, Rome and Genova, 1972,* vol. 1, 203–212. Genova.

Pincemin Deliberos, Sophia, and Mauricio Rosas Kifuri

2000 Iconografia del agua en los Codices Mayas. *Los investigadores de la cultura Maya* 8(1):100–113.

Prufer, Keith M.

2001 Archaeological Findings. In *Report of the New Millennium Expedition Year 2000 Joint Services Scientific Expedition to the Upper Raspaculo, Maya Mountains, and Limestone Karst of the Western Chiquibul Area, Belize,* ed. Lt. Col. Alastair Rodgers. The Brake Colaton Raleigh, Devon, UK.

2002 Communities, Caves, and Ritual Specialists: A Study of Sacred Space in the Maya Mountains of Southern Belize. Ph.D. Dissertation. Department of Anthropology, Southern Illinois University, Cabondale.

2005 Shamans, Caves and the Roles of Ritual Specialists in Maya Society. In *In the Maw of the Earth Monster: Mesoamerican Ritual Cave Use,* eds. James E. Brady and Keith M. Prufer, 186–222. University of Texas Press, Austin.

Rands, Robert L.

1953 The Water Lily in Maya Art: A Complex of Alleged Asiatic Origin. *Bureau of American Ethnology Bulletin* 151:75–153.

1955 Some Manifestations of Water in Mesoamerican Art. *Smithsonian Institution Anthropological Papers* 48:265–393.

Redfield, Robert, and Alphonso Villa Rojas

1934 *Chan Kom: A Maya Village*. University of Chicago Press, Chicago.

Reents-Budet, Dorie J.

1994 *Painting the Maya Universe: Royal Ceramics of the Classic Period.* Duke University Press, Durham.

Rice, Don S.

1997 Ingeniera hidraulica en Peten Central, Guatemala. In *Simposio de investigaciones arqueológicas en Guatemala, 1996,* 533–544. Ministerio de Cultura y Deportes, Instituto de Antropologia e Historia, Asociacion Tikal, Guatemala.

Rivera Dorado, Miguel

1987 El Satunsat o Laberinto. *Oxkintok* 1:18–29. Misión Arqueológica de España en México, Madrid.

Rivera Dorado, Miguel, and Ascensión Amador Naranjo

1993 El Laberinto de Oxkintok. In *VII Simposio de investigaciones arqueológicas en Guatemala*, eds. Juan Pedro Laporte and Héctor L. Escobedo, 727–735. Ministerio de Cultura y Desportes, Instituto de Antropología e Historia, Asociación Tikal, Guatemala.

Sahagún, Bernardino de

1950–1982 *Florentine Codex: General History of the Things of New Spain.* Translated from the Aztec Into English With Notes and Illustrations by Arthur J.O. Anderson and Charles E. Dibble. School of American Research, University of Utah Press, Santa Fe.

Sanders, William T.

1957 Tierra y Agua (Soil and Water), a Study of the Ecological Factors in the Development of Meso-American Civilizations. Ph.D. Dissertation, Parts 1–2. Department of Anthropology, Harvard University, Cambridge.

1968 Hydraulic Agriculture Economic Symbiosis and the Evolution of States in Central Mexico. In *Anthropological Archaeology in the Americas,* ed. B. J. Meggers, 88–107. Anthropological Society of Washington, Washington, D.C.

Sandstrom, Alan R.

1991 *Corn Is Our Blood: Culture and Ethnic Identify in a Contemporary Aztec Indian Village*. University of Oklahoma Press, Norman.

2005 The Cave-Pyramid Complex Among Contemporary Nahuas of Northern Veracruz. In *In the Maw of the Earth Monster: Studies of Mesoamerican Ritual Cave Use,* eds. James E. Brady and Keith M. Prufer, 35–68. University of Texas Press, Austin.

Scarborough, Vernon L.

1996 Reservoirs and Watersheds in the Central Maya Lowlands. In *The Managed Mosaic: Ancient Maya Agriculture and Resource Use,* ed. Scott L. Fedick, 304–314. University of Utah Press, Salt Lake City.

1998 Ecology and Ritual: Water Management and the Maya. *Latin American Antiquity* 9(2):135–159.

Schavelzon, Daniel

1980 Temples, Caves, or Monsters? Notes on Zoomorphic Facades in Pre-Hispanic Architecture. In *Third Palenque Round Table, 1978, Part 2,* ed. Merle Greene Robertson, 151–162. University of Texas Press, Austin.

Schele, Linda, and Mary E. Miller

1986 *Blood of Kings: Dynasty and Ritual in Maya Art.* Kimbell Art Museum, Fort Worth.

Smith, A. Ledyard

1955 *Archaeological Reconnaissance in Central Guatemala,* Publication 608. Carnegie Institution of Washington, Washington, D.C.

Spranz, Bodo

1967 Descubriemiento en Totimehuacan, Puebla. *Boletín del Instituto Nacional de Antropología e Historia* 27:19–22.

Stuart, David

1987 *Ten Phonetic Syllables.* Research Reports on Ancient Maya Writing 14. Center for Maya Research, Washington, D.C.

1997 The Hills Are Alive: Sacred Mountains in the Maya Cosmos. *Symbols* (Spring): 13–17.

Stuart, David, and Stephen D. Houston

1994 *Classic Maya Place Names.* Studies in Pre-Columbian Art and Archaeology 33. Dumbarton Oaks Research Library and Collection, Washington, D.C.

Tedlock, Barbara

1992 *Time and the Highland Maya.* University of New Mexico Press, Albuquerque.

Thompson, J. Eric S.

1959 Role of Caves in Maya Cuture. *Mitteilungen der Museum für Völkerkunde und Vorgeschichte* 25:122–129.

Toor, Frances

1947 *A Treasury of Mexican Folkways.* Crown, New York.

Tozzer, Alfred M.

1907 *A Comparative Study of the Mayas and the Lacandones.* Macmillan, New York.

Villa Rojas, Alfonso

1969 Maya Lowlands: The Chontol, Chol, and Kekchi. In *Handbook of Middle American Indians,* Volume 7, Ethnology, ed. Evon Z. Vogt, 230–240. University of Texas Press, Austin.

Vogt, Evon Z.
1964 Ancient Maya and Contemporary Tzotzil Cosmology: A Comment on Some Methodological Problems. *American Antiquity* 30:192–195.
1976 *Tortillas for the Gods: A Symbolic Analysis of Zinacanteco Rituals.* Harvard University Press, Cambridge.

Vogt, Evon Z., and David Stuart
2005 Some Notes on Ritual Caves Among the Ancient and Modern Maya. In *In the Maw of the Earth Monster: Mesoamerican Ritual Cave Use,* eds. James E. Brady and Keith M. Prufer, 155–185. University of Texas Press, Austin.

Ximénez, Francisco
1967 Historia natural del reino de Guatemala, compuesto por Fray Francisco Ximénez . . . escriba en el pueblo de Sacapulas en el año de 1722, Publicación especial, 14 Sociedad de Geografía e Historia de Guatemala, Guatemala.

Chapter Three

Caves and Artificial Caves in Late Postclassic Maya Ceremonial Groups

by Timothy W. Pugh

Maya ceremonial groups are well-known for their monumental constructions, built as microcosmic images of the universe. Such ritual assemblages often represent creation places from which the universe emerged (Freidel, Schele, and Parker 1993: 123–172; Schele and Mathews 1998: 36–40). Caves are critical places in Maya creation events and the subsequent universe; hence, one would expect to find these features incorporated into monumental constructions. Yet, many archaeologists ignore the subterranean features in their fieldwork and discount them in their interpretations. This chapter investigates some of the ways the Late Postclassic (A.D. 1200 to 1540) Maya incorporated caves into their built environment. This point will be primarily illustrated through an examination of Late Postclassic temple assemblages and related groups, although I will also discuss some Colonial and modern uses of caves as analogies for the interpretation of archaeological materials.

Temple assemblages were originally defined at Mayapán in Yucatán, Mexico (Figure 3.1) and include five

FIGURE 3.1. *Selected Maya sites.*

ritual buildings in a specific arrangement (Figure 3.2) (Proskouriakoff 1962: 91). In these groups a raised shrine, an opposing temple, and a statue shrine standing between these structures form the primary axis, which generally extends east to west. The temple is a god house on an artificial mountain in the form of a pyramid (Carmack 1981: 186; Schele and Mathews 1998: 29). Statue shrines often held statues of human, animal, and anthropomorphized figures composed of stucco and

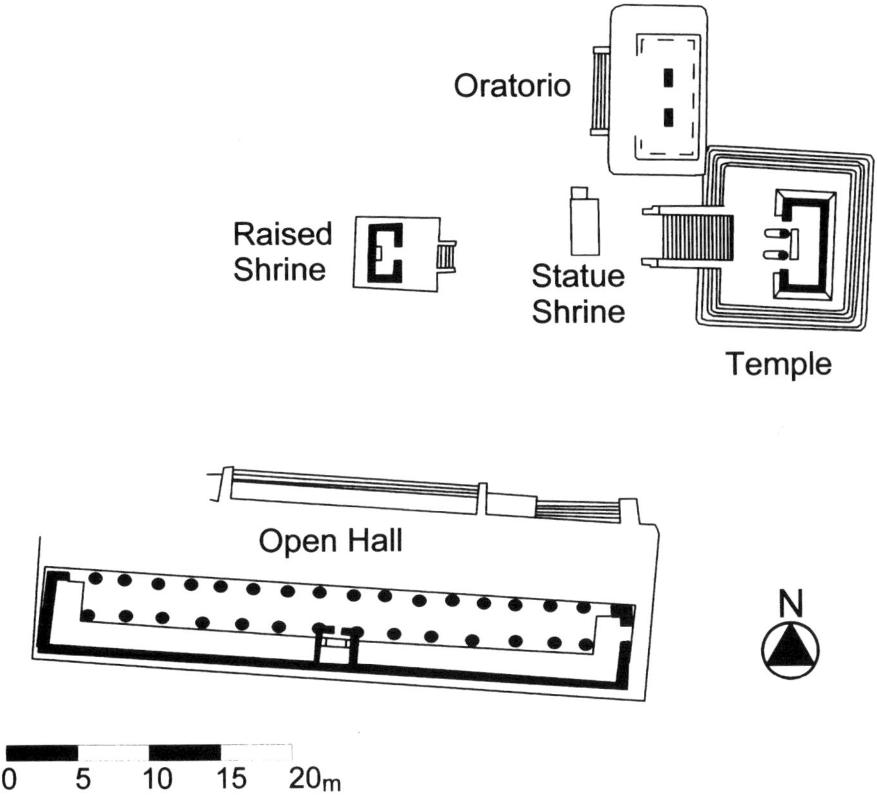

FIGURE 3.2. *Mayapán temple assemblage (redrawn from Proskouriakoff 1957).*

stalactites (Proskouriakoff 1962: 136), depicting the same personages found on image censers inside the temples (Winters 1955: 403). Raised shrines may have been dedicated to ancestor veneration, although the exact use of these structures is uncertain (Pugh 2003a: 946). To the right and facing in the same direction as the temple is an oratorio, which is a smaller god house. At a right angle to the temple stands an open hall. Such halls appear to have been lineage halls (Carmack 1981: 287–290). Temple assemblages are exaggerated variants of another type of ceremonial assemblage known as the basic ceremonial group, which is limited to an open hall, raised shrine, and oratorio (Proskouriakoff 1962: 91). Each of the buildings had particular meanings and uses; hence, temple assemblages and basic ceremonial groups, like most other Maya ritual areas, are composed of interrelated ritual symbols and settings. Included in many such configurations of symbols and ritual actions were natural and artificial caves.

CAVE SYMBOLISM

Caves were important symbols in Late Postclassic to Colonial period Maya ritual performances, and like most ritual symbols they were multivocal (Stone 1995: 34). Cave entrances are naturally liminal icons, as one can pass from the light surface of the earth into the dark underworld (Stone 1995: 34–39). Caves are decidedly peculiar relative to the surface world. They are also important sources of water, especially in Yucatán where surface water is scarce; hence, part of their significance is obviously related to their role as crucial resources. Caves were also associated with wind, a multidimensional force that could be either positive or negative. Winds move water from subterranean passages into the sky (Hanks 1990: 306), but wind blowing from water inside caves can cause sickness (Redfield and Villa Rojas 1934: 165; Villa Rojas 1945: 135).

As naturally "in-between" or liminal icons, caves were ideal ritual spaces for negotiating the boundaries of cosmic planes. In some myths, entrance into a cave initiates travel to another world occupied by supernatural beings. For example, the Itza describe that the realm of the Lord of the Deer could be accessed through a cave, but in his domain, time functioned differently than in the material world (Hofling 1991: 141–148). Such beliefs may be quite old because carvings at Late Preclassic Izapa depict monster mouths, likely representations of caves, which frame or contain mythological events (V. G. Smith 1984). In Yucatán, one must avoid injuring tortoises, as doing so will ultimately compel one to leap into a *cenote* occupied by a large tortoise guarding an entrance into the underworld (Redfield and Villa Rojas 1934: 207–208). Caves and artificial pits were also places where negative beings such as monstrous animals (Hofling 1991: 186–192) and evil winds (Hanks 1990: 348) could be trapped.

In addition to vertical boundaries, caves help to mark and mediate horizontal social boundaries. Boundary points on Colonial maps include large trees, boulders, *cenotes,* and caves with springs, wells, towns, and ruins (Roys 1943: figure 1 and 176–190). Crosses, symbols of *tzuk* or "division," and representations of the world tree (Freidel, Schele, and Parker 1993: 73) marked these important places, which were visited cyclicly on ceremonial circuits that renewed the social group and the land contained by the boundaries (Marcus 1993: 126).

For the Maya and other Mesoamerican groups, the reciprocity of life and death occurs along borders between this world and the otherworld; hence, caves vocalize both life and death. The life aspect of caves is evident in their role as birthplaces. The features could represent wombs and vaginas and were the origin places of group ancestors (Brady 1988: 52; Heyden 1981: 20). Cave imagery is often paralleled with flowers (Hunt 1977: 107), and some apical ancestors and deities are born from the latter rather than the former (see Davis 1978: 21; Tozzer 1907: 94–95). The Maya of Yucatán believed the sun and moon were born from the underworld in the east (Sosa 1985: figure 11; Villa Rojas 1945: 155).

Maya groups do not strongly differentiate caves and artificial pits (Brady 1991: 6–7), and this holds true with regard to cave births as well. In Yucatán, indigenous accounts describe that many powerful crosses were found/born in forest caves or borrow pits (Redfield and Villa Rojas 1934: 108–109). Similar beliefs exist in the highlands at Zinacantan, Mexico (Vogt 1981: 128), and Esquipulas, Guatemala (Brady and Veni 1992: 155). Chan Santa Cruz, the renowned speaking cross of the Caste War in Yucatán, was "born" from a mahogany tree growing on the edge of Cenote Chan Santa Cruz (Reed 1964: 135–136). The mahogany tree, which the Cruzob Maya believed had given birth to many crosses, was venerated as "the Mother of the Crosses" until the Mexican army cut it down in 1852 (Reed 1964: 144). The descendants of the Cruzob Maya claim that the present cross in the Santuario de la Cruz Parlante was part of the original tree and was "found" while excavating a well for drinking water; hence, it was born from both an artificial penetration in the earth and a tree that once stood next to a water-filled *cenote.* Like the original Mother of Crosses, the modern cross is considered to be female and is clearly an aspect of the Virgin Mary.

The importance of trees growing on cave mouths is widespread and extends back to at least the Middle Preclassic period. Relief I and Relief IX of Chalcatzingo, Morelos, Mexico, depict cave/monster mouths with plants growing at their edges (Joralemon 1971: 49). On Relief IX, the plants at the mouths of the caves are four in number and lie at the four directions, indicating that they were world trees. World trees are usually depicted with reptilian/cave imagery at their bases, as one can observe on Late Preclassic Stela 25 at Izapa (Taube 1988: figure 58).

Cenotes and cave springs were important water sources for the Maya. When new communities were established in nineteenth-century Yucatán, they settled around *cenotes* and water was one of the primary concerns (Redfield and Villa Rojas 1934: 18). Clifford Brown (1999: 583) recently expounded on A. L. Smith's (1962: 210) observation that the density of settlement at Late Postclassic Mayapán roughly correlates with the frequency of *cenotes* by suggesting that lineage settlements might have clustered around the water sources. The presence of water within the subterranean features obviously led to their symbolic connection with rain and the rain deity Chaak (see Stone 1995: 35–43) and later the Virgin Mary (Villa Rojas 1945: 102). However, the ideological significance of caves was not simply a by-product of being water sources. In fact, the contrary is often the case, as many caves that center settlements are dry, especially artificial grottos. The life symbolism of caves extends well beyond their role as water sources.

Caves were also associated with death and the underworld. When the sun died to the west, it passed through the cavernous underworld until reborn in the east (Sosa 1985: 397). The sarcophagus lid of Pakal, who ruled Palenque from A.D. 615 to 683 (Martin and Grube 2000: 162–168), eulogizes the death and underworld aspects of cave symbolism. In the relief sculpture, the world tree, the sun, and the dying ruler, Pakal, descend into the maw of the underworld—a cave. Caves were also strongly connected with sacrificial death. A well-known example of cave sacrifice occurred at Chichén Itzá, where persons were thrown into a large water-filled *cenote* (Landa 1941: 180). Numerous Late Postclassic period offerings recovered from the Sacred Cenote (Coggins and Shane 1984: 111–155) support ethnohistoric accounts of its use as an offering place, although human sacrifice is difficult to document. During the revolt at Sacalum in 1623, after sacrificing and dismembering Spaniards and indigenous converts, Maya revolutionaries placed the bodies of the Spanish leaders in a "hole of white earth," probably a borrow pit, and the bodies of other victims in caves (G. D. Jones 1989: 180–182). In 1696, after reportedly sacrificing two Dominican priests, the Itza of Petén placed their remains in an island cave (G. D. Jones 1998: 303–304). These Colonial accounts resemble imagery on Stela 14 of Uxmal, which depicts two nude males with their arms tied behind their backs lying in a *cenote,* or another "opening in the earth" (Figure 3.3) (Kowalski 1987: 166; Schele and Mathews 1998: 45). The monument, which dates to around A.D. 900, includes the ruler, Lord Chaak, standing above the captives holding an ax and wearing a large plumed headdress (Kowalski 1987: 37–39). Lord Chaak appears as a world tree above an earthly penetration. The "opening in the earth" may be Ek'Waynal, or "the black transformer place," a portal into another cosmic plane (Schele and Mathews 1998: 45).

Cave deposits parallel caches, indicating that materials placed in them were offerings (Stone 1995: 36). Both burials and the deposition of offerings into caves are part of a reciprocal arrangement in which human life is exchanged for world renewal. Northern Lacandon practices differ slightly from this pattern, as they utilize caves and overhangs to depose of "dead" deity effigy censers called "god pots" (Davis 1978: 76).

The incorporation of caves in architectural groups reflects that some were considered buildings—the houses of gods (Stone 1995: 35–37). *Aktun,* or "cave," includes the numeral classifier *ak*, which appears to be applied to objects such as caves, towns, and canoes that contain people or objects (Stone 1995: 35). Among the Lacandon, deities live in caves or in archaeological ruins (Tozzer 1907: 88–89, 148). The Lacandon have a principle of inversion between existential planes—items that appear in one form on one plane are transformed into another form in the otherworld. For example, wood and thatch houses appear to the deities as caves, but they discern caves and vaulted stone ruins as wood and thatch houses (Davis 1978: 24–25). Various supernatural animal protectors were venerated in Yucatán, and the lairs of some are described as resembling "a subterranean ant colony" (Villa Rojas 1945: 103). Guardians of communities and milpas called *balam* live in caves to the west. *Balam* return to their homes through a network of tunnels similar to the interior of wasps' nests (Sosa 1985: 246–248). Many protectors of forests and rain deities also live in caves. Kulubtun, the deity of honeybees, ruled a large *cenote* full of honey that lay somewhere to the east (Villa Rojas 1945: 101–155). The Yukatekos also believed the Late Classic to Late Postclassic inhabitants of much of Yucatán, the Itza, continued to live in caves beneath their former cities (Villa Rojas 1945: 153). Classic period imagery depicts similar housing for divine beings (see Stone 1995: 35). Whereas Westerners classify caves as natural features, the Maya considered them to have been houses of the gods and other powerful beings and, therefore, the divinely built environment.

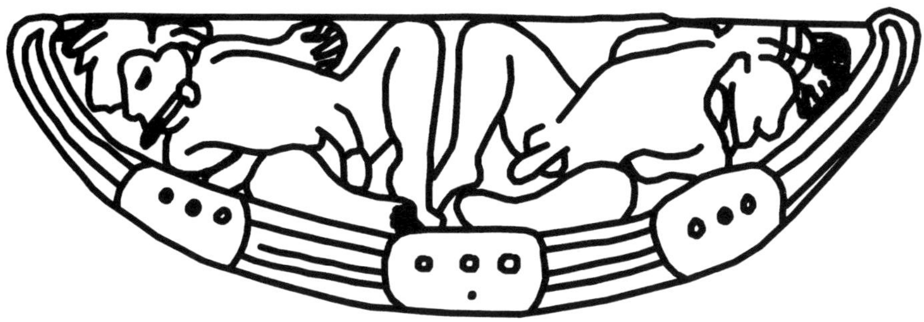

FIGURE 3.3. *Sacrificial cave imagery at the base of Stela 14, Uxmal (redrawn from Schele and Mathews 1998: Figure 1.19).*

The role of caves as houses was also likely incorporated into Late Postclassic deity imagery of Yucatán. The Northern Lacandon emerged from populations that fled the conquest and colonialization of Petén and Yucatán and took advantage of a portion of Chiapas that the Spaniards had cleared of Chol Maya (De Vos 1980: 223–224). The Lacandon used god pots with images of deities. The bowls of the censers represent the depicted deity's cave (Davis 1978: 151). A small stone at the base of the censer bowl, which was taken from the actual house of the deity—either a cave or archaeological ruins—helps ensoul the vessel and represents the deity's bench (McGee 1998: 43). Lacandon god houses include several god pots representing various deities; however; the owner of the god pot had to make a pilgrimage to the deity's house/cave to acquire the stone that activates the vessel (Davis 1978: 77; McGee 1998: 44–45). Late Postclassic Lowland Maya temples also included god pots representing various deities and therefore may have incorporated caves and the sacred landscape into the god house, like the Lacandon vessels.

Frequently, the inclusion of caves and the underworld in ritual spaces is even more subtle than the Lacandon example. The people of San Andrés, Petén, Guatemala, venerated a clothed wooden effigy of San Simón, which combined pre-Columbian and Catholic symbolism (Schwartz 1983: 152–154). San Simón was associated with the underworld, rain, and crops and was "bathed" during droughts (Schwartz 1983: 164). The bathing rite occurred at night on the western side of the plaza, opposite the main doorway of the church to the east, and involved pouring water over the figure three times. This portion of the plaza was considered dangerous by older people (Schwartz 2004: personal communication). Although no cave rested on the western side of the plaza, San Simón acted as an analogue, perhaps interacting on behalf of the people with underworld deities in that location (Schwartz 1983: 165).

CAVES IN LATE POSTCLASSIC TEMPLE ASSEMBLAGES

Late Postclassic ceremonial groups differ from those of the Classic period, as they are smaller and the masonry tends to be more poorly shaped, if not rubble. Despite these differences, certain qualities continue into the Late Postclassic, including the centrality of temples and caves. As mentioned, temples are god houses, places constructed so humans could communicate with the gods. Ceremonial groups were often built around caves, *cenotes,* or borrow pits to incorporate the significance of such features into the assemblages.

Yucatán Peninsula

Late Postclassic Mayapán in Yucatán, Mexico, contains numerous *cenotes,* many of which were incorporated into ceremonial groups. In the center of the ceremonial core rests a radial temple called the Castillo. The Cenote Ch'en Mul stands at the city's core approximately 10 m east of the Castillo. Constructions adjacent to the feature diverted water from the large central plaza into the mouth of the *cenote* (P. E. Smith 1955: 114). A branch of the cave leads northeast to a small chamber that rests directly below a circular west-facing temple called the Round Temple (Figure 3.4) (Pugh 2001b: 251). Excavations did not discern extensive deposits of ceremonial artifacts or human remains in the *cenote,* although water pools within the chamber were utilized in the Classic and Postclassic periods (R. E. Smith 1953b: 223–224).

The Cenote Ch'en Mul is a crucial component of the ceremonial architecture in the core of Mayapán, as demonstrated by its relationships with the Castillo and Round Temple. The Castillo is loaded with underworld and calendrical symbolism (Milbrath and Peraza Lope 2003: 16–17), and the western-facing Round Temple was likely a temple of Ehecatl-Quetzalcoatl, the wind deity, who was associated with caves (Aveni, Milbrath, and Peraza Lope 2004: 133; Miller and Taube 1993: 85). The Cenote Ch'en Mul was also incorporated into a smaller ceremonial group (Pugh 2003b: 416). This group is a temple assemblage with Str. Q-143 standing as the central temple. In front of the temple stand a raised shrine (Str. Q-149) and a statue shrine (Str. Q-146). On the right side of the temple is an oratorio (Str. Q-142a), and at a right angle stands an open hall (Str. Q-145). The Ch'en Mul group appears to incorporate the *cenote* as a second temple (Pugh 2003b: 416). On its right side is an oratorio (Str. Q-153), and at a right angle to the oratorio is an open hall (Str. Q-151). The raised shrine (Str. Q-148) faces into the hall rather than the *cenote.*

The Cenote Itzmal Ch'en and Cenote X-Coton groups, which are lesser ceremonial groups distant from the central ceremonial area of Mayapán, also incorporate *cenotes* into their ceremonial architecture (Brown 1999: 183). The Itzmal Ch'en group (Figure 3.5) is a complex arrangement of buildings that combines a temple assemblage with a basic ceremonial group (Proskouriakoff 1962: 127). The temple assemblage includes a temple (Str. H-17) on the north side of the plaza facing south toward a radial shrine with a circular superstructure (Str. H-18) and an open hall (Str. H-15). The temple assemblage shares the oratorio (Str. H-14) with the basic ceremonial group. The basic ceremonial group includes the oratorio (Str. H-14) aligned with and facing an open hall (Str. H-16), with the circular raised shrine between them. The axis bisecting the medial features of the oratorio and open hall also bisects the

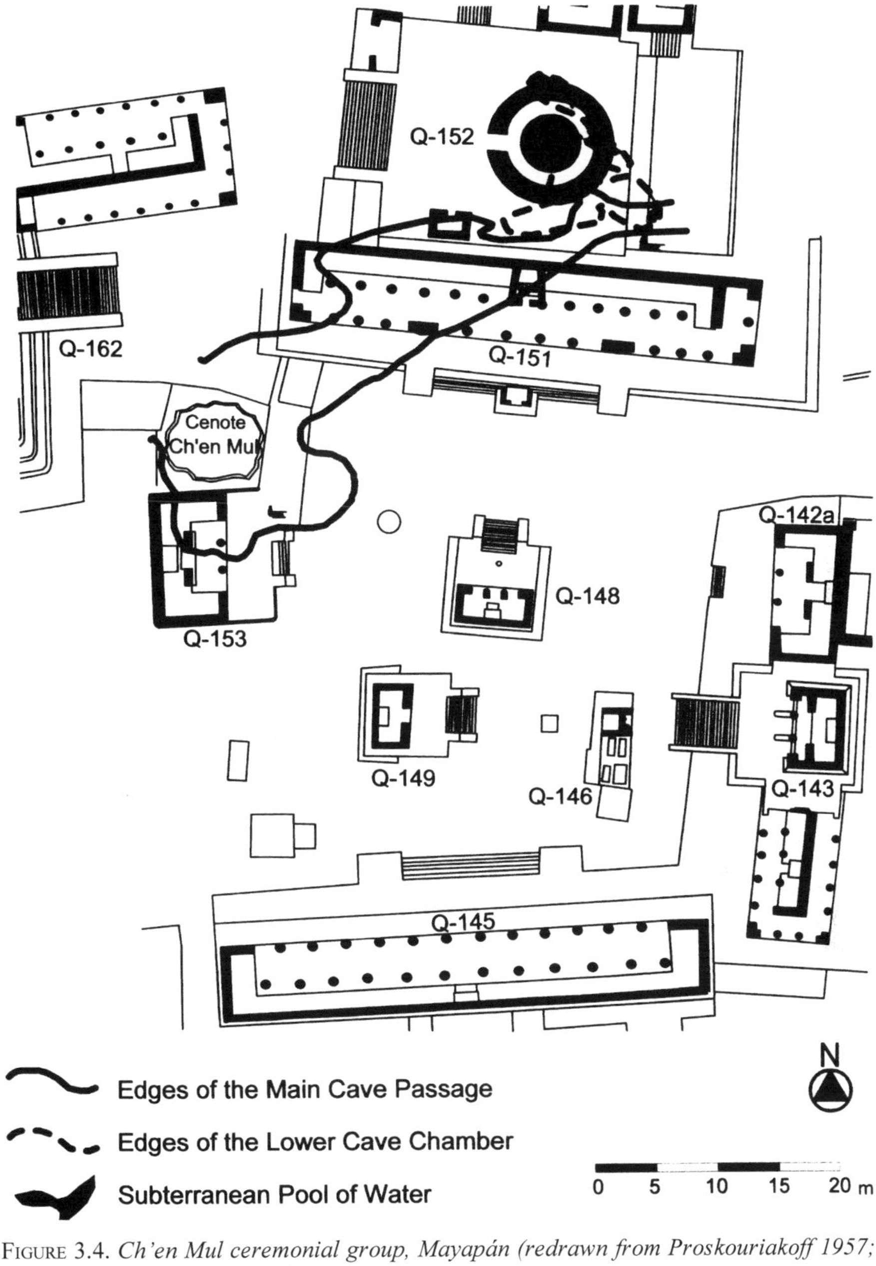

FIGURE 3.4. *Ch'en Mul ceremonial group, Mayapán (redrawn from Proskouriakoff 1957; Smith 1953b; and Pugh 2001b: Figure 4).*

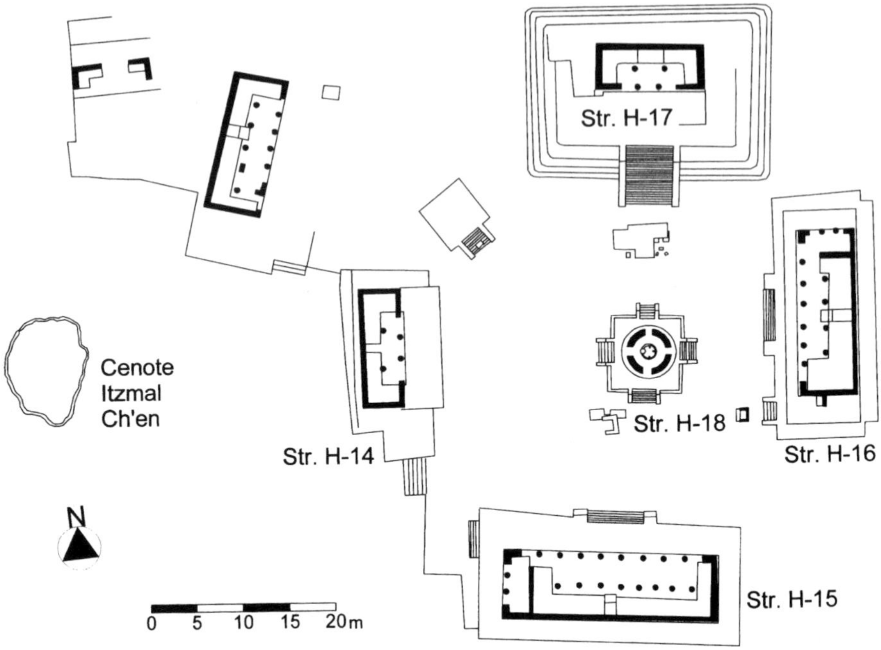

FIGURE 3.5. *Itzmal Ch'en group, Mayapán, Yucatán (redrawn from Proskouriakoff 1962: Figure 1).*

Cenote Itzmal Ch'en, indicating that this feature helped determine the arrangement of the group. Excavations were not conducted in the *cenote,* but modern Maya held rituals there (Proskouriakoff 1962: 128–129).

The Cenote X-Coton group of Mayapán (Figure 3.6) rests 1.4 km east of the central group near one of the city's gates. It is not a temple assemblage, as it does not have an open hall, but a temple (Str. T-72) lies on the south side of the plaza facing north toward the Cenote X-Coton. The temple held numerous Ch'en Mul effigy censers, dating it to the Late Postclassic period, as well as a shaft with cremated human remains (Shook 1953: 208–209). Northeast of the temple is a pair of ceremonial buildings resting on a shared platform (Str. T-70) facing west. These buildings include architectural elements of both temples and raised shrines and do not neatly fit in either category (Proskouriakoff 1962: 130). Ch'en Mul effigy censers were associated with the buildings' fifth and final construction phase (Shook 1953: 216), indicating that they were in use during the Late Postclassic period. West of the southern shrine/temple are three rectangular platforms and a stela.

Inside the Cenote X-Coton stands a small shrine with heavy use in the Late Postclassic period, also demonstrated by large numbers of Ch'en Mul effigy censer sherds. The skeletal remains of numerous animals were found around the shrine

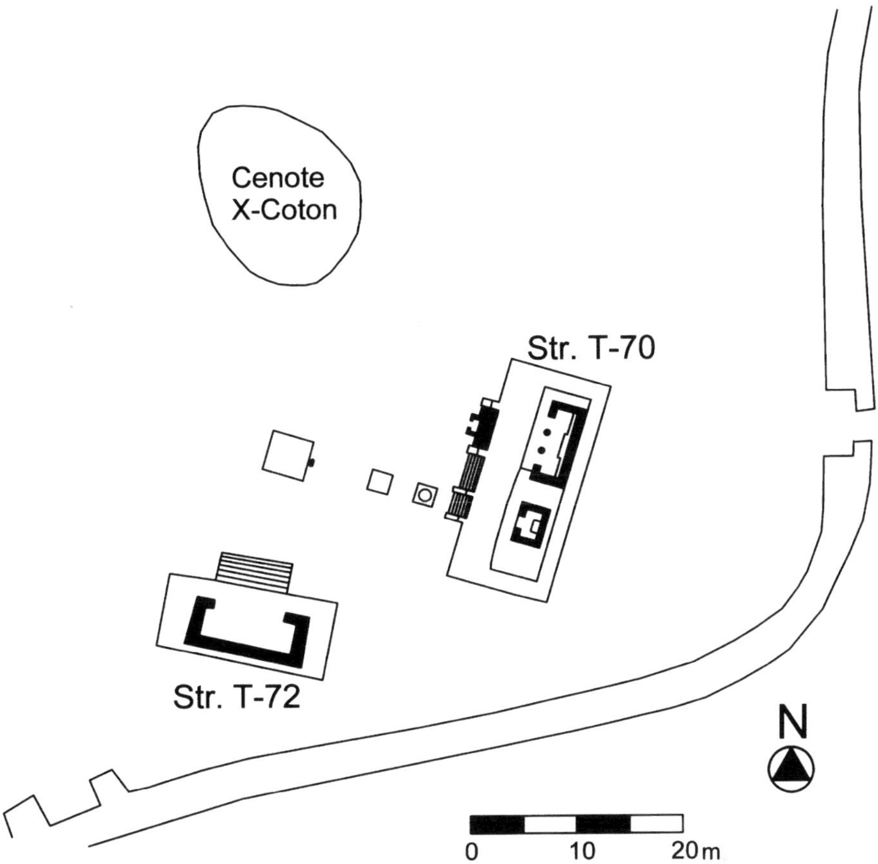

FIGURE 3.6. *X-Coton group, Mayapán, Yucatán (redrawn from Shook 1953: figure 1; and Jones 1952).*

(R. E. Smith 1953a: 69–70). Northeast of the platform was a stairway leading to the water source. In the southwest corner of the *cenote* lay a passage leading to a water hole, which had been intentionally blocked with large stones. This blockage contained the disarticulated remains of more than twelve humans, including children and adults (R. E. Smith 1953a: 72; 1971: 116). A niche in the southern wall of the *cenote* held a human figure sculpted from stone surrounded by numerous censer sherds (R. E. Smith 1953a: 71). The figure is making an offering and wears an animal skin, possibly a jaguar, with the human face protruding from its mouth (R. E. Smith 1953a: figure 6d). Depictions of humans dressed as animals are likely representations of *aj way* (Freidel, Schele, and Parker 1993: 260–262). *Way* refers to a variety of related things including dreams, shaman, sleep, and the transformation into an animal companion (Freidel, Schele, and Parker 1993: 442). A second niche in Cenote X-Coton held animal bones and a dog carved from stone (R. E. Smith 1953a: 71). The *cenote* seems to have been utilized for rituals associated with water, sacrifice, and *way* transformations. "Transformation" is commonly associated with caves and may illuminate their importance to rites of passage (Stone 1995: 38).

Although Ch'en Mul is the only *cenote* in the central group, two temples incorporated cavities accessed by vertical shafts within the structure that may have been artificial caves. These cavities were much larger than that of Str. T-72, described previously. Both cavities held the remains of numerous humans, animals, and other offerings (Shook 1954: 254–274), which parallels them with Cenote X-Coton and cave deposits described later. A similar shaft-accessed cavity that denominated "the High Priest's Grave" at Chichén Itzá held human remains and what appear to be modeled Late Postclassic effigy censers (Thompson 1938: 46–48), although temporal affiliation of ceramics at Chichén Itzá remains contentious.

In the Ch'en Mul, Itzmal Ch'en, and X-Coton groups at Mayapán, *cenotes* stand in the western portion of the ceremonial group. In the Itzmal Ch'en group, the *cenote* determined the east-west axis of the assemblage. In the Ch'en Mul and X-Coton groups, the *cenote* stands in the northwest quadrant of the ceremonial area. In all three assemblages, the *cenote* stands in the quadrant immediately counterclockwise of the medial axis extending from a temple. Therefore, although the orientation of the main temple of Itzmal Ch'en differs from those of the other two groups, the *cenote* is in the same position relative to the temple. The Late Postclassic temporal affiliation of these groups was designated in part by virtue of the presence of Ch'en Mul effigy censer sherds. As mentioned, such censers are likely related to Lacandon deity effigy censers. Hence, caves may also be incorporated into the groups at Mayapán through the censers' bowls. Caves were also incorporated into deity effigies composed of plaster, which were partially composed of speleothems and stood in statue shrines (Proskouriakoff 1962: 136).

Many Late Postclassic temples in Yucatán were topped by churches or cathedrals after the conquest. By doing so, the Spaniards incorporated indigenous layouts of sacred space into the Colonial designs. Cenotes and caves are still found to the west of churches at Chumayel, Telchaquillo, the Santuario de la Cruz Parlante, Izamal, and many other sites. The features are now associated with Chaak, lesser chaaks, and the Virgin Mary (Villa Rojas 1945: 102).

Petén

At present, no natural caves have been recorded in association with Late Postclassic ceremonial groups in Petén, Guatemala. The discrepancy is likely a sampling error that will normalize with continued Late Postclassic research in the region, as caves and tunnels are associated with Late Classic period architecture (see Brady 1997). An artificial pit at Zacpetén in Petén, Guatemala, manifests striking similarities with natural *cenotes* in Yucatán. The pit, designated as Op. 1000,

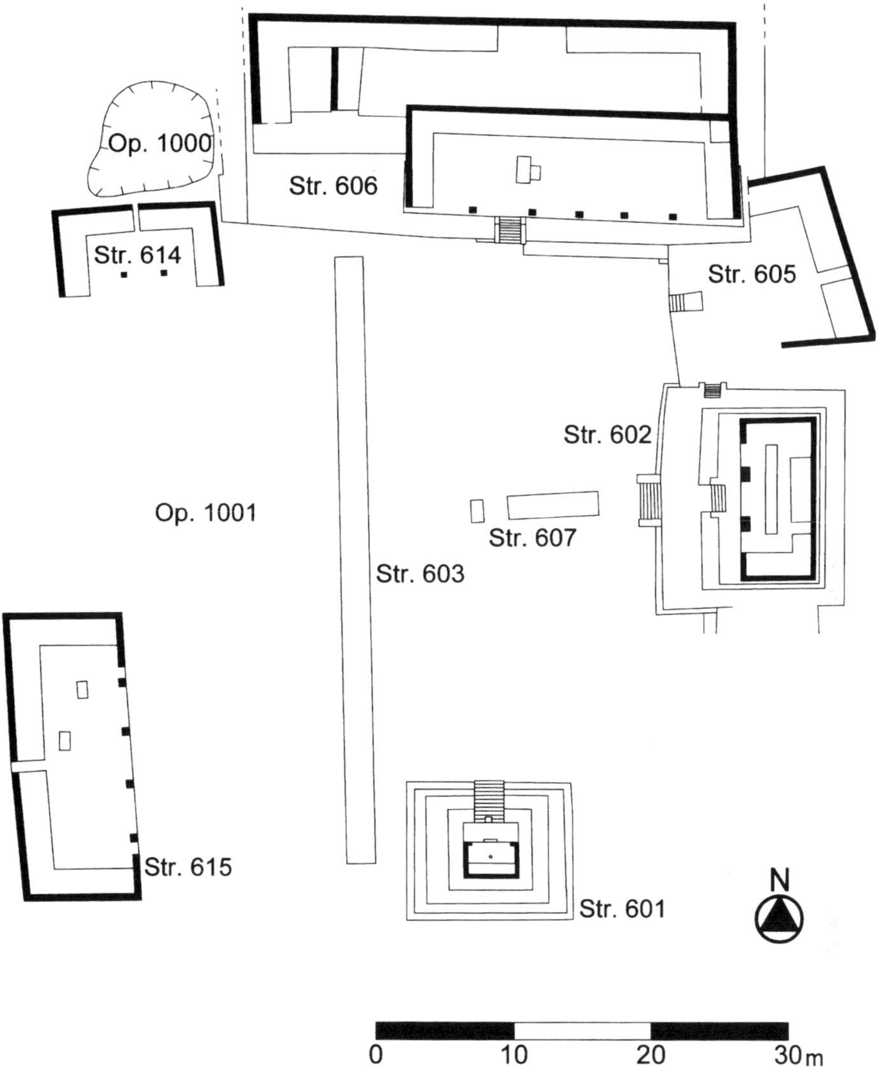

FIGURE 3.7. *Group A, Zacpetén, Petén, Guatemala.*

rests in the northwest corner of Group A (Figure 3.7). Group A contains a temple assemblage constructed similar to those of Mayapán (Pugh 2001a: 573–575; 2003b: 423; Pugh and Rice 1997; Rice 1988: 234; Rice, Rice, and Pugh 1998: 229–230). Like some groups at Mayapán, Group A at Zacpetén contains a penetration into the earth, Op. 1000 (Pugh 2003b). Op. 1000 held a large deposit of dismembered human remains that included dismembered but articulated remains of adults and children.

Cut marks on the remains (Duncan 1999 n.d.) and their articulations indicate that the individuals were dismembered before the decay of flesh.

The dismembered remains were not tossed unceremoniously into the Op. 1000. Before their deposition, a fire was burned in the artificial pit. An accelerator mass spectrometry (AMS) analysis (Beta-112318) of fragments of wood from the deposit indicated a Conventional Age of 540 ± 30 BP calibrated (2 sigma, 95 percent probability) to A.D. 1310–1360 and A.D. 1380–1440, with the latter intercept having a higher relative probability (68.9 percent). The dismembered remains were placed on the burned wood and ash and were subsequently covered with limestone rubble and crushed limestone. A substantial amount of eroded soil eventually capped the limestone debris.

Topoxté, located approximately 28 km northeast of Zacpetén, has three islands: Topoxté proper, Paxte, and Cante, each of which contains a temple assemblage. Topoxté Island includes the most elaborately constructed temple assemblage known in Petén (Figure 3.8). The site contains no obvious caves or artificial pits, but it does include numerous *chultuns,* which are cavities excavated into bedrock. *Chultuns* have traditionally been interpreted as storage pits of food resources; however; unless human remains fall into the latter category, these are not storage pits of the materialistic sort. Many of the multichambered *chultuns* at Topoxté include burials, dismembered remains including crania of human adults and children, and other offerings (Hermes and Calderón 2000: 66–74). The *chultuns* were concentrated beneath the central ceremonial area of Topoxté; however, most were Protoclassic and Classic period constructions. It is possible that the late occupants of the site knew of these features, although it seems more likely that the association was spurious.

Although Topoxté lacks open cave features, northwest of the temple (36 degrees clockwise from the medial axis) on the western edge of the plaza lays a Late Postclassic platform (Str. L) (Figure 3.8) containing:

> rocks and earth and mixed with the fill are bones from children and adults. Occasional limb bones are articulated, but the skeletons are not intact and the remains do not appear to be formalized burials. They may be the dismembered bodies of sacrificial victims. (Bullard 1970: 267)

The deposit in Str. L is obviously similar to that in Op. 1000 at Zacpetén and lies in the same position, northwest of the temple. Although no caves were encountered in the central group of Topoxté, it certainly possesses analogous sacrificial/death symbolism. Furthermore, the structure rests on the western edge of the plaza, which may also signify descent into chthonic realms.

The borrow pit at Zacpetén and Str. L at Topoxté were large caches (Stone 1995: 35), perhaps dedicating the Late Postclassic construction of the ceremonial groups. Although the overall theme of Op. 1000 appears to have been death-related, including the underworld symbolism of the pit and the dismembered individuals, the cache represented one side of an exchange between humans and the deities in

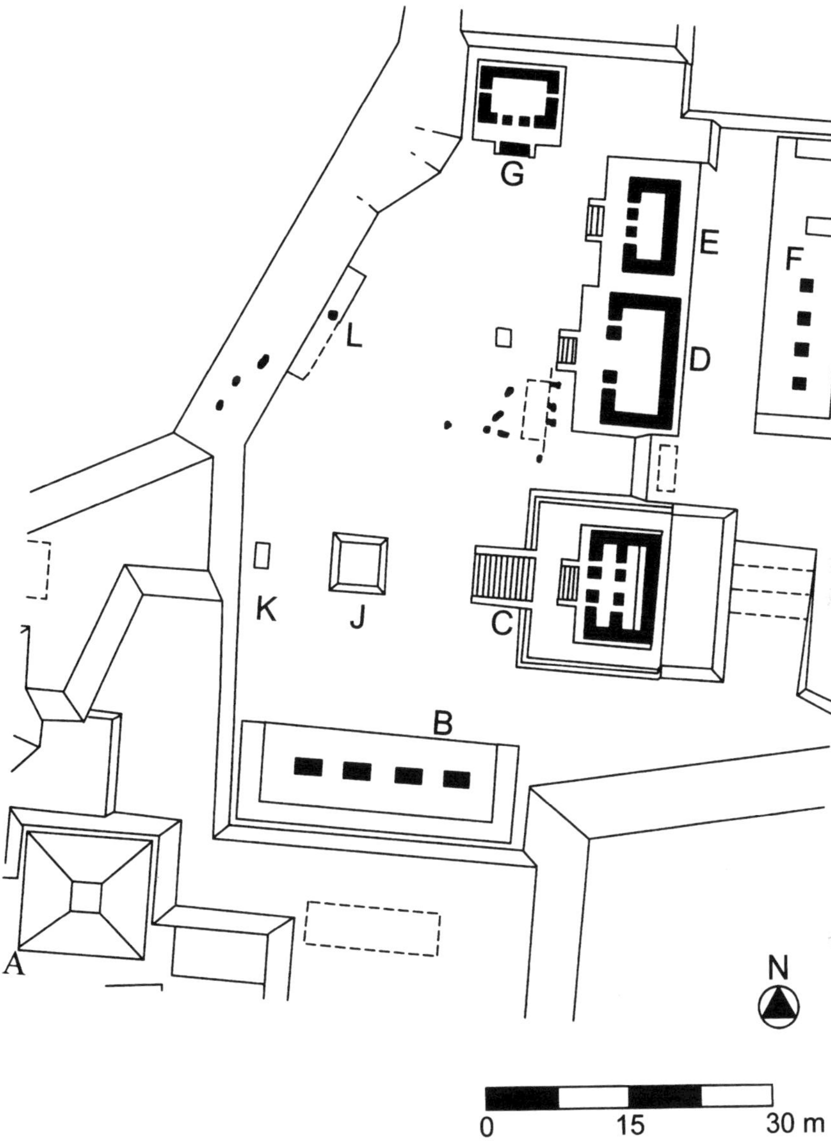

FIGURE 3.8. *Central group, Topoxté Island, Petén, Guatemala (redrawn from Bullard 1970: Figure 3).*

return for renewed life. In both cases, the deposits lie on the western side of the plaza, matching the groups at Mayapán, and they rest in the northwest quadrant of each group, similar to the Ch'en Mul and X-Coton groups. The similarity between the assemblages at the two sites is likely the result of historic connections and, therefore, shared cosmologies (Pugh 2003b).

Guatemalan Highlands

Many sites in the Guatemalan Highlands include artificial caves (Brady 1991; Brady and Veni 1992). The central group at Utatlán contains a temple assemblage, and northwest of the temple rest the mouths of two artificial caves, one of which has tunnels ending near a circular temple (Fox 1991: 221–232; 1994: 164) similar to the Cenote Ch'en Mul at Mayapán. The western-facing Round Temple at Mayapán may have been dedicated to Ehecatl-Quetzalcoatl (Aveni, Mibrath, and Peraza Lope 2004: 133) and that of Utatlán to K'ucumatz, the highland manifestation of the former (Carmack 1981: 41, 275). If these presumed associations are correct, then patterned connections between the round structures and caves at the two sites may have materialized the creation myth describing the descent of Ehecatl-Quetzalcoatl into the underworld.

Late Postclassic artificial caves are found elsewhere in the Guatemalan Highlands, including Mixco-Viejo and Esquipulas, although neither site contains a temple assemblage. Some of the caves at the Late Postclassic Pokomam capital, Mixco Viejo, were artificially enlarged and are still used for ritual events (Brady and Veni 1992: 150–154). Countless pilgrims visit Esquipulas to venerate the Black Christ, and locals believe the cross was originally "found" in a nearby artificial cave. It is unknown when the caves were constructed, but a Late Postclassic site, Yzquipulas, rests nearby (Brady and Veni 1992: 155–156). The reason for the various *Cuevas de las Minas* at Esquipulas is uncertain; however, some mines in the area were literally consumed by devotees of the Black Christ (Hunter, Horst, and Thomas 1989: 281–285). These mines follow veins of white clay, which are believed to have medicinal value, especially in regards to pregnancy, childbirth, and the health of newborns. Locals believe the "raw clay . . . is holy," and its extraction is conducted by men in a ritualized manner (Hunter, Horst, and Thomas 1989: 285). It is uncertain whether the pre-conquest Maya participated in similar geophagic practices.

DISCUSSION AND CONCLUSION

Not all temple assemblages or other types of Late Postclassic ceremonial groups include caves or artificial penetrations into the earth. However, the central groups at Mayapán, Zacpetén, Topoxté, and Utatlán do include such features. Furthermore, the penetrations lie to the west in all and in the northwest quadrant in most of the groups. Were it not for Utatlán, one could ascribe the similarities to historic connections, as Zacpetén, Topoxté, and Mayapán all included members of a social group called the Kowoj (Pugh 2003b). The artificial cave on the west side of the plaza at Utatlán and the *cenotes* to the west of churches and cathedrals in Yucatán, many of which were likely built on Late Postclassic temples, demonstrate that the pattern is more widespread than the Late Postclassic Kowoj. The reason for the striking similarity between the temple assemblage at Utatlán and the groups at Zacpetén and Mayapán is unknown but may have resulted from direct contact between the occupants of Utatlán and one or both of the lowland sites. Alternatively, Utatlán may have been influenced by the same site from which the occupants of Mayapán obtained their model. "Influence" here includes information exchange or migration events.

The preceding discussion of caves in Late Postclassic ceremonial groups might give one a false sense that the features were universal aspects of temple assemblages; however, many such groups do not contain the features. Nevertheless, when present, caves tend to be located in the northwest quadrant of temple assemblages. The west is paralleled with death and the underworld, both of which are associated with caves. Hence, the orientation of temple assemblage architecture so that caves are located in a specific position indicates a particular construction of architectural grammar that redundantly and circularly declares that the western space within the assemblage parallels the underworld, death, darkness, the womb, and so on. The speaking cross of the Caste War is venerated on a shrine to the east of the Cenote Chan Santa Cruz (Reed 1964: 135–136); hence, the orchestration of ritual action to the east of caves has continued into modern times.

When caves were not present at a particular site, they were often constructed, and the Maya did not differentiate these features from natural caves. As mentioned, such differentiation is a product of the Western mind-set and not of Maya cosmology—caves were the homes of the deities and therefore constructed features. Borrow pits were, in fact, used to remove limestone for construction, but materialistic use did not undermine the ritual significance of the features—in fact, it may have added to it. The removal of limestone and subsequent use of the material to create a "creation mountain" may have been a ritual action, as construction events occurred at important calendrical junctures (Love 1986: 177). Similar to world trees/crosses, the artificial mountains of temple pyramids were "born" from borrow pits.

Caves in temple assemblages were ritual spaces similar to other buildings within the groups. They were places that were both ritual icons and spaces for ritual activity. In fact, in some cases, such as Str. L at Topoxté, a building fulfilled the role accomplished by *cenotes* and borrow pits in temple assemblages at other sites. Since the penetrations into the earth often helped determine the placement of the assemblages, they can be seen as grounding points, points of origin, and emblems of creation. Creation, however, establishes an insatiable responsibility to reciprocate (Godelier 1999: 171–199). Hence, although these sacred features gave life to the community, they required payment in return. Furthermore, they filled a void in human consciousness—the memory that humans had historically constructed their own social realities. This forgotten detail was substituted with divine cosmogony and ethnogenesis (Godelier 1999: 171–199).

Previous research has suggested reciprocity between the eastern and western sides of many temple assemblages, which are clearly demarcated by the small *sakbe* in Group A at Zacpetén (Figure 3.7) (Pugh 2003b). Offerings placed in caves include dismembered human and animal remains, censers, and other materials. Western sacrificial death allows eastern birth and life. John Sosa (1985) defined not one primordial cave but two, one to the west and the other to the east. The sun passed through these openings each day as it died and was reborn. Passing through holes results in transformations, as is evident from the planting of decapitated heads/seed and the resulting fertility and political succession (Freidel 1992: 108; Sosa 1985: 278; Stone 1995: 38). Hence, the temple in Late Postclassic groups substituted for the eastern cave and its associated attributes such as life, rebirth, light, males, and up. The penetration into the earth represented by the *cenote* or artificial cave represented death, darkness, females, and down (Pugh 2003b: 420–426). These western locations were not static locations but "black transformer" places (Schele and Mathews 1998: 45) that helped perpetuate the cosmos.

The eastern and western sides are not diametrically opposed but include many of the same elements. The sun, moon, and rain were tied to both directions. Many modern Maya towns in Yucatán, such as Telchaquillo, the Santuario de la Cruz Parlante, and Izamal, place the Virgin Mary in both locations as well. These eastern and western penetrations into the earth may also prevent cosmic destruction. Apparently, the black horse ridden by the Virgin as she crossed the sky produced massive amounts of rain, which drained from the surface of the earth into two *cenotes,* although Alfonso Villa Rojas (1945: 102) did not note the location of these features. However, Cenote Ch'en Mul at Mayapán and Cenote Chan Santa Cruz at the Santuario de la Cruz Parlante are equipped with drains that draw water off the plaza into the *cenotes,* and water would also have poured into Op. 1000 at Zacpetén as well. Hence, these features might have replicated the western *cenote* of the prehistoric parallel of the Virgin Mary, as well as the earthly penetrations' ability to prevent a catastrophic deluge.

As microcosms, Late Postclassic temple assemblages were the centers of the built environment; however, they often incorporated *cenotes* and caves, and when those were not available the Maya often created artificial penetrations into the earth. Although *cenotes* and caves were not built by humans, they were constructed by deities or ancestors, and it was from these features that humans emerged. These features, along with associated temples, formed a dynamic axis between life and death, which made the rest of the built environment possible.

REFERENCES CITED

Aveni, Anthony F., Susan Milbrath, and Carlos Peraza Lope

2004 Chichén Itzá's Legacy in the Astronomically Oriented Architecture of Mayapan. *RES* 45:123–143.

Brady, James E.

1988 The Sexual Connotation of Caves in Mesoamerican Ideology. *Mexicon* 10(3):51–53.

1991 Caves and Cosmovision at Utatlan. *California Anthropologist* 18(1):1–10.

1997 Settlement Configuration and Cosmology: The Role of Caves at Dos Pilas. *American Anthropologist* 99(3):602–618.

Brady, James E., and George Veni

1992 Man-Made and Pseudo-Karst Caves: The Implications of Subsurface Features Within Maya Centers. *Geoarchaeology* 7(2):149–167.

Brown, Clifford T.

1999 Mayapán Society and Ancient Social Organization. Ph.D. Dissertation. Department of Anthropology, Tulane University, New Orleans.

Bullard, William R.

1970 Topoxte: A Postclassic Maya Site in Peten, Guatemala. In *Monographs and Papers in Maya Archaeology,* ed. William R. Bullard, 245–308. Peabody Museum of American Archaeology and Ethnology, Cambridge.

Carmack, Robert M.

1981 *The Quiché Mayas of Utatlán: The Evolution of a Highland Guatemala Kingdom.* University of Oklahoma Press, Norman.

Coggins, Clemency C., and Orrin C. Shane III

1984 *Cenote of Sacrifice: Maya Treasures From the Sacred Well at Chichén Itzá.* University of Texas Press, Austin.

Davis, Virginia Dale

1978 Ritual of the Northern Lacandon Maya. Ph.D. Dissertation. Department of Anthropology, Tulane University, University Microfilms International, Ann Arbor.

De Vos, Jan

1980 *La Paz de Dios y del Rey: La Conquista de la Selva Lacandona 1525–1821.* Fondo de Cultura Económica, México.

Duncan, William

1999 Postclassic Mortuary Practices in Civic/Ceremonial Contexts in Peten, Guatemala. Paper presented at the 64th Annual Meeting of the Society for American Archaeology, Chicago.

n.d. Understanding Veneration and Violation in the Archaeological Record. In *Understanding Ritual Violence in the Archaeological Record: Behavior and Meaning,* eds. Gordon F.M. Rakita, Jane E. Buikstra, Lane A. Beck, and Sloan R. Williams. University Press of Florida, Gainesville.

Fox, John W.

1991 The Lords of Light Versus the Lords of Dark: The Postclassic Highland Maya Ballgame. In *The Mesoamerican Ballgame,* eds. Vernon Scarborough and David R. Wilcox, 213–238. The University of Arizona Press, Tucson.

1994 Political Cosmology Among the Quiché Maya. In *Factional Competition and Political Development in the New World,* eds. Elizabeth Blumfield and John W. Fox, 158–170. Cambridge University Press, New York.

Freidel, David A.

1992 Children of the First Father's Skull: Terminal Classic Warfare in the Northern Maya Lowlands and the Transformation of Kingship and Elite Hierarchies. In *Mesoamerican Elites: An Archaeological Assessment,* eds. Diane Z. Chase and Arlen F. Chase, 99–117. University of Oklahoma Press, Norman.

Freidel, David, Linda Schele, and Joy Parker
1993 *Maya Cosmos: Three Thousand Years on the Shaman's Path*. William Morrow and Company, New York.

Godelier, Maurice
1999 *The Enigma of the Gift*. University of Chicago Press, Chicago.

Hanks, William F.
1990 *Referential Practice: Language and Lived Space Among the Maya*. University of Chicago Press, Chicago.

Hermes, Bernard, and Zoila Calderón
2000 Chultunes. In *El Sitio Maya de Topoxte: Investigaciones en una isla del lago Yaxhá, Petén, Guatemala,* ed. Wolfgang W. Wulster, 66–74. Verlag Philipp von Zabern, Mainz am Rhein.

Heyden, Doris
1981 Caves, Gods, and Myths: World-View and Planning in Teotihuacan. In *Mesoamerican Sites and World-Views,* ed. Elizabeth P. Benson, 1–39. Dumbarton Oaks Research Library, Washington, D.C.

Hofling, Charles A.
1991 *Itzá Maya Texts With a Grammatical Overview*. University of Utah Press, Salt Lake City.

Hunt, Eva
1977 *The Transformation of the Hummingbird: Cultural Roots in a Zinacantan Mythical Poem*. Cornell University Press, Ithaca.

Hunter, John M., Oscar H. Horst, and Robert N. Thomas
1989 Religious Geophagy as a Cottage Industry: The Holy Clay Tablet of Esquipulas, Guatemala. *National Geographic Research* 5(3):281–295.

Jones, Grant D.
1989 *Maya Resistance to Spanish Rule: Time and History on a Colonial Frontier.* University of New Mexico Press, Albuquerque.
1998 *The Conquest of the Itza*. Stanford University Press, Stanford.

Jones, Morris R.
1952 *Map of the Ruins of Mayapan, Yucatan, Mexico.* Current Report 1. Carnegie Institution of Washington, Washington, D.C.

Joralemon, Peter D.
1971 *A Study of Olmec Iconography.* Studies in Precolumbian Art and Archaeology Number Seven. Dumbarton Oaks, Washington, D.C.

Kowalski, Jeff K.
1987 *The House of the Governor: A Maya Palace at Uxmal, Yucatán, Mexico.* University of Oklahoma Press, Norman.

Landa, Diego de
1941 Relación de las Cosas de Yucatán (1566). In *Landa's Relación de las Cosas deYucatán,* ed. Alfred M. Tozzer, 3–208. Peabody Museum of American Archaeology and Ethnology, Cambridge.

Love, Bruce
1986 Yucatec Maya Ritual: A Diachronic Perspective. Ph.D. Dissertation. Department of Anthropology, University of California, Los Angeles.

Marcus, Joyce

1993 Ancient Maya Political Organization. In *Lowland Maya Civilization in the Eighth Century A.D.,* eds. Jeremy A. Sabloff and John S. Henderson, 111–183. Dumbarton Oaks Research Library and Collection, Washington, D.C.

Martin, Simon, and Nikolai Grube

2000 *Chronicle of the Maya Kings and Queens.* Thames and Hudson, London.

McGee, R. Jon

1998 Lacandon Incense Burner Renewal Ceremony: Termination and Dedication Ritual Among the Contemporary Maya. In *The Sowing and the Dawning: Termination, Dedication, and Transformation in the Archaeological and Ethnographic Record of Mesoamerica,* ed. Shirley B. Mock, 41–46. University of New Mexico Press, Albuquerque.

Milbrath, Susan, and Carlos Peraza Lope

2003 Revisiting Mayapán: Mexico's Last Maya Capital. *Ancient Mesoamerica* 14:1–46.

Miller, Mary, and Karl Taube

1993 *The Gods and Symbols of Ancient Mexico and the Maya.* Thames and Hudson, London.

Proskouriakoff, Tatiana

1957 *Mayapan, Plan of the Main Group of Ruins.* Carnegie Institution of Washington Publication 619. Carnegie Institution of Washington, Washington, D.C.

1962 Civic and Religious Structures of Mayapán. In *Mayapán Yucatán México,* eds. H.E.D. Pollock, Ralph L. Roys, T. Proskouriakoff, and A. Ledyard Smith, 87–164. Carnegie Institution of Washington, Washington, D.C.

Pugh, Timothy W.

2001a Architecture, Ritual, and Social Identity at Late Postclassic Zacpetén, Petén Guatemala: Identification of the Kowoj. Ph.D. Dissertation. Department of Anthropology, Southern Illinois University at Carbondale, University Microfilms International, Ann Arbor.

2001b Flood Reptiles, Serpent Temples, and the Quadripartite Universe: The Imago Mundi of Late Postclassic Mayapán. *Ancient Mesoamerica* 12(2):247–258.

2003a A Cluster and Spatial Analysis of Ceremonial Architecture at Late Postclassic Mayapán. *Journal of Archaeological Science* 30:941–953.

2003b The Exemplary Center of the Late Postclassic Kowoj Maya. *Latin American Antiquity* 14(4):408–430.

Pugh, Timothy W., and Prudence M. Rice

1997 Arquitectura estilo Mayapan y evidencias de organización dual en el sitio postclásico de Zacpeten, Peten, Guatemala. In *Simposio de investigaciones arqueológicas en Guatemala,* 521–532. Ministerio de Cultura y Deportes, Instituto de Antropologia e Historia, Asociacion Tikal, Guatemala.

Redfield, Robert, and Alfonso Villa Rojas

1934 *Chan Kom: A Maya Village.* The University of Chicago Press, Chicago.

Reed, Nelson

1964 *The Caste War of Yucatan.* Stanford University Press, Stanford.

Rice, Don S.
1988 Classic to Postclassic Maya Household Transition in the Central Peten, Guatemala. In *Household and Community in the Mesoamerican Past,* ed. Rick Wilk, 227–248. University of New Mexico Press, Albuquerque.

Rice, Don S., Prudence M. Rice, and Timothy W. Pugh
1998 Settlement Continuity and Change in the Central Peten Lakes Region: The Case for Zacpetén. In *Anatomía de una civilización: approximaciones interdisciplines a la cultura Maya,* eds. Andrés Ciudad Riuz, Yolanda Fernández Marquínez, José García Campillo, Josefa Iglesias Ponce de León, Alfonso L. García-Gallo, and Luis T. Saenz Castro, 207–252. Sociedad Española de Estudios Mayas, Madrid.

Roys, Ralph L.
1943 *The Indian Background of Colonial Yucatan.* Carnegie Institution of Washington, Washington, D.C.

Schele, Linda, and Peter Mathews
1998 *The Code of Kings: The Language of Seven Sacred Maya Temples and Tombs.* Scribner, New York.

Schwartz, Norman
1983 San Simon: Ambiguity and Identity in Petén, Guatemala. *Sociologus* 33:152–173.

Shook, Edwin M.
1953 *The X-Coton Temples at Mayapán.* Current Reports No. 11. Carnegie Institution of Washington, Washington, D.C.
1954 *Three Temples and Their Associated Structures at Mayapan.* Current Reports No. 14. Carnegie Institution of Washington, Washington, D.C.

Smith, A. Ledyard
1962 Residential and Associated Structures at Mayapán. In *Mayapán Yucatán México,* eds. H.E.D. Pollock, Ralph L. Roys, T. Proskouriakoff, and A. Ledyard Smith, 166–277. Carnegie Institution of Washington, Washington, D.C.

Smith, Philip E.
1955 *Excavations in Three Ceremonial Structures at Mayapan.* Current Reports No. 21. Carnegie Institution of Washington, Washington, D.C.

Smith, Robert E.
1953a *Cenote X-Coton at Mayapan.* Current Reports No. 5. Carnegie Institution of Washington, Washington, D.C.
1953b *Cenote Explorations at Mayapan and Telchaquillo.* Current Reports No. 12. Carnegie Institution of Washington, Washington, D.C.
1971 *The Pottery of Mayapan.* Papers of the Peabody Museum of Archaeology and Ethnology, Vol. 66. Harvard University, Cambridge.

Smith, Virginia G.
1984 *Izapa Relief Carving: Form, Content, Rules for Design, and Role in Mesoamerican Art History and Archaeology.* Dumbarton Oaks, Washington, D.C.

Sosa, John R.
1985 The Maya Sky, The Maya World: A Symbolic Analysis of Yucatec Maya Cosmology. Ph.D. Dissertation. Department of Anthropology, State University of New York at Albany, University Microfilms International, Ann Arbor.

Stone, Andrea J.
1995 *Images From the Underworld: Naj Tunich and the Tradition of Maya Glyph Painting*. University of Texas Press, Austin.

Taube, Karl A.
1988 The Ancient Maya New Year Festival: The Liminal Period in Maya Ritual and Cosmology. Ph.D. Dissertation. Department of Anthropology, Yale University, University Microfilms International, Ann Arbor.

Thompson, Edward H.
1938 *The High Priest's Grave: Chichen Itza, Yucatan, Mexico.* Anthropological Series, Field Museum of Natural History 27(1), Chicago.

Tozzer, Alfred
1907 *A Comparative Study of the Mayas and the Lacandon.* MacMillan Company, New York.

Villa Rojas, Alfonso
1945 *The Maya of East Central Quintana Roo.* Publication 559. Carnegie Institution of Washington, Washington, D.C.

Vogt, Evon Z.
1981 Some Sacred Aspects of the Sacred Geography of Highland Chiapas. In *Mesoamerican Sites and World-Views,* ed. Elizabeth P. Benson, 119–142. Dumbarton Oaks, Washington, D.C.

Winters, Howard D.
1955 *Three Serpent Column Temples and Associated Platforms at Mayapán.* Current Report 32. Carnegie Institution of Washington, Washington, D.C.

Chapter Four

Social Power and Sacred Space at Actun Nak Beh, Belize

by Christina T. Halperin

Archaeologists have documented the presence of caves under and near Maya settlement centers for some time (Digby 1958; Joyce 1929; E. H. Thompson 1938), but the relationship between the two is only now being examined as more attention is devoted to cave studies and as archaeologists consider both the material and sociosymbolic aspects of landscape. Recent investigations of the integration of caves and settlements have indicated that the sacred nature of caves and other natural features of the landscape aided in settlement site selection and development, as well as in the legitimization of elite status and power (Brady 1997; Brady and Ashmore 1999; Brady and Bonor Villarejo 1993; Brady et al. 1997).

A newly discovered cave, Actun Nak Beh, and settlement site, Cahal Uitz Na, Belize, provide a heretofore unreported method of integrating caves with settlement sites (Figure 4.1). The Western Belize Regional Cave Project (WBRCP), directed by Dr. Jaime Awe, reported the sites to the Department of Archaeology, Belize, in 1996 and has since conducted preliminary research at the cave and the site's center (Awe 1999; Awe and Helmke 1998; Conlon and Ehret 1999; Ehret and Conlon 1999; Ferguson 1999; Halperin 2002; Helmke et al. 1999; Hodgman 2001; Mirro, Owen, and Helmke 1999). Actun Nak Beh is connected to the ceremonial center of Cahal Uitz Na by a 240-m causeway, a layout unique in the southern Maya Lowlands. Nonetheless, the site layout of Cahal Uitz Na, like others throughout Mesoamerica (cf. Brady and Veni 1992; Heyden 1975, 1981, 2000; King and Shaw 2003; Reeder 1993; Reeder et al. 1995), reveals a mixing of what A. Bernard Knapp and Wendy Ashmore (1999: 10–11) call "constructed" and "conceptualized" landscapes. It exhibits both material features formed by humans and natural features imbued with religious symbolism and cultural meaning.

This chapter examines two models relating sacred sites to the formation of social power: the legitimization of elite authority and power and the creation of community solidarity. These models are then examined in reference to Actun Nak Beh through a comparison of the cave's and Cahal Uitz Na's layouts and documentation of their archaeological remains. I argue that power struggles at Actun Nak Beh served to simultaneously unite and divide the Cahal Uitz Na community.

SACRED SITES AND SOCIAL POWER

Individuals and groups exercise, acquire, and negotiate social power using diverse methods and forms (Comaroff and Comaroff 1992; Foucault 1977, 1978, 1980; Mann 1986; Miller and Tilley 1984; Wolf 1990). Scholarly definitions of power often focus on asymmetrical relationships, when an individual or group possesses power "over" another individual or group (Miller and Tilley 1984: 5–9). Eric Wolf (1990: 586), for example, suggests that power is the ability to impose one's will on another individual, to control the settings of human interaction, or to control the direction of energy flow (e.g., economic resources). John and Jean Comaroff (1992: 28–30) suggest that power is the means by which humans can obtain their goals and shape the lives of others. It is acquired through control over how symbols and materials are created, disseminated, and used. These forms of power formulate a practice of domination and resistance based on historically contingent circumstances and human agency.

Elite control over sacred sites to legitimize social relations provides an example of how such domination can take shape. Although ideas and meanings are difficult to control, their symbolic, material correlates are more easily regulated. Symbols not only express the social structure of a society; they shape, mold, and reinvent it (Turner 1967: 20). Manifestations of symbolism are seen in various forms, including but not limited to rituals and ceremonies, writing systems, icons or other symbolic objects, and cultural landscapes. Because these "materialized" forms (in particular the last three, which can be detected archaeologically) can be used, owned, transferred, and controlled, they can be manipulated as sources of political and social power (DeMarrais, Castillo, and Earle 1996: 15; Earle 1997: 153; Godelier 1999; Helms 1988).

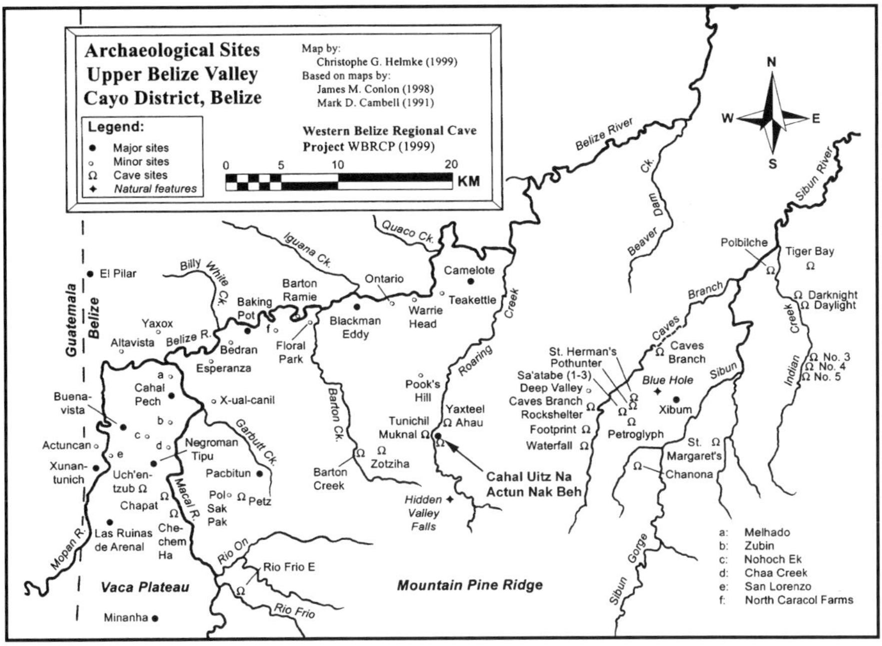

FIGURE 4.1. *Map of the Upper Belize Valley (adapted from map by C. Helmke).*

Caves, as sacred spaces, provided "materialized" symbols of significant aspects of Maya cosmology and worldview. In turn, cave ceremonies and the material objects displayed in such ceremonies also provided symbolic manifestations of Maya concepts and beliefs. Access to or control over sacred spaces, such as caves, and associated rituals served as a fundamental strategy for displaying, legitimizing, and negotiating social power. Large monumental architecture communicates an accumulation of power and wealth that can be read visually regardless of the audience's language, age, gender, or status differentiation (Earle 1997: 156). The placement of monumental architecture over or near caves implies control over the latter by the elites who lived in and provided the financial backing for the former. As Mark Leone (1984: 26) asserts, such spatial ordering "takes social relations and makes them appear to be resident in nature or history, which makes them apparently inevitable."

In addition, ritual dramatization of power plays a central role in defining political and social hierarchies within complex societies. In some cases, it may provide a more effective means of communicating power differences than verbal declarations. As David Kertzer (1988: 30) argues, "[D]irect verbal expression of status differences is more likely to create overt conflict among those in lower ranks than is ritual expression of the same message."

The use of sacred features to validate Mesoamerican elite authority is also indicated by the emulation of sacred features (e.g., caves and mountains) and cosmology (e.g., the structuring of the universe) in monumental architecture and site layouts (Ashmore 1989, 1991; Bassie Sweet 1991, 1996; Brady and Ashmore 1999; Schele and Freidel 1990; Vogt 1981, 1992). These architectural arrangements symbolically equate civic centers with the center of the universe, or *axis mundi*, thereby mapping social relations onto cosmological spheres. Andrea Stone (1992) has argued that these architectural metaphors legitimized elite corporate rituals that were conducted within urban settings and served as a means of controlling commoners whose folk rituals probably incorporated the "real" version of such natural features. She suggests that instead of competing with elite practices, however, folk practices reinforced the sacred meanings and sentiments associated with the urban symbols (Stone 1992: 127).

The benefits of caves and cave ceremonies were not exclusive to elite members of society. As mentioned, many Mesoamerican caves were used as regional and local pilgrimage sites by both commoners and elites (Brady and Stone 1986; Stone 1992). At an individual level, pilgrimages to and worship at sacred sites provide a way to influence one's fate or personal needs (Morinis and Crumrine 1991: 14). These rituals, conducted either individually or collectively, possess liminal phase attributes, in that they represent a release from everyday social activities and structures. Thus, hegemonic power relations, albeit only temporarily, may become inverted or annulled (Turner 1979: 152–153).

Collective ritual experiences also foster community identity. These practices transcend social status boundaries and blur asymmetric power relations. In Zinacantan, Chiapas, the year-renewal ceremony not only provides a "symbolic way of relating the outlying hamlets to the tribal ancestral gods in the Center . . . it also links together the top-ranking shamans and top-ranking cargo holders through their shared experience of praying and conducting the ceremonies" (Vogt 1970: 99). These types of communal gatherings reinforce group identity and social values through shared practices and a belief in the protective power of divinity (Durkheim 1915: 59; Mach 1993: 80; Morinis and Crumrine 1991: 16; Turner 1969: 96; 1979: 207–208). In turn, the physical setting (e.g., caves) and materials used during these gatherings become symbolic of the group's collective affiliation.

The formation of community solidarity, however, does not negate a simultaneous reinforcement and legitimization of social divisions. For example, M. J. Sallnow's (1981) research on Ccamahuara pilgrimages in the Andes revealed that detachment of individuals from their local settings did upset normal hierarchical relations and reinforce sentiments of egalitarianism and solidarity. At the same time, these expressions were crosscut and sometimes enhanced by intercommunity conflict, pilgrimage-contingent factionalism, and ethnically based hierarchies. Similarly, Edward Schortman et al. (2001) argue that for leaders to be successful, they must draw from two such contradictory processes: they must both reinforce their privileged status through restrictive access and use of symbols pertinent to an elite social identity *and* foster a local corporate identity through a commonality of symbolic expression.

ACTUN NAK BEH AND CAHAL UITZ NA SITE LAYOUTS

Actun Nak Beh as a setting for social power struggles is first considered by the cave's location in relation to Cahal Uitz Na's layout. These architectural and spatial configurations clearly link Cahal Uitz Na elites to the cave site. They also appear to indicate that the cave was publicly accessible and thus a locus for communal activities.

Cahal Uitz Na is a medium-sized site located in the Roaring Creek Valley, Belize, at the foothills of the Maya Mountains. The center, surrounded by numerous *plazuela* groups and isolated house mounds, was the primary administrative center for the Upper Roaring Creek Valley during the Classic period (ca. A.D. 250–900). It is considered a "major center" within the Belize Valley because of the site's size and abundance of stone monuments (Awe and Helmke 1998: 213; Awe, Helmke, and Griffith 1998: 234).

The Roaring Creek Valley, like much of the Maya area, is composed of a heavily karsted, Cretaceous limestone riddled with caves. Cahal Uitz Na is surrounded by dozens of caves, many of which contain Preclassic and Classic period archaeological remains (Awe, Helmke, and Griffith 1998) (Figure 4.2). Actun Nak Beh is the closest known cave to the site's ceremonial core. Beyond physical proximity, Actun Nak Beh is clearly integrated into the layout of the center by the presence of a causeway that runs from Cahal Uitz Na's main plaza to the entrance of the cave (Figure 4.3). The causeway is 240 m long and approximately 10 m wide (Awe and Helmke 1998: 205; Conlon and Ehret 1999). Its construction is typical of other causeways in the Maya area (Shaw 2001: 261): limestone-facing stones lined the causeway edges; limestone and river cobblestones were used as fill; above which sat a layer of smaller stones or ballast; and the top was coated with limestone plaster (Halperin 2002: 68).

The layout of the center shares some attributes with a site layout template identified by Wendy Ashmore (1989, 1991) in which site planning is thought to incorporate features from Maya cosmology. It includes an emphasis on construction alignments along a north-south axis, with underworld symbolism in the southern realm of sites and overworld or heavenly symbolism in the northern realm of sites. Causeways were often used to connect these symbolic features. Cahal Uitz Na also possesses a north-south alignment, which is emphasized by the site's only known causeway. In addition, Actun Nak Beh with its supposed underworld associations is located in the south, and the site's elite residences and public ceremonial architecture are located in the north.

The causeway connects two public, ceremonial loci: Cahal Uitz Na's Plaza A and Actun Nak Beh's Entrance 1. Although public and private designations of space are often culturally subjective, these designations focus primarily on scale (number of people involved, few or many) and access. Ceremonial use of these

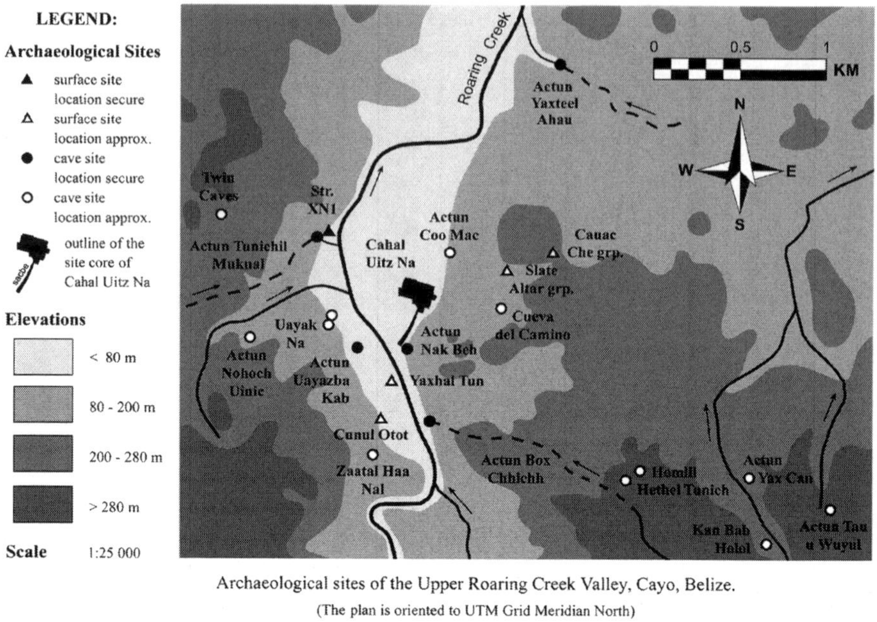

FIGURE 4.2. *Map of the Upper Roaring Creek Valley showing the locations of cave sites near Cahal Uitz Na (adapted from map by C. Helmke).*

spaces is inferred from the size and type of architecture, as well as the material remains recovered.

James Conlon and Jennifer Ehret (1999: 38) have noted a dichotomy between public and private areas of Cahal Uitz Na's principal architecture. Access to Plazas C and D was restricted by pyramidal and range type structures. These areas were probably more private sectors of the site. Plazas E and F, although easily accessible, were very small and located on the site's periphery.

Plazas A and B, on the other hand, were easily accessible. Openings at their corners allowed individuals to enter from outside the site core. They are the two largest plazas at the site and could have accommodated large crowds of people. The two plazas also contain architecture that is typical of public ceremonial zones within Classic period centers. Plaza B includes the site's only ball court, and Plaza A contains two of the largest pyramidal structures at the site (Conlon and Ehret 1999: 38, table 2). All four of Cahal Uitz Na's stelae (uncarved) and most of its slate monuments are situated in Plaza A (Awe and Helmke 1998).

James Brady (1989: 402–405) has suggested that spatial patterns of rituals within caves are similar to those of rituals on surface sites. Large, spacious cave entrances are thought to be analogous to large, easily accessible plazas on surface sites, and the dark interior areas of caves are thought to be analogous to restricted

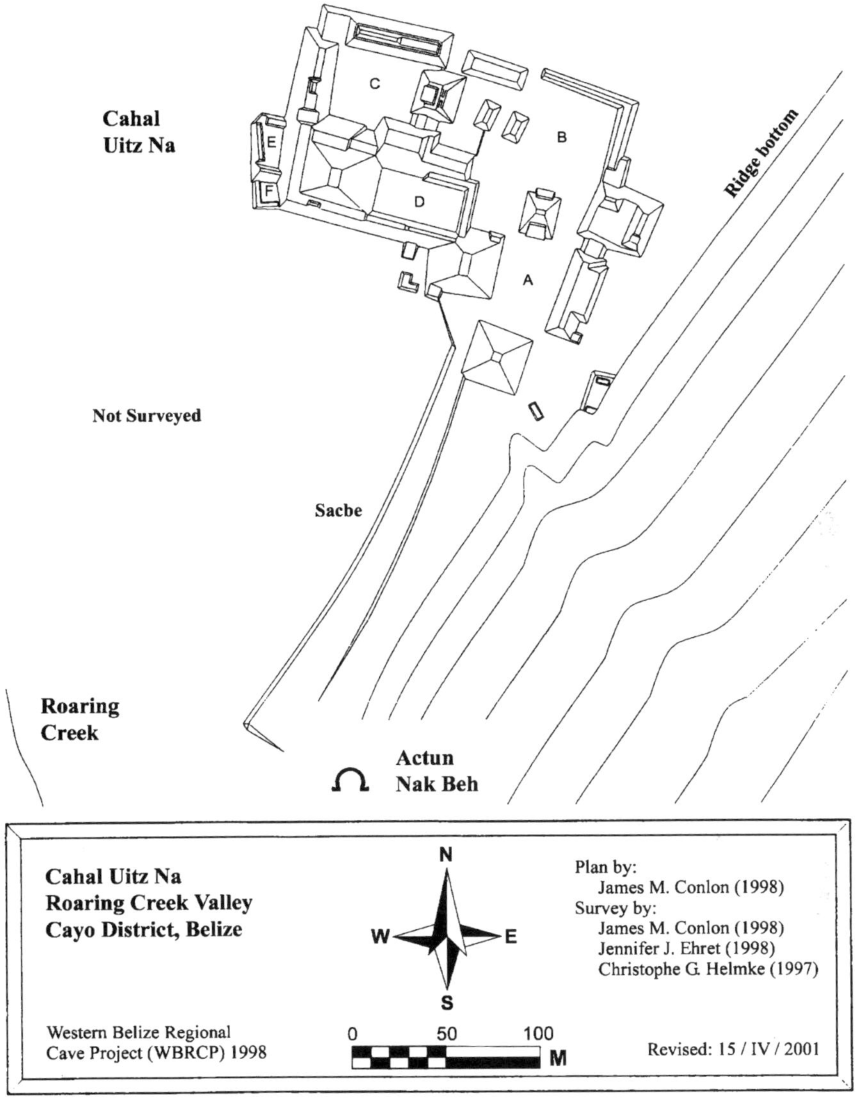

FIGURE 4.3. *Plan map of Cahal Uitz Na in relation to Actun Nak Beh (after Conlon and Ehret 1999: figure 3).*

areas on surface sites, such as those within structures or inaccessible plazas. This dichotomy of space can be applied to Actun Nak Beh: Entrance 1 could accommodate a large crowd of people, and its dark interior was limited in space to fewer than six to seven individuals in any given area.

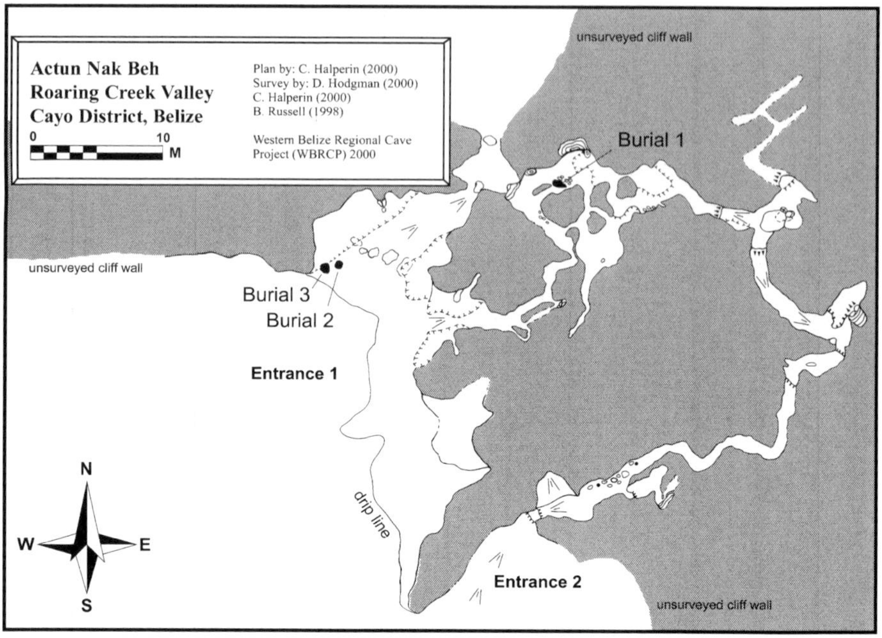

FIGURE 4.4. *Plan map of Actun Nak Beh showing locations of burials (adapted from Halperin 2002: figure 2.4).*

The cave site is small and "dry," lacking an underground river or substantial water seepage. The cave has two entrances, Entrance 1 and Entrance 2 (Figures 4.4 and 4.5). Entrance 1 resembles the morphology of a rockshelter in shape and size. It is located at the base of a cliff face and is characterized by a 5- to 7-m-high overhang or "roof," which extends out from the cave wall approximately 5 m. A breakdown slope of large (1–2 m) limestone boulders, rocks, and pebbles extends 40 degrees upward at the northernmost point of the entrance area. At the base of this large rockshelter-like opening in the cliff face is a flat, alluvial floodplain large enough to have held a crowd of people.

In contrast to Entrance 1, Entrance 2 and the cave interior are small and restrictive. Entrance 2 has no overhang and consists of a small opening less than 1 m in diameter. The interior of the cave is shaped like a U, consisting of a narrow "loop" of passage that connects the two entrances. Five small chambers, no larger than 5 m in diameter, are dispersed along the passage. The cave's narrow passage measures approximately 1 m in width. Its height varies between approximately 1 and 8 m.

Aside from the availability or lack of space, the causeway, which stops at Entrance 1, provides the most compelling evidence for the use of this area by a large group of people or a "public" audience. Causeways functioned to funnel and direct the movement of people through space (Ashmore 1989, 1991; Jackson 1994: 189–

FIGURE 4.5. *Actun Nak Beh's Entrance 1 (photo by E. White).*

205). Unlike large interregional and intersite causeways, intrasite roads, such as the Cahal Uitz Na–Actun Nak Beh causeway, were used for the procession of people during festivals, ceremonies, and daily activities (Awe 1999; Folan 1991; Keller 1994, 1997; Shaw 2001).

SITE CHRONOLOGY

Analysis of ceramics recovered from Actun Nak Beh and Cahal Uitz Na further confirms the integration of the cave and settlement by demonstrating their simultaneous use. Surface collections (Awe and Helmke 1998) and test-pit excavations (Conlon and Ehret 1999; Ehret and Conlon 1999; Ferguson 1999) established a preliminary chronology dating from the Middle Preclassic to the Late Classic period. The principal construction phases of the plaza platforms and the ball court occurred during the Classic period.

Ceramic analysis from Actun Nak Beh (n = 71 diagnostic sherds) indicates that the cave was used primarily during the Classic period, although one Middle Preclassic and one Late Preclassic sherd were recovered (Halperin 2002: 72–73). The ceramics were recovered from surface collections, four excavation units placed in Entrance 1, and three excavation units placed in the interior, dark zone of the cave. Although the location and architecture associated with the cave suggest it was intensively used, the low number of ceramics (and other artifacts) recovered from this small cave may indicate that the ritual site was swept clean, as seen among contemporary Zinacantecos (Vogt 1970: 102), or periodically looted. The low number of artifacts recovered from the Cahal Uitz Na causeway is not surprising among Maya causeways (see, for example, Keller 1994, 1997) and may also indicate ritual sweeping or cleaning.

ARCHAEOLOGICAL FINDS AT ACTUN NAK BEH

Although Actun Nak Beh contained a low number of material remains in reference to other, more inaccessible caves in the area, these finds indicate that the site was used for ceremonial activities (Halperin 2002). The most pervasive evidence of this assertion is the recovery of three burials. None of the burials was articulated or complete, although all appeared to be deliberate, if perhaps secondary, burials. The extremely poor preservation of the bones impeded extensive analysis. The deposition of secondary burials is lengthy and involves at least two stages of mortuary ritual, so it may have permitted the scheduling of the second stage of burial to coincide with agrarian cycles or public ceremonies (McAnany, Storey, and Lockard 1999: 131).

Burial 1 contained a single adult individual and was encountered in a small chamber in the interior of the cave (Figure 4.4). It was uncovered in a clay matrix under a pile of large rocks and a lens of pine (*Pinus* sp.) charcoal. The charcoal lens was mixed with Early Classic period dish sherds and broken obsidian blades. A small jade bead (0.8 by 0.5 cm) and three broken speleothems (cave formations) were also encountered with the human remains. The speleothems, in particular, do not appear to be a coincidental part of the burial because they were recovered interspersed with the bones rather than on or around the bones like the jade bead.

Burials 2 and 3, located in Entrance 1 under the rockshelter-like overhang, also contained poorly preserved bones. These burials dated to the Late to Terminal Classic period. Burial 2, capped by river cobble and limestone rocks, contained a thoracic vertebra and rib bones of a single adult individual. A large piece of quartz crystal, a slate pendant, obsidian, and partial remains of a Belize molded-carved vase were encountered interspersed with the capstones of the burial.

Burial 3 contained partial remains of an infant and an adult. They were found among chert flakes, a sliver of quartz crystal, and the remains of Late Classic polychrome and monochrome serving vessels. Matrix samples from Burial 3 contained remains of fruit (Sapotaceae family), pits of nance (*Byrsonima crassifolia*), the endocarps of the cohune palm (*Attalea cohune*), and pine (*Pinus* sp.) charcoal (Morehart 2002; Morehart, this volume).

Ceremonial activity at Actun Nak Beh may have also involved the use of ceramics for offering items. The Actun Nak Beh ceramic assemblage includes a lower percentage of jars than of open-form vessels within both burial and nonburial contexts. The frequency of jars (22 percent, n = 114) in the Actun Nak Beh assemblage is lower than those in typical domestic contexts (cf. Deal 1998: 52; LeCount

1996: 264) and many cave contexts (cf. Brady 1990: 442; Ishihara 2000; Moyes 2000; Pendergast 1969, 1971, 1974; Reents-Budet and MacLeod 1997: 50–58).

Most of the vessel forms in the ceramic assemblage consist of bowls (38 percent) and dishes (24 percent), classified as "open forms" according to a ratio of vessel height to maximum width (Rice 1987: 216; Sabloff 1975: 23). These vessels have large, open mouths, which suggests easy access to the vessel's contents (Rice 1987: 237–242). Although multiple functions can be attributed to these vessel forms, ethnographic and iconographic evidence suggests that they could have been used to serve or present items and were therefore ideal for offerings as they provide easy visibility and accessibility to their contents. Vessels of all form types are found in elite and commoner burials as offerings, for the deceased. Jars are less likely than vessels of other forms to appear in burials (Welsh 1991). Thus, the high frequency of open forms, predominately bowls and dishes, may suggest that ceramics were used for offerings. Their fragmentary state, however, may also suggest that the ceramics were ritually smashed before deposition (cf. J.E.S. Thompson 1975).

DISCUSSION

The layout of Cahal Uitz Na in reference to Actun Nak Beh follows a site pattern found throughout Mesoamerica in which ancient peoples strategically incorporated caves into their settlements. Unlike Mesoamerican sites that include architecture built over or near caves, as seen at the sites of Dos Pilas and Las Pacayas (Brady 1997; Brady and Ashmore 1999; Brady et al. 1997), Ma'ax Na (King and Shaw 2003), Nacimiento (Eberl 2002; Montenegro 2002), Oxkintok (Brady and Bonor Villarejo 1993), Teotihuacan (Heyden 1975, 1981, 2000), Utatlan (Brady 1991), Xochicalco (Hirth 2000), and Xochitecatl (Serra Puche 2001) (see also Brady and Bonor Villarejo 1993; Brady 1997 for a synthesis), the site of Cahal Uitz Na contains a causeway between a public, ceremonial zone of the site and the entrance of a cave. This pattern is parallel to the Terminal and Postclassic period site of Chichén Itzá in the northern Maya Lowlands. Several causeways radiate from Chichén Itzá's Plaza of the Castillo, the heart of the city. One of these roads, Causeway 1, links the Plaza of the Castillo with the Sacred Cenote, a large sinkhole known for its ceremonial significance and ritual offerings including human bones, ceramic vessels, metal artifacts, jadeite carved plaques, shell, and textiles (Cobos and Winemiller 2001; Coggins and Shane 1984).

The site layout at Cahal Uitz Na indicates that the site's leaders appropriated and controlled a significant sacred "resource." By means of the cave's physical presence and the rituals conducted therein, this resource provided a medium in which elite members could spatially and metaphorically link themselves with the supernatural and thus naturalize their privileged status as leaders and tribute extractors. In this sense, their link to the sacred foraged a division between the elites of the center and the commoners integrated into the Cahal Uitz Na polity.

On a larger scale, Cahal Uitz Na leaders may have used Actun Nak Beh and other nearby caves as a means to compete with other Belize Valley centers. Angel García-Zambrano's (1994) analysis of early-sixteenth-century Mesoamerican land and town titles indicates that rulers' conquest of neighboring groups and consolidation of territory and captives were contingent on the performance of "rituals of foundation" at caves and other sacred features at the heart of settlements and on settlement boundaries. In reviewing ethnographic literature on the relationship between caves and settlements, Brady (1997: 604) also notes that caves serve as a symbol for "an unwritten contract between the settlement and the earth in which the community's right to the land is validated by cave ritual." Similarly, Actun Nak Beh, as an important sacred "resource," and the caves surrounding Cahal Uitz Na may have increased the center's ceremonial prosperity and legitimacy needed to claim land rights and amass tribute.

The closest major centers to Cahal Uitz Na are situated in the alluvial bottom along the Belize River (Figure 4.1). These centers did not have easy access to cave sites and therefore had to rely on other mechanisms for alliance building. Competition for social status and power is most intense among similarly structured entities (Brumfiel 1994: 4). Other Classic period centers in the Belize Valley that were surrounded by caves, such as those in the Sibun River Valley (McAnany, Berry, and Thomas 2003), may have served as important competitors to Cahal Uitz Na because they may have had access to similar sacred "resources."

The spatial layout of Cahal Uitz Na and Actun Nak Beh also indicates that ceremonies at the cave were communal affairs, probably involving participation from residents both within and outside the center's site core. On one hand, Cahal Uitz Na's civic dominance could not be expressed without the counterweight of its subjects, who provide both the consent and challenge to its authority. On the other hand, the gathering of diverse social groups and classes to participate in communal religious events promotes social cohesion and identity among those who attend. Cahal Utiz Na's ceremonial center and associated cave may have provided an appropriate setting for such social unification. This phenomenon can be seen at other public cave sites, such as Naj Tunich. Epigraphic texts painted on its cave walls reveal that the cave was visited by a number of noblemen, dignitaries, and ritual specialists from various regional polities. Andrea Stone (1995: 183) argues that some of these pilgrimages were conducted as "cooperative enterprises," suggesting that the site played a role in securing political alliances and fostering regional integration.

CONCLUSION

Sacred landscapes are simultaneously contentious and communal. Leaders at Cahal Uitz Na gained and legitimized their social power by writing it into the landscape. They physically aligned themselves with a sacred cave site, Actun Nak Beh, through the construction of a causeway and thus linked themselves with the sacred emotions and meanings embedded in it. Such claims of legitimacy appear to have been transmitted broadly, as spatial and archaeological research indicates that the cave was used, at least in part, for public ceremonies. From a regional perspective, Cahal Uitz Na's control of the cave may have provided one avenue to create alliances and compete with other, similarly structured centers in the valley. In turn, the cave's public nature suggests that it played a key role in the formation of community solidarity and identity. Shared experiences strengthen bonds that crosscut social hierarchies. Taken together, these processes form a web of social negotiations whose lines both merge and divide.

ACKNOWLEDGMENTS

I would like to thank the Department of Archaeology, Belize, for its support of the Western Belize Regional Cave Project and project director, Jamie Awe, for his support and guidance. This research would have not been possible without financial assistance from the Social Sciences and Humanities Research Council of Canada (to Jaime Awe). I extend my thanks to all Western Belize Regional Cave Project staff, students, and workers, especially co-workers at Actun Nak Beh during the 2000 field season: Megan Bassendale, Oscar Chi, Ventura Chi, Sherry Gibbs, Christophe Helmke, Daniel Hodgman, Reiko Ishihara, Harri Kettunen, José Mai, Aguapeto, Christopher Morehart, Placido, Jeffrey Ransom, Don Valentine, and Eric White.

I am also grateful for the helpful comments of Wendy Ashmore, Chelsea Blackmore, James Brady, Christopher Morehart, and master's committee members Mary Pohl, Kathryn Josserand, Nicholas Hopkins, and Michael Uzendowski on earlier drafts of this chapter. All errors are the sole responsibility of the author.

REFERENCES CITED

Ashmore, Wendy

1989 Construction and Cosmology: Politics and Ideology in Lowland Maya Settlement Patterns. In *Word and Image in Maya Culture: Explorations in Language, Writing, and Representation,* eds. William F. Hanks and Don S. Rice, 272–286. University of Utah Press, Salt Lake City.

1991 Site-planning Principles and Concepts of Directionality Among the Ancient Maya. *Latin American Antiquity* 2:199–226.

Awe, Jaime J.

1999 The Distribution of Caves and Surface Sites in the Roaring Creek Valley, Belize: Implications for Sacred Geography. Paper presented at the 64th Annual Meeting of the Society for American Archaeology, Chicago.

Awe, Jaime J., and Christophe G.B. Helmke

1998 Preliminary Report on the Reconnaissance of Cahal Uitz Na, Roaring Creek Valley, Cayo District, Belize. In *The Western Belize Regional Cave Project: A Report of the 1997 Field Season,* Occasional Paper No. 1, ed. Jaime J. Awe, 200–215. Department of Anthropology, University of New Hampshire, Durham.

Awe, Jaime J., Christophe G.B. Helmke, and Cameron S. Griffith
1998 Archaeological Reconnaissance in the Roaring Creek Valley: Caves, Rockshelters, and Settlement Architecture. In *The Western Belize Regional Cave Project, A Report of the 1997 Field Season,* Occasional Paper No. 1, ed. Jaime J. Awe, 216–236. Department of Anthropology, University of New Hampshire, Durham.

Bassie Sweet, Karen
1991 *From the Mouth of the Dark Cave: Commemorative Sculpture of the Late Classic Maya.* University of Oklahoma Press, Norman.
1996 *At the Edge of the World, Caves and Late Classic Maya World View.* University of Oklahoma Press, Norman.

Brady, James E.
1989 An Investigation of Maya Ritual Cave Use With Special Reference to Naj Tunich, Peten, Guatemala. Ph.D. Dissertation. Interdisciplinary Archaeology Program, University of California, Los Angeles.
1990 Investigaciónes en la Cueva de la Sangre y otras cuevas de la región de Petexbatún. In *Proyecto Arqueologico Regional Petexbatún, Informe Preliminar #2, Segunda Temporada, 1990,* eds. Arthur A. Demarest and Stephen D. Houston, 438–489. Instituto de Antropología e Historia, Guatemala City.
1991 Caves and Cosmovision at Utatlan. *California Anthropologist* 18(1):1–20.
1997 Settlement Configuration and Cosmology: The Role of Caves at Dos Pilas. *American Anthropologist* 99:602–618.

Brady, James E., and Wendy Ashmore
1999 Mountains, Caves, Water: Ideational Landscapes of the Ancient Maya. In *Archaeologies of Landscape, Contemporary Perspectives,* eds. Wendy Ashmore and A. Bernard Knapp, 124–148. Blackwell, Oxford.

Brady, James E., and Juan L. Bonor Villarejo
1993 Las cavernas en la geografía sagrada de los Mayas. In *Perspectivas antropológicas en el mundo Maya,* eds. M. J. Iglesias and F. Ligorred, 75–95. Sociedad Española de Estudios Mayas, Madrid.

Brady, James E., Ann Scott, Allan Cobb, Irma Rodas, John Fogarty, and Monica Urquizú Sánchez
1997 Glimpses of the Dark Side of the Petexbatun Project: The Petexbatun Regional Cave Survey. *Ancient Mesoamerica* 8:353–364.

Brady, James E., and Andrea J. Stone
1986 Naj Tunich: Entrance to the Maya Underworld. *Archaeology* 39(6):18–25.

Brady, James E., and George Veni
1992 Man-Made and Pseudo-Karst Caves: The Implication of Subsurface Features Within Maya Centers. *Geoarchaeology* 7(2):149–167.

Brumfiel, Elizabeth M.
1994 Factional Competition and Political Development in the New World: An Introduction. In *Factional Competition and Political Development in the New World,* eds. Elizabeth M. Brumfiel and John W. Fox, 3–13. Cambridge University Press, Cambridge.

Cobos, Rafael, and Terance L. Winemiller
2001 The Late and Terminal Classic Period Causeway Systems of Chichen Itza, Yucatan, Mexico. *Ancient Mesoamerica* 12:283–291.

Coggins, Clemency C., and Orrin C. Shane III

1984 *Cenote of Sacrifice: Maya Treasures From the Sacred Well at Chichén Itzá,* eds. Clemency C. Coggins and Orrin C. Shane III. University of Texas Press, Austin.

Comaroff, John, and Jean Comaroff

1992 *Ethnography and the Historical Imagination.* Westview Press, Boulder.

Conlon, James M., and Jennifer J. Ehret

1999 Survey at the Major Center of Cahal Uitz Na, Cayo District, Belize. In *The Western Belize Regional Cave Project, A Report of the 1998 Field Season,* Occasional Paper No. 2, ed. Jaime J. Awe, 33–44. Department of Anthropology, University of New Hampshire, Durham.

Deal, Michael

1998 *Pottery Ethnoarchaeology in the Central Maya Highlands.* University of Utah Press, Salt Lake City.

DeMarrais, Elizabeth, Luis Jaime Castillo, and Timothy Earle

1996 Ideology, Materialization and Power Strategies. *Current Anthropology* 37:15–31.

Digby, Adrian

1958 A New Maya City Discovered in British Honduras: First Excavations at Las Cuevas and an Underground Necropolis Revealed. *Illustrated London News* 232:274–275.

Durkheim, Emile

1915 *The Elementary Forms of the Religious Life.* George Allen & Unwin, New York.

Earle, Timothy

1997 *How Chiefs Come to Power: The Political Economy in Prehistory.* Stanford University Press, Stanford.

Eberl, Markus

2002 Excavaciones en el "Area de La Barranca Escondida" de Aguateca. Paper presented at the XX Simposio de Investigaciones Arqueológicas, Museo Nacional de Arqueología y Etnología, Guatemala City.

Ehret, Jennifer J., and James M. Conlon

1999 Plaza Excavations at Cahal Uitz Na, Cayo District, Belize: Preliminary Report. In *The Western Belize Regional Cave Project, A Report of the 1998 Field Season,* Occasional Paper No. 2, ed. Jaime J. Awe, 53–68. Department of Anthropology, University of New Hampshire, Durham.

Ferguson, Josalyn

1999 Salvage Excavations at the Ballcourt at Cahal Uitz Na. In *The Western Belize Regional Cave Project, A Report of the 1998 Field Season,* Occasional Paper No. 2, ed. Jaime J. Awe, 45–52. Department of Anthropology, University of New Hampshire, Durham.

Folan, William L.

1991 *Sacbes* of the Northern Maya. In *Ancient Road Networks and Settlement Hierarchies in the New World,* ed. Charles D. Trombold, 222–229. Cambridge University Press, Cambridge.

Foucault, Michel
1977 *Discipline and Punish: The Birth of the Prison.* Pantheon Books, New York.
1978 *The History of Sexuality: An Introduction,* Vol. 1. Random House, New York.
1980 *Power/Knowledge: Selected Interviews and Other Writings, 1972–1977.* Pantheon Books, New York.

García-Zambrano, Angel J.
1994 Early Colonial Evidence of Pre-Columbian Rituals of Foundation. In *Seventh Palenque Round Table, 1989,* eds. Merle Greene Robertson and Virgina M. Fields, 217–227. Pre-Columbian Art Research Institute, San Francisco.

Godelier, Maurice
1999 *The Enigma of the Gift.* University of Chicago Press, Chicago.

Halperin, Christina T.
2002 Caves, Ritual, and Power: Investigations at Actun Nak Beh, Cayo District, Belize. Master's Thesis. Department of Anthropology, Florida State University, Tallahassee.

Helmke, Christophe G.B., David M. Cruz, Michael J. Mirro, and Amelia L. Jacobs
1999 Investigations at the Slate Altar Group in the Eastern Periphery of Cahal Uitz Na, Cayo District, Belize. In *The Western Belize Regional Cave Project, A Report of the 1998 Field Season,* Occasional Paper No. 2, ed. Jaime J. Awe, 53–68. Department of Anthropology, University of New Hampshire, Durham.

Helms, Mary W.
1988 *Access to Origins: Affines, Ancestors, and Aristocrats.* University of Texas Press, Austin.

Heyden, Doris
1975 An Interpretation of the Cave Underneath the Pyramid of the Sun in Teotihuacan, Mexico. *American Antiquity* 40(2):131–147.
1981 Caves, Gods, and Myths: World-view and Planning at Teotihuacan. In *Mesoamerican Sites and World-Views,* ed. Elizabeth P. Benson, 1–39. Dumbarton Oaks Research Library and Collection, Washington, D.C.
2000 From Teotihuacan to Tenochititlan. In *Mesoamerica's Classic Heritage: From Teotihuacan to the Aztecs,* eds. Davíd Carrasco, Lindsay Jones, and Scott Sessions, 165–184. University Press of Colorado, Boulder.

Hirth, Kenneth
2000 *Ancient Urbanism at Xochicalco: The Evolution and Organization of a Pre-Hispanic Society.* University of Utah Press, Salt Lake City.

Hodgman, Daniel
2001 Actun Nak Beh and Cahal Uitz Na: Evidence for Sacred Geography and Regional Lattice. Undergraduate Honors Thesis. Department of Anthropology, University of Pennsylvania, Philadelphia.

Ishihara, Reiko
2000 Ceramics From the Darkness: An Investigation of Ancient Maya Ritual Activity at Chechem Ha, Cayo District, Belize. Undergraduate Honors Thesis. Manuscript on file, Department of Archaeology, Belize.

Jackson, John Brinckerhoff
1994 A *Sense of Place, A Sense of Time.* Yale University Press, New Haven.

Joyce, T. A.
1929 Report on the British Museum Expedition to British Honduras, 1929. *Journal of the Royal Anthropological Institute* 59:439–459.

Keller, Angela H.
1994 The Xunantunich Sacbe Project 1994. In *Xunantunich Archaeological Project: 1994 Field Season,* ed. Richard M. Leventhal, 74–92. Manuscript on file, Institute of Archaeology, University of California, Los Angeles, and Belmopan, Belize.
1997 Testing and Excavation Around *Sacbe* II and Group C. In *Xunantunich Archaeological Project: 1997 Field Season,* ed. Richard M. Leventhal, 97–115. Manuscript on file, Institute of Archaeology, University of California, Los Angeles, and Belmopan, Belize.

Kertzer, David I.
1988 *Ritual, Politics, and Power.* Yale University Press, New Haven.

King, Eleanor M., and Leslie C. Shaw
2003 A Heterarchical Approach to Site Variability: The Maax Na Archaeology Project. In *Heterarchy, Political Economy, and the Ancient Maya: The Three Rivers Region of the East-Central Yucatán Peninsula,* eds. Vernon L. Scarborough, Fred Valdez Jr., and Nicholas Dunning, 64–76. University of Arizona Press, Tucson.

Knapp, A. Bernard, and Wendy Ashmore
1999 Archaeological Landscapes: Constructed, Conceptualized, Ideational. In *Archaeologies of Landscape,* eds. Wendy Ashmore and A. Bernard Knapp, 1–30. Blackwell Publishers, Oxford.

LeCount, Lisa J.
1996 Pottery and Power: Feasting, Gifting, and Displaying Wealth Among Late and Terminal Classic Lowland Maya. Ph.D. Dissertation. Department of Anthropology, University of California, Los Angeles.

Leone, Mark
1984 Interpreting Ideology in Historical Archaeology: The William Paca Garden in Annapolis, Maryland. In *Ideology, Power and Prehistory,* eds. Daniel Miller and Christopher Tilley, 25–36. Cambridge University Press, Cambridge.

Mach, Zdzislaw
1993 *Symbols, Conflict, and Identity: Essays in Political Anthropology.* State University of New York Press, Albany.

Mann, Michael
1986 *The Sources of Social Power: A History of Power From the Beginning to* A.D. *1760,* Vol. 1. Cambridge University Press, Cambridge.

McAnany, Patricia A., Kimberly A. Berry, and Ben S. Thomas
2003 Wetlands, Rivers, and Caves: Agricultural and Ritual Practice in Two Lowland Maya Landscapes. In *Perspectives on Ancient Maya Rural Complexity,* eds. Gyles Iannone and Samuel V. Connell, 71–81. The Costin Institute of Archaeology, University of California, Los Angeles.

McAnany, Patricia A., Rebecca Storey, and Angela K. Lockard
1999 Mortuary Ritual and Family Politics at Formative and Early Classic K'axob, Belize. *Ancient Mesoamerica* 10:129–146.

Miller, Daniel, and Christopher Tilley

1984 Ideology, Power, and Prehistory: An Introduction. In *Ideology, Power, and Prehistory,* eds. Daniel Miller and Christopher Tilley, 1–16. Cambridge University Press, Cambridge.

Mirro, Michael J., Vanessa A. Owen, and Christophe G.B. Helmke

1999 The Western Belize Regional Cave Project Reconnaissance Expeditions: Results of the 1998 Field Season. In *The Western Belize Regional Cave Project, A Report of the 1998 Field Season,* Occasional Paper No. 2, ed. Jaime J. Awe, 8–32. Department of Anthropology, University of New Hampshire, Durham.

Montenegro, Gustavo Adolfo

2002 Nacimiento Maya. *Revista Domingo, Revista semanal del Prensa Libre* 1099:8–11.

Morehart, Christopher T.

2002 Ancient Maya Ritual Cave Utilization: A Paleoethnobotanical Perspective. Master's Thesis. Department of Anthropology, Florida State University, Tallahassee.

Morinis, Alan, and N. Ross Crumrine

1991 *La Peregrinación:* The Latin American Pilgrimage. In *Pilgrimage in Latin America,* eds. N. Ross Crumrine and Alan Morinis, 1–18. Greenwood Press, New York.

Moyes, Holley

2000 The Cave as a Cosmogram: Function and Meaning of Maya Speleothem Use. In *The Sacred and the Profane: Architecture and Identity in the Maya Lowlands,* Acta Mesoamericana, Vol. 10, eds. Pierre R. Colas, Kai Delvendahl, Marcus Kuhnert, and Annette Schubart, 137–148. Anton Saurwein, Germany.

Pendergast, David M.

1969 *The Prehistory of Actun Balam, British Honduras.* Art and Archaeology Occasional Papers No. 16. Royal Ontario Museum, Toronto.

1971 *Excavations at Eduardo Quiroz Cave, British Honduras (Belize).* Art and Archaeology Occasional Paper No. 21. Royal Ontario Museum, Toronto.

1974 *Excavations at Actun Polbilche. British Honduras.* Art and Archaeology Occasional Papers No. 16. Royal Ontario Museum, Toronto.

Reeder, Philip

1993 Cave Exploration and Mapping on the Northern Vaca Plateau. *NSS News* 51(11):296–300.

Reeder, Philip, Edward Alt, Brian Nichols, William Reynolds, and James Webster

1995 *Annual Report on Multidisciplinary Research Activities on the Northern Vaca Plateau.* Manuscript on file, Institute of Archaeology, Belmopan, Belize.

Reents-Budet, Dorie, and Barbara MacLeod

1997 *The Archaeology of Petroglyph Cave, Cayo District, Belize.* Manuscript on file, Department of Archaeology, Belmopan, Belize.

Rice, Prudence M.

1987 *Pottery Analysis: A Sourcebook.* University of Chicago Press, Chicago.

Sabloff, Jeremy A.

1975 *Excavations at Seibal, Department of Peten, Guatemala: The Ceramics*. Peabody Museum of Archaeology and Ethnology Memoirs 13(2). Harvard University, Cambridge.

Sallnow, M. J.

1981 Communitas Reconsidered: The Sociology of Andean Pilgrimage. *Royal Anthropological Institute* 16(2):163–182.

Schele, Linda, and David Freidel

1990 *The Forest of Kings*. Quill William Morrow, New York.

Schortman, Edward M., Patricia A. Urban, and Marne Ausec

2001 Politics With Style: Identity Formation in Prehispanic Southeastern Mesoamerica. *American Anthropologist* 103(2):312–330.

Serra Puche, Mari Carmen

2001 The Concept of Feminine Places in Mesoamerica: The Case of Xochitecatl, Tlaxacala, Mexico. In *Gender in Pre-Hispanic America,* eds. Cecelia F. Klein and Jeffrey Quilter, 255–284. Dumbarton Oaks, Washington, D.C.

Shaw, Justine M.

2001 Maya *Sacbeob*: Form and Function. *Ancient Mesoamerica* 12:261–272.

Stone, Andrea J.

1992 From Ritual in the Urban Landscape to Capture in the Urban Center: The Recreation of Ritual Environments in Mesoamerica. *Journal of Ritual Studies* (6)1:109–130.

1995 *Images From the Underworld: Naj Tunich and the Tradition of Maya Cave Painting.* University of Texas Press, Austin.

Thompson, Edward H.

1938 The High Priest's Grave, Chichen Itza, Yucatan, Mexico. Prepared for publication with notes and introduction by J. Eric Thompson. *Field Museum of Natural History, Anthropology Series* Vol. 27, No. 1.

Thompson, J. Eric S.

1975 Introduction to the Reprint Edition. In *The Hill-Caves of Yucatan,* by Henry C. Mercer. University of Oklahoma Press, Norman.

Turner, Victor W.

1967 *Forest of Symbols.* Cornell University Press, Ithaca.

1969 *The Ritual Process: Structure and Anti-Structure.* Aldine Press, Chicago.

1979 *Process, Performance, and Pilgrimage: A Study in Comparative Symbology.* Concept Publishing Company, New Delhi.

Vogt, Evon Z.

1970 *The Zinacantecos of Mexico: A Modern Maya Way of Life.* Holt, Rinehart and Winston, New York.

1981 Some Aspects of the Sacred Geography of Highland Chiapas. In *Mesoamerican Sites and World-Views,* ed. Elizabeth P. Benson, 119–142. Dumbarton Oaks, Washington, D.C.

1992 The Persistence of Maya Tradition in Zinacantan. In *The Ancient Americas: Art From Sacred Landscapes,* ed. Richard F. Townsend, 60–69. The Art Institute of Chicago, Chicago.

Welsh, William B.M.

1991 *An Analysis of Classic Lowland Maya Burials.* BAR International Series 409.

Wolf, Eric R.

1990 Distinguished Lecture: Facing Power—Old Insights, New Questions. *American Anthropologist* 92:586–596.

Chapter Five

Pilgrimage and Caves on Cozumel

by Shankari Patel

Spanish sources document a rich history of pre-Columbian pilgrimage at Cozumel, centered on the Maya deity Ix Chel, the goddess of fertility, childbirth, divination, and medicine. Yet despite this well-documented evidence, previous archaeological interpretations of Cozumel have focused exclusively on the island's assumed significance to Postclassic trade. Although a review of the model employed by the Harvard Arizona project to study the island demonstrates that data did not support such an interpretation, Cozumel is often cited as an example of a Maya trading center. A focus on trade has structured subsequent research away from the examination of those features that might be expected to be associated with pilgrimage.

My recent research into the caves and *cenotes* of Cozumel documents the widespread cultural modification of these features, which highlights the importance of these natural landmarks in the religious life of the ancient Maya. It also suggests that the original pilgrimage circuit may have been laid out around landscape features such as caves and *cenotes* that were known to have been associated with Ix Chel (Milbrath 1999). The landscape approach adopted by this project appears to hold promise for illuminating pre-Columbian pilgrimage at Cozumel.

HISTORIC BACKGROUND

Because of Cozumel's proximity to Cuba, it was a favored supply stop for the conquistadors. Juan de Grijalva, who commanded the second expedition to Yucatán in 1518, explored the island's interior along paved roads known as *sacbeob,* finding an abundance of fish and honey products in the empty towns (Wagner 1942). Hernán Cortés's 1519 expedition regrouped at Cozumel after being separated by a *norte*. Naum Pat, the lord of Cozumel, kept his people neutral when bargaining with the Spaniards. He provided Cortés with information on the two shipwrecked Spaniards living on the mainland in exchange for a document protecting the islanders from future harassment.

Francisco López de Gómara, who chronicled the Cortés expedition, described the island, known as Acuzamil, as consisting of three towns with an estimated 3,000 residents. The natives were expert fishermen who also produced maize and honey. There were numerous temples throughout the island where the Maya offered copal and fruit and occasionally sacrificed birds, dogs, children, and adults to the idols. A temple near the coast, with a hollow ceramic idol fastened to the temple wall with mortar, appeared different than the rest. In the back of this idol, an entrance allowed the native priests to converse directly with the worshippers. The multitude of chapels and temples attracted a great number of "devout and superstitious" pilgrims who came from distant lands to worship at Cozumel. When Cortés destroyed the idols at the coastal temple and replaced them with images of the cross and the Virgin Mary, Gómara (Simpson 1964) recorded that the islanders enthusiastically brought the same offerings of birds, fruit, and copal to the image of the Virgin Mary that they had provided to their own idols.

According to the Bishop Diego de Landa, Cozumel served as a pilgrimage center devoted to the goddess Ix Chel. Landa wrote, "And they held Cozumel and the well of Chichén Itzá in the same veneration as we have for pilgrimages to Jerusalem and Rome, and so they used to go to visit these places and to offer presents there, especially to Cozumel, as we do to holy places" (in Tozzer 1941: 109).

Ethnohistoric sources record that Cozumel received pilgrims from distant lands. Diego de Contreras Duran, who inherited the island from his father as part of his *encomienda,* noted in 1579 that the Maya journeyed in great numbers from Tabasco, Xicalango, Champoton, and Campeche to worship Ix Chel (Roys, Scholes, and Adams 1940: 5).

The pilgrimage center at Cozumel was so important that Spanish sources suggest that *sacbeob* on the mainland were constructed expressly to accommodate religious traffic to the island. Diego López de Cogolludo noted (in Tozzer 1941: 109):

> There are remains of paved highways which traverse all this kingdom and they say they ended in the east on the seashore where it crosses an arm of the sea for

> the distance of four leagues which divides the mainland from that island. These highways were like the *caminos reales*, which guided them with no fear of going astray so that they might arrive at Cozumel for the fulfillment of their vows, to offer their sacrifices, to ask for help in their needs, and for the mistaken adoration of their false gods.

Cozumel continued its tradition of supplying the conquistadors during the conquest. Francisco de Montejo's fleet stopped in Cozumel in 1527 on its way to secure the Yucatán Peninsula. The fleet received supplies from Naum Pat, the Maya lord who had assisted Cortés. When Montejo and his men ventured north, Naum Pat, who was on the mainland attending a wedding, reportedly saved them from starvation (Clendinnen 1987: 21). The cooperation of the Cozumel Maya throughout the conquest (and the island's location along the periphery of the Maya realm) resulted in little Spanish interference with native religious practices during the Colonial era (Roys, Scholes, and Adams 1940: 8).

Although the early conquistadors may have made a display of casting down idols and replacing them with the icons of Christianity, the Maya continued to practice their native religious rituals well into the Colonial period (Lothrop 1924). Many of the colonial letters to the crown reported Cozumel's Indians' continued adherence to native rituals at sanctuaries "hidden" within the forest. Requests from officials for the appointment of a priest to instruct the Cozumel Maya in Christianity rarely yielded results.

There is little information concerning Cozumel during the seventeenth and eighteenth centuries. The island suffered from piratical raids in the late sixteenth century, which is thought to have led the Maya to abandon the island in the eighteenth century (Antochiw and Dachary 1991). Court documents describe two towns on the island in 1673, yet maps from 1766 and 1801 list the island as uninhabited (Roys, Scholes, and Adams 1940: 10).

Spanish sources paint a vivid picture of Cozumel Island as a religious center that drew pilgrims from all parts of Yucatán. Indeed, Cogolludo's description seems to suggest that the *sacbe* system in the interior of the peninsula was transportation infrastructure specifically constructed to serve pilgrimage. Furthermore, the economy appears to have been oriented around subsistence with maize and fish listed as the principal products (Simpson 1964; Wagner 1942). The frequent references to the production of honey on the island could be tied specifically to the brewing of the ritual alcoholic beverage *balche*. Interestingly, no mention is made of the importance of markets or trade centers. Thus, according to the conquest and ethnohistoric records the island's economy appears to have facilitated pilgrimage, and this is what structured secondary production as well.

A HISTORY OF MODERN INVESTIGATION

Cozumel's fame as a pilgrimage center lured John Lloyd Stephens and Frederick Catherwood to the island in 1842. Barred from the interior by vegetation and encountering no occupants, Stephens and Catherwood assumed it to be uninhabited and confined their investigations to the ruins of San Miguel on the west coast (Stephens 1962: 236–246). William Henry Holmes (1895: 66) spent time at the west coast shrine known as Miramar whose interesting feature was a sculptured pillar of a kneeling woman grasping her abdomen in a birthing position (Figure 5.1). A similar column in the interior of the island also caught the attention of George Howe (1911: 549–550) (Figure 5.2).

Channing Arnold and Frederick J. Tabor Frost visited Cozumel in 1908, searching explicitly for what they described as "the Mayan Mecca." Because only ruins accessible from the port of San Miguel had been described, they reasoned that previous explorers had seen just a fraction of the pre-Columbian architecture. They were convinced that the true pilgrimage center lay in the "heart of the island" hidden by the dense forest. If Cozumel was the *Isla Sagrada,* Arnold and Frost expected to find elaborate architecture rivaling or surpassing structures on the mainland. Over the course of several weeks they hacked through miles of thick brush searching for religious architecture, eventually discovering San Gervasio, the largest site on the island. Nevertheless, the explorers were disappointed with San Gervasio, which could not compare in size or grandeur to Chichén Itzá (Arnold and Frost 1909).

Additional sites on Cozumel were recorded by the Mason-Spinden Expedition to Yucatán led by Gregory Mason and Herbert J. Spinden and described in the *Silver Cities of Yucatan* (Mason 1927). This expedition accessed the northern part of the island by anchoring at Punta Molas. Venturing inland they came upon a lagoon with the remains of an ancient *sacbe,* described as

> A viaduct made of great stone slabs, which had been built by ancient Mayas. It was raised two feet above the water. For a quarter mile it could still be used, but the balance was disintegrating for a considerable distance. The slabs had either been worn smooth by pedestrians or had been chosen for their smoothness to the bare feet of pilgrims coming to Cozumel's shrines as Greeks sought the shrine of Apollo at Delphi. (Mason 1927: 276)

The nineteenth and early twentieth centuries saw a steady stream of explorers attracted to Cozumel because of its reputation as a great pilgrimage center. Most left frustrated by their inability to penetrate the dense jungle and discouraged because the architecture was not on the grand scale they had expected. This led later archaeologists to dismiss Cozumel's religious history and focus instead on the island's role as a pre-Columbian trading center. These modern studies mark a new period of exploration centered on economic models.

Harvard University and the University of Arizona initiated an extensive island-wide archaeological project in 1972. Over the course of two field seasons, over thirty sites were carefully examined to understand "the role of long-distance trade in the rise, maintenance, and fall of Mesoamerican civilizations" (Sabloff and Rathje 1975: 455). The project's elaborate mercantile model, constructed before the inves-

FIGURE 5.1. *"La Parturienta Columna" at Miramar (from Holmes 1895).*

tigation, remains the most influential and most frequently cited interpretation of Cozumel and will be discussed in detail later.

Excavations at San Gervasio continued into the 1980s (Robles Castellanos 1986) and 1990s (Azcárate Soto and Ramírez Ramírez 2000; Ramírez Ramírez and Azcárate Soto 2000, 2002) to restore the site for the growing number of tourists visiting the island and to test a number of ideas regarding its political and economic

FIGURE 5.2. *"La Parturienta Columna" at Santa Rita (from Howe 1911).*

autonomy. Rather than seeing Cozumel as a port controlled by the Toltec at Chichén Itzá during the Early Postclassic, INAH (Instituto Nacional de Antropología y Historia) archaeologists sought evidence to prove the island prospered not from the fall of Chichén Itzá but as a result of increased maritime trade after Coba collapsed (Sierra Sosa 1994; Sierra Sosa and Robles Castellanos 1988).

THE MERCANTILE MODEL

Because sources state that the island received pilgrims from key trading ports on the mainland and because of its seemingly convenient location along the Maya sea-trade route, the Harvard Arizona Archaeological Project assumed Cozumel's chief function was in relation to trade. Since previous archaeological surveys had documented occupation extending from the Late Preclassic to the conquest, it was also believed that the island's importance to the trading system was rather ancient. Cozumel had persisted while its notable neighbors, such as Coba and Chichén Itzá, had been abandoned. Cozumel appeared to be the ideal place to test how mercantile systems adapted to change and to understand aspects of the larger trading network.

The project hypothesized that Cozumel would have first operated as a neutral port of trade controlled by Toltec Chichén Itzá during the Early Postclassic. After

Chichén Itzá collapsed it was thought the island reemerged as an independent trading port during the Late Postclassic. Because Cozumel would no longer be protected by Chichén Itzá, the project speculated that security "[w]as reinforced religiously through the institution of a pilgrimage route which exactly paralleled the principal trading route" (Sabloff et al. 1974: 403). The trading port was thought to predate the pilgrimage tradition, and therefore the investigators explicitly predicted that the pilgrimage center at Cozumel would not date to a period earlier than the Late Postclassic (Sabloff et al. 1974: 414).

A close examination of both the assumptions and the results of the Harvard Arizona project raises serious doubts about the mercantile model. The basic premise that Cozumel's location made it a natural and important port is highly questionable. Although the island lies only 20 km from the coast, a deep channel with a strong current separates it from the mainland. As Clinton Edwards (1957: 13–14) warns,

> Through the channel, called the Canal de Cozumel, flows a swift, north-setting current of from four to six knots, and small craft which ply between mainland ports to the north and the harbor at San Miguel must hug the coast of the peninsula as far south as Playa del Carmen before attempting a dash across the channel. If the wind or motor fails, the navigator may find himself rapidly carried back towards his last port of call.

The Maya were well aware of this difficulty. Colonial documents note, "When they have to cross over to the town of Polé, which is on the mainland, they employ many superstitions before embarking and crossing that strait, which flows with greater velocity than a mighty river" (Roys, Scholes, and Adams 1940: 9). The settlement surveyors of the Harvard Arizona project similarly concluded, "The channel separating Cozumel from the mainland is difficult and dangerous to cross even with modern craft" (Freidel and Leventhal 1975: 65). The difficulty in reaching Cozumel needs to be stressed because the island produced the same goods that were readily available on the mainland, so its importance as a trade center has always rested primarily on its seemingly ideal location for seafaring trade. Since sailing to the island was more hazardous than staying close to the coast, what was the incentive for traders to risk their wares in getting there? Trade alone appears to be an inadequate explanation.

Archaeological data suggest that the initial port-of-trade model cannot be applied to Cozumel for a number of reasons. The first assumption, that all of Yucatán had been under the central control of Chichén Itzá during the Early Postclassic, proved to be incorrect based on subsequent work in Yucatán and Quintana Roo in the late 1970s (Andrews 1983; Robles Castellanos 1980). Ceramic evidence from the mainland indicated that the peninsula had been divided between two distinct political and commercial spheres of Chichén Itzá and Coba, with Cozumel most likely falling under the influence of Coba (Phillips 1979: 261). Although Peto Cream ceramics recovered from subsequent excavations at San Gervasio reveal an Itzá link, Anthony Andrews (1990: 164) believes the evidence is insufficient to confirm an

Itzá commercial or military presence on the island. Furthermore, Andrews and Fernando Robles Castellanos (1985: 67–68) note the problems involved in applying J. Eric Thompson's historic arguments to the archaeological record:

> Another fundamental problem is our adherence to quasi-historical sequences of events which offer felicitous, but somewhat simplistic, accounts of the arrival of foreign groups in northern Yucatán in the ninth and tenth centuries of the Christian era. Because such reconstructions fail to clarify the archaeological record, we must assume that a far more complex series of events took place. In this respect, we are not alluding to the old Quetzalcoatl-Kulkulcan migration myth, but rather to the more intricate "Putun models" proposed in the early 1970's (Thompson 1970; Ball 1974). These models offer only a superficial explanation of the social, economic, and political processes underlying events, and fail to deal adequately with the interaction between foreign groups and local polities in the course of those changing times.

In addition, the central proposition that Cozumel had been an important trading center in the Early Postclassic proved untenable. The majority of the material recovered by the project dated to the Late Postclassic. A lack of secular remains from the Early Postclassic led David Phillips (1979: 257) to conclude that "Cozumel was not a major center before the Decadent period," and evidence for trade could only be found in Late Postclassic lots. Phillips (1979: 263) found that

> The lack of pre-Decadent remains on Cozumel belies the supposed importance of the island in Early Postclassic trade; because of strategic factors, it may be that Cozumel was not as advantageously sited relative to trade routes as it was during the Decadent. In other words, Cozumel is not the ideal place to test the port-of-trade model.

The conclusion of the ceramic analysis sounded a similar note. Judith Connors (1983: 365–374) says,

> Ceramic evidence does not strongly support the dynamic port of trade model as proposed by the investigators (Rathje and Sabloff 1973; Sabloff and Rathje 1975). The absence of ceramics indicating the presence of foreign groups on the island in Early Postclassic times tends to reduce the likelihood that Cozumel was a port of trade in the purest sense, as defined in the Cozumel research design.

Not only did the archaeological remains negate the hypothesis that Cozumel was an early trading center, they also did not support the expectation that the pilgrimage cult was a late development. All of the material recovered from earlier lots was "biased towards ritual" (Phillips 1979: 235), indicating a ceremonial significance to Cozumel before the establishment of trade in the Late Postclassic. An analysis of the artifacts suggests that the market on Cozumel may have been significantly different than those found on the mainland in being structured around pilgrimage activity. The most common artifacts recovered were net sinkers (1979: 246) and plugs for hollow log beehives (1979: 251), confirming the conquistadors' accounts that fish and honey were the island's main products (Maudslay 1996; Pagden 1986; Simpson 1964; Wagner 1942).

Unfortunately, the mercantile model never acknowledged that the evidence for mercantile activity resembled a secondary development associated with pilgrimage. Furthermore, the bulk of the data recovered suggests an economic system structured around servicing the needs of pilgrims. Although the mercantile model was unable to provide a convincing explanation for developments on Cozumel, it has regrettably shifted attention away from the religious function of the island. Thus, Cozumel was classified as an example of a typical Late Postclassic trading center that took advantage of its prime location along an important sea-trade route to participate in the commerce of the region (Sabloff 1977, 2001; Sabloff and Freidel 1975; Sabloff and Rathje 1975).

PILGRIMAGE AND TRADE

Despite the fact that the ethnohistoric sources identify Cozumel as a pilgrimage center, an archaeological project has yet to investigate the implication. This appears to reflect a wider anthropological bias. Victor Turner (1973: 209) criticized anthropology for neglecting pilgrimage as an important area of study, citing anthropology's obsession with "pragmatics" over "symbolics." Yet it is the symbolic that draws people to sacred centers and, in the process, creates a number of cultural systems of interest to even the most pragmatic anthropologist. Pilgrimage centers embrace both spiritual and secular activities. As a phenomenon that attracts some of the largest gatherings of people on the planet (Morinis 1992), pilgrimage encourages mercantile activities. Large transient populations engaged in any type of activity require food, lodging, and items acquired in markets. Sacred centers stimulate the trade of ritual and utilitarian items, incorporating financial activities into the ideological interests of the center (Rinschede and Sievers 1987; Sopher 1967).

In addition to providing goods and services to pilgrims, religious markets have an impact on local and regional economies (Rinschede and Sievers 1987). As Gisbert Rinschede (1992: 65) notes,

> On the whole, the economy of an entire city and its surroundings (Fatima and Lourdes) and sometimes of an entire country (Mecca in Saudi Arabia) can be influenced by the pilgrim stream. Until the end of the Second World War, when the oil industry developed dramatically, the income produced by the Mecca pilgrims was the backbone of Saudi Arabian economy.

A. J. Wensinck (1966: 32) points out the close relationship between religious celebrations and economic activity. He notes, "Great fairs were from early times associated with the hajj, which was celebrated on the conclusion of the date harvest." Besides utilitarian goods, pilgrimage markets also provide pilgrims with ritual objects for use on-site or as mementos, ideological symbols embodying the ideals of the center. Miles Richardson (1997: v) views the trade of religious articles as inevitable "since the sacred has a physical presence, copies can be made, and if copies can be made, they can be sold and a profit turned." This need for mementos appears to be universal and has been called the "cult of traces" (Morinis 1992: 6). As Simon Coleman and John Elsner (1995: 100) elaborate, "One of the most characteristic aspects of pilgrimage art in all the world religions is the proliferation of objects made available to pilgrims and brought home by them as reminders and even as tangible channels of connection with the sacred experience."

The connection between pilgrimage and commerce has been recognized in the Mesoamerican area as well. It is interesting to compare A. P. Maudslay's description of Esquipulas over a hundred years ago to Wensinck's analysis of the hajj cited previously. Maudslay (quoted in McBryde 1947: 83) says,

> The great festival of the year is held in January, and then for a week or more the usually half-deserted little town of Esquipulas swarms with pilgrims. In old days its fame was so great that it attracted worshippers all the way from Mexico and Panama and the fair, which was carried out at the same time, was the great commercial event of the year. Thither the English merchants from Belize brought their wares and carried on what was practically the whole of the foreign business of Honduras, Salvador and Guatemala, taking in exchange the native grown indigo.

Interregional commerce has been linked to the fairs and fiestas surrounding pilgrimage sites in Guatemala (McBryde 1969: 248–249). Walter Randolph Adams (1991: 120) observed that institutions like pilgrimages do not stand alone but are a part of other social processes. Among the Tzeltales and Tojolabales he noted, "A market was held concurrently which included products from throughout the catchment area, as well as products from Taiwan and other foreign countries. This market, its co-occurrence with the pilgrimage, and the range of products offered for sale again point to the economic functions of pilgrimages" (Adams 1991: 113). Thompson (1970: 138) believed modern religious markets in Guatemala likely mirrored pre-Columbian practices. As with other areas of the world, Mesoamerican pilgrimage and markets were symbiotic. "Pilgrimage devotion, the market, and fair are all connected with voluntary, contractual activities (the religious promise, the striking of a bargain, the penny ride on the merry-go-round)" (Turner and Turner 1978: 37).

In the model I have developed, it is clear that, cross-culturally, pilgrimage produces markets that are only explainable in relation to the sacred site. The dominant trend has been to study trade on Cozumel independently from the pilgrimage function. In reviewing the data analyses from the Harvard Arizona project, it is interesting that little evidence of trade is produced and the data recovered point to religious activity. The project concluded that "[a]lthough Cozumel's role as a pilgrimage shrine is made quite clear in the ethnohistoric literature, its role as a trading center is more ambiguous" (Freidel and Sabloff 1984: 179). With the close association between pilgrimage and economic activity in Mesoamerica, it makes more sense to see trade on Cozumel as an outgrowth of religious traffic surrounding pilgrimage to Ix Chel. By investigating the ideological reasons for traveling to Cozumel, we would gain a better picture of its mercantile activity.

THE CAVES OF COZUMEL

Landscape features figured prominently in Mesoamerican pilgrimage sites. A number of these sites consisted of caves and *cenotes,* which received offerings in propitiation of the rain or water deities (Martínez Marin 1972; Turner 1973). A review of the literature indicates considerable evidence of cave utilization on Cozumel. For instance, several early explorers described altars and structures built in, over, or next to caves (Arnold and Frost 1909; Mason 1927). William Davidson (1967) also recorded a number of small cave shrines that seem to be situated in relation to water found deeper within the cave. In describing the temple at San Francisco Cave, Davidson (1967: 52, 56) noted,

> Northwest of Cedral three-fourths of mile inland from Punta Tunich is a filled-in *cenote* which has a cave ruin in one side. Due to the protection afforded by the cave, the structure is in excellent condition, and painted figures are clearly visible to the left of the door. The small oratorio, which measures thirty inches long, twenty-four inches wide, and seventeen inches high, guards the potable water found deeper in the cave.

Wyllys Andrews IV (1955–1956: 8) documented a cave/*cenote* temple at Chen Pita, in the southern portion of the island. The site consisted of two caves, each containing large pools of water. Within the sheltered overhang of the caves a number of fire opals, sourced to an area hundreds of kilometers away from the island (Phillips 1979: 290), were cached under an altar. The pattern of building miniature temples and platforms in caves and *cenotes* on Cozumel has counterparts at other sites along the east coast (Andrews and Corletta 1995).

Several archaeological surveys and projects have recovered religious artifacts from the island's *cenotes* (Luna Erreguerena 1989), and INAH has identified several of the island's caves as serving a ceremonial function (Velázquez Morlet et al. 1988). An underwater archaeological project in the 1980s discovered ceramics and jade axes dating to the Late Classic period (Delgado 1998: 276) within the *cenote* at Chankanaab (Luna Erreguerena 1989: 150), and divers exploring the *cenote* of Chu-Ha near the airport in 1996 found intact ceramic vessels (Sterner 1997). The Island Caves Research Center (ICRC) has spent the past twenty years mapping an underwater cave system on Cozumel known as Cueva Quebrada. At a surface opening in this system, 5,000 m from the west coast entrance, divers discovered pottery, human bones, and a number of other artifacts. As they exited this cave entrance they were surprised to discover a previously unrecorded surface site (Bozanic 1991).

Based on the literature, I suspected that a pilgrimage circuit involving landscape features was once the focus of religious devotion on Cozumel and that these features may hold critical data on the importance of the Ix Chel cult. Therefore, I chose to reexamine a number of caves on Cozumel precisely because they had been so badly ignored in the past. The cave sites I visited were accessible to areas restored for tourism and exhibited evidence of ancient ritual use.

SAN GERVASIO

San Gervasio, one of the larger settlements on Cozumel, served as the main administrative and ceremonial center (Freidel and Sabloff 1984; Sierra Sosa and Robles Castellanos 1988: 9). Although only a fraction of the site has been excavated, there are three prominent caves in the restored section of the site. During the restoration, archaeologists collected human bones, ceramics, and conch shells from the floors of these caves (Sierra Sosa 1994: 80).

The first cave I investigated was directly behind Structure 30a near the entrance to the San Gervasio archaeological zone.[1] This building was identified as an oratory. A culturally modified hole in the bedrock gives access to the cave. This opening may have been the only entrance during the pre-Columbian period (Figure 5.3). The cave consists of a single chamber with a collapsed ceiling. Thelma Sierra Sosa (1994: 80) proposed that a masonry wall once encircled the interior of the cave. During my examination I noticed masonry blocks strewn around the cave's interior, but only the western wall remained discernible. Because this cave yielded a large ceramic sample, the Harvard Arizona project speculated that it had been used "extensively as a dump" (Gregory 1975: 97).

In a smaller cave located 72 m east of the first, Sierra Sosa (1994: 80) noted the presence of a staircase providing access to the surface. Although I noted a number of masonry fragments against the southern wall that appear to suggest its existence, the staircase is no longer obvious. Other architectural features observed included two field walls terminating at the cave's northern and southern boundaries. Adjacent to this cave were two unexcavated masonry structures. A third cave, 120 m east of the second, contained masonry modifications to its interior, but given the state of deterioration it was difficult to determine the original form of these alterations.

In addition to the three caves, a *cenote* temple was also examined at San Gervasio. The Harvard Arizona project speculated that this *cenote* "played an important role in the activities of the center" (Freidel and Sabloff 1984: 154) because a *sacbe* terminated at a staircase descending into it. Although the staircase is gone, I noted that Structures 37a and 38a, which appear to be temples, were adjacent to this *cenote*. Structure 38a, which was not excavated or included in the San Gervasio restoration plans, towers over the western wall of the well. Aside from a prominent looters' hole, Structure 38a is still in good condition. The placement of this temple is reminiscent of the Casa del Cenote at Tulum (Lothrop 1924: 109–111). The only other building in the vicinity is Structure 41a, one of the largest temples on the island, constructed during the Late Classic period. David Freidel (1975) speculated that this temple housed Ix Chel's oracle at San Gervasio.

FIGURE 5.3. *Cave entrance in relation to San Gervasio structure (photo by S. Patel).*

CELERAIN I

Celerain I, in the Punta Sur Ecological Park at the southern point of the island (Punta Celerain), is another *cenote* historically associated with both a temple and *sacbe*. Hebert Spinden and Ludlow Griscom described the *cenote* shrine in 1926 as "[a] temple built over the entrance to a cave which contained a permanent fresh pool. Stairs from the doorway descended to the cavern" (in Mason 1927: 278). When William Sanders mapped the site (Figure 5.4) in 1954 he noted, "A special feature is a four-step stairway which goes 1.2 meters under the floor of the back room and has its entrance in the back room doorway. It descends into what evidently was a *cenote* below the temple, now filled with rubble" (Sanders 1955: 191–192). Sanders collected fragments of incense burners from the floor of the temple. When William Davidson (1967: 52–53) visited the site, also known as Chen David, in 1967, the temple structure had collapsed but the staircase was clearly visible. Other than Sanders's map and the descriptions given previously, little is written about this site.

Following Sanders's distances from the modern lighthouse, the remains of the site were relocated in 2001. The temple has been completely destroyed, its masonry blocks scattered around the *cenote,* which still contains water (Figure 5.5). A wooden bridge now provides a walkway over the water. A sizable mound of rubble frames the southern portion of the well. Two additional entrances to the *cenote* were located along the southeastern and southwestern boundaries of the cave. Its companion temple, Celerain II, has also deteriorated into obscurity, and efforts to relocate it failed. Neither site was included in the restorations plans for the ecological park.

DISCUSSION

The archaeological evidence for the importance of cave/*cenotes* is not limited to architecture found within them or artifacts recovered from them. The presence of powerful landmarks, such as caves and *cenotes,* was a matter of first importance in any decision about land utilization, especially for religious purposes. Although the Harvard Arizona project investigated the island for information on trade, its settlement analysis found the majority of masonry structures to be religious constructions. Not surprisingly, these

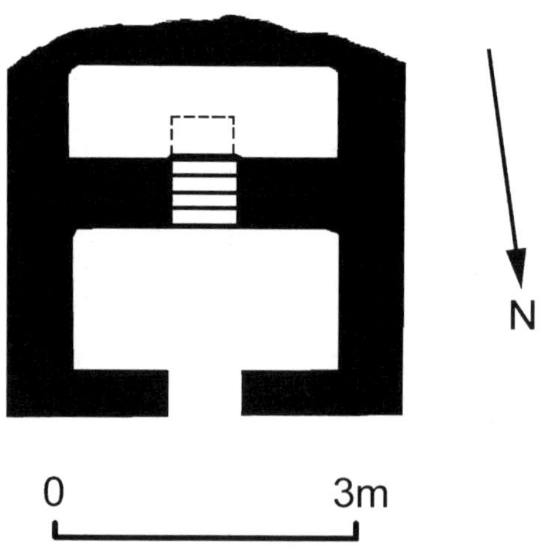

FIGURE 5.4. *Celerain I. Map of* cenote *temple (after Sanders 1955).*

FIGURE 5.5. *Celerain I (photo by S. Patel).*

buildings were associated with an island-wide *sacbe* network, which outlined a ceremonial circuit tying together the island's sacred geography (Freidel and Sabloff 1984: 183). The project also noted a number of religious structures adjacent to, within, or above the island's caves and *cenotes*. In addition, an extensive field wall network demarked space throughout much of the island. A number of these walls were not only near caves but actually appeared to delimit many of the large *cenotes* (Friedel and Sabloff 1984: 33). Thus, a number of lines of evidence suggest that caves and *cenotes* were features of first importance that structured the utilization of space around them.

Religious activity may have persisted at *cenotes* on Cozumel even after the Maya resettled the island in the 1850s. A female statue situated at a *cenote* (Figure 5.6) near the island's Late Classic center received offerings up until its removal in the 1940s for display at the museum in San Miguel. The idol described as "*La Xnuc*," "*La Vieja*," and "*La Virgen de Santa Rita*" held a special place of veneration among the people of Cozumel, and local informants attested the *cenote* had received patrons for at least fifty years before the idol's removal from the site (Escalona Ramos 1946: 559–560).

CONCLUSIONS

The results of my recent cave survey on Cozumel indicate that these features were far more important than currently appreciated. The time and effort involved in

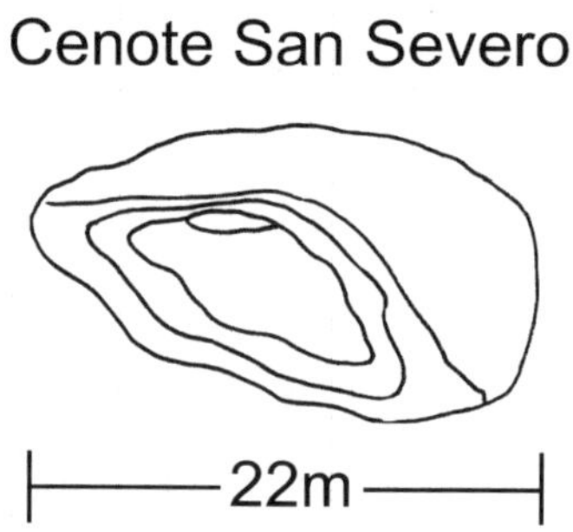

Figure 5.6. *"La Xnuc," "La Vieja" (after Escalona Ramos 1946).*

modifying such landmarks seem out of keeping with previous archaeological interpretations, which list the Cozumel caves as dumps, quarries, or places of refuge (Freidel and Sabloff 1984: 71; Gregory 1975: 97; Rathje and Phillips 1975: 77; Sierra Sosa 1994: 80). There appears to be a pattern of widespread cultural modification directly associated with caves and *cenotes* on Cozumel. Architecture was built in or above these features, and staircases facilitated access. The failure to appreciate the significance of the association between shrines, caves, and *cenotes* and the cult of Ix Chel at sites like San Gervasio and Celerain I is a central reason religious motivation did not receive greater attention. The thinking of the Harvard Arizona project was clear in stating that "structures within the architectural comparative type of shrine have been located upon *sacbeob*, next to *cenotes*, and along the coastlines of both Cozumel and the east coast which seem to be unlikely locations for structures with solely a religious purpose" (Freidel and Leventhal 1975: 72). Yet we now know these are precisely the places where sacred landmarks are expected, and this relationship has been extensively documented on the east coast of the mainland at Xcaret, Tulum, and Tancah (Andrews and Andrews 1975; Miller 1977).

Pilgrimage figured prominently in all activities on the island and according to the Spanish records was the incentive for Maya travel to Cozumel. The Harvard Arizona project also recovered evidence that established the ritual center at Cozumel before the trading activities of the Late Postclassic. My recent reexamination of cave features on Cozumel has shown that they are the focus of a degree of modification that is inconsistent with their supposed utilitarian and domestic functions. Instead, they appear to be integrated as focal points of ritual/ceremonial architectural complexes. This is consistent with the growing literature on Maya caves suggesting that they were among the most important landmarks in the ancient sacred landscape. These features were accessible from the *sacbe* network, whose primary function, according to Freidel, was to provide a ceremonial circuit for pilgrims to Cozumel. These data tentatively support the hypothesis that an ancient pilgrimage circuit was once laid out in relation to the island's caves and *cenotes*. These findings indicate that the landscape approach may be the most profitable means for investigating and reconceptualizing pilgrimage at Cozumel.

NOTE

1. The structure nomenclature is taken from the Harvard Arizona project.

REFERENCES CITED

Adams, Walter Randolph

1991 Social Structure in Pilgrimage and Prayer: Tzeltales as Lords and Servants. In *Pilgrimage in Latin America,* eds. N. Ross Crumine and Alan Morinis, 109–121. Greenwood Press, New York.

Andrews, Anthony P.

1983 *Maya Salt Production and Trade*. University of Arizona Press, Tucson.

1990 The Role of Trading Ports in Maya Civilization. In *Vision and Revision in Maya Studies,* eds. Flora S. Clancy and Peter D. Harrison, 159–168. University of New Mexico, Albuquerque.

Andrews, Anthony P., and Fernando Robles Castellanos

1985 Chichén Itzá and Coba: An Itzá-Maya Standoff in Early Postclassic Yucatan. In *The Lowland Maya Postclassic,* eds. Arlen F. Chase and Prudence M. Rice, 62–71. University of Texas Press, Austin.

Andrews, Anthony P., and Roberta Corletta

1995 A Brief History of Underwater Archaeology in the Maya Area. *Ancient Mesoamerica* 6(2):101–117.

Andrews, E. Wyllys, IV

1955–1956 Xcaret Journal. Manuscript on file, Middle American Research Institute, Tulane University, New Orleans.

Andrews, E. Wyllys, IV, and Anthony P. Andrews

1975 *A Preliminary Study of the Ruins of Xcaret, Quintana Roo, Mexico: With Notes on Other Archaeological Remains on the Central East Coast of the Yucatán Peninsula.* Middle American Research Institute, Publication 40, New Orleans.

Antochiw, Michel, and Alfredo César Dachary

1991 *Historia de Cozumel*. Consejo Nacional para la Cultura y las Artes, Mexico.

Arnold, Channing, and Frederick J. Tabor Frost

1909 *American Egypt: A Record of Travel in Yucatán*. Hutchinson and Row, London.

Azcárate Soto, Antonieta, and Demetrio Ramírez Ramírez
2000 Trabajos de Reconocimiento en el Grupo VI (Complejo el Ramonal) de San Gervasio, Cozumel, Q. Roo. *Actualidades Arqueológicas* 4(22):12–16.

Ball, Joseph W.
1974 A Coordinate Approach to Northern Maya Prehistory: A.D. 700–1000. *American Antiquity* 39(1):85–93.

Bozanic, Jeffrey
1991 Cozumel Pottery Report. Paper on file, The Island Caves Research Center, Cozumel.

Clendinnen, Inga
1987 *Ambivalent Conquests: Maya and Spaniard in Yucatán*. Cambridge University Press, Cambridge.

Coleman, Simon, and John Elsner
1995 *Pilgrimage: Past and Present in the World Religions*. Harvard University Press, Cambridge, Massachusetts.

Connors, Judith
1983 The Ceramics of Cozumel, Quintana Roo, Mexico. Ph.D. Dissertation. Department of Anthropology, University of Arizona, Tucson.

Davidson, William
1967 Study of Settlement Patterns, Cozumel Island, Quintana Roo, Mexico. Masters Thesis. Department of Geography, Memphis State University, Memphis.

Delgado, James P.
1998 *Encyclopedia of Underwater and Maritime Archaeology,* ed. James P. Delgado. Yale University, New Haven.

Edwards, Clinton R.
1957 Quintana Roo: Mexico's Empty Quarter. Masters Thesis. Department of Geography, University of California, Berkeley.

Escalona Ramos, Alberto
1946 Algunas ruinas prehistoricas en Quintana Roo. *Boletín de la Sociedad Mexicana de Geografía y Estadística* 61(3):513–628.

Freidel, David A.
1975 The Ix Chel Shrine and Other Temples of Talking Idols. In *A Study of Changing Pre-Columbian Commercial Systems: The 1972–1973 Seasons at Cozumel, Mexico,* eds. Jeremy A. Sabloff and William L. Rathje, 107–113. Monographs of the Peabody Museum, no. 3. Peabody Museum of Archaeology and Ethnology, Cambridge.

Freidel, David A., and Richard M. Leventhal
1975 The Settlement Survey. In *A Study of Changing Pre-Columbian Commercial Systems: The 1972–1973 Seasons at Cozumel, Mexico,* eds. Jeremy A. Sabloff and William L. Rathje, 60–87. Monographs of the Peabody Museum, no. 3. Peabody Museum of Archaeology and Ethnology, Cambridge.

Freidel, David A., and Jeremy A. Sabloff
1984 *Cozumel: Late Maya Settlement Patterns.* Academic Press, New York.

Gregory, David A.

1975 San Gervasio. In *A Study of Changing Pre-Columbian Commercial Systems: The 1972–1973 Seasons at Cozumel, Mexico,* eds. Jeremy A. Sabloff and William L. Rathje, 88–106. Monographs of the Peabody Museum, no. 3. Peabody Museum of Archaeology and Ethnology, Cambridge.

Holmes, William H.

1895 *Archaeological Studies Among the Ancient Cities of Mexico, Part I. Monuments of Yucatan.* Field Museum of Natural History Anthropological Series 1, Chicago.

Howe, George

1911 The Ruins of Tulum. *American Anthropologist,* N.S. 13:539–550.

Lothrop, Samuel K.

1924 *Tulum: An Archaeological Study of the East Coast of Yucatán.* The Carnegie Institution of Washington, Washington, D.C.

Luna Erreguerena, Pilar

1989 Underwater Archaeology in Mexico. In *Underwater Archaeology Proceedings of the Society for Historical Archaeology Conference,* ed. J. Barto Arnold III, 149–151. Society for Historical Archaeology, Tucson, Arizona.

Martínez Marin, Carlos

1972 Santuarios y peregrinaciones en el Mexico prehispanico. In *Religión en Mesoamerica,* eds. Jaime Litvak King and Noemi Castillo Tejeros, 161–176. XII Mesa Redonda Sociedad Mexicana de Antropología, Mexico, D.F.

Mason, Gregory

1927 *Silver Cities of Yucatan.* Putnam, New York.

Maudslay, A. P.

1996 [1956] *The Discovery and Conquest of Mexico by Bernal Díaz del Castillo.* Translated and edited by A. P. Maudslay. Da Capo, New York.

McBryde, Felix Webster

1947 *Cultural and Historical Geography of Southwest Guatemala.* Institute of Social Anthropology, Pub. 4. Smithsonian Institution, Washington, D.C.

1969 *Geografía cultural e historica del sureste de Guatemala.* Seminario de Integración Social Guatemalteca, No. 24. Guatemala.

Milbrath, Susan

1999 *Star Gods of the Maya: Astronomy in Art, Folklore, and Calendars.* University of Texas Press, Austin.

Miller, Arthur G.

1977 The Maya and the Sea: Trade and Cult at Tancah and Tulum, Quintana Roo, Mexico. In *The Sea in the Pre-Columbian World,* ed. Elizabeth P. Benson, 97–138. Dumbarton Oaks Research Library and Collections, Washington, D.C.

Morinis, Alan

1992 Introduction. In *Sacred Journeys: The Anthropology of Pilgrimage,* ed. Alan Morinis, 1–29. Greenwood Press, Westport.

Pagden, Anthony

1986 *Hernan Cortés: Letters From Mexico.* Trans. and ed. Anthony Pagden. Yale University Press, New Haven.

Phillips, David A.

1979 Material Culture and Trade of the Postclassic Maya. Ph.D. Dissertation. Department of Anthropology, University of Arizona, Tuscon.

Ramírez Ramírez, Demetrio, and Antonieta Azcárate Soto

2000 Recientes investigaciones en el grupo II, o Mayapan de San Gervasio, Cozumel, Q. Roo. *Actualidades arqueológicas* 5(23):10–13.

2002 Investigaciones receientes en Cozumel. *Arqueología Mexicana* 9(54):46–49.

Rathje, William L., and David A. Philips

1975 The Ruins of Buena Vista. In *A Study of Changing Pre-Columbian Commercial Systems: The 1972–1973 Seasons at Cozumel, Mexico,* eds. Jeremy A. Sabloff and William L. Rathje, 77–86. Monographs of the Peabody Museum, No. 3, Peabody Museum of Archaeology and Ethnology, Cambridge.

Rathje, William L., and Jeremy A. Sabloff

1973 Ancient Maya Commercial Systems: A Research Design for Island of Cozumel, Mexico. *World Archaeology* 5:221–231.

Richardson, Miles E.

1997 Prologue, in Geography and Pilgrimage: A Review. In *Sacred Places, Sacred Spaces: The Geography of Pilgrimages,* eds. Robert H. Stoddard and Alan Morinis, v–vii. Geoscience and Man, vol. 34. Louisiana State University, Baton Rouge.

Rinschede, Gisbert

1992 Forms of Religious Tourism. *Annals of Tourism Research* 19(1):51–67.

Rinschede, Gisbert, and Angelika Sievers

1987 The Pilgrimage Phenomenon in Socio-Geographical Research. *The National Geographical Journal of India* 33(2):213–217.

Robles Castellanos, Fernando

1980 *La secuencia cerámica de la región de Coba, Quintana Roo.* Tesis Profesional. Escuela Nacional de Antropología e Historia, Mexico.

1986 *Informe anual del Proyecto Arqueológico Cozumel: temporada 1980.* Fernando Robles Castellanos (coordinador). Instituto Nacional de Antropología e Historia, México.

Roys, Ralph L., Frances V. Scholes, and Eleanor B. Adams

1940 *Report and Census of the Indians of Cozumel 1570.* Carnegie Institution of Washington Publication No. 523, Contribution 30, Washington, D.C.

Sabloff, Jeremy A.

1977 Old Myths, New Myths: The Role of Sea Traders in the Development of Ancient Maya Civilization. In *The Sea in the Pre-Columbian World,* ed. Elizabeth P. Benson, 67–88. Dumbarton Oaks Research Library and Collections, Washington, D.C.

2001 Cozumel Island. In *Archaeology of Ancient Mexico and Central America: An Encyclopedia,* eds. Susan Toby Evans and David L. Webster, 189–191. Garland, New York.

Sabloff, Jeremy A., and David A. Freidel

1975 A Model of a Pre-Columbian Trading Center. In *Ancient Civilization and Trade,* eds. Jeremy A. Sabloff and C. C. Lamberg-Karlovsky, 369–408. University of New Mexico, Albuquerque.

Sabloff, Jeremy A., and William L. Rathje
1975 *Study of Changing Pre-Columbian Commercial Systems. The 1972–1973 Seasons at Cozumel, Mexico. A Preliminary Report,* eds. Jeremy A. Sabloff and William L. Rathje. Monographs of the Peabody Museum, No. 3. Peabody Museum of Archaeology and Ethnology, Cambridge.

Sabloff, Jeremy A., William L. Rathje, David A. Friedel, Judith G. Connor, and Paula L.W. Sabloff
1974 Trade and Power in Postclassic Yucatán: Initial Observations. In *Mesoamerican Archaeology: New Approaches,* ed. Norman Hammond, 397–416. University of Texas, Austin.

Sanders, William T.
1955 *An Archaeological Reconnaissance of Northern Quintana Roo.* Carnegie Institution of Washington Current Report No. 24, Washington, D.C.

Sierra Sosa, Thelma Noemi
1994 *Contribucion al Estudio de los Asentamientos de San Gervasio, Isla de Cozumel.* Instituto Nacional de Antropologia e Historia, Mexico.

Sierra Sosa, Thelma Noemi, and Fernando Robles Castellanos
1988 Investigaciones Arqueologicas en San Gervasio, Isla de Cozumel. In *Cozumel, Un Encuentro en la Historia,* coords. Eva Saavedra Silva and Jorge Sobrino Sierra, 1–13. Fondo de Publicaciones y Ediciones de Quintana Roo.

Simpson, Lesley Byrd
1964 *Cortés: The Life of the Conqueror by His Secretary Francisco López de Gómara.* Trans. and ed. Lesley Byrd Simpson. University of California, Berkeley.

Sopher, David E.
1967 *Geography of Religions.* Prentice-Hall, Englewood Cliffs, NJ.

Stephens, John Lloyd
1962 [1843] *Incidents of Travel in Yucatán. Volume 2.* University of Oklahoma Press, Norman.

Sterner, Bob
1997 The Cenotes of Cozumel. *Immersed,* Fall:52–56.

Thompson, J. Eric S.
1970 *Maya History and Religion.* University of Oklahoma Press, Norman.

Tozzer, Alfred
1941 *Landa's Relación de las Cosas de Yucatán,* ed. Alfred M. Tozzer. Papers of the Peabody Museum of Archaeology and Ethnology, vol. 18. Peabody Museum of Archaeology and Ethnology, Cambridge.

Turner, Victor
1973 The Center Out There: Pilgrim's Goal. *History of Religions* 12:191–230.

Turner, Victor, and Edith Turner
1978 *Image and Pilgrimage in Christian Culture.* Columbia University, New York.

Velázquez Morlet, Adriana, Casado Lopez, Maria del Pilar, and Edmundo Lopez de la Rosa
1988 *Zonas Arqueologicas. Yucatán,* eds. Adriana Velázquez Morlet, Casado Lopez, Maria del Pilar, and Edmundo Lopez de la Rosa. Instituto Nacional de Antropología e Historia, Mexico.

Wagner, Henry R.
1942 *Discovery of New Spain in 1518 by Juan de Grijalva.* The Cortes Society, Berkeley, California.

Wensinck, A. J.
1966 Hadjdj. *Encyclopedia of Islam.* Brill, Leiden.

II

Reconstructing Ritual and Cosmology

Chapter Six

The Impact of Ritual on Ancient Maya Economy

by James E. Brady

Because of particular theoretical interests in archaeology, research on ancient Maya economics has lagged (McAnany 1989). Even now, when archaeologists speak of ancient Maya economy, the discussion tends to focus on interregional exchange of items such as obsidian or jade that can be chemically sourced or that are obvious foreign imports. The interest here has been in locating points of origin and destination for goods so that routes of exchange can be reconstructed. As Patricia McAnany (1989: 359) notes, questions concerning the distribution within sites of some of these items, such as obsidian, have yet to be resolved; therefore, archaeologists have not reached a consensus on some basic questions of the circulation of goods within Maya society. It is not surprising, then, that there have been few attempts to deal with the allocation of economic resources.

With direct access to the data, anthropologists have a somewhat easier time addressing these issues and have produced considerably more literature on Mesoamerican economics. These anthropological works should be of interest to the archaeologist, at the very least, as guides to potentially important areas of investigation. Eric Wolf (1966), for instance, has analyzed peasant economy in terms of production for particular areas of allocation, which he calls the rent, market, and ceremonial funds. The designation of the ceremonial fund as a major area of allocation is of special interest because the materialist bias of archaeology in general, and of cultural ecology in particular, has tended to minimize the importance of religion and ritual in society. This bias was unusually well illustrated when an archaeologist attempted to deal with ethnographic data. Barbara Price (1974) dismissed the very existence of a ceremonial fund simply because the items purchased were of extra-local origin. She clearly missed the point. Even if her assertion was true, it does not change the nature of the allocation. Furthermore, if true, it should make the ceremonial fund an area of particular interest because it would be one of the allocations most directly responsible for generating and maintaining interregional trade. It is not difficult to find examples of trade in ritual items that were of such importance that they became economic and political issues as well. One has only to look at the trade in frankincense and myrrh in the Old World to appreciate this point (Groom 1981; Van Beek 1958, 1960).

This chapter attempts to examine the nature of the allocation for the ceremonial fund and determine the extent to which the allocations might have been economically significant. Although theoretical bias may play a part, the main reason little progress has been made in assessing the economic impact of religion is the presence of a number of knotty methodological problems. One of the most serious is the difficulty in isolating the ritual component in multiuse sites. The inability to clearly distinguish the ceremonial assemblage precludes any type of more detailed analysis. This is a problem Maya cave archaeology was forced to confront and was able to resolve because of the unique nature of the cave environment. It is recognized cross-culturally that the dark zone of caves is generally reserved for religious ritual. The growing sophistication in reading cave context also permits researchers to increasingly establish cave function in the twilight and light zones as well. The consensus among Maya cave specialists is that, by and large, these were purely religious spaces. Thus, the artifacts within the cave can be taken as forming a ceremonial assemblage.

Interestingly, cave assemblages share many elements with surface—presumably utilitarian—assemblages, so that function is not implicit in the artifact itself but is interpretable only within a context. This should hardly be surprising. Brian Hayden and Aubrey Cannon (1984: 96) documented in ethnographic situations that "artifacts rarely function in the utilitarian, social, or ideological domain to the exclusion of the others." This may mean, unfortunately, that multifunction contexts will provide several, possibly conflicting interpretations for the same assemblage. Single-function, purely ceremonial features such as caves certainly provide the surest and easiest context for analyzing a host of problems associated with religion and ritual. Although there is a growing awareness of the importance of caves in Maya religion (Brady 1997), there appears to be little appreciation of the potential of these features for contributing to our analysis of Maya economics.

The reason the economic component of cave assemblages has gone unrecognized lies in the nature of cave investigations. First, cave studies have generally been carried out as salvage projects, so few represent even a week of field investigation. Few caves have therefore been investigated intensively enough to produce artifact assemblages sufficiently impressive to call attention to their economic importance. Second, cave reports frequently lack the complete or detailed artifact descriptions necessary for making such an analysis.[1] Finally, the caves that have been investigated are not, on the whole, closely associated with excavated surface sites; therefore, it is difficult, if not impossible, to make meaningful quantitative comparisons between cave assemblages and those recovered from surface sites.

THE PETEXBATUN REGIONAL CAVE SURVEY

Because the Petexbatun Regional Cave Survey worked as a closely integrated component of Vanderbilt University's Petexbatun Regional Archaeological Project, many of the problems mentioned previously have been mitigated. Both projects, for example, expended their greatest effort at the site of Dos Pilas. Thus, the cave artifact assemblage can be assessed within the context of the overall Dos Pilas assemblage. A rough assessment of the economic importance of the cave component can be derived by comparing the quantity of material in various artifact categories recovered by the cave project to that recovered by the Dos Pilas surface project.

Before beginning, however, it should be emphasized that I am not attempting to minimize the still substantial problems in making comparisons between these very different types of sites. For one thing, the larger project had already begun its investigation when its director, Arthur Demarest, invited me to initiate a cave survey. Thus, when the cave project[2] completed its investigation after two and a half seasons, the surface project already had four years of work at Dos Pilas. Additionally, the cave component was always considerably smaller. On these grounds alone, one would expect the cave assemblage to represent only a minor component of the overall assemblage. Recovery methods also differed considerably. Almost all material recovered by the surface project came from excavation, whereas the majority of cave artifacts were surface collected. The fact that the cave deposits tended to be more concentrated aided in recovery and offset some of the differences in work time and personnel. At the same time, preservation in many cave contexts is superior to that on the surface, so caves produced bone and shell artifacts that had simply disappeared from the surface.

A common perception was that the cave survey had cleared a larger percentage of the total artifact inventory than the surface project had. This is an important point because it would indicate that the cave and surface assemblages are not comparable as samples of their respective artifact inventories. A number of lines of evidence suggest that this is not the case, but there is no way to completely resolve the issue. First, it is now clear that the cave survey located only a small percentage of all the caves in the area. Therefore, the twenty-two caves investigated represent a sample of the area's caves, just as the surface project only sampled a portion of the architecture. Areas within the caves containing rivers were not intensively collected because the ceramics and artifacts tended to be of limited value as a result of extreme erosion. Since such riverine areas formed a large part of each major cave, it is clear that the cave survey only collected a portion of each of its sites. Finally, specialized excavation methods using wet screening of riverine sands and employing chemical deflocculants to highly plastic clays demonstrated that the surface collection had left large quantities of artifacts just below the surface in waterlogged areas (Brady and Scott 1997; Urquizú Sánchez 1996). Thus, once again, the artifact assemblage recovered from the caves represents only a small sample of all the artifacts in the cave.

In sum, it appears that valid comparisons can be made between the cave and surface collections and that because all the work was done as part of a single large archaeological project, the problems are fewer and less severe than with any cave investigation conducted to date. Nevertheless, this analysis is not without serious problems, so the results should be taken as indicating nothing more than general orders of magnitude. For this reason, simple percentages or raw figures will be used, which readers will have to weigh for themselves.

ASSEMBLAGE COMPARISONS

As in most excavations, pottery is the most commonly encountered artifact at Dos Pilas. The surface project recovered 128,000 sherds (Foias 1992: 251), and the cave survey analyzed over 64,000. In other words, approximately one-third of all the pottery from the combined projects was recovered in caves. Cave sherds tend to be much larger than those recovered in surface excavation, so the percentage by sherd weight would be even higher. The large percentage the cave component forms of the project's overall assemblage raises questions as to whether the Dos Pilas caves are representative of caves in general. My experience at Naj Tunich was similar to that at Dos Pilas, and a comparable-sized assemble was also amassed at that site (Brady 1989). At Mayapán, where a fair amount of work was expended in caves, an assemblage of over 55,000 sherds was recovered (Smith 1971: 106). Although he spent a far shorter time in the field, David Pendergast collected about 23,000 sherds each from Actun Balam and Eduardo Quiroz Cave (Pendergast 1969: 58; 1971: 23). E. Wyllys Andrews (1965) does not give sherd counts from the Gruta de Chac, but it is obvious that the amount of ceramic present is enormous. This same point can be made for the Pusilha Caves, where, because of the period when they were excavated, a quantitative analysis of the ceramics was not conducted (Joyce 1929; Joyce et al. 1928). Thus, the evidence suggests that caves regularly produce sizable ceramic assemblages, so the quantity collected at Dos Pilas is understandable in terms of the size and duration of the project.

Although a third of the project ceramic assemblage came from caves, this chapter does not claim that one of every three vessels produced at the site ended

FIGURE 6.1. *The fact that many vessels could be restored indicated that sherd counts represented fewer vessels than would be the case in surface contexts.*

up in the caves. The fact that large portions of many cave vessels can be restored clearly indicates that fewer vessels were present than suggested by the sherd count (Figure 6.1). Nevertheless, even if the cave assemblage amounted to 10 percent of total production, this would translate into a significant increase in demand over simple domestic utilization. Polychrome, painted, and fine ceramics account for about 15 percent of the total assemblage, indicating that workshops producing these ceramics were also affected by cave ritual. If the highest level of ceramic specialization is reflected in vessels with hieroglyphic texts produced for specific occasions, then the presence of the earliest dynastic text from Dos Pilas on one cave vessel and another recording the capture of a prisoner suggests that this level of specialist was also involved in production for cave ceremonies. The large assemblage of ceramic drums and whistles found in the Cueva de los Quetzales also suggests there was specialty production for ritual activities (Helton 1997) (Figure 6.2).

The economic importance of cave ritual is more apparent in dealing with artifacts produced by specialists or involving the use of imported raw materials. The most common artifact in this class is obsidian. Excluding the material overlaying the royal tomb in Structure L5-1,[3] 1,212 obsidian artifacts were recovered from various surface contexts at Dos Pilas (Stiver 1992: 290), and the caves produced another 325, or about 21 percent of the obsidian. A third of the blade cores were also found in caves. Whereas it was noted that sherd counts from the caves suggested greater pottery utilization than was probably the case, the same cannot be said for obsidian. The small size and dark color of the artifacts make it less likely that they would be discovered on muddy cave floors during surface survey. In the Cueva de Sangre, surface mud, never more than 10 cm deep, was cleared from a 4-m by 2.5-m area and dissolved in a chemical deflocculant. This process recovered ten obsidian blades from an area where none had been found by the surface collection and suggests that obsidian may be heavily underrepresented in the cave assemblage (Brady and Scott 1997: 20).

Obsidian prismatic blades have been reported from at least twenty-eight Maya caves,[4] so they appear to be a common part of cave artifact assembles. The fact that Naj Tunich is the only other cave reporting more than 100 blades is once again explainable in terms of the size and intensity of the investigation. It is generally assumed that obsidian was used in blood-letting rituals (Brady 1989: 324; Brady and Stone 1986; MacLeod and Puleston 1978; J.E.S. Thompson 1975: xix), which is supported by use-wear analysis that has detected little or no utilization on cave blades (Aoyama 2001; Reents-Budet and MacLeod 1986: 89). The large number of blades recovered at Dos Pilas argues that the prevalence of blood letting in cave ritual may be underappreciated. One of the economic implications is that a significant amount of a site's obsidian was disposed of without ever having been used in the utilitarian realm.

Although chert is locally available, the production of large, bifacially flaked blades required the skill of a specialist. Therefore, they may have been items of intraregional trade, which had a restricted distribution (Gibson 1989). Ninety-four whole or broken blades and points have been recovered from noncache[5] contexts at Dos Pilas (Stiver 1992: 287), and another seventy-two, or 43 percent, have been found in caves. The cave specimens are statistically longer and thinner than those from the surface (Brady et al. 1991: 710), indicating that the finest examples are disposed of in caves (Figure 6.3). Such artifacts appear to be a common element in cave assemblages, with at least seventeen other caves reporting examples.[6] Some of the larger blades were almost certainly hafted and used as knives similar to the one recovered from the Cenote of Sacrifice (Coggins and Ladd 1992: 262–263) and the three blades, attached to pre-Columbian wooden handles, still being used for sacrificial purposes in the Cuicatec area when discovered in a ceremonial cave in 1957 (Holland and Weitlaner 1960). Since several dozen blades were recovered in

FIGURE 6.2. *The large number of sherds from ceramic drums in the Cueva de los Quetzales indicates that there was specialty production in items for ritual use.*

caches at Dos Pilas (Palka 1990) and the caching of blades decorated with anthropomorphic faces has been reported from sites such as the Templo Mayor, it may be that many of the cave blades were simply deposited as valuable offerings, similar in intent to the cached examples.

Among the imported stones, jade is the most valuable, but surprisingly not a great deal has been recovered at Dos Pilas. The royal tomb in Structure L5-1, for instance, accounts for 86 percent by weight of all the jade found by the surface project. The caves account for only 5 percent of the site's jade but for 28 percent of the jade found outside of this one tomb. There is reason to believe jade is also underrepresented in the cave assemblage. The jade from the cave is composed mainly of jade beads, some of which have been broken. A number of the copal lumps recovered from the Cenote of Sacrifice contain beads that had been embedded in the incense, and it was noted that many of the beads had broken as a result of burning (Proskouriakoff 1974: 4). Burned jade beads were also found in and around the *incensarios* at Balankanche (Andrews 1970: 12). The Dos Pilas Cave jade indicates a similar practice. If jade beads were added to burning incense, these would tend to be buried in the cave mud when the ceramic vessels in which the copal was burned were smashed at the end of ceremonies. Small pieces of jade were found in two of the seven test pits that used chemicals to dissolve cave mud, suggesting that there is considerably more jade in the caves, but without the use of these chemicals it is unlikely that it can be recovered (Urquizú Sánchez 1996). Jade has been reported from sixteen other caves (Brady 1989: 290–298), so it is a frequent cave offering.[7]

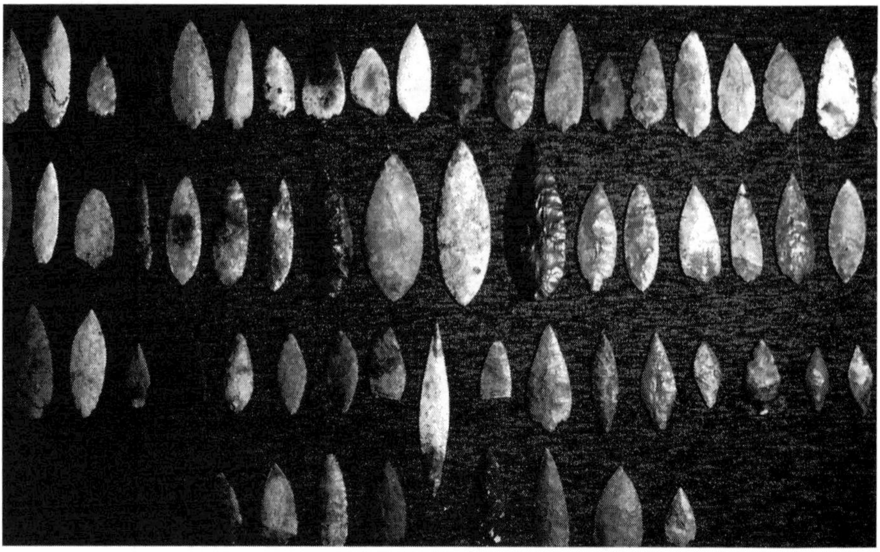

FIGURE 6.3. *Over 40 percent of the large, bifacially chipped blades were recovered from caves.*

Far more significant in terms of weight is the use of dark green or black jade, as well as other fine-grained imported stones, in the manufacture of *hachas*. Fifty-seven percent of all *hachas* have come from caves; that is, more have been found in caves than on the surface. Because the cave *hachas* are larger and more complete, this represents 88 percent by weight of the imported stone. *Hachas* are reported almost as frequently as other artifacts, being noted in twelve cave deposits.[8]

Polished hematite plaques, which probably formed parts of mirrors, are another imported item found both on the surface and in caves. As with jade, the simple comparison of artifact numbers is misleading, since many of the plaques found on the surface have been broken into a number of fragments. By comparing weights, we find that about 46 percent of the hematite comes from caves (Figure 6.4). A complete slate backing for a mirror was also found in one of the caves. Hematite plaques and slate backs are not as common in caves as the artifacts noted previously, but they have been reported at seven other caves.[9]

Items of worked bone form a major class of cave artifacts that do not have counterparts on the surface, probably because of poor preservation. The surface project recorded only eleven artifacts, including a fragment of worked bone that was unidentifiable as to original form. The only artifact type to have more than a single example is needles/awls, of which there are seven. The Dos Pilas caves, by contrast, have produced thirteen awls, thirty-three needles, and seventy-four bone artifacts in total. The surface project also lists three perforated animal canine teeth, as compared to forty-six recovered from the caves. If anything, bone artifacts are underrepresented in the cave collection. Experiments using chemicals to dissolve

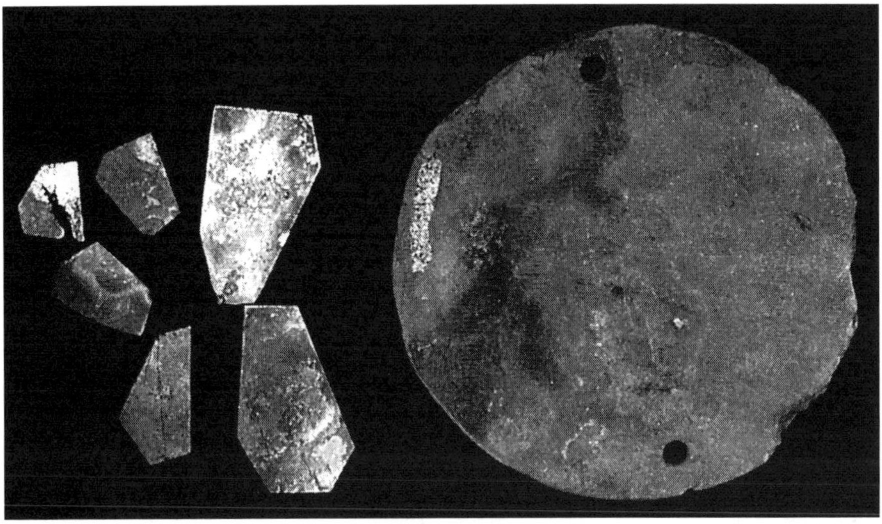

FIGURE 6.4. *This slate mirror back and polished hematite plaques were found in the Cueva de Río Murciélago.*

cave mud produced much larger quantities of worked bone than found during our regular survey (Brady and Scott 1997: 19). Worked bone artifacts in general are common in caves, with awls reported from at least six sites and needles from seven (Brady 1989: 270–272). Cached animal teeth have also been reported from caves, with the most spectacular case being two caches at Actun Polbilche containing 528 whole and 384 fragmentary teeth (Pendergast 1974: 55–58).

Worked shell is a difficult category to compare between cave and surface, in part because the assemblages are quite different. Fifty-three of the sixty shell artifact cards from the surface describe material recovered from only three burials, including the royal tomb in Structure L5-1. Thus, there is no counterpart in caves to the many pieces of shell that formed the mosaic headdress in the royal tomb. Because of the nature of the finds, it is also difficult to make comparisons using the artifact cards. The cards can refer to a single item or to several pieces, which were part of a single necklace, for instance. Other times, because of the condition of the remains, the cards will refer to "many" pieces of mosaic or "many" fragments of burned shell. The Dos Pilas caves have produced 365 shell beads of various types. These include forty-seven *Oliva* shells and sixty-eight of *Marginella,* both imported from the ocean. In total there are nearly 400 artifacts, which include several elaborate pendants, rosettes, and a conch trumpet. As with worked bone, the chemical processing of cave mud recovered large numbers of shell artifacts, indicating that this item is actually underrepresented in the cave assemblage (Figure 6.5). Although exact figures are not available, it seems apparent that shell artifacts from the caves form a high percentage of all the shells from the site. Shell artifacts are

FIGURE 6.5. *This large quantity of worked shell was recovered when mud from a single lot in the Cueva de Sangre was broken down with a chemical deflocculant. The experiment indicated that worked shell was underrepresented in the cave assemblage.*

once again commonly reported. (For a description of types and distribution, see Brady 1989: 281–287.)

DISCUSSION

For archaeologists with only a passing familiarity with the cave literature, the sheer size of the Dos Pilas cave artifact assemblage is startling. In the different artifact categories, the cave component accounts for 20 percent to over 50 percent of the total site assemblage on this very large project. An immediate question is whether the Dos Pilas assemblage is comparable to other cave assemblages. In the discussion of the ceramics, examples of other large cave collections were produced to show that the size of the Dos Pilas cave assemblage is not without precedent. In other categories, it was shown that the same types of artifacts found at Dos Pilas have been reported from a number of other caves, indicating that the material is part of a generalized cave assemblage. Although the Dos Pilas cave assemblage may differ in size from those at other sites, this difference is explainable in terms of the project's size and duration. Since no comparable study has been carried out, there is no way to resolve the question of representativeness. Nevertheless, at this moment I see no reason to suggest that the basic quantitative relationship between surface and cave would necessarily be radically different at another site. Thus, the results presented for Dos Pilas appear to have a general applicability.

Although I am not attempting to minimize the problems of comparison between cave and surface, the high percentages reported from caves suggest that the allocation of goods for cave ritual was substantial. The economic impact of the expenditure would have been broadly felt within Maya society, since it affected producers of such basic commodities as utilitarian ceramics as well as common polychrome pottery. Even the demand for the more common imported commodities like obsidian would have been impacted. The effect would have been greatest, however, in small, highly specialized crafts, suggested by the high percentages of hematite mirrors, imported stone *hachas,* very fine chert blades, and objects of bone and shell. Percentages are not available, but the presence of large numbers of sherds with hieroglyphs also suggests a significant demand for specialized painted vases. Finally, although the percentage of jade is lower than other categories, there are reasons, such as the physical conditions in the caves and our recovery techniques, for believing the caves contain a larger quantity of this material than was actually recovered.

Although cave artifact assemblages contain many types of artifacts, the presence of large numbers of wealth items appears notable. Much of this is because items of personal adornment appear to have favored offerings (Brady 1989: 322). Thus, it is not surprising that perhaps the largest collection of Maya jade from any site is the one recovered from the Cenote of Sacrifice at Chichén Itzá, a cave feature (Proskouriakoff 1974). Large jade caches have been recovered in other caves as well (Núñez Chinchilla 1972; Pendergast 1970). Although not considered previously, metal assumes a value on a par with jade during the Postclassic. Once again, some of the largest collections of metal objects have come from the Cenote of Sacrifice (Lothrop 1952; Piña Chán 1970: 38) and a number of "bell" caves in western Honduras (Bray 1977: 393–394). The cursory investigation of the Quemistlan bell cave yielded over 800 bells, sheets of worked copper, and a mosaic mask (Blackiston 1910), and Tauleve Cave was supposed to have had a similar quantity (Stone 1957: 63). Thus, the caching of large quantities of wealth items in caves appears to have been a fairly common practice. This is interesting in that the Earth Lord is often portrayed in ethnographic sources as having incredible wealth hoarded within his cave (Holland 1963: 93; Vogt 1969: 302). These native accounts may have grown out of the long-held knowledge of the offerings that had been placed there.

The economic implications do not stop with the documentation that considerable wealth had been deposited in caves. As noted earlier, most economic studies focus on interregional exchange, but there is no agreement on the degree to which items circulate within the society, and little systematic thought has been given to how goods leave the system. Certain items, such as jade used in jewelry, are practically indestructible, so there is little demand for replacement based on pieces "wearing out." If there were no mechanism for the removal of this material from the system, concentrations would reach a level where demand for additional pieces would drop and the exchange system would break down. Economic anthropologists note that one of the functions of certain types of institutions, such as the

Northwest Coast potlatch, is to remove goods from circulation within the society to force their replacement. Did such institutions exist among the ancient Maya, and what were they? In the case of jade, offerings placed in burials and caches are obvious mechanisms of removal. One economic function of caves was clearly to remove goods from circulation on a large scale. The data presented here indicate that caves were far more important in this respect than either caches or burials, the two most commonly considered mechanisms. The fact that many of the items were imported or made of imported materials indicates that ritual was an important factor in the maintenance of demand for items of interregional exchange.

CONCLUSION

In defining the ceremonial fund as one of the basic components of the economy, David Wolf (1966) recognized that in living societies where actual human behavior is observed, religion and ritual play a very obvious economic role. The Dos Pilas data, for the first time, allow us to form an idea of the size of the economic allocation made to cave ritual in ancient Maya society. Given the centrality of caves in Maya ideology, the economic evidence presented is exactly what one would expect of sites of major ritual significance. On the archaeological side, Price (1974: 455) echoes this point with her proposal that archaeological remains represent fossilized energy flow through the social system. The amount of energy passing through a given part of the system reflects the relative importance of that institution or subsystem. Applying Price's model to the findings of the Petexbatun Regional Cave Survey clearly indicates that this area of the social system was of enormous importance.

The society's ceremonial fund was obviously expended on much more than just cave ritual, but if the size of this one component is any indication, archaeologists have yet to appreciate the tremendous economic importance of ritual in Maya society. Why this should be is uncertain. The largest and most elaborately furnished structures in all parts of the world that we, as archaeologists, excavate (temples, churches, and pyramids) tend to be those with a religious function. Throughout much of the history of our own tradition, the Catholic Church was the wealthiest social institution, and the tithe was a well-recognized practice that directed a sizable percentage of the society's wealth into religion. One must suspect that obstinacy is playing a role in preventing archaeologists from accepting the obvious economic importance of religion. It is hoped that the present study represents a small contribution to the development of a more well-rounded consideration of both Maya economics and religion.

NOTES

1. The work of David Pendergast is a notable exception to this generalization.

2. To prevent further skewing of the comparison, artifact quantities reported for the surface project do not include material recovered during the 1994 season, since the cave

survey ended in 1993. The inclusion of the later material would have increased the disparity in time and personnel between the surface and the cave projects and exacerbated problems of comparability. It has meant, however, that this chapter has had to rely on the preliminary reports published after the 1993 season.

3. The obsidian overlaying the tomb was excluded from consideration because the size of this single deposit obscures comparisons with other contexts. Furthermore, the comparison between surface and cave contexts generally corresponds to utilitarian as opposed to ritual utilization. Since the L5-1 deposit is ceremonial in nature, the obsidian does not logically belong with material collected from utilitarian contexts.

4. Obsidian is reported from the following cave sites: BELIZE: the Pusilha Caves (Joyce 1929: 446; Joyce et al. 1928: 344), Actun Balam (Pendergast 1969: 53), Actun Dzib (Walters 1988), Eduardo Quiroz (Pendergast 1971: 66), Actun Polbilche (Pendergast 1974: 51, 53), Caves Branch caves (MacLeod and Puleston 1978: 72, 75), Petroglyph Cave (Reents-Budet and MacLeod 1986: 66), Actun Tunichil Muknal (Moyes 2001: 157), Uayak Na (Awe, Helmke, and Griffith 1998: 219), Actun Uayazba Kab (Ferguson and Gibbs 1999: 137–139), Actun Yaxteel Ahau (Mirro and Awe 1999: 184), Glenwood Cave (Peterson 2001: 46), Pine Torch Cave (Peterson 2001: 46), and five caves from the Maya Mountains Archaeological Project (Prufer 2002: 239); YUCATÁN: Actun Spukil (Mercer 1975: 30), Cenote X-Coton (Smith 1953: 70), Ch'en Mul and Telchaquillo (Smith 1954), Balankanche (Andrews 1970: 52), the Cenote of Sacrifice (Ediger 1971: 112; Sheets 1991: 172; Sievert 1992); GUATEMALA: Naj Tunich (Brady 1989: 326), the Rio Candelaria caves (Carot 1989: 116; Pope and Sibberensen 1981: 20), Lanquin (Gurnee 1968: 165); HONDURAS: Gordon Cave 3 at Copan (Brady 1995). The term *cave* is used here in the sense of the Maya word *ch'een,* which means a hole or a cavity that penetrates the earth. As such it includes caves, grottoes, *cenotes,* sinkholes, many springs, places where rivers emerge from or disappear into the earth, crevices, and any number of other holes. It is for that reason that the Cenote of Sacrifice at Chichén Itzá is considered as a cave feature.

5. Several dozen blades recovered from caches were excluded from consideration because the ceremonial context made them functional more akin to the cave blades than those found in residential or defensive contexts. If these blades had been included with the cave assemblage, the majority of the overall project assemblage would have been associated with ritual contexts.

6. Chert blades and points are reported from the following sites: BELIZE: Actun Balam (Pendergast 1969: 53), Eduardo Quiroz (Pendergast 1971: 65), Pusiha (Joyce 1929: 446), Cueva de los Muertos (Rushin-Bell 1982: 13), Petroglyph Cave (Reents-Budet and MacLeod 1986: 66), Actun Yaxteel Ahau (Mirro and Awe 1999: 184; Roberts 1990: 125), and an unnamed cave (Rushin-Bell 1982: 17); YUCATÁN: Balankanche (Andrews 1970: 52), the Cenote of Sacrifice (Coggins and Shane 1984: 47; Sievert 1992: 57), Xhambak (Mercer 1975: 36), Mayapán (Proskouriakoff 1962: figures 28–29; Smith 1954: 228), Loltun (González Licón 1986: 47; Mercer 1975: 107, 110; E. H. Thompson 1897: plate 7), San Pablo (Lee and Hayden 1988: 54); GUATEMALA: Naj Tunich (Brady 1989), Cueva de las Pinturas (Brady et al. 1997: 94), Alta Verapaz (Seler 1904: 90); HONDURAS: Rio Chamelcon (Blackiston 1910: 539).

7. Jade artifacts have been recovered from: BELIZE: Batty's Cave (Pendergast 1974: 85), Rio Frio Cave C (Mason 1928: 31–36; 1940: 114–115), Rio Frio Cave E (Pendergast 1970: 47–48), Eduardo Quiroz Cave (Pendergast 1971: 70), Benque Viejo (Gann 1925: 110), Cueva de los Muertos (Rushin-Bell 1982: 13), Actun Yaxteel Ahau (Owen and Gibbs 1999: 191); YUCATÁN: Balankanche (Andrews 1970: 52), the Cenote of Sacrifice (Piña Chán

1970: 38; Proskouriakoff 1974), Loltun (E. H. Thompson 1897: 20) Actun Toh (Rissolo 2003: 127), San Pablo (Lee and Hayden 1988: 47); GUATEMALA: Naj Tunich (Brady 1989), Balam Na Cave 4 (Garza, Brady, and Christensen 2001: 19); HONDURAS: Gordon's Cave in Copan, Cueva Votiva at Copan (Núñez Chinchilla 1972: 103–104).

8. *Hachas* have been recovered from: BELIZE: Actun Balam (Pendergast 1969: 53), Rio Frio Cave E (Pendergast 1970: 47), Eduardo Quiroz Cave (Pendergast 1971: 67–68), Las Cuevas, Blancaneaux Cave, and Petroglyph Cave (Reents-Budet and MacLeod 1986: 68–71), Actun Tunichil Muknal (Moyes 2001: 157), Actun Yax Tun (Peterson 2001: 47), Xmuqlebal Xheton and Wood Bench Cave (Prufer 2002: 237); YUCATÁN: the Cenote of Sacrifice (Moholy-Nagy and Ladd 1992: 100); GUATEMALA: Naj Tunich produced four specimens (Brady 1989: 298–300).

9. Hematite has been recovered from: BELIZE: Blancaneaux Cave, Petroglyph Cave (Reents-Budet and MacLeod 1986: 69–71), Cueva de los Muertos (Rushin-Bell 1982: 13), Actun Tunichil Muknal (Moyes 2001: 157); YUCATÁN: the Cenote of Sacrifice (Moholy-Nagy and Ladd 1992: 100–102); GUATEMALA: Naj Tunich (Brady 1989), Cueva de los Quetzales (Brady 1994: 604; Brady and Rodas 1995: 21).

REFERENCES CITED

Andrews, E. Wyllys, IV

1965 *Explorations in the Gruta de Chac, Yucatan, Mexico.* Middle American Research Institute, Publication 31. Tulane University, New Orleans.

1970 *Balankanche, Throne of the Tiger Priest.* Middle American Research Institute, Publication 32. Tulane University, New Orleans.

Aoyama, Kazuo

2001 Ritos de plebeyos Mayas en la Cueva Gordon No. 3 de Copán (Honduras) Durante el periodo clásico: análsis de los microhuellas de Uso Sobre la Lítica Menor de Obsidiana. *Mayab* 14:5–16.

Awe, Jaime J., Christophe G.B. Helmke, and Cameron S. Griffith

1998 Archaeological Reconnaissance in the Roaring Creek Valley: Caves, Rockshelters, and Settlement Architecture. In *The Western Belize Regional Cave Project: A Report of the 1997 Field Season,* ed. Jaime J. Awe, 216–236. Department of Anthropology Occasional Paper No. 1. University of New Hampshire, Durham.

Blackiston, A. Hooton

1910 Recent Discoveries in Honduras. *American Anthropologist* 12:536–541.

Brady, James E.

1989 An Investigation of Maya Ritual Cave Use With Special Reference to Naj Tunich, Peten, Guatemala. Ph.D. Dissertation. Archaeology Program, University of California, Los Angeles.

1994 Petexbatun Regional Cave Survey Artifacts. In *Proyecto Arqueológico Regional Petexbatun, Informe Preliminar #6,* eds. Arthur A. Demarest, Juan Antonio Valdés, and Héctor Escobedo, 571–641. Vanderbilt University, Nashville.

1995 A Reassessment of the Chronology and Function of Gordon's Cave #3, Copan, Honduras. *Ancient Mesoamerica* 6:29–38.

1997 Settlement Configuration and Cosmology: The Role of Caves at Dos Pilas. *American Anthropologist* 99(3):602–618.

Brady, James E., and Irma Rodas
1995 Maya Ritual Cave Deposits: Recent Insights From the Cueva de los Quetzales. *Institute of Maya Studies Journal* 1(1):17–25.

Brady, James E., Irma Rodas, Lori Wright, Katherine Emery, Nora María López, Laura Stiver, and Robert Chatham
1991 Proyecto Aqueológico Regional de Cuevas Petexbatún. In *Proyecto Arqueológico Regional Petexbatún, Informe Preliminar #3,* eds. Arthur A. Demarest, Takeshi Inomata, Héctor Escobedo, and Joel Palka, 652–748. Vanderbilt University, Nashville.

Brady, James E., and Ann Scott
1997 Excavations in Buried Cave Deposits: Implications for Interpretation. *Journal of Cave and Karst Studies* 59(1):15–21.

Brady, James E., and Andrea Stone
1986 Naj Tunich: Entrance to the Maya Underworld. *Archaeology* 39(6):18–25.

Brady, James E., Gene A. Ware, Barbara Luke, Allan Cobb, John Fogarty, and Beverly Shade
1997 Preclassic Cave Utilization Near Cobanerita, San Benito, Peten. *Mexicon* 19(5):91–96.

Bray, Warwick
1977 Maya Metalwork and Its External Connections. In *Social Process in Maya Prehistory,* ed. Norman Hammond, 365–403. Academic Press, London.

Carot, Patricia
1989 *Arqueología de la cuevas del norte de Alta Verapaz.* Cuadernos de Estudios Guatemaltecos 1, Centre D'Études Mexicaines et Centraméricaines, México.

Coggins, Clemency Chase, and John M. Ladd
1992 Wooden Objects. In *Artifacts From the Cenote of Sacrifice, Chichen Itza, Yucatan,* ed. Clemency Chase Coggins, 235–344. Peabody Museum of Archaeology and Ethnology, Harvard University, Cambridge.

Coggins, Clemency Chase, and Orrin C. Shane III
1984 *Cenote of Sacrifice: Maya Treasures From the Sacred Well at Chichen Itza.* University of Texas Press, Austin.

Ediger, Donald
1971 *The Well of Sacrifice.* Doubleday and Company, Garden City.

Ferguson, Josalyn M., and Sherry Gibbs
1999 Report on the 1998 Excavations at Actun Uayazba Kab, Roaring Creek Valley, Belize. In *The Western Belize Regional Cave Project: A Report of the 1998 Field Season,* ed. Jaime J. Awe, 112–145. Department of Anthropology Occasional Paper No. 2. University of New Hampshire, Durham.

Foias, Antonia
1992 Análisis preliminar de la cerámica del Petexbatún. In *Proyecto arqueológico regional Petexbatún, informe preliminar #4,* eds. Arthur A. Demarest, Takeshi Inomata, Héctor Escobedo, and Joel Palka, 250–285. Vanderbilt University, Nashville.

Gann, Thomas W.F.
1925 *Mystery Cities: Exploration and Adventure in Lubaantun*. Duckworth, London.

Garza, Sergio, James E. Brady, and Christian Christensen
2001 Balam Na Cave 4: Implications for Understanding Preclassic Cave Mortuary Practices. *California Anthropologist* 28(1):15–21.

Gibson, Eric C.
1989 The Organization of Late Pre-Classic Maya Lithic Economy in the Eastern Lowlands. In *Prehistoric Maya Economies of Belize*, ed. Patricia A. McAnany, 115–138. JAI Press, Greenwich, CT.

González Licón, Ernesto
1986 *Los Mayas de la gruta de Loltún, Yucatán, a través de sus materiales arqueológicos*. Instituto Nacional de Antropología e Historia, Mexico.

Groom, Nigel
1981 *Frankincense and Myrrh: A Study of Arabian Incense Trade*. Longman, London.

Gurnee, Russell H.
1968 Maya Cave Discoveries. *Explorers Journal* 46:146–186.

Hayden, Brian, and Aubrey Cannon
1984 *The Structure of Material Systems: Ethnoarchaeology in the Maya Highlands*. SAA Papers, No. 3. Society for American Archaeology, Washington, D.C.

Helton, Clint
1997 An Analysis of Polychrome Ceramics From Los Quetzales Cave at the Site of Las Pacayas, Guatemala: Typology, Structure and Design. M.A. Thesis. Department of Anthropology, Brigham Young University, Provo.

Holland, William R.
1963 *Medicina Maya en los altos de Chiapas: un estudio del Cambio socio-cultural*. Instituto Nacional Indigenista, Mexico.

Holland, William R., and Robert J. Weitlaner
1960 Modern Cuicatec Use of Prehistoric Sacrificial Knives. *American Antiquity* 25:392–396.

Joyce, T. A.
1929 Report on the British Museum Expedition to British Honduras, 1929. *Journal of the Royal Anthropological Institute* 59:439–459.

Joyce, T. A., T. Gann, E. L. Gruning, and R.C.E. Long
1928 Report on the British Museum Expedition to British Honduras, 1928. *Journal of the Royal Anthropological Institute* 58:323–349.

Lee, Thomas A., and Brian Hayden
1988 *San Pablo Cave and El Cayo on the Usumacinta River, Chiapas, Mexico*. Papers of the New World Archaeological Foundation No. 53. Brigham Young University, Provo.

Lothrop, Samuel Kirkland
1952 *Metals From the Cenote of Sacrifice, Chichen Itza, Yucatan*, Vol. 10, No. 2. Memoirs of the Peabody Museum of Archaeology and Ethnology. Harvard University, Cambridge.

MacLeod, Barbara, and Dennis E. Puleston

1978 Pathways Into Darkness: The Search for the Road to Xibalba. In *Tercera Mesa Redondade Palenque, Vol. 4,* eds. Merle Greene Robertson and Donnan Call Jeffers, 71–78. Herald Printers, Monterey, CA.

Mason, Gregory

1928 *Pottery and Other Artifacts From Caves in British Honduras and Guatemala.* Indian Notes and Monographs No. 47. Museum of the American Indian, New York.

1940 *South of Yesterday.* Henry Holt, New York.

McAnany, Patricia

1989 Economic Foundations of Prehispanic Maya Society: Paradigms and Concepts. In *Prehistoric Maya Economies of Belize,* ed. Patricia A. McAnany, 347–372. JAI Press, Greenwich, CT.

Mercer, Henry C.

1975 *The Hill-Caves of Yucatan.* University of Oklahoma Press, Norman (original 1896).

Mirro, Michael J., and Jaime J. Awe

1999 Report of Investigations on Ledge 1 at Actun Yaxteel Ahau, Roaring Creek Valley, Belize. In *The Western Belize Regional Cave Project: A Report of the 1998 Field Season,* ed. Jaime J. Awe, 166–185. Department of Anthropology Occasional Paper No. 2. University of New Hampshire, Durham.

Moholy-Nagy, Hattula, and John M. Ladd

1992 Objects of Stone, Shell, and Bone. In *Artifacts From the Cenote of Sacrifice, Chichen Itza, Yucatan,* ed. Clemency Chase Coggins, 99–152. Peabody Museum of Archaeology and Ethnology, Harvard University, Cambridge.

Moyes, Holley

2001 The Cave as a Cosmogram: The Use of GIS in an Intrasite Spatial Analysis of the Main Chamber of Actun Tunichil Muknal, a Maya Ceremonial Cave in Western Belize. M.A. Thesis, Florida Atlantic University, Boca Raton.

Núñez Chinchilla, Jesús

1972 Reconocimiento y exploración de una "Cueva Votiva" en la zona arqueológica de las ruinas de Copán. *Anales de la sociedad de geografía e historia de Guatemala* 45:102–105.

Owen, Vanessa, and Sherry Gibbs

1999 Report of Investigations on Ledge 2 at Actun Yaxteel Ahau, Roaring Creek Valley, Belize. In *The Western Belize Regional Cave Project: A Report of the 1998 Field Season,* ed. Jaime J. Awe, 186–204. Department of Anthropology Occasional Paper No. 2. University of New Hampshire, Durham.

Palka, Joel

1990 Operación DP10: excavaciones en la estructura L5-49. In *Proyecto arqueologico regional Petexbatun, informe preliminar #2, segunda temporada, 1990,* eds. Arthur A. Demarest and Stephen D. Houston, 225–234. Vanderbilt University, Guatemala City.

Pendergast, David M.

1969 *The Prehistory of Actun Balam, British Honduras.* Art and Archaeology Occasional Paper 16. Royal Ontario Museum, Toronto.

1970 *A. H. Anderson's Excavations at Rio Frio Cave E, British Honduras (Belize).* Art and Archaeology Occasional Paper 20. Royal Ontario Museum, Toronto.

1971 *Excavations at Eduardo Quiroz Cave, British Honduras (Belize).* Art and Archaeology Occasional Paper 21. Royal Ontario Museum, Toronto.

1974 *Excavations at Actun Polbilche, Belize.* Monograph 1. Royal Ontario Museum, Toronto.

Peterson, Polly A.

2001 Shedding Light on Xibalba Through Cave Survey and Surface Collection. In *Sacred Landscape and Settlement in the Sibun River Valley: XARP 1999 Archaeological Survey and Excavation,* ed. Patricia A. McAnany, 41–64. Department of Archaeology, Boston University, Boston.

Piña Chán, Román

1970 *Informe preliminar de la reciente exploración del cenote Sagrado de Chichén Itzá.* Investigaciones, No. 24. Instituto Nacional de Antropología e Historia, Mexico.

Pope, Kevin O., and Malcolm B. Sibberensen

1981 In Search of Tzultacaj: Cave Explorations in the Maya Lowlands of Alta Verapaz, Guatemala. *Journal of New World Archaeology* 4(3):16–54.

Price, Barbara J.

1974 The Burden of the Cargo: Ethnographic Models and Archaeological Inference. In *Mesoamerican Archaeology: New Approaches,* ed. Norman Hammond, 445–465. University of Texas Press, Austin.

Proskouriakoff, Tatiana

1962 The Artifacts of Mayapan. In *Mayapan, Yucatan, Mexico,* Publication 619, eds. H.E.D. Pollock, Ralph L. Roys, T. Proskouriakoff, and A. Ledyard Smith, 321–442. Carnegie Institution of Washington, Washington, D.C.

1974 *Jades From the Cenote of Sacrifice, Chichen Itza, Yucatan.* Memoirs of the Peabody Museum of Archaeology and Ethnology, Vol. 10, No. 1. Harvard University, Cambridge.

Prufer, Keith Malcolm

2002 Communities, Caves and Ritual Specialists: A Study of Sacred Space in the Maya Mountains of Southern Belize. Ph.D. Dissertation. Department of Anthropology, Southern Illinois University, Carbondale.

Reents-Budet, Dorie, and Barbara MacLeod

1986 The Archaeology of Petroglyph Cave, Belize. In *The Underground Maya,* eds. David M. Pendergast and Andrea Stone. Royal Ontario Museum, Toronto (manuscript in author's possession).

Rissolo, Dominique A.

2003 *Ancient Maya Cave Use in the Yalahau Region, Northern Quintana Roo, Mexico.* Association for Mexican Cave Studies, Bulletin 12. Association for Mexican Cave Studies, Austin.

Roberts, Charlotte A.

1990 Observations of Mayan Cave Archaeology in Belize. *Cave Science* 17(3):123–129.

Rushin-Bell, CarolJo

1982 The Living Caves of the Dead. *Caving International* 14:12–18.

Seler, Eduard

1904 Antiquities of Guatemala. In *Mexican and Central American Antiquities, Calendar Systems and History,* Bulletin 28: 77–121, ed. Charles P. Bowditch. Bureau of American Ethnology, Washington, D.C.

Sheets, Payson

1991 Flaked Lithics From the Cenote of Sacrifice, Chichén Itzá, Yucatán. In *Maya Stone Tools: Selected Papers From the Second Maya Lithic Conference,* eds. Thomas R. Hester and Harry J. Shafer, 163–188. Monographs in World Archaeology, No. 1. Prehistory Press, Madison.

Sievert, April Kay

1992 *Maya Ceremonial Specialization: Lithic Tools From the Sacred Cenote at Chichen Itza, Yucatan.* Prehistory Press, Madison.

Smith, Robert E.

1953 *Cenote X-Coton at Mayapan.* Current Report 5: 67–81. Department of Archaeology, Carnegie Institution of Washington, Washington, D.C.

1954 *Cenote Exploration at Mayapan and Telchaquillo.* Current Report 12: 222–233. Department of Archaeology, Carnegie Institution of Washington, Washington, D.C.

1971 *The Pottery of Mayapan: Including Studies of Ceramic Material From Uxmal, Kabah, and Chichen Itza,* Vol. 66. Papers of the Peabody Museum of Archaeology and Ethnology, Harvard University, Cambridge.

Stiver, Laura

1992 La Litica del Proyecto Petexbatun: Analisis de Laboratorio, 1992. In *Proyecto Arqueológico Regional Petexbatun, Informe Preliminar #4,* eds. Arthur A. Demarest, Takeshi Inomata, Héctor Escobedo, and Joel Palka, 286–296. Vanderbilt University, Guatemala.

Stone, Doris Z.

1957 *The Archaeology of Central and Southern Honduras,* Vol. 49, No. 3. Papers of the Peabody Museum of Archaeology and Ethnology, Harvard University. Cambridge.

Thompson, Edward H.

1897 *Cave of Loltun,* Volume 1:52–72. Memoirs of the Peabody Museum of American Archaeology and Ethnology, Harvard University, Cambridge.

Thompson, J. Eric S.

1975 Introduction. In *The Hill-Caves of Yucatan,* by Henry C. Mercer, vii–xliv. University of Oklahoma Press, Norman.

Urquizú Sánchez, Mónica Claudina

1996 Una aplicación metodológica para la recuperación e interpretación de rasgos culturales en Cuevas. Tesis de Licenciatura, Universidad de San Carlos, Guatemala.

Van Beek, Gus W.

1958 Frankincense and Myrrh in Ancient South Arabia. *Journal of American Oriental Society* 78:141–151.

1960 Frankincense and Myrrh. *The Biblical Archaeologist* 23:69–95.

Vogt, Evon Z.

1969 *Zinacantan: A Maya Community in the Highlands of Chiapas.* Harvard University Press, Cambridge.

Walters, Gary Rex
1988 *Maya Ceremonial Caves Project, 1988, Belize, Central America.* Triad Research Services, Columbia, MO.

Wolf, Eric R.
1966 *Peasants*. Prentice-Hall, Englewood Cliffs, NJ.

Chapter Seven

Scribes and Caves in the Maya Lowlands

by Andrea Stone

There can be little doubt that in ancient Maya society, forms of elite cave ceremonialism coexisted alongside those of the agrarian commoner. Caves were not the poor man's cathedral, with the upper class having impressive stone temples to fulfill *their* religious obligations. Quite the contrary, caves and other topographic features had inherent powers to open lines of communication with spirits and ancestors and to invoke a communal sense of the past that could not be duplicated in the built environment (Stone 1992). This made it as necessary for the elite as for the peasantry to renew their ties with the sources of sacred power found in the landscape. Pilgrimages to natural sanctuaries of renown, such as caves, were also exploited by the elite to buttress their claims of divine status.

Regrettably, the difficulty of reconstituting the motivation of cave ritual from archaeological remains, which tend on the whole to reflect nonspecific patterns of ritual behavior (e.g., deposition of offerings, burning incense, human sacrifice), means we have only the vaguest notion of the specialized rituals that may have been practiced by the elite in caves. Karen Bassie-Sweet (1991) has argued that royal period-ending, accession, and preaccession rituals were regularly conducted in caves by rulers, but these claims have yet to be substantiated. Maya cave art provides particularly important evidence for helping us understand the specific motivation of elite cave rituals (Stone 1989). Bassie-Sweet and several associates have recently been investigating a cave, Jolja', Chiapas, that has preserved cave paintings and inscriptions, dating from the inception of the Early Classic, that refer to ritual feasting by secondary nobility who may have been on a long-distance pilgrimage (Zender, Bassie, and Pérez de Lara 2001). The idea that secondary nobles, not just the rulers, participated in cave ceremonialism, which they commemorated in cave art, seems likely since they, too, had to support their own social and political agendas.

In this chapter I argue that one member of this secondary tier of nobles, the scribes who both created and interpreted hieroglyphic inscriptions, practiced some form of cave ceremonialism aimed at affirming the sacred status of their scribal office and their near suprahuman abilities. That scribes were perceived as such by the ancient Maya is now obvious. Recent research has shown that scribes were people of high rank, sometimes the sons of kings (Coe and Kerr 1998: 96; Reents-Budet 1994: 58); had supernatural patrons (Coe and Kerr 1998); bore epigraphic titles, also borne by gods, that touted their extraordinary skill and sagacity (Reents-Budet 1994: 49); and were prime targets of enemy capture because of the enormous prestige they lent to a polity (Johnston 2001). Their artistic endeavors were likened to cosmogonic events as if they conceived of themselves as creator gods (Reents-Budet 1998: 76). The evidence is irrefutable that scribal office in Classic Maya society had a powerful mystique that relied on identification with the supernatural. Scribes may have had a system of divine right to hold their office not unlike the office of the *k'uhul ajaw*. Scribes had ample opportunity to reinforce these ideas symbolically since they exerted so much control over representational media, particularly pictorial vases. It is no wonder so many vases portray supernatural patrons of scribes as well as scribal self-portraits, which were essentially self-serving. But scribes' associations with the supernatural world must have also been acted out in real rituals that could affirm the divine inspiration of their craft in a tangible way. In this regard, scribes may have made pilgrimages to important sacred caves. This proposal, admittedly, remains in the realm of speculation, garnering support mainly from iconographic and epigraphic evidence. However, some of the latter comes directly from caves, notably the cave Naj Tunich. The evidence is suggestive enough to warrant putting forth a cohesive argument about the relationship between scribes and caves that can be tested against future discoveries.

THE SCRIBE AND CAVE IN LOU 16

The most compelling case for scribal cave pilgrimage comes from a Late Classic vase scene published in Michael Coe's 1978 *Lords of the Underworld*, Vase No. 16 (referred to henceforth as LOU 16). As others have suggested (Bassie-Sweet 1991:

FIGURE 7.1. *Detail of LOU 16 showing a scribe, wearing a traveler's hat, emerging through a cave entrance. God N hands him a shell paint container (drawing from Coe 1978, no. 16).*

124; Houston 2001), this scene seems to take place in a cave (Figure 7.1, see color rollout photograph in Coe 1978 for all other details). The lower left and right edges are occupied by two large Witz Monsters, known to represent both mountains and their cavernous interiors. In the mouth of these Witz Monsters is a large half crescent that resembles a half lunar glyph. This motif, with its curved, pointed upper tip, also characterizes the skeletal maw glyph, T769 (Figure 7.2a–c), and the Postclassic *cenote* glyph, T591 (Figure 7.2d), which will be discussed later. Glyphs bearing this type of crescentic contour, including the glyph for the moon (Figure 7.2e), seem to describe cavelike enclosures. The version on LOU 16 is festooned with corn kernels and leaves. Since the Witz Monster is a mountain, the crescent in its mouth could represent a maize-associated cave inside the mountain. The heads floating in the cave enclosure could be a form of personified maize seed.

The central deity figure (Figure 7.1) sits on a peculiar projection with two volutes that may represent a convoluted speleothem, although the Maya usually do not depict speleothems in such naturalistic terms. The Witz Monster heads have pronounced water symbolism, with repeated water lilies and water stacks. Cave formations portrayed in Maya iconography generally merge stone, water, and death symbols, all of which are pertinent to caves (Stone 2005). Even the yellow undulating pattern at the bottom of the scene recalls the irregular surfaces of limestone cave walls.

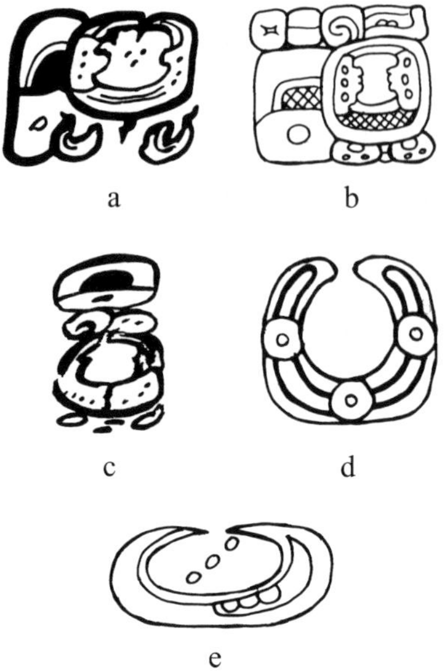

FIGURE 7.2. *a. T769, or skeletal maw glyph, compounded with "black" and -ya subfix. Note three dots on the interior (author drawing from Kerr Vase 1440, Kerr 1989: 83). b. T769 from Quirigua, Stela C, A9, compounded with "black" and -nal affixes (author drawing after Stuart and Houston 1994: figure 85b). c. T769, or skeletal maw glyph, from Drawing 19, Naj Tunich, compounded with "black" and -nal affixes (author drawing). d. T591, or* cenote *glyph (author drawing after Thompson 1962: 453). e. T683, or lunar glyph, from Altar de Sacrificios St. 6 (drawing after Thompson 1971: figure 22, no. 46).*

In the center of this mythical cave environment is a figure emerging through a quatrefoil opening, a conventional representation of a cave entrance with a long history in Mesoamerican art, extending back to the time of the Olmec (Figure 7.1). That this is a portal into a cave is reinforced by the "cluster of grape" stone markings appearing inside the portal, specifying a rocky place. Coming through the quatrefoil cave entrance is a human figure wearing a wide-brimmed woven hat over a cloth head wrap, which can be seen underneath. In Maya art, cloth head wraps are worn by court functionaries, including scribes.[1] Often identifying hunters and traveling merchants in Maya art, the wide-brimmed hat is sometimes called a "hunter's hat." But, as I recently argued (Stone 2000), the wide-brimmed hat has more general associations with people traveling long distances, including pilgrims on a religious mission. Indeed, I aver that this particular figure is a pilgrim, specifically a scribe, entering a cave.

Identification of this court functionary as a scribe is based on the presence of several other actors who are known supernatural patrons of scribes and carry scribal paraphernalia. In the upper left is a "Monkey-man" scribe (Coe and Kerr 1998: 106) holding a codex, and next to him is a young god with a "number tree" associated with scribes, holding a shell paint pot. Both of these characters wear the "deer ear" device above their ears, which Justin Kerr (n.d.) recently identified as a stylized shell paint container. In the center of the scene (Figure 7.1) is another scribal patron, an old god, often called God N or Pawahtun (Coe and Kerr 1998: 104). A three-dimensional stone sculpture of this same god was found in the fill of Structure 9N-82 at Copan, believed to have served as the palace of several generations of a family of scribes (Fash 1991: 120–122). The old god proffers a shell paint container toward the man entering the cave, who simultaneously reaches for it. As Kerr (n.d.) notes, the shell paint pot is the quintessential badge of scribal office. In my mind, the underlying message of this vignette is that scribal craft has its ultimate origins with the gods and is bestowed on humans by their beneficence. It is further significant that the scribe is shown as having journeyed to a cave to participate in this supernatural encounter wherein he accepts his badge of office.

In published comments of which I was unaware at the original writing of this chapter, Stephen Houston (2001) also recognized the importance of this vase for our understanding of the origins of scribal office. He interprets the scene as one showing the gods offering writing to humankind and further notes its gendered context; that is, writing is bestowed on a male protagonist. He observes that a female protagonist sits to the right of the quatrefoil, suggesting some kind of dualistic thematic contrast with the emerging male figure. My own take on the vase differs somewhat from Houston's in that I believe the scene portrays the culmination of a man's pilgrimage to a cave, as indicated by the traveler's hat. My interpretation stresses the divine origins of scribal office rather than archetypal gender roles. I argue that LOU 16 provides evidence that a divine right system for scribes was in place during the Classic period; that is, scribal status and legitimacy, like those of Maya kings, rested on an intimate affiliation with the supernatural. Dorie Reents-Budet (1994: 46) has also made a case that scribes claimed suprahuman status, claims that were not totally unfounded since scribes were exceptionally well trained and highly skilled at what they did, as evidenced in the extraordinary vases they painted.

SCRIBES AND CAVES IN MAYA ICONOGRAPHY

The argument that scribes made pilgrimages to caves to reconnect with the divine source of their office receives further support from other works of art. Maya iconography demonstrates a linkage between scribal office and the supernatural power of caves. Some ethnohistoric evidence for this linkage can be found in the sixteenth-century writings of Diego de Landa. Michael Coe and Justin Kerr (1998: 169–170) mention Landa's (in Tozzer 1941: 153) description of the purification of hieroglyphic books as part of the ceremonies held during the month Wo. Landa states that virgin water, which must have come from a cave or *cenote,* as J.E.S. Thompson (1959) proved long ago, was mixed with pigment and sprinkled over the wooden book covers. The scribe-priests were likely the ones who collected the virgin water, illustrating one reason why scribes may have journeyed to caves.

We can begin approaching the linkage between scribes and caves iconographically by examining the glyph T769, a logograph depicting a frontal skeletal lower jaw (Figure 7.2a–c). Although the glyph is variously stylized and abbreviated, its canonical form includes a U-shaped mandible marked by black bands (shown as cross-hatching in sculpted media) and bearing several disks or plates marked by a line of dots. These are also standard elements of certain types of long bones in Maya art (for instance, the "bone throne" glyph, T150, also has these traits). The tips of the U either terminate in extended fangs or taper and curl inward, giving them a hooked appearance, similar to the full lunar glyph (Figure 7.2e). The discs with lines of tiny circles seem to be bony plates marking the jaw. Many have recognized the fact that T769 is morphologically and conceptually related to the *cenote* glyph (Schele and Mathews 1998: 45; Stuart and Houston 1994: 71–72). Indeed, the *cenote* glyph, T591 (Figure 7.2d), seems to be a northern Yucatecan transformation of T769 in which the skeletal jaw retains its U shape but always ends in inward-curving tips and never fangs. The U is always marked by thin black bands, and, in the codices, the bony plates are replaced by jadelike disks. The derivation of the *cenote* glyph from T769 helps explain the meaning of the latter.

David Stuart and Stephen Houston (1994: 71–72) identify T769 as a logograph for a depression or hole and note that it is usually compounded with the glyph for "black," making it a "black hole" (see examples compounded with "black" in Figure 7.2a–c). Linda Schele and Peter Mathews (1998: 45), on the other hand, outright identify T769 as an abstract form of "cenotes, caves, and other openings in the earth." They basically see the glyph and its iconographic equivalents as cosmic portals, an idea followed by Michael Carrasco and Kerry Hull (2002). However, contextual evidence indicates that T769 is an enclosure rather than strictly a portal.

I concur with Schele and Mathews that T769 refers to a cave or *cenote,* although I believe it specifically connotes a water-filled hole in the earth. Hence, the glyph could serve in Yucatán as the symbol of a *cenote,* which, by definition, has water. Late Classic iconography confirms the aquatic associations of T769, where it is often associated with water. Examples can be seen in the "Cosmic Plate" (Schele and Miller 1986: plate 122), where Chaak stands in water framed by a zoomorphic version of T769, and on Copan St. 11, where the protagonist standing above T769, which serves as a toponym, is flanked by water scrolls (Fash 1991: figure 108). Furthermore, some examples of T769, such as on Kerr Vessel 1440 (Figure 7.2a) and Lacanha Panel 1, N5 (Coe and Benson 1966: figures 10 and 11), have three dots inside, recalling the three dots encircled by the lunar glyph, T683 (Figure 7.2e). The dots in the lunar glyph refer to water (Bassie-Sweet 1991: 95). The lunar glyph, which is morphologically related to T769, also represents a water-filled well, the home of the Moon Goddess (Stone 1985; Thompson 1971: 236), who is often shown residing within it. Clearly, the dots in T769 demonstrate parallelism with the lunar glyph as a water-filled cave, *cenote,* or other terrestrial depression.

Further support that T769 refers to a cavelike setting, associated with water, comes from the inscriptions of Naj Tunich. In Drawing 19, T769, with a "black" prefix and the *-nal* superfix associated with toponyms (Stuart and Houston 1994), meaning something like "place," occurs after the verb *pak-xi* (Figure 7.2c and MacLeod and Stone 1995: figure 7-14). Barbara MacLeod (MacLeod and Stone 1995: 178) translates *pak-xi* as "he returned," one of several verbs common at Naj Tunich that describe the pilgrimage event. The protagonist, at A5, who can be identified as Ruler 3 from Dos Pilas,[2] is stated to have returned to the "black skeletal maw," no doubt a reference to Naj Tunich. The toponym characterizes Naj Tunich as a watery, subterranean environment; and it is noteworthy that there is a large pool of water just inside the cave's dark zone (Stone 1995: figure 5-5).

a

b

c

Figure 7.3. *a. Figure from the facade of Structure 9N-82, Copan (author redrawing of Schele and Miller 1986: figure III.8). b. Carved bone from Burial 116, Temple I, Tikal, shows scribe's hand emerging from zoomorphic maw, which may represent a cave (author drawing after Coe and Kerr 1998: figure 65). c. Madrid Codex page 73b shows Chaak as scribe inside a* cenote. *The bird perching on the edge may be a messenger of auguries (drawing after Lee 1985: 121).*

How is T769, demonstrated to be a logograph for a water-filled cave or *cenote,* relevant to the iconographic issues at hand? This stems in part from the association of scribal imagery with a skeletal jaw, which I regard as an iconographic variant of T769. One such case is the sculptures on the facade of the earlier-mentioned scribal palace, Structure 9N-82 at Copan. Here we see two frontal views of a scribe holding a paint pot and brush (Figure 7.3a). The head in both examples is destroyed (although reconstructed in the drawing), so it is unclear whether the scribes portrayed were human or gods. These bust-length figures reside in a U-shaped skeletal maw, which, on the face of it, recalls T769.

Recently, certain skeletalized snakelike creatures in Maya art have been identified as centipedes (Boot 1999; Grube and Nahm 1994: 702). Because of this, U-shaped skeletal maws, such as that on the Palenque Sarcophogus Lid, are increasingly being reinterpreted as this self-same creature, known as the *sak bak nah chapaht* ("white bone house centipede"). It is possible that the skeletal maw of T769 is also that of a centipede as opposed to a serpent, but the relevance of this distinction is not clear for the understanding of T769. Schele and Mathews (1998: 45) assert that this skeletalized zoomorph (which they identify as a snake rather than a centipede) is an iconographic version of the more abstract T769. Accepting this assessment allows us to interpret the skeletal U-shaped maw in which the scribe sits on the facade of Structure 9N-82 as a water-filled terrestrial depression, such as a cave.

That the U-shaped jaw on the Structure 9N-82 facade does refer to a cave can be substantiated by looking at Structure 10L-22, Copan. The top steps of the entrance to the inner sanctum of the superstructure are sculpted into a skeletal mandible (Freidel, Schele, and Parker 1993: figure 3.20). This is a striking example of a symbolic cave entrance in the form of a zoomorphic maw, a well-known ploy in Mesoamerican architecture (Schavelzon 1980). Details of the mandible, such as the cartouches with interior dots that line the jaw and extended fangs, relate the jaw to the glyph T769 and to the facade of Structure 9N-82. In Structure 10L-22, the corners of the building portray stacked Witz Monster heads, symbolically converting the building into a sacred mountain, whereas the skeletal maw doorway expresses its cavernous interior (Freidel, Schele, and Parker 1993: 151 and figure 3:18).

Another example of scribal imagery associated with a skeletal maw is seen on a carved bone from Burial 116, Tikal. Here a scribe's hand emerges from a profile skeletalized zoomorphic head, either a snake or a centipede, with extended fangs (Figure 7.3b). As in the case of the Copan facade, I interpret this imagery as a reference to the scribe's association with caves as the locus of the supernatural origins of his craft. In a similar vein, Allen Christenson (2001: figure 1.1) says his the carved bone "depicts the hand of a divine artist holding a paintbrush emerging from the open maw of a serpent, symbolic of a portal giving access to the underworld where gods and sacred ancestors live." Christenson's remarks echo my own sentiments; however, I believe the framing of a scribe in a cavelike setting also served to mystify and exalt the scribe's role.

The scribe-in-cave theme is also represented on page 73b of the Madrid Codex (Figure 7.3c). Chaak is shown as a painter and calendar priest sitting in a *cenote* glyph. The "print-out" scroll emerging from his mouth shows him to be an interpreter of sacred books as well as a painter of them, both important scribal duties. A bird is perched at the edge of the *cenote.* This is interesting, since a bird is also shown hovering over the edge of the cave portal on LOU 16. Houston (2001) suggests that the bird on the vase refers to revelatory messages given to scribes in light of the fact that birds are seen as messengers in Maya thought. One could interpret the bird perched at the edge of the *cenote* as having this same function, a purveyor of esoteric knowledge to the scribe. That Chaak is placed in a *cenote* on Madrid 73b provides further evidence for a linkage between scribes and caves.

SCRIBES AT NAJ TUNICH

It is a well-established fact that the cave paintings of Naj Tunich, Guatemala, register the presence of the artists/scribes themselves, in the form of both figural representations, what can be construed as self-portraits, and in texts where they mention their own names. The role of scribes in the cave paintings was first signaled in David Stuart's (1987) *Ten Phonetic Syllables,* in which he deciphered the word for writing, *tz'ihb'.* Stuart identified an example of the phrase *u-tz'ihb'*, "he writes" or "his writing," in one of the cave paintings (drawing 66; Stone 1995: figure 7-12). He further showed that the subject of this clause—what must be the scribe's name—makes up the entirety of another text, Drawing 30 (Figure 7.4). Stuart reasoned that Drawing 30 reflects a situation in which a scribe deigned to write his name on the cave wall for his own sake, not merely to acknowledge authorship of an inscription. We now know that the name of this scribe occurs in three separate inscriptions at Naj Tunich. In one, Drawing 28 (Stone 1995: figure 10), the name is accompanied by a standard scribal title at A16, *itz'at,* or "sage," so there can be no doubt that this individual was a scribe. The scribe is listed in this case as one of three protagonists who came to "see" Naj Tunich, a metaphor for the pilgrimage. A scribe is also mentioned in Drawing 88 where an *u-tz'ihb'* compound appears at B9, followed by the scribe's name (Stone 1995: figure 7-3).

FIGURE 7.4. *Drawing 30, Naj Tunich, is a scribe's stand-alone signature (author's drawing).*

In another discovery related to scribes at Naj Tunich, Stuart asserted that one of the painted seated figures depicts a scribe in light of the fact that he is portrayed sitting in front of a shell, meant to show a paint container, a standard feature of scribes in Classic Maya art (Figure 7.5a). Since the publication of Michael Coe and Justin Kerr's *The Art of the Maya Scribe* (1998), it seems clearer than ever that scribes played a role of uncommon importance in the paintings of Naj Tunich. Coe identifies new features of scribal costume seen mainly on pictorial ceramics (Coe and Kerr 1998: 92). For instance, scribes often wear cloth head wraps into which they tuck their painting implements. Bundles of stumpy quill pens are attached to the scribe's headgear by knotted cords. Many scribes sport hairdos with jagged ends that poke through their head cloths. The Drawing 22 figure exhibits several of these traits, namely, the twisted cord and large front knot securing the head cloth, as well as the jagged hairdo poking through the top (Michael Coe 1997: personal communication). This hairdo may also be present in another cave portrait (Figure 7.5b), and other headgear associated with scribes can be seen among the Naj Tunich figures. For instance, the dwarf in Drawing 83 has a twisted hank of hair protruding straight up, another of Coe's proposed scribal traits (Figure 7.5c). Coe indicated to me several years ago that he believes a preponderance of the painted human figures at Naj Tunich represent scribes. Although this idea cannot be proved beyond the few concrete examples already mentioned, it is intriguing given the foregoing discussion. The scribal portrait in Drawing 22 (Figure 7.5a) and the stand-alone signature in Drawing 30 (Figure 7.4) go beyond mere notations of authorship. This would be true as well for other scribal portraits that may exist at Naj Tunich. They are, rather, independent memorializations. Yet, do they reflect a "Kilroy was here" impulse, the painters

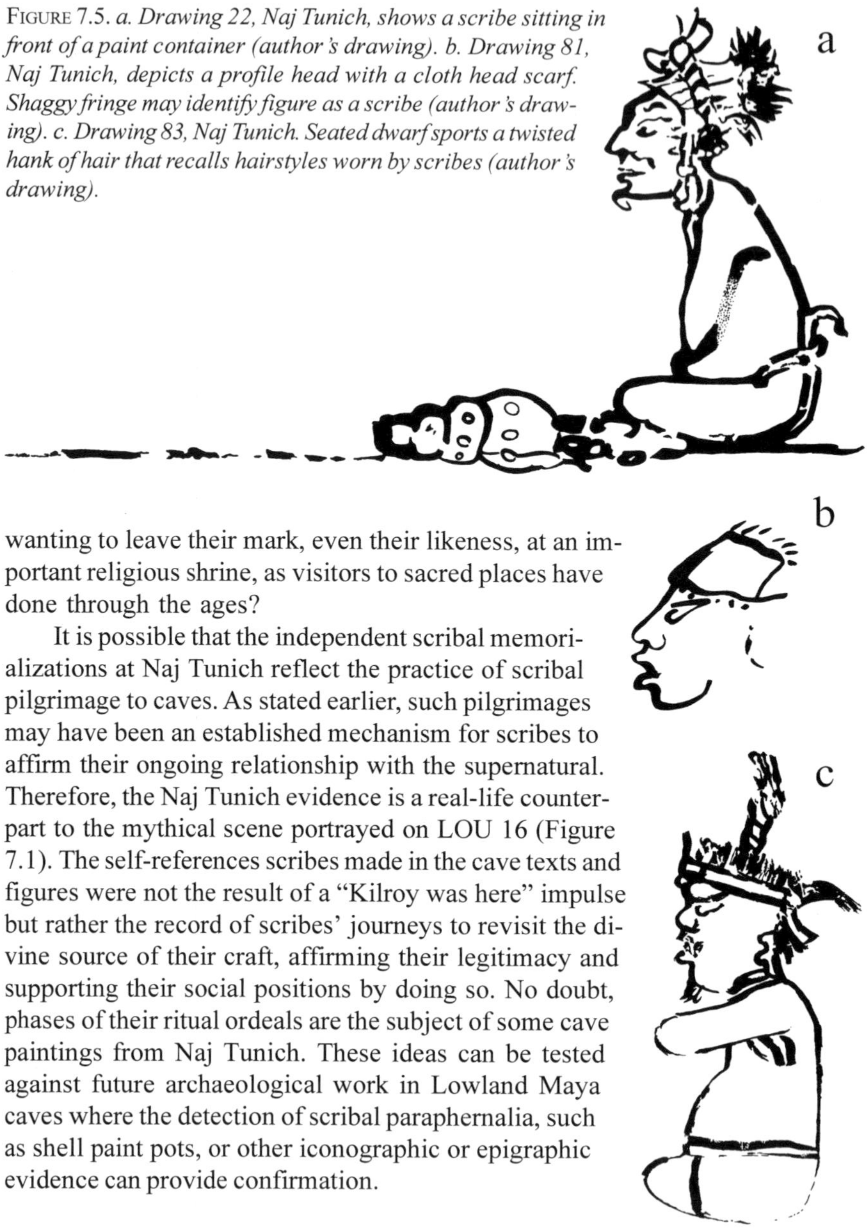

Figure 7.5. *a. Drawing 22, Naj Tunich, shows a scribe sitting in front of a paint container (author's drawing). b. Drawing 81, Naj Tunich, depicts a profile head with a cloth head scarf. Shaggy fringe may identify figure as a scribe (author's drawing). c. Drawing 83, Naj Tunich. Seated dwarf sports a twisted hank of hair that recalls hairstyles worn by scribes (author's drawing).*

wanting to leave their mark, even their likeness, at an important religious shrine, as visitors to sacred places have done through the ages?

It is possible that the independent scribal memorializations at Naj Tunich reflect the practice of scribal pilgrimage to caves. As stated earlier, such pilgrimages may have been an established mechanism for scribes to affirm their ongoing relationship with the supernatural. Therefore, the Naj Tunich evidence is a real-life counterpart to the mythical scene portrayed on LOU 16 (Figure 7.1). The self-references scribes made in the cave texts and figures were not the result of a "Kilroy was here" impulse but rather the record of scribes' journeys to revisit the divine source of their craft, affirming their legitimacy and supporting their social positions by doing so. No doubt, phases of their ritual ordeals are the subject of some cave paintings from Naj Tunich. These ideas can be tested against future archaeological work in Lowland Maya caves where the detection of scribal paraphernalia, such as shell paint pots, or other iconographic or epigraphic evidence can provide confirmation.

NOTES

1. Some Chama vases depict processions with figures wearing precisely the same headgear: a wide-brimmed traveling hat worn over a cloth head wrap. These figures are also court functionaries. For illustrations, see Danien 1997.

2. The author learned that Stanley Guenter earlier identified this glyph as the name of Ruler 3 from Dos Pilas (Marc Zender 2002: personal communication), although MacLeod's observations were independent. The identification of the Dos Pilas ruler in this inscription is important in that Drawing 19 was one of several texts submitted to radiocarbon analysis by Marvin Rowe and colleagues at Texas A&M University (Armitage et al. 2001: table 1). Their proposed dates were, on the whole, significantly older than dates proposed by Stone (1995) based on calendrical evidence. Stone's (MacLeod and Stone 1995: table 1) reconstructed date for Drawing 19 is A.D. 738, whereas radiocarbon analysis yielded A.D. 610. Apparently, the radiocarbon date is inaccurate because the reign of Ruler 3, between A.D. 727 and 741 (Martin and Grube 2000: 60), coincides precisely with the reconstructed glyphic date.

REFERENCES CITED

Armitage, Ruth, James Brady, Allan Cobb, John Southon, and Marvin Rowe

2001 Mass Spectrometric Radiocarbon Dates From Three Rock Paintings of Known Age. *Latin American Antiquity* 66(3):471–480.

Bassie-Sweet, Karen

1991 *From the Mouth of the Dark Cave: Commemorative Sculpture of the Late Classic Maya.* University of Oklahoma Press, Norman.

Boot, Erik

1999 Of Serpents and Centipedes: The Epithet Wuk Chapaht Chan K'inich Ahaw. *Notes on Maya Hieroglyphic Writing* 25. Center for Maya Research, Washington, D.C.

Carrasco, Michael, and Kerry Hull

2002 The Cosmogonic Symbolism of the Corbeled Vault in Maya Architecture. *Mexicon* 24(2):26–32.

Christenson, Allen J.

2001 *Art and Society in a Highland Maya Community: The Altarpiece of Santiago Atitlán.* University of Texas Press, Austin.

Coe, Michael D.

1973 *The Maya Scribe and His World.* The Grolier Club, New York.

1978 *Lords of the Underworld: Masterpieces of Classic Maya Ceramics.* Princeton University Press, Princeton, N.J.

Coe, Michael, and Elizabeth Benson

1966 Three Maya Relief Panels at Dumbarton Oaks. *Studies in Pre-Columbian Art and Archaeology No. 2.* Dumbarton Oaks, Washington, D.C.

Coe, Michael, and Justin Kerr

1998 *The Art of the Maya Scribe.* Abrams, New York.

Danien, Elin

1997 The Ritual on the Ratlinixul Vase: Pots and Politics in Highland Guatemala. *Expedition* 39(3):37–48.

Fash, William

1991 *Scribes, Warriors, and Kings: The City of Copán and the Ancient Maya.* Thames and Hudson, London.

Freidel, David, Linda Schele, and Joy Parker

1993 *Maya Cosmos: Three Thousand Years on the Shaman's Path.* William Morrow, New York.

Grube, Nikolai, and Werner Nahm

1994 A Census of Xibalba: A Complete Inventory of Way Characters on Maya Ceramics. In *The Maya Vase Book, Volume 4,* ed. Justin Kerr, 686–715. Kerr Associates, New York.

Houston, Stephen

2001 Comments on paper by Takeshi Inomata, The Power and Ideology of Artistic Creation. *Current Anthropology* 42(3):321–349.

Johnston, Kevin

2001 Broken Fingers: Classic Maya Scribe Capture and Polity Consolidation. *Antiquity* 75(288):373–381.

Kerr, Justin

1989 *The Maya Vase Book, Volume 1.* Kerr Associates, New York.

n.d. *Where Do You Wear Your Paint-Pot?* Manuscript posted on mayavase.com.

Lee, Thomas A., Jr.

1985 *Los Códices Mayas.* Universidad Autónoma de Chiapas. Tuxtla Gutiérrez, Mexico.

MacLeod, Barbara, and Andrea Stone

1995 The Hieroglyphic Inscriptions of Naj Tunich. In *Images From the Underworld: Naj Tunich and the Tradition of Maya Cave Painting,* by Andrea J. Stone, 155–184. University of Texas Press, Austin.

Martin, Simon, and Nikolai Grube

2000 *Chronicles of the Maya Kings and Queens: Deciphering the Dynasties of the Ancient Maya.* Thames and Hudson, London.

Reents-Budet, Dorie

1994 *Painting the Maya Universe: Royal Ceramics of the Classic Period.* Duke University Art Museum, Durham.

1998 Elite Maya Pottery and Artisans as Social Indicators. In *Craft and Social Identity,* eds. Cathy Lynne Costin and Rita P. Wright, 71–89. Archaeological Papers of the American Anthropological Association 8. American Anthropological Association, Arlington.

Schavelzon, Daniel

1980 Temples, Caves, or Monsters? Notes on Zoomorphic Façades in Pre-Hispanic Architecture. In *Third Palenque Round Table, 1978, Part 2,* ed. Merle Greene Robertson, 151–162. University of Texas Press, Austin.

Schele, Linda, and Peter Mathews

1998 *The Code of Kings: The Language of Seven Sacred Temples and Tombs.* Scriber, New York.

Schele, Linda, and Mary Ellen Miller

1986 *The Blood of Kings: Dynasty and Ritual in Maya Art.* George Braziller, New York.

Stone, Andrea

1985 The Moon Goddess at Naj Tunich. *Mexicon* 7(2):23–29.

1989 The Painted Walls of Xibalba: Maya Cave Painting as Evidence of Cave Ritual. In *Word and Image in Maya Culture: Explorations in Language, Writing and Representation,* eds. William F. Hanks and Don S. Rice, 319–335. University of Utah Press, Salt Lake City.

1992 From Ritual in the Landscape to Capture in the Urban Center: The Recreation of Ritual Environments in Mesoamerica. *Journal of Ritual Studies* 6(1):109–132.

1995 *Images From the Underworld: Naj Tunich and the Tradition of Maya Cave Painting*. University of Texas Press, Austin.

2000 Spiritual Journeys, Secular Guises: Rock Art and Elite Pilgrimage at Naj Tunich Cave. In *Pilgrimage and Sacred Landscape in the Americas,* eds. John Carlson and Jeffery Quilter. Dumbarton Oaks, Washington, D.C. (volume under review).

2005 Divine Stalagmites: Modified Speleothems in Maya Caves and Aesthetic Variation in Classic Maya Art. In *Aesthetics and Rock Art,* eds. Thomas Heyd and John Clegg, 215–233. Ashgate, Hampshire, England.

Stuart, David

1987 Ten Phonetic Syllables. *Research Reports on Ancient Maya Writing 14*. Center for Maya Research, Washington, D.C.

Stuart, David, and Stephen Houston

1994 *Classic Maya Place Names*. Studies in Pre-Columbian Art and Archaeology 33. Dumbarton Oaks, Washington, D.C.

Thompson, J.E.S.

1959 The Role of Caves in Maya Culture. *Mitteilungen aus dem Museum für Völkerkunde in Hamburg* 25:122–129.

1962 *A Catalog of Maya Hieroglyphs*. University of Oklahoma Press, Norman.

1971 *Maya Hieroglyphic Writing,* third edition. University of Oklahoma Press, Norman.

Tozzer, Alfred

1941 *Landa's relación de las cosas de Yucatán*. Papers of the Peabody Museum of Archaeology and Ethnology 18. Harvard University, Cambridge, MA.

Zender, Marc, Karen Bassie, and Jorge Pérez de Lara

2001 Art and Ritual in Jolja' Cave, Chiapas, Mexico. Paper presented at the 66th Annual Meeting of the Society for American Archaeology, New Orleans.

Chapter Eight

Nikte' Mo' Scattered Fire in the Cave of K'ab Chante'

by James E. Brady
Pierre R. Colas

Epigraphic and Archaeological Evidence for Cave Desecration in Ancient Maya Warfare

Historians and political scientists have always been fascinated by warfare because of the dramatic changes in power and abrupt shifts of fortune that occur. Military conquest has implications for a city, however, that go beyond simply questions of power. Human beings live in a world of symbols and ideology, and settlements are always enveloped in these. Eduardo Matos Moctezuma (1987: 191) says, "As Mircea Eliade has noted, the founding or first settlement of every city is accompanied by signs and, in general, the sacred space is made into a defined area that transforms it into an 'inexhaustible source' of sacralty. This place is always 'discovered' by humans through certain symbols laden with mystic meaning." In preindustrial societies, settlements have a semisacred quality, as Joseph Campbell notes in comparing the founding of cities to the building of a temple. He states, "Ancient cities are built like temples, having their portals to the four directions, while in the center place stands the major shrine of the divine city founder. The citizens live and work within the confines of this symbol" (Campbell 1956: 43). Much of the city's power resides in the strength of the residents' attachment to these symbols. Conquerors have always shown great awareness of this, so a central element of any victory is the destruction of those symbolic devices held most dear by the vanquished or perhaps the appropriation of the elements by the victor.

In this chapter we present evidence of Classic Maya warfare aimed at one of the most important symbols for the legitimation of settlement and rulership: the cave. Archaeological and epigraphic evidence of this aspect of Maya warfare will be presented that not only expands our underdeveloped knowledge of the ideological side of indigenous warfare but also provides insights into the ideological bases of political and even settlement legitimacy.

CAVES IN THE IDEOLOGY OF SETTLEMENT AND RULERSHIP

It has long been recognized that caves play a significant role in the ideology of Mesoamerican groups. Human beings are generally thought to have been created within the earth and then to have emerged from caves onto the earth's surface (Heyden 1987: 128). Geographer Erich Isaac (1962) has pointed out that in many religions cross-culturally, the act of creation is the central justification of human existence. Societies holding this belief tend to be those that practice large-scale religious landscape modification with the intent of modeling the primordial scene that existed when the world was created. Angel García-Zambrano (1994) has shown independently that in founding new settlements, Mesoamerican groups look for locations that possess attributes of the primordial landscape. Caves, as one of the central motifs in creation, become pivotally important to group ideology. García-Zambrano (1994: 218) sums up this importance by saying, "These cavities, when ritually dedicated to the divinities, became the pulsating heart of the new town, providing the cosmogonic referents that legitimized the settlers' rights for occupying that space and for the ruler's authority over that site."

The cave as a focus of community identity survived into modern times. Alfonso Villa Rojas (1947: 579) has noted among the Tzeltal, "[E]ach rural settlement is tied by religious bonds to a certain cave where a cross is kept as the main symbol of its sacred importance. Usually the ranchería is known by the name of the cave to which it belongs; thus the ranchería of Dzajalchen (Red Cave) is connected with the cave of that name." The same association was found in the community of Larrainzar. Before the 1930s the town was known as San Andrés Istacostoc, with *Istacostoc* a Nahuatl translation of its sixteenth-century Maya name, *Zacanch'en,* or "White Cave" (Holland 1963: 27).

Whereas certain sacred landmarks might have been the focus of community identity, others served a more restricted audience. C. Guiteras Holmes (1947: 1) noted that the Tzotzil lineages are formed into clans, and each clan is associated with a particular cave. The cave is the place where the ancestors of a particular lineage emerged and where the souls of members returned at death. Individuals whose ancestors emerged from the same cave refer to each other as "brothers."

Evon Vogt (1976: 99) recorded that lineages take their names from their waterholes, which are cave features. Patricia McAnany (1995: 159) has argued that Maya lineages are intimately connected to the land they inhabited, especially because the lineages' predecessors were buried in that place (McAnany 1995: 100). Caves are particularly important in this respect. At the end of the seventeenth century, Bishop Núñez de la Vega discovered the bones of lineage founders in caves in Chiapas and reported that they were venerated "as though they had been saints" (in Thompson 1975: xxxiii). This practice appears to have continued into modern times. Villa Rojas (1969: 215) recorded that the Tzeltal buried the most distinguished members of each lineage in a cave up until the beginning of the twentieth century. The importance of these caves in indigenous society cannot be overestimated. In discussing the cave dedicated to the founding couple in Santa Eulalia, Oliver LaFarge (1947: 128) says, "I suspect from these indications that the cave is the true center of the ceremonial and that there are probably yet other rites performed there." Thus, through use, caves became places where the ancestors lived. They molded sacred space around themselves and became the focus of social identity for kin groups (McAnany 1995: 110).

Caves are also powerful political symbols that are as old as Mesoamerican civilization. David Grove (1973) sees the motif of cave emergence as central to the ideological justification of Olmec kingship. In his analysis of Altar 4 at La Venta, Grove demonstrates, based on the murals at Oxtotitlan Cave, that the Olmec monuments called altars are in fact thrones. The most prominent motif on the thrones is a central figure emerging from a niche portrayed as the open mouth of a jaguar. Grove notes that the iconographic motifs surrounding the central figure resemble those that, in later Mesoamerican cultures, deal with authority. The open mouth of the jaguar represents a cave, and Grove (1973: 134; 1981: 61) theorizes that the emergence from the cave is a statement of the king's mythical underworld origins and therefore a statement about his right to rule based on divine status.

The situation is very much analogous in Maya art. A common representation shows a man or a god emerging from the open mouth of the kawak monster, which Dicey Taylor (1978: 83) explicitly identifies as a cave symbol. David Stuart's (1987: 17–20) reading of the kawak head as *wits,* or "hill," appears to substantiate this. One of the major uses of the kawak mask in Maya art is as a throne for gods or rulers (Tate 1980: 15), which makes it iconographically similar to the Olmec scene at Oxtotitlan Cave. In her analysis of several Maya stela, Carolyn Tate (1980: 16–17) concludes that the presence of the kawak mask is used to buttress the ruler's claim to office.

Furthermore, rulership is often pictured as being conferred within the earth. In Central Mexican legend, the ritual perforation of the septum that transformed the Chichimec chiefs into *tlatoanis* was performed in Chicomoztoc. This symbolized the conversion of the nomadic Chichimecs into the civilized Toltecs. In much the same way, the K'iche' kings received their right to rule from the god Tohil in the Wukub-Pek (Recinos, Goetz, and Morley 1950: 180). These myths were then played out in ritual. Richard Townsend (1987: 398) notes, "There is abundant evidence for the use of caves and cave-temples as places for the confirmation of new rulers."

The final act in the coronation of the Aztec *tlatoani* was a prayer and blood-letting vigil in the temple of Yopico. Townsend (1987: 397) says, "Yopico was an earth cult temple, which Sahagún describes as having a sunken receptacle or hole within the inner chamber. In the Nahuatl text this hole is named *oztoc*, at the cave." He concludes, "It was through sacrifice to the earth that the transfer of power to the new *tlatoani* was consecrated and made legal" (Townsend 1992: 204).

The desecration of this sacred space would have had serious repercussions for the religious as well as ideological underpinnings of a site's inhabitants and its ruling lineage. Based on what has been said, the acts might have struck at the symbol of the settlers' right to occupy the land. The destruction of the place of the founding ancestors might have compromised or at least weakened the ruling lineage's claim to legitimacy. In the next section we will present evidence to show that the deliberate destruction of caves may have been a widespread practice in the wake of a military victory.

ARCHAEOLOGICAL EVIDENCE OF CAVE DESECRATION

Although archaeological studies of caves before 1980 tended not to be particularly intensive, they occasionally noted the presence of stone walls closing a cave entrance or blocking a passage. Perhaps the best-known example is the passage discovered in 1959 at Balankanche (Andrews 1970: 5). A masonry and mortar wall appears to have been strategically placed to block a tightly restricted point in the tunnel system where the passage was only 30 cm high by 60 cm wide (Andrews 1970: 6). Several other walls were recorded at the cave, but they all employed different construction methods, suggesting that they had been built at different times or for different purposes. The most intensive utilization of the cave dates to the Modified Florescent period (A.D. 900–1150), which coincides with the heyday of nearby Chichén Itzá. Since most of the material in the blocked passage dates to this period, the wall closing off the passage must have been constructed after this time. Interestingly, at the close of the Modified Florescent period, Andrews (1970: 8) notes that "use of the cave was abruptly curtailed." He assumed that the wall sealing the passage had been constructed by the residents of Chichén Itzá as the site was being abandoned (Andrews 1971: 256).

As investigations became more intensive after 1980, evidence of a pattern of possible acts of violence directed against caves began to emerge. The evidence included the blocking of entrances and passages as well as the looting of sites. The discussion here will focus on evidence recovered at Naj Tunich, Balam Na, and Dos Pilas. At Naj Tunich a restricted opening that was the sole passage between the entrance chamber and the tunnel system had been blocked at one time by a stack of neatly cut speleothems. It is noteworthy that this was one of the few places sufficiently small in Naj Tunich to permit closure. Other evidence suggests that this was part of widespread violence against the site. All seven of the tombs in the entrance chamber had been looted. A large stalagmite growing on the tumbled wall of Structure 6 clearly shows that the looting had occurred in antiquity (Brady 1989: 147). Structures 2–4 are elaborate Late Classic tombs, clearly associated with elite individuals, and a hieroglyphic inscription on ceramics from Structure 2 indicates that the occupant held an important political office. The remains of monochrome slipped bowls used for burning incense were also found in front of Structures 1 and 4 and may have been used in rituals before the looting. If rituals in Naj Tunich had been directed to a former ruler, these rites may have had a heavy political overtone and thus provided an additional motive for the looting.

Balam Na is a small hill located 16 km northwest of Poptun, Petén, Guatemala. The hill contains at least six caves, four of which were investigated in 2001 (Garza, Brady, and Christensen 2001). The entrances to Caves 2 and 4 appear to have been blocked by the Maya. Cave 4 contained a number of Late Preclassic burials that had been laid in natural alcoves, which were then closed by stone walls. The blocked alcove-tombs appear stylistically similar to three tombs at Naj Tunich thought to date to the same time period. All appear to have been looted in antiquity. The presence of jade, pyrite, and other stone beads suggests that these had been elaborately furnished elite interments.

As might be expected, the Petexbatun Regional Cave Survey recovered some of the most extensive evidence of cave blockage. The Cueva de Sangre, located slightly more than 2 km southeast of the central plaza at Dos Pilas, appears to have been an important sacred landmark based on the architectural elaboration surrounding the main entrance. A small platform had been built directly over the entrance, a low wall enclosed both the entrance and mound, and two other mounds appeared to have spanned the normal approach to the cave. At the time the cave was investigated, the restricted 5-m-long tube that gave access to the tunnel system was completely choked with rock, providing clear evidence that it had been deliberately blocked. Beneath the rubble, an extremely large (115 by 22 cm) metate was found on the original ground surface in a number of pieces, suggesting that it had been deliberately broken. A thick layer of ash was found on the floor of the tube, indicating some type of burning event.

The largest and most impressive architectural complex at Dos Pilas is associated with the El Duende Pyramid, a natural hill that had been modified into a huge pyramidal base for a large masonry temple. During the second season, the project discovered the Cueva del Río El Duende, which runs directly under the hill and contains a large underground lake. This latter feature is probably the basis of the toponym for the complex (Stuart and Houston 1994: 85). At the back of the hill is a second cave, the Cueva de El Duende. A large plazuela group containing four masonry range structures was built next to the cave, so the plaza was situated directly above the cave's main chamber. Excavations in this chamber during the first season recovered sherds containing the earliest dynastic text from the site, as well as ceramics dating to the Middle Preclassic. The location of the Cueva de El Duende in direct association with four palace-type structures and next to the largest pyramid at the site clearly links the use of the cave to the high elite. The

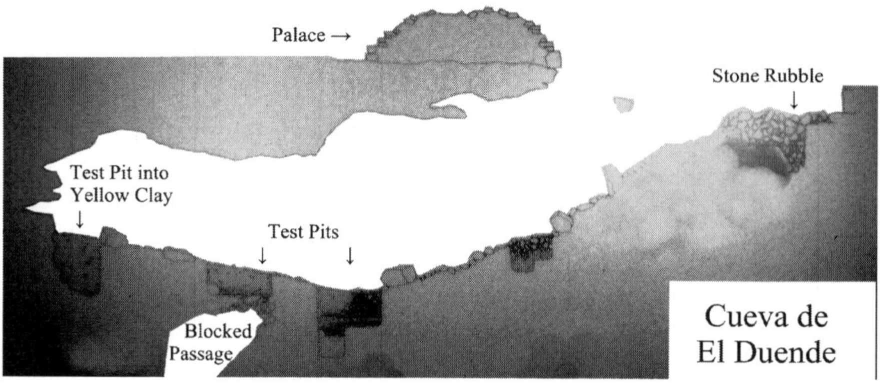

FIGURE 8.1. *Cross section of the main chamber of the Cueva de El Duende showing the location of the entrance to the blocked passage, the deposits of yellow clay, and the stone rubble at the mouth of the cave.*

presence of the dynastic text reinforces this impression (Houston 1993: 102).

During the second season of work at the Cueva de El Duende, a number of anomalous features appeared (Figure 8.1). During the first year, it was noted that a thick layer of sterile yellow clay overlay the cultural deposits in the eastern side of one test pit. This clay extended all the way to the back of the main chamber but was not found in the side passage. A looter's pit dug into the clay at the back of the chamber was excavated to bedrock during the second season to assess the extent of the deposit. This clay was 2 m deep, indicating that an impressive amount of soil had been brought into the cave. The fact that the clay overlay the cultural material was clear evidence that it postdated the ritual use of the cave. The function of the clay was resolved when a third pit came down on two large rocks that covered the entrance to the longest tunnel in the cave. This tunnel goes directly under the hill and appears to have connected to the Cueva del Río El Duende. The clay, therefore, appears to have been laid down to bury and block that entrance. The discovery initially created high expectations that the passage might have been blocked to protect an important feature such as an elite burial.

The complete absence of any artifacts of value caused us to reevaluate the passage in the larger context of other features in the entrance chamber. A circular depression at the entrance to the cave was filled with rock. Because many of the blocks were well cut and finished, it was assumed that they belonged to some badly deteriorated architectural feature that had been constructed in the depression. When the rocks were cleared, however, it was apparent that there was nothing more than a jumble of stone. In reexamining the placement, it now appears that the stone had completely filled the depression at one time, closing off the entrance to the cave. Excavations in the palace group directly above the cave suggest that the stone blocking the cave entrance had been pulled from these structures.

One reason we had not originally considered the possibility that the entrance had been blocked was that the present configuration of the ceiling would make that difficult to do. Several large blocks of ceiling collapse noted on the cave floor, however, raised the possibility that the entrance was somewhat smaller in the Late Classic. To test this, a small pit was excavated at the base of one of the large pieces of fallen ceiling. It was found to be resting on Late Classic material and so must have fallen after that time. It is suspected that the entrance was reopened when the collapse of the ceiling caused the blockage to shift downward into the entrance chamber.

Thus, it appears that someone went to great lengths to put an end to the use of the Cueva de El Duende. Many cubic meters of clay were hauled in to completely cover the floor of the cave and bury the entrance to the principal passage. This act taken alone could be interpreted as a simple termination ritual conducted by the inhabitants of Dos Pilas and reflect the evolving use of the cave over time. This, however, was not an isolated event and appears to have accompanied the blocking of the entrance by ripping down major public architecture. The evidence of significant associated destruction suggests the events were likely linked to warfare.

EPIGRAPHIC EVIDENCE

Recent advances in the decipherments of Maya hieroglyphic texts appear to explain these archaeological interpretations by revealing instances of desecration of caves as one of the acts carried out by one polity against another in the context of warfare.

This discussion was stimulated by a recent decipherment made by David Stuart (Vogt and Stuart 2005). Based on phonetic complementation and circumstantial evidence, Stuart read the signs HH2 (designations refer to the Macri and Looper [2003] catalog of hieroglyphs) and the sign BT6 as a head variant for CH'EEN (Figure 8.2). This reading is based on the ubiquitous occurrence of 1G1 *na* as phonetic complement to the logograph. A Jolja' Cave text contains an instance of the glyph 3M4.HH2 behind the verb "to arrive" (Stuart 1999: personal communication). Stuart read the whole compound *huliy tu ???-n* ("he arrives at his ???").

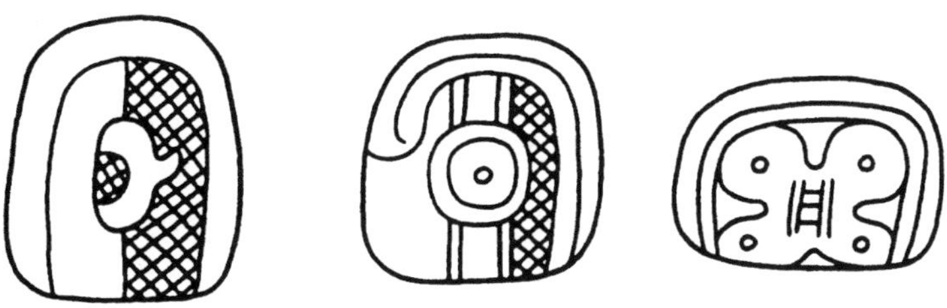

FIGURE 8.2. *Examples for the* ch'een *hieroglyph (redrawn from Macri and Looper 2003: 108f).*

Stuart concluded that the object of arrival must be the cave itself. *Ch'een,* the word for "cave" or "well" in all Maya languages, ends with the consonant n, so Stuart concluded that *ch'een* must be the value for HH2 and its equivalent signs. Unfortunately, there are no phonetic complements for the beginning of this logograph, and no syllable for *ch'e* has been recognized. The reading, therefore, is open to question, but we find Stuart's argument convincing and have accepted his suggested reading of the hieroglyph as cave. Based on this decipherment, we will address several hieroglyphic texts that date from Classic times.

THE DESTRUCTION OF THE CAVE: "STAR OVER" *U-CH'EEN*

One of the most enigmatic verbs for a war is the "Star Over" hieroglyph, which occurs many times in inscriptions. Its significance as a verb for war was first proposed by Berthold Riese (1982), who demonstrated its use in describing warlike actions between two cities. The sign always consists of ZQE, a sign for a star with two appendixes, and the sign ZUH yi, probably either a verbal suffix or a phonetic complement. The main sign can vary, as Riese demonstrated, among main signs for earth, shells, and emblem glyphs. As such, Riese semantically interpreted the glyph as "was attacked place X." The phonetic reading of the glyph still remains in doubt, although Stuart (1995: 311ff.) ventured a HUBUY, "to fall," reading; Erik Boot and Alfonso Lacadena suggested a HAY, "to destroy," reading; and Marc Zender (2004: personal communication) recently proposed a CH'AY, "to devastate, to sink," reading. Since there are no phonetic clues to decipher the verb, we use Riese's interpretation of the glyph as "to destroy" while acknowledging other possible meanings such as "to sink" within this complex verb. Of interest here is its occurrence with the cave glyph on Tonina Monument 122 (Figure 8.3).

On this monument the Palenque king K'an Joy Chitam can be seen with ropes binding his arms, obviously designating him as a prisoner of Tonina. The text starts with the calendar round 13 Ak'bal 16 Yax (9.13.19.13.3), corresponding to August 30, 711.

FIGURE 8.3. *Tonina Monument 122 (redrawn after Graham and Mathews 1999: 153).*

The next hieroglyph is the star over earth glyph carrying the combination u-CH'EEN-*na.* The whole compound might be translated as "was attacked his cave." The text goes on to specify the owner of this cave, K'an Joy Chitam B'aakal Ajaw, the lord of Palenque, stripped of his *K'inich* royal epithet and his *K'uhul* emblem glyph prefix, indicating his lowered status in the wake of his defeat (Colas 2003). The text clearly relates that the cave of the king of Palenque was destroyed and the king was taken to Tonina as prisoner.

This section has often been interpreted rather loosely as "was attacked his place" instead of literally "his cave." Considering, however, that the "star over" glyph seems to refer to the most decisive of all actions in describing the conquest of cities (Martin and Grube 2000: 16), it is noteworthy that the city of Palenque itself appears archaeologically not to have been physically affected by this event. We tentatively propose that the previous section has to be read literally as "was attacked his cave," referring to the destruction of an important symbol of rulership: the cave.

THE SCATTERING OF FIRE INTO THE CAVE: *U CHOK K'AK TU CH'EEN*

Three different looted panels, thought to come from the Piedras Negras region, record a series of war events in the mid-seventh century (Mayer 1995: plate 75; Schele and Grube 1994: 116). The text starts with an unknown event involving Ruler 1, Yo'nal Ahk K'in Ajaw, from Piedras Negras. The unknown event is undertaken by Ka "K'atun" Ajaw K'ab Chante', a ruler of the site of Sak Tz'i. A distance number leads to the date 9.10.8.6.2 13 Ik' 5 Zip (April 17, 641). The recorded event (Figure 8.4) consists of three securely deciphered signs that can be read as u-CHOK-K'AK', "he scatters fire." The subject of this intransitive sentence follows immediately. His name is given as Nikte' Mo' Petun? Ajaw (Flower Parrot, Lord of Petun). His name is followed by a prepositional phrase tu-CH'EEN-*na,* "into his cave." The owner of the cave is named afterward, K'ab Chante' Sak Tz'i Ajaw Bakab (Hand Sky Tree? Sak Tz'i Lord Bakab). The text, therefore, states that on April 17, Nikte' Mo' scattered fire into the cave of K'ab Chante'.

The text goes on to record a beheading event (Orejel 1990) on 9.10.8.6.3 1 Ak'bal 6 Zip (April 18, 641) against an individual Nikte' Mo' Petun Ajaw, most likely the same Nikte' Mo' who scattered fire into K'ab Chante's cave a day earlier. The actor of the beheading event is Ka "K'atun" Ajaw K'ab Chante' u Ajaw K'in, the same person whose cave was the object of fire throwing. The text continues with the recording of a capture event a day later against Ek' Mo', Lord of Bonampak, and ends with two undeciphered events.

The series of known events (not counting the unknown event involving Piedras Negras Ruler 1) starts with Nikte' Mo' throwing fire into the cave of K'ab Chante'. A day later Nikte' Mo' is beheaded by K'ab Chante'. One is inclined to see a direct causal relation between Nikte' Mo' throwing fire into the cave and the beheading a

FIGURE 8.4. *Lintel of unknown provenance from the Piedras Negras region (drawing by Colas).*

day later. This strongly suggests that the fire throwing is some kind of war event that is answered by a reprisal from K'ab Chante'. Our interpretation is in accord with the overall account of the inscription that records only war events. The question is whether the expression "throwing fire into the cave" is meant as a metaphor for war or as actual event that precipitated war. We believe it might be both. The burning of the cave could actually have occurred, and K'ab Chante' took revenge by beheading Nikte' Mo' for burning his cave a day earlier. It might also be that "burning" here represents more a term for destruction and desecration of the cave.

THE BURNING OF THE CAVE: *PULUUY U CH'EEN*

An event, very similar to that on the looted panels from the Piedras Negras region, is recorded on Naranjo Stela 23 (Figure 8.5). The left side of Stela 23 starts with the initial series 9.13.18.4.18 8 Etz'nab 16 Uo (March 23, 710). The verb appears in E9 as PULUUY, deciphered by Stuart (Grube and Martin 1998: 61). This hieroglyph is a clear verb for a war, meaning "to burn" in Cholan languages, and has been noted in many war contexts (Grube and Martin 1998) and some death phrases (Fitzsimmons 1998). The object of this burning event is written in F9 as a possessive phrase u-CH'EEN, "his cave." In E10 to E11 follows the eroded nominal phrase of a Yaxhá king, who is the possessor of the cave. The actor of this event is Ruler 2, K'ak' Tiliw Chan Chaak, of Naranjo (Martin and Grube 2000: 76). The text goes on to record the exhumation of the skull and bones of an important king of Yaxhá (Yax Bolon Chaak) and the subsequent scattering of the human remains on an island. The text on the right side of the stela goes on to record a war event against the site Sakha' (Martin and Grube 2000: 76).

The hieroglyph in E9 PULUUY is a well-accepted verb for war. As such, the phrase has been interpreted as a "burning of Yaxhá" (Martin and Grube 2000: 76). We emphasize that the object of the burning is specified explicitly as the impinged bone sign read by Stuart as CH'EEN, meaning "cave." Since Stuart and Houston's (1994) study of toponyms, the impinged bone sign has been regarded as a general

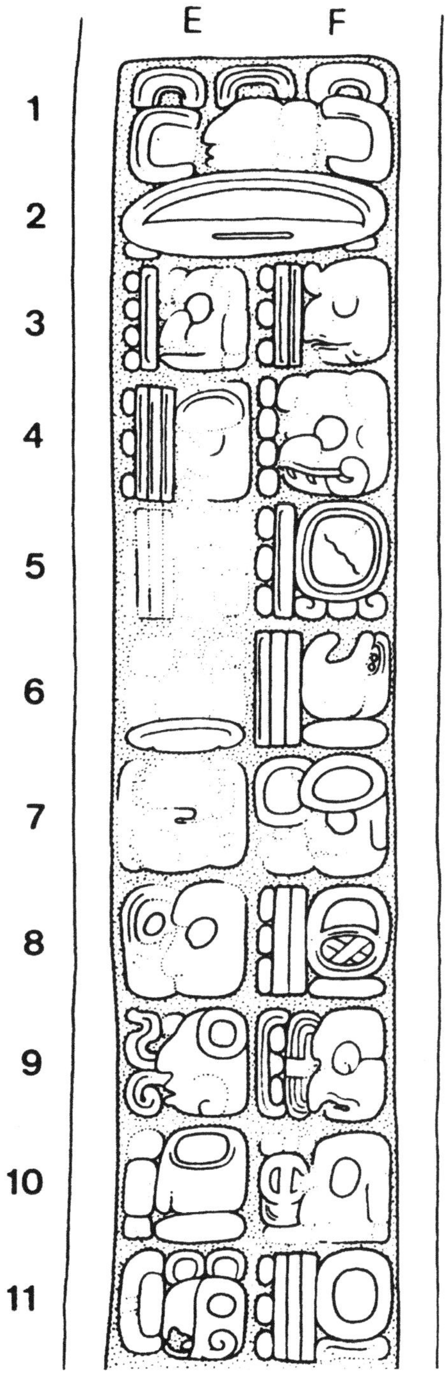

FIGURE 8.5. *Section from Stela 23, Naranjo (redrawn after Graham and von Euw 1975: 60).*

glyph for "place" in combination with a prefixed CHAN hieroglyph (Stuart and Houston 1994: 11). It should be noted that in this case the CHAN glyph is lacking. Furthermore, the CH'EEN hieroglyph is directly possessed through the ergative prefix. We believe the meaning "his cave" should be taken literally. The actual burning of the cave of the Yaxhá ruler may describe an actual act in a war, although the possibility exists that "burning" again represents a metaphor for destruction.

THE CARRYING OF FIRE INTO THE CAVE: *TOK(?)*

A somewhat related event can be identified on the cave walls of Naj Tunich in Drawing 82 (Figure 8.6). The text starts with the calendar round date 13 Ix and 4 Zak. The long count position remains unclear, although the most accepted dating is 9.15.13.3.14 (August 27, 744). The reading of the verb in position A2 is still uncertain, although one of the authors (Colas 1998) has raised the possibility of reading it as TOK-ku, *tok*, meaning "invasion." The sign consists of a seated human figure bearing the sign for fire K'AK' (T122:563) on its back. Beneath this fire sign, T528 is visible and can be either the logograph for TUUN, "stone," or the phonetic complement ku. Depending on the choice of interpretations, this sign can be interpreted iconically as a human figure carrying fire on a stone. As such, it has been interpreted as meaning that "fire

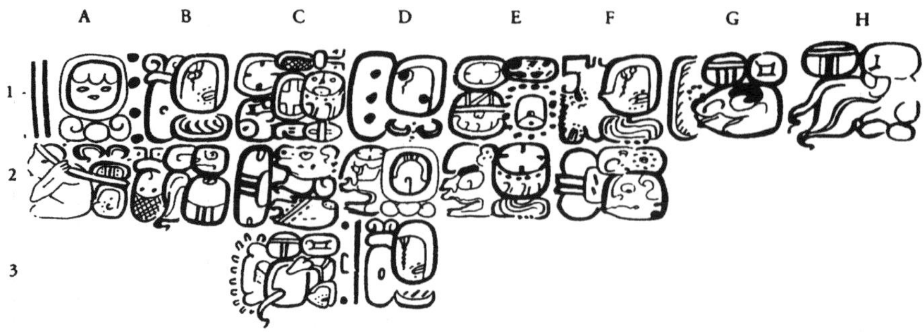

FIGURE 8.6. *Drawing 82, Naj Tunich (redrawn after MacLeod and Stone 1995: 179).*

was carried on a stone object into the cave" (Christian Prager 1997: personal communication). It could also be interpreted logographically-phonetically as a logograph ending with k, possibly *tok*, meaning both "fire" and "invasion" in the Yucatecan and Mopan languages. Given the close connection already noted between fire and warfare, the two possible interpretations, of an unspecified fire event or of an invasion, probably had much the same meaning to a native reader. There is no definite proof for a TOK reading of the "fire bearer" in Drawing 82. Therefore, we interpret the hieroglyph iconographically as a human figure carrying fire on a stone into a cave. The object of this event is stated in B2-C1 as Tum y-Ohl K'inich, a person of Caracol. The actor is introduced by an *u kabhi* verb in D2 as Chak-?-Took', holy lord of Ixkun (C2-C3).

As has been pointed out (Colas 1998: 101f.), the nature of the "fire bearer" verb is clarified by the inscription on Ixkun Stela 2, the only other occurrence of this verb. Here, the "fire bearer" is embedded in an account of wars. The first event occurs in B11 and can be identified as a PULUUY burning event on 9.17.9.0.13 3 Ben 6 K'ayab (December 21, 779) against Ixkun (A12). The next event is the "fire bearer" event (C3) that takes place in the night (Colas 1998: 101). The following day a *ch'ak* event (C4), meaning "beheading" or by extension "defeating" (Orejel 1990), is mentioned against an unknown place. A distance number leads to yet another PULUUY "burning" event against Ucanal on 9.17.9.3.4 (February 10, 780). As has been proposed earlier (Colas 1998), the account on Stela 2 from Ixkun makes the interpretation of the "fire bearer" as a verb for a war quite likely. If the "fire bearer" is interpreted iconographically as carrying fire into a cave, this expression obviously relates to an act of war. The "fire bearer" verb could very well be interpreted as a burning of a cave describing an act of war.

DISCUSSION

The deliberate destruction of caves as an act of war sheds light on the special nature of Mesoamerican warfare. Although Maya warfare certainly involved the direct confrontation of warriors on opposing sides, the determination of the victor may have had nothing to do with the number of casualties inflicted. The capture of objects or places important to the enemy may have been crucial in who claimed victory. This is clear in the now famous clash between the two Classic Maya giants, Tikal and Calakmul. Although the latter had exercised power over much of the Maya region for many centuries, Tikal overthrew Calakmul in A.D. 695, "bringing down the flint and shield," in the words of the inscriptions, of its king, Y Ich'aak K'ak' (Martin and Grube 2000: 110f.). However, Y Ich'aak K'ak' is buried in a richly furnished tomb at Calakmul (Carrasco Vargas et al. 1999: 49ff.), so obviously, despite losing a decisive battle to his archenemy, the king himself appears not to have been harmed. Thus, the capture of the king was not the decisive act in the war but rather the taking of his war paraphernalia: the flint and shield.

Another example can be found in the clashes between Tikal and Naranjo that are vividly described in the inscriptions (Martin 1996). In one battle, certain palanquins with a statue of a deity had been captured (Martin 1996: 227). The figure is said to have been taken captive just like a human being. The taking of gods is also reported for the Aztecs (Hassig 1988: 184). There were obviously numerous ways of conducting a war in Classic Maya times. Tikal captured a highly regarded sacred object and thus deprived Naranjo of an important source of religious strength and perhaps legitimation.

The desecration of a cave was probably less like the capture of an object, however, and more akin to the desecration of a temple. In sixteenth-century Yucatán, the Maya used the term *aktun* to refer to both caves and stone buildings, which suggests that caves and temples may have been conceptually linked in native thought (Thompson 1959: 124). The practice of burning an enemy's temple is well documented for the Aztecs (Hassig 1988: 150, 166, 173, 184, 204, 207) and a common symbol of conquest in the codices is a burning temple. It could be that among the Classic Maya an analogous symbol of conquest was the desecration of a cave.

Although we believe the archaeological evidence previously presented indicates a violent desecration of caves, other forms of termination rituals are known among the Maya. The practice of destroying buildings accompanied by complex ritual activities is widely recognized in the context of construction. These termination rituals include the deliberate damaging or destruction of architecture or artifacts, accompanied by burning and censing. In special cases a building, rather than being destroyed, was buried in *saskab* (white clay), and a new structure emerged over it, indicating a special kind of *rite de passage* (Wagner 2002). In this case, the termination would not be connected with warfare but would be a simple ritual act. Thus, there could be two possible reasons for sealing caves. The first would be conducted by the inhabitants during a termination ritual that indicated a transition rite, as seen in architectural construction. The second would be an attack in the context of warfare to desecrate a symbol at the heart of one's enemies' claim to political legitimacy.

Although the inscriptions speak of burning a cave, the detection of an actual burning event in connection with an act of war would be difficult. Garrett Cook (1986: 139) points out that burning is such an integral part of all K'iche' Maya rituals that the ceremonies are referred to as "burnings" and the altars on which rituals are performed are called "burning places" (Bunzel 1952: 431). Therefore, one would expect quantities of charcoal to be present in caves simply as a by-product of religious rituals. The burning of large amounts of copal during ceremonies also tends to blacken walls and formations as well as the soil on the floor. Movement within the dark zone of a cave required the use of torches and deposited yet more evidence of burning. Given all these sources of burning, the identification of burning in connection to desecration would require some extraordinary context. We suspect, however, that the use of the term *burning* is probably a gloss for sundry acts of desecration, looting, and mayhem.

As noted, archaeologists have only begun to recognize evidence of termination of caves in recent years. One of the indications in caves, the blocking of entrances or passages, could be associated with a (peaceful) ritual termination. Advocates of that position, however, must explain the fact that no new construction has been detected around the terminated caves, and utilization of the site appears to cease after the sealing of the cave. In point of fact, the interpretation of the termination being associated with warfare is quite clear because most well-investigated cases have clear evidence of other forms of violence. At the Cueva de El Duende, public architecture was torn down to fill the depression in front of the cave and close the entrance. At both Balam Na and Naj Tunich, the closing of passages or entrances was accompanied by the looting of the tombs in the caves. Evidence of such termination events has been detected archaeologically at surface sites. David Freidel (1992) has suggested the widespread termination of Cerros during the Late Preclassic following a military defeat. Shirley Mock (1998) has described a deposit of thirty skulls, some of which show cranial flaying, which she feels was part of that termination event. The Late Preclassic date at Cerros makes it more or less contemporaneous with the looting and closure of Balam Na. Evidence of a Classic period termination event was also found at Yaxuna (Freidel, Suhler, and Cobos Palma 1998; Suhler and Freidel 2000) and Teotihuacan (Sugiyama 1998).

CONCLUSIONS

In this chapter we have presented epigraphic evidence for the desecration of caves in the context of Maya warfare. We have also presented possible archaeological evidence of such desecration in the form of looted tombs and blocked cave entrances and passages. In our discussion we have shown that Maya warfare is not directed solely against a person or people but against objects and places as well. This is hardly new. The burning of the enemy's main temple is a well-recognized coup de grâce after a major military victory. It signaled the termination of the battle, with the complete victory of the enemy. Although the temple is a religious structure, archaeologists have never had difficulty understanding the political and social implications of the destruction of a site's largest religious structure.

What is new is the proposal that caves were one of the major features against which war was waged. An implication is that caves were considered elements on a par in importance with pyramids. In the section on the role of caves in the ideology of settlement and rulership, we have stressed that point. The fact that caves were the focus of indigenous attention in warfare is a substantiation of our point. Caves were specifically targeted because of the role they played in sanctifying and legitimizing both settlement and rulership.

REFERENCES CITED

Andrews, E. Wyllys, IV

1970 *Balankanche, Throne of the Tiger Priest,* Publication 32. Middle American Research Institute, New Orleans.

1971 Balankanche—Throne of the Tiger Priest. *Explorers Journal* 49(4):254–262.

Brady, James E.

1989 An Investigation of Maya Ritual Cave Use With Special Reference to Naj Tunich, Peten, Guatemala. Ph.D. Dissertation. Archaeology Program, University of California, Los Angeles.

Bunzel, Ruth

1952 *Chichicastenango: A Guatemalan Village.* J. J. Augustine Publisher, Locust Valley, New York.

Campbell, Joseph

1956 *The Hero With a Thousand Faces.* Meridian Books, New York.

Carrasco Vargas, Ramón, Sylviane Boucher, Paula Alvarez González, Vera Tiesler Blos, Valeria García Vierna, Renata García Moreno, and Javier Vázquez Negrete

1999 A Dynastic Tomb From Campeche, Mexico: New Evidence on Jaguar Paw, a Ruler of Calakmul. *Latin American Antiquity* 10(1):47–58.

Colas, Pierre Robert

1998 Ritual and Politics in the Underworld. *Mexicon* 20(5):99–104.

2003 K'inich and King: Naming Self and Person Among Classic Maya Rulers. *Ancient Mesoamerica* 14:269–283.

Cook, Garrett

1986 Quichean Folk Theology and Southern Maya Supernaturalism. In *Symbol and Meaning Beyond the Closed Community: Essays in Mesoamerican Ideas,* ed. Gary H. Gossen, 139–153. Institute of Mesoamerican Studies, State University of New York, Albany.

Fitzsimmons, James

1998 Classic Maya Mortuary Anniversaries at Piedras Negras, Guatemala. *Ancient Mesoamerica* 9:271–278.

Freidel, David A.

1992 Krieg, Mythos und Realitat. In *Die Welt der Maya,* eds. Eva Eggebrecht and Arne Eggebrecht, 158–176. Verlag Phillip von Zabern, Mainz am Rhein.

Freidel, David A., Charles K. Suhler, and Rafael Cobos Palma

1998 Termination Deposits at Yaxuna. In *The Sowing and the Dawning: Termination, Dedication, and Transformation in the Archaeological and Ethnographic Record of Mesoamerica,* ed. Shirley Boteler Mock, 135–144. University of New Mexico Press, Albuquerque.

García-Zambrano, Angel J.

1994 Early Colonial Evidence of Pre-Columbian Rituals of Foundation. In *Seventh Palenque Round Table, 1989,* eds. Merle Greene Robertson and Virginia Fields, 217–227. Pre-Columbian Art Research Institute, San Francisco.

Garza, Sergio, James E. Brady, and Christian Christensen

2001 Balam Na Cave 4: Implications for Understanding Preclassic Cave Mortuary Practices. *California Anthropologist* 28(1):15–21.

Graham, Ian, and Peter Mathews

1999 *Corpus of Maya Hieroglyphic Inscriptions,* Vol. 6, No. 3. Peabody Museum of Archaeology and Ethnology, Harvard University, Cambridge.

Graham, Ian, and Eric von Euw

1975 *Corpus of Maya Hieroglyphic Inscriptions,* Vol. 2, No. 1. Peabody Museum of Archaeology and Ethnology, Harvard University, Cambridge.

Grove, David C.

1973 Olmec Altars and Myth. *Archaeology* 26(2):128–135.

1981 Olmec Monuments: Mutilation as a Clue to Meaning. In *The Olmec and Their Neighbors: Essays in Memory of Matthew W. Sterling,* ed. Elizabeth P. Benson, 49–68. Dumbarton Oaks Research Library and Collection, Washington, D.C.

Grube, Nikolai, and Simon Martin

1998 Deciphering Maya Politics. In *Notebook for the XXIInd Maya Hieroglyphic Forum at Texas,* 61–64. Department of Art and Art History, University of Texas, Austin.

Guiteras Holmes, C.

1947 Clanes y sistema de parantesco de Cancuc (México). *Acta Americana* 5:1–17.

1961 *Perils of the Soul: The World View of a Tzotzil Indian.* The Free Press, New York.

Hassig, Ross

1988 *Aztec Warfare: Imperial Expansion and Political Control.* University of Oklahoma Press, Norman.

Heyden, Doris

1987 Caves. In *Encyclopedia of Religion,* ed. Mircea Eliade, 3:127–133. Macmillan, New York.

Holland, William R.

1963 *Medicina Maya en los altos de Chiapas: Un estudio del cambio socio-cultural.* Instituto Nacional Indigenista, Mexico.

Houston, Stephen D.

1993 *Hieroglypha and History at Dos Pilas: Dynastic Politics of the Classic Maya.* University of Texas Press, Austin.

Isaac, Erich

1962 The Act and the Covenant. *Landscape* 11:12–17.

LaFarge, Oliver

1947 *Santa Eulalia: The Religion of a Cuchumatan Indian Town.* University of Chicago Press, Chicago.

MacLeod, Barbara, and Andrea Stone
1995 The Hieroglyphic Inscriptions of Naj Tunich. In *Images From the Underworld: Naj Tunich and the Tradition of Maya Cave Painting,* ed. Andrea J. Stone, 155–184. University of Texas Press, Austin.

Macri, Martha, and Mathew Looper
2003 *The New Catalog of Maya Hieroglyphs. Volume 1, The Classic Inscriptions.* University of Oklahoma Press, Norman.

Martin, Simon
1996 Tikal's "Star War" Against Naranjo. In *Eighth Palenque Round Table, 1993,* ed. Merle Greene Robertson, 223–235. Pre-Columbian Art Research Institute, San Francisco.

Martin, Simon, and Nikolai Grube
2000 *Chronicle of the Maya Kings and Queens. Deciphering the Dynasties of the Ancient Maya.* Thames & Hudson, London.

Matos Moctezuma, Eduardo
1987 Symbolism of the Templo Mayor. In *The Aztec Templo Mayor,* ed. Elizabeth Hill Boone, 185–209. Dumbarton Oaks Research Library and Collection, Washington, D.C.

Mayer, Karl-Herbert
1995 *Maya Monuments VII: Sculptures of Unknown Provenience, Supplement 4.* Academic Publishers, Graz, Austria.

McAnany, Patricia A.
1995 *Living With the Ancestors: Kinship and Kingship in Ancient Maya Society.* University of Texas Press, Austin.

Mock, Shirley Boteler
1998 The Defaced and the Forgotten: Decapitation and Flaying/Mutilation as a Termination Event at Colha, Belize. In *The Sowing and the Dawning: Termination, Dedication, and Transformation in the Archaeological and Ethnographic Record of Mesoamerica,* ed. Shirley Boteler Mock, 113–123. University of New Mexico Press, Albuquerque.

Orejel, Jorge
1990 *The "Axe-Comb" Glyph (T 333) as ch'ak.* Research Reports on Ancient Maya Writing, No. 32. Center for Maya Research, Washington, D.C.

Recinos, Adrian, Delia Goetz, and Sylvanis G. Morley
1950 *Popol Vuh: The Sacred Book of the Ancient Quiché Maya.* University of Oklahoma Press, Norman.

Riese, Berthold
1982 Kriegsberichte der Klassischen Maya. *Baessler Archiv* 30 (2):255–321.

Schele, Linda, and Nikolai Grube
1994 *Tlaloc-Venus Warfare: The Peten Wars 8.17.0.0.0–9.15.13.0.0.* Notebook for the XVIIIth Maya Hieroglyphic Workshop. University of Texas Press, Austin.

Stuart, David
1987 *Ten Phonetic Syllables.* Research Reports on Maya Writing No. 14. Center for Maya Research, Washington, D.C.
1995 A Study of Maya Inscriptions. Ph.D. Dissertation. Department of Anthropology, Vanderbilt University, Nashville.

Stuart, David, and Stephen D. Houston
1994 *Classic Maya Place Names.* Studies in Pre-Columbian Art and Archaeology, No. 33. Dumbarton Oaks Research Library and Collection, Washington, D.C.

Sugiyama, Saburo
1998 Termination Programs and Prehistoric Looting at the Feathered Serpent Pyramid in Teotihuacan, Mexico. In *The Sowing and the Dawning: Termination, Dedication, and Transformation in the Archaeological and Ethnographic Record of Mesoamerica,* ed. Shirley Boteler Mock, 147–164. University of New Mexico Press, Albuquerque.

Suhler, Charles K., and David A. Freidel
2000 Rituales de terminación: implicaciones de la guerra Maya. In *La guerra entre los antiguos Mayas*. Memorias de la Primera Mesa Redonda de Palenque, ed. Silvia Trejo, 73–104. Conacutla, Instituto Nacional de Antropología e Historia, México, D.F.

Tate, Carolyn
1980 The Maya Cauac Monster: Visual Evidence for Ancestor Veneration Among the Ancient Maya. Master's Thesis. Department of Art History, University of Texas, Austin.

Taylor, Dicey
1978 The Cauac Monster. *Tercera Mesa Redonda de Palenque, Vol. 4,* eds. Merle Greene Robertson and Donnan Call Jeffers, 79–89. Pre-Columbian Art Research, Monterey.

Thompson, J. Eric
1959 The Role of Caves in Maya Culture. *Mitteilungen aus dem Museum für Völkerkunde in Hamburg* 25:122–129.
1975 Introduction to the Reprint Edition. In *The Hill-Caves of Yucatan,* by Henry C. Mercer, vii–xliv. University of Oklahoma Press, Norman.

Townsend, Richard F.
1987 Coronation at Tenochtitlan. In *The Aztec Temple Mayor,* ed. Elizabeth Hill Boone, 373–410. Dumbarton Oaks Research Library and Collection, Washington, D.C.
1992 *The Aztecs.* Thames and Hudson, New York.

Villa Rojas, Alfonso
1947 Kinship and Nagualism in a Tzeltal Community, Southeastern Mexico. *American Anthropologist* 49:578–587.
1969 The Tzeltal. In *Handbook of Middle American Indians, Vol. 7: Ethnology,* ed. Evon Z. Vogt, 195–225. University of Texas Press, Austin.

Vogt, Evon Z.
1976 *Tortillas for the Gods: A Symbolic Analysis of Zinacantan Ritual.* Harvard University Press, Cambridge.

Vogt, Evon Z., and David Stuart
2005 Some Notes on Ritual Caves Among the Ancient and Modern Maya. In *In the Maw of the Earth Monster: Mesoamerican Ritual Cave Use,* eds. James E. Brady and Keith M. Prufer, 155–185. University of Texas Press, Austin.

Wagner, Elisabeth
2002 White Earth Bundles—The Symbolic Sealing and Burial of Buildings Among the Ancient Maya. Paper presented at the 7th European Maya Conference, London.

Chapter Nine

Plants and Caves in Ancient Maya Society

by Christopher T. Morehart

The growing field of Maya cave archaeology has brought caves to the forefront as essential, sacred features of the ancient Maya landscape and has established caves as significant loci for serious archaeological study (Awe 1998; Brady 1989, 1997; Brady et al. 1997a; MacLeod and Puleston 1978; Pohl and Pohl 1983; Prufer 2002; Rissolo 2001; Stone 1995, 1997). By examining archaeological data of caves in conjunction with ethnographic, ethnohistoric, iconographic, and epigraphic records, caves can be seen as transitional loci between structurally opposite cosmological spheres—namely, earth and underworld, night and day, and life and death. This liminal quality (Turner 1969) made caves an effective stage for symbolically laden ritual activities.

Researchers have proposed a number of interpretations for the kinds of rituals performed in caves. The majority of these focus either on fertility rites, emphasizing the relationship between caves and deities associated with rain, agriculture, and the forces of creation (Awe 1998; Brady 1988, 1989; MacLeod and Puleston 1978; Morehart 2002b), or on political rituals, examining the acquisition of symbolic space by ruling elites and the negotiation of socioeconomic and political power (Brady 1997; Brady and Ashmore 1999; Halperin 2002; Helmke 1999; Morehart 2002b; Pohl 1983). However, these theories of cave use are not necessarily distinct and conceptually exclusive; fertility rites may have had broader political implications, and political rituals were likely tied to notions of fertility and creation. This assessment underscores the high level of integration among many facets of indigenous, non-Western cultures that anthropologists often separate into distinct cultural categories such as economics, politics, social organization, and religion—a traditional methodology that has been etically useful but that in some cases may hinder emically viable reconstructions of the past.

Most interpretations of Maya cave utilization have been based predominantly on observations of durable artifactual assemblages, to the virtual exclusion of botanical remains. The systematic recovery, analysis, and interpretation of botanical remains will shed light on the nature of Maya cave activities by contributing an overlooked source of data to archaeologically derived inferences. Furthermore, few investigations of ancient ritual practices at surface sites have employed archaeobotanical data. Thus, cave contexts offer an unparalleled opportunity to obtain broader understandings of the use of plants in ancient Maya ritual experience.

In response to this paucity of studies on plant remains recovered from ritual contexts, paleoethnobotanical research was initiated between June and August 2000, in a series of caves in the greater Upper Belize Valley of western Belize, as part of the Western Belize Regional Cave Project, directed by Dr. Jaime Awe (Morehart 2001, 2002a, 2002b). Because of length restrictions, it is not possible to present this research in its entirety (see Morehart 2002b for a more in-depth discussion of this research). This chapter presents some interesting aspects of the botanical assemblage, focusing predominantly on food remains, from four of these caves: Actun Nak Beh in the Roaring Creek Valley, Barton Creek Cave in the Barton Creek Valley, and Actun Chapat and Actun Chechem Ha in the Macal River Valley (Figure 9.1). Interpretations are made by comparing archaeobotanical data with analogous information contained in the ethnographic and ethnohistoric record of the Maya and, to a limited extent, with iconography from the Classic period. Remains of foods are interpreted as remnants of offerings to sacred entities associated with the earth and other natural forces. Furthermore, an attempt is made to explore possible regional patterns in ritual activities reflective of wider social, political, and economic conditions by integrating the botanical assemblage within larger archaeological contexts.

PALEOETHNOBOTANICAL INVESTIGATIONS

Paleoethnobotanical investigations involved recovering macrofloral and, to a limited extent, microfloral material. Macrofloral remains were yielded by water-floating 1-liter soil samples from archaeological deposits and by collecting in situ carbonized macroremains. Microfloral analysis was focused on extracting, isolating, and

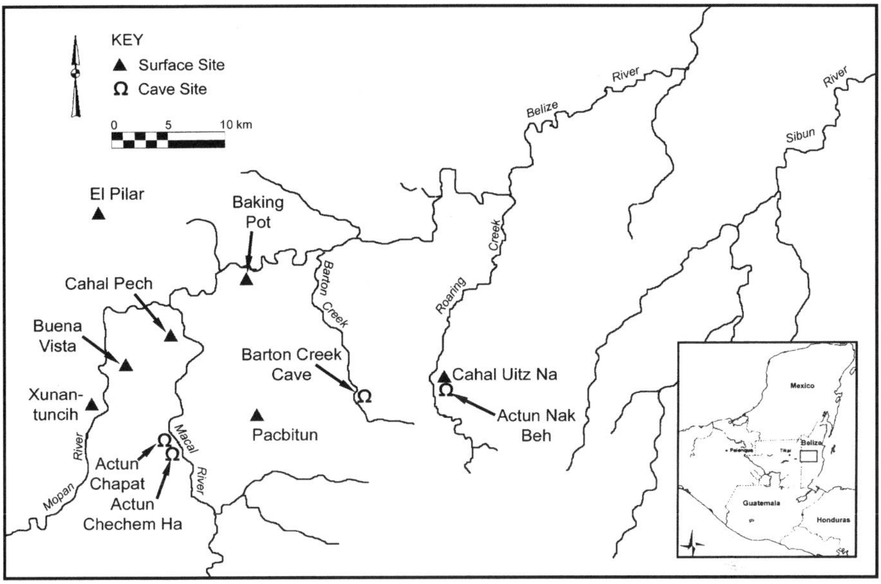

FIGURE 9.1. *Map of the Upper Belize Valley showing cave sites discussed in the text.*

identifying starch grains from soil collected from the interiors of complete ceramic vessels and on residues adhering to ceramic sherds found at Actun Chechem Ha. Identification of plant remains was undertaken at the paleoethnobotanical laboratory at the New York Botanical Garden and the archaeology laboratories at Florida State University. Botanical material was compared to modern comparative samples and, especially in the case of wood charcoal, to descriptions and photomicrographs of plant structural anatomy contained in several reference texts (e.g., Camacho Uribe 1988; Carreras and Dechamps 1995; Détienne and Jacquet 1983).

Archaeobotanical sampling yielded a number of well-preserved plant and organic materials, including a textile fragment, domesticated crops, the fruits of economically useful trees, and numerous species of wood charcoal. The degree of preservation of plant and organic remains from the caves was remarkable, although preservation varied between sites. In general, however, preservation was considerably greater than what is commonly encountered at surface sites. This factor emphasizes not only the productivity of archaeobotanical studies in caves in the Maya Lowlands but also the importance of cave sites for Maya paleoethnobotanical research in general.

Food Remains

Remains of botanical food items are one of the most interesting aspects of the archaeobotanical assemblage. This material consists of domesticated plants—such

FIGURE 9.2. Zea mays *(maize) remains from Actun Chapat. Marks indicate 1 mm.*

as maize (*Zea mays*), beans (*Phaseolus* sp.), squash (*Cucurbita* sp.), and chile peppers (*Capsicum annuum*)—and the carbonized fruit remains from economically useful trees.

Domesticated plants were found at Actun Chapat, Actun Chechem Ha, and Barton Creek Cave. Evidence of domesticated crops from Actun Chapat consists of charred maize fragments, bean cotyledons, and squash rinds recovered from excavations in several artificial terraces. The terraces may have served as key foci for the placement of food offerings. Because of poor preservation, it was not possible to identify the species of bean, and the absence of seeds or peduncle remains prevented species-level identification of the squash. Maize was the most abundant cultigen from Actun Chapat (Figure 9.2). The maize consists of cob fragments, individual cupules and glumes, and kernel fragments. Although most of the maize specimens from Actun Chapat were fragmentary, maize-yielding deposits generally contained many parts of the maize ear, suggesting that complete ears may have been offered that only fragmented following burning and decomposition over time. All undisturbed deposits sampled, ranging in date from the Early Classic period (perhaps earlier for some deposits) to the Late Classic period, contained maize remains. Because of incomplete preservation of maize from later contexts, morphological measurements of the maize were restricted to specimens from a level radio-

FIGURE 9.3. Zea mays *(maize) cobs from Actun Chechem Ha.*

carbon dated to the Early Classic period (A.D. 410–650, two-sigma calibration), as well as to maize from an undated level directly below the Early Classic deposit. These specimens are small, with mean cupule widths between 2.5 and 3.86 mm, comparable in size to maize from Formative period sites in Lowland Mesoamerica, such as Cuello in northern Belize (Miksicek 1991; Miksicek et al. 1981) and La Venta in the Gulf Coast region of Mexico (Rust and Leyden 1994: 196). This may be a reflection of the size of maize cultivated during early periods in this region of Belize, it may indicate that immature ears were deposited in the cave, or it may be the result of the fragmented and incomplete nature of the maize collection from Actun Chapat.

Domesticated plant remains from Actun Chechem Ha are more limited in number and consist solely of maize. In 1998, researchers collected several intact, uncarbonized maize cobs from two Late Classic period *ollas* located on two of the cave's ledges (Figure 9.3). The original number of cobs collected is not certain, but it appears that some disintegrated before 2000. Only seven cobs were available for analysis. The small size of the cobs is notable. The average length is 18.22 mm, and the longest individual is only 22.01 mm in length. The reduced size is not the result of postdepositional shrinkage because the maize is not carbonized, and the cobs are likely underdeveloped. The only other macroremains of maize include extremely fragmented maize kernels collected from a surface hearth feature in Crawl 3, one of the cave's inner tunnels that Holley Moyes (2001) proposed was modified in antiquity to be used as a ritual sweatbath. Lastly, starch grains morphologically similar to maize starch were identified in residues and soil samples from intact vessels and ceramic sherds. The grains range between 15 and 26 μ, are simple and spherical, and have spherical central hilums—all characteristics of maize starch (Reichert 1913). Because of the small sample size, it was not possible to determine any associative patterns between vessel types and maize starch, although maize starch grains were recovered from a variety of vessel types, including jars, bowls, and a miniature vessel.

The best-preserved domesticated food remains were found at Barton Creek Cave. Maize and beans were found in hearthlike features and burials distributed throughout the cave. A single, large hearthlike feature (Feature 23) at Barton Creek Cave—associated with Late Classic period, Spanish Lookout Phase ceramics (A.D. 600–800)—yielded an amazing assemblage of domesticates, including squash rinds and the seeds of two species of squash, *Cucurbita moschata* and *C. pepo*. The assemblage also included forty-one chile pepper seeds and the calyxes of chile peppers, as well as maize remains (Figure 9.4). The maize remains consist of complete and fragmented cobs and kernels. Some cobs have intact kernels and husks, whereas others are small, underdeveloped basal cobs. Also, maize stem fragments were found in abundance. The numerous maize stems in conjunction with the entirely unprocessed ears and basal cobs suggest that entire maize plants were deposited. The same observation can be made of the squash and chile peppers because the seeds of each were found in association with fragments of their fruits. A carbonized cotton textile fragment also was recovered from the same feature. The cloth is composed of Z-spun, S-plied warp and weft elements woven into a twill pattern.

The remains of edible tree fruits were not particularly common in the archaeobotanical assemblage. Actun Nak Beh was the only cave where the carbonized remains of tree fruits from economically significant trees[1] were found, consisting of the pits of nance (*Byrsonima crassifolia*) and the endocarps of the cohune palm (*Attalea cohune*) (Figure 9.5). These remains were recovered from a Late Classic burial located in the cave's entrance at the termination of a causeway leading to the nearby ceremonial center Cahal Uitz Na (Awe and Helmke 1998; Halperin 2002). The possibility that these remains were deposited naturally by animals can be ruled out. Although cohune endocarps were found in other deposits in the entrance, nance pits were only recovered associated with the burial. A more common occurrence of nance pits would be expected had they been a regular aspect of the diets of the animals inhabiting the cave. Furthermore, both nance and avocado (*Persea* cf. *americana*) wood charcoal were found in the same burial, which strengthens the notion that the nance was intentionally deposited and suggests that avocado may have had a similar function, although no actual avocado pits were found.

FIGURE 9.4. Zea mays *(maize) remains from Barton Creek Cave.*

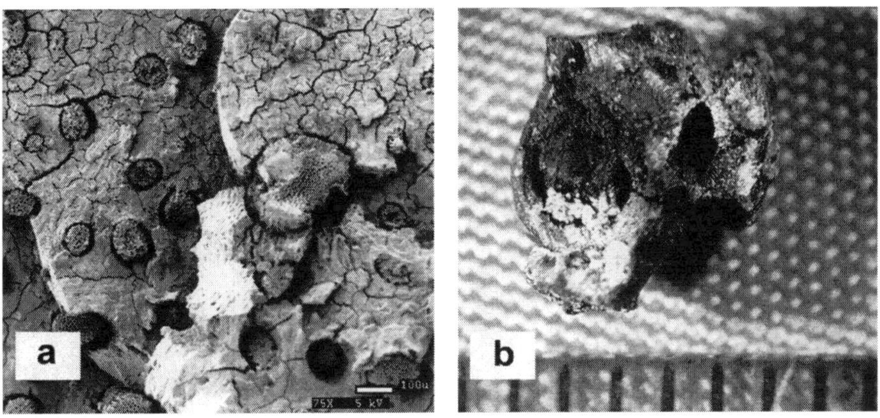

FIGURE 9.5. *Tree fruit remains from Actun Nak Beh. a. SEM of* Attalea cohune *(cohune palm) endocarp; b.* Byrsonima crassifolia *(nance) pit. Marks indicate 1 mm.*

Woods

In addition to the avocado and nance wood charcoal just discussed, several other taxa of wood charcoal were identified in the archaeobotanical assemblage. It is not possible to present all these data here, but some very general statements can be made (see Morehart 2002b and Morehart, Prufer, and Lentz 2003 for more information on the characteristics of the charcoal remains and interpretations of their cultural significance). Pine (*Pinus* sp.) was the most common wood charcoal recovered. All the caves yielded pine remains, and pine was the most ubiquitous taxa of wood charcoal at the intrasite level. A wide variety of hardwoods were identified also, including avocado, nance, *habín* (*Piscidia* sp.), copal (*Protium* cf. *copal.*), *balche'* (*Lonchocarpus* sp.), Spanish cedar (*Cedrela* sp.), malady (*Aspidosperma* sp.), cacao (*Theobroma* sp.), and many others (Morehart 2002b).

INTERPRETATIONS

The discovery of domesticated crops—especially maize—at Actun Chapat, Actun Chechem Ha, and Barton Creek Cave reveals a widespread practice of offering agricultural products in caves. In addition, maize remains have been found in many other caves in the Maya Lowlands, spanning from the Middle Formative period to the Late Classic period, including Cueva de las Pinturas (Brady et al. 1997b) and Naj Tunich (Brady 1989; Brady and Stone 1986) in Petén, Guatemala; Gordon's Cave 3, located near Copán, Honduras (Brady 1995); Cueva del Río Talgua, in northeastern Honduras (Brady et al. 2000); and Mayahak Cab Pek, a rockshelter in the Maya Mountains of Belize (Prufer and Goldstein 1999). It is not surprising that maize is common at these sites. Among the contemporary Maya, maize is believed to have had a subterranean origin (Thompson 1970: 348–354), and iconography from the Classic period often depicts the Maize God emerging from a fissure in the earth's surface (Taube 1985: 175). The belief that maize originated in a cave ties caves with the act of creation and the source of life in Maya mythology. In the Popul Vuh, for instance, humans were made from maize dough, and the Postclassic Mother goddess, Xmucane, ground the maize for humans nine times—a number often associated with the underworld (D. Tedlock 1985).

Domesticated plants found at cave sites in the Maya Lowlands are likely the remnants of rites conducted to appease deities associated with agricultural fertility and, thus, the maintenance of life. Many modern Maya groups hold that caves, *cenotes,* and mountains are the dwelling places of earth deities associated with rain and agriculture, and rituals are conducted at these sacred features to ensure a productive harvest (Alcorn 1984; Cruz Guzmán, Josserand, and Hopkins 1980; Gossen 1974; Redfield and Villa Rojas 1934; Thompson 1930; Vogt 1969, 1976; Wisdom 1940). There is a central belief that to use the products of the earth and maintain agricultural productivity, proper rituals must be made to acquire the earth deities' permission before planting and to repay them for use of their domain after harvest. The contemporary Tzotzil Maya of Zinacantan, located in Highland Mexico, make pilgrimages to the caves and mountains surrounding Zinacantan during maize field ceremonies to communicate with and repay the Earth Lord, who is described as a greedy Ladino in control of rain and all the products of the earth (Vogt 1969: 457; 1976: 17). Among the Yukatek (Redfield and Villa Rojas 1934: 205) and Lacandon (McGee 1990: 7), caves and *cenotes* are dwelling places for *chaaks,* traditional rain deities, and the sixteenth-century Yukatek offered human sacrifices in *cenotes* to appease rain gods (Tozzer 1941: 223).

Examination of the archaeobotanical specimens in conjunction with ethnographic information provides some support for the interpretation that fertility rites were conducted at these caves. There appears to be a preference for offerings of unprocessed, domesticated crops in the caves. This observation is especially salient with the botanical remains from Barton Creek Cave, where maize stalks and cobs with intact husks were recovered. Ethnographic accounts of the ritual use of unprocessed maize are often associated with agricultural rituals. For instance, K'iche' priest-shamans of Momostenango, Guatemala, collect armloads of corn stalks and arrange them around shrines to ask deities for agricultural productivity (B. Tedlock 1982: 80), and the Mam Maya of Highland Guatemala leave dedicatory offerings of roasted ears in the local church for their patron saints (Stadelman 1940: 123).

The symbolism of unprocessed "raw" food can be found in many cultures. Raw food can represent social cooperation for a community of agriculturalists (Firth 1973: 255), suggesting that the communal effort and labor expended in the agricultural cycle are metaphorically bound up in the unprocessed food. Structurally, raw or uncooked food is associated with the realm of "nature," which is in opposition to the realm of "culture" (Levi-Strauss 1969). Because Maya earth deities are associated with nature in contrast to culture (e.g., Redfield and Villa Rojas 1934: 111–116; Vogt 1976: 32), the unprocessed condition of the agricultural products may have symbolized their relationship to Earth Gods.

Interestingly, wood charcoal from *habín* (*Piscidia* sp.) was found in abundance at both Barton Creek Cave and Actun Chapat in association with the remains of cultigens. The modern Yukatek use branches, wood, and bark from this tree during both first fruit rites and the *ch'a chaak*, a traditional rain ceremony (Barrera Marin, Barrera Vasquez, and López Franco 1976; Flores and Kantún Balam 1997; Redfield and Villa Rojas 1934). It is considered a "cold" tree in the Yukatek humoral system because it stays green longer than other trees and often grows near water, making it a symbolically effective plant to use during rain ceremonies.

The immaturity of maize cobs from Actun Chechem Ha might be evidence that young ears of maize were offered as part of first fruit rites. The modern Lacandon and Yukatek (Boremanse 1993: 334; Redfield and Villa Rojas 1934: 127) commonly offer young, "green" ears of maize to earth deities during first fruit ceremonies. The Lacandon believe the Earth Gods must consume these first fruits of harvest before the community can eat. Some Early Classic period maize from Actun Chapat may also have been from young ears, although it is possible that their size reflects the cultivation of maize with smaller ears during this time.

It is of particular interest that no remains of domesticated plants were recovered from Actun Nak Beh. Instead, the discovery of nance and cohune fruits from a burial in the cave's entrance may suggest a qualitative distinction in the type or form of rituals conducted at this cave. A causeway connects the entrance of Actun Nak Beh to the medium-sized ceremonial center Cahal Uitz Na, the dominant organizational

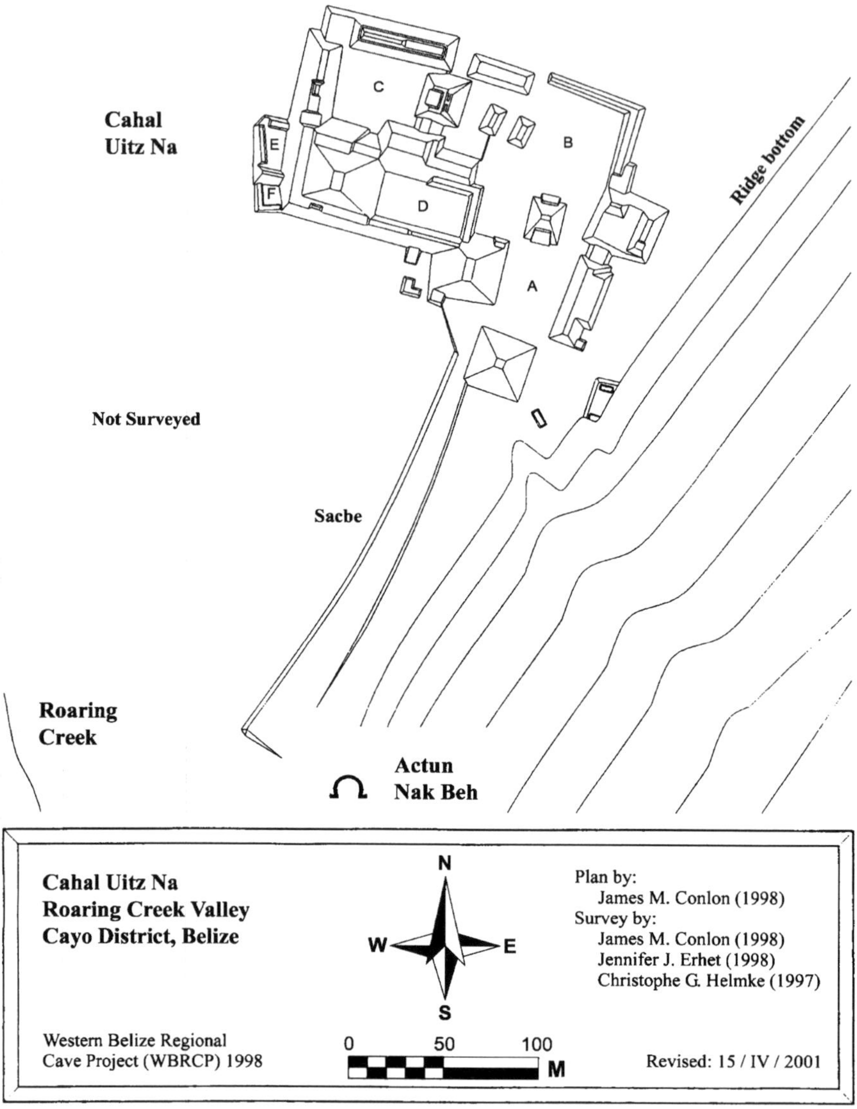

FIGURE 9.6. *Map of Cahal Uitz Na, Cayo District, Belize.*

node for the Late Classic period inhabitants of the Roaring Creek Valley (Awe and Helmke 1998) (Figure 9.6). The direct association of the cave with the surface site suggests that the ideological potency of caves was crucial to the legitimization and maintenance of political authority for the rulers of Cahal Uitz Na (Halperin 2002).

Perhaps socially and ideologically dominant groups at Cahal Uitz Na utilized the causeway and the open space of Actun Nak Beh's entrance for public rituals that symbolically tied the cave with the surface site and provided cosmological justification for the power of Cahal Uitz Na's rulers (Halperin 2002).

Ceremonial events that function to establish socioeconomic and political differences commonly incorporate wealth items or prestige goods. Such objects perceived to be valuable become a source of metaphors for evaluating the people who have access to them (Douglas and Isherwood 1979: 62; Lesure 1999: 24). Although traditional artifactual forms of wealth in ancient Maya society, such as jade and exotic ceramic wares, are not abundant at Actun Nak Beh (Halperin 2002: 125), the botanical food remains from the site can be interpreted as symbols of wealth and power. As with any form of material culture, access to botanical resources and foods can be restricted and controlled by individuals and groups in dominant social, economic, and political positions. The nance, the cohune, and perhaps the avocado remains may be evidence that the rulers of Cahal Uitz Na owned orchards of economically useful trees, although this interpretation must be tempered by the fact that no botanical data are currently available from Cahal Uitz Na itself. Although speculative, their presence in a burial in Actun Nak Beh's entrance might suggest offerings to an ancestral figure (Halperin 2002: 107–108) responsible for establishing sources of economic and political power for the elites at Cahal Uitz Na.

This interpretation does have some basis in the ethnohistoric and iconographic records of the Maya. Bishop Landa recorded that sixteenth-century Yukatek elites maintained orchards of economically useful trees that were an inheritable source of both wealth and prestige (in Tozzer 1941: 64). A more illustrative Classic period example of this practice is found in the iconography of Pakal's tomb at Palenque, where Pakal's ancestors are depicted with economically useful fruit trees (Robertson 1983: figures 181–186). Pakal's father, Kan Bahlum Mo', is associated with a nance tree, and his great-grandmother, Lady Yohl Ik'nal, is associated with an avocado tree. The association between Pakal's ancestors and orchard species metaphorically links these trees to inheritable sources of social, political, and economic power (McAnany 1995: 75; Schele and Mathews 1998: 120–123).

PLANTS AND CAVES IN PERSPECTIVE

A potentially significant pattern observable among the plant remains from the cave sites as presented is the dichotomy between those caves yielding domesticated crops and Actun Nak Beh, where orchard species were recovered in association with a burial. The difference between Actun Nak Beh and the other caves is manifest in other ways as well. Actun Nak Beh is the only cave site investigated that is directly associated with a ceremonial center. The construction of a causeway between Cahal Uitz Na and Actun Nak Beh suggests rulers intentionally appropriated sacred features to legitimize their dominance (Halperin 2002), creating a structured landscape that materialized an ideology (DeMarrais, Castillo, and Earle 1996; Earle

1997: 151–158; cf. Geertz 1973: 127) in which certain groups controlled the forces of nature and life that caves were thought to contain. Actun Chapat, Actun Chechem Ha, and Barton Creek Cave are not directly associated with a ceremonial center. Instead, these caves are located in more "rural" loci in the surrounding valleys and foothills of the Upper Belize Valley.

It is possible that this dichotomy contributed to qualitatively different types of ritual activity such that "rural" caves were the focus of rites conducted toward earth deities and agricultural success, whereas rituals at more "urban" caves, such as Actun Nak Beh, were public performances that achieved a greater articulation with broader hegemonic processes of Maya political systems. This assessment may be parallel to contemporary Maya cosmological beliefs that emphasize structural contrasts between the village or town, the "domesticated" realm of humans and culture, and the surrounding forests, the wild, "undomesticated" realm of nature inhabited by spirits and deities (Alcorn 1984: 86; Redfield and Villa Rojas 1934: 107, 111–116; Vogt 1976: 32).

The dichotomy between "rural" and "urban" caves is a potentially useful model for future research, but it is particularly difficult to document for multiple reasons, and caution must be employed when exploring this avenue not to make large inferential leaps concerning the social statuses of groups that used these caves. Although the archaeological characteristics of Actun Nak Beh are strong evidence that the cave was used and symbolically appropriated by the inhabitants of Cahal Uitz Na, it is more difficult to ascertain the status and sociopolitical affinities of groups that used the other cave sites. Given the incomplete nature of the research conducted at these cave sites and the often problematic ambiguity in obtaining socioeconomic and political insight from archaeological data recovered from caves, it would be premature and misleading to conclude that these caves were used solely by common, politically subordinate peasant farmers simply because they are not associated clearly with a larger site. Without careful study of this question, such a conclusion may create an inaccurate regional picture of cave utilization and may simplify understandings of a complex ritual system in general.

Although there are differences in the types of botanical food items from the caves in this study, domesticated agricultural products versus orchard species, as food offerings they likely served similar symbolic functions. The domesticated cultigens belonged to gods who controlled the forces of nature, and they were offered to these earth deities as symbolic payments to compensate for the use of their domain. The individual interred in the burial at Actun Nak Beh, from which the fruit remains of orchard species were discovered, may have been an ancestral figure associated with the rulers of Cahal Uitz Na (Halperin 2002: 107–108). Although the fruits possibly served as a symbolic metaphor for wealth, power, and dynastic descent, they were ultimately offerings to deified ancestors who were the source of the ruling group's continued wealth and power.

This assessment underscores the likelihood that there were extensive similarities in ancient Maya perceptions of caves and in cave rituals. The belief that caves were associated with creation and that they were dwelling places for powerful deities was probably shared by most of Maya society, although the manner in which this symbolic system was set in motion through rituals varied depending on a number of factors. Even in the case of politically motivated public rites, as proposed for Actun Nak Beh (Halperin 2002), their impact would have been reduced greatly without a wider social audience capable of understanding or at least acknowledging the power of caves. In short, elucidating distinctions in ancient Maya cave utilization that reflect variable social and political conditions on a regional level is a crucial aspect for future investigations in Maya cave archaeology, but it is equally important to document commonalities among cave assemblages that may suggest shared traditions in ritual and symbolic life.

ACKNOWLEDGMENTS

I would like to thank the editors, Dr. James Brady and Dr. Keith Prufer, for inviting me to contribute to this volume. The data for this chapter were collected while I was a member of the Western Belize Regional Cave Project (WBRCP). I am grateful to the project's director, Dr. Jaime Awe, for the opportunity to conduct research and to the Department of Archaeology of Belize for its support. The WBRCP was supported by a grant (to Awe) from the Social Sciences and Humanities Research Council of Canada. The paleoethnobotanical research was partially funded by a grant from the Foundation for the Advancement of Mesoamerican Studies, Inc. (Grant 00097). I would also like to thank Dr. Mary Pohl and Dr. David Lentz for the advice and resources they provided during this study. Finally, thanks to Dr. Mary Glowacki and Christina Halperin for their editorial comments on an earlier draft of this chapter.

NOTES

1. By economically significant trees, I refer to trees that were used for food, construction materials, medicine, or fuel throughout Maya prehistory (see Lentz 1999 for a list of common tree species recovered from Maya archaeological sites). Many trees may have been deliberately cultivated in managed orchards, a practice referred to as arboriculture or tree cropping (see Cliff and Crane 1989; Gómez-Pompa, Salvador Flores, and Aliphat F. 1990; Lentz 1990; McKillop 1994, 1996; Morehart 2002b, 2003; Puleston 1982 for discussions on the significance of arboriculture in Maya society and specific tree species that were likely cultivated). Nance and cohune have complex ethnobotanical histories and have been recovered from Maya archaeological sites from the Formative period to the Colonial period. The fruits of nance are commonly sold in modern markets, and it is cultivated by many Maya groups who eat the raw fruits, make it into a fermented beverage, and use it for medicines (Atran and Ucan Ek' 1999: table 2.2; Berlin, Breedlove, and Raven 1974: 289; Breedlove and Laughlin 1993: 151–152; Roys 1931: 234–235, 306; Wisdom 1940: 62). The sixteenth-century Yukatek Maya cultivated nance trees for the edible fruits and used the bark to tan animal skins (Marcus 1982: 242; Tozzer 1941: 199). The leaves of cohune palms are widely

used as a source of thatch, and the fruits are eaten raw and provide a useful source of cooking oil (Atran and Ucan Ek' 1999: table 2.2; McKillop 1996: 290; McSweeney 1995: 165–168). Commercial trade in the "heart" or *palmito* of the cohune palm, composed of the tree's apical meristem and undeveloped leaves, is a lucrative business (McSweeney 1995: 168–169). Cohune hearts can be eaten raw or cooked and can be processed into wine (Balick 1990: 93; McKillop 1996: 291; McSweeney 1995: table 1), a use that characterizes other neotropical palms such as coyol (*Acrocomia aculeata*) (Balick 1990; Lentz 1990: 185).

REFERENCES CITED

Alcorn, Janis B.

1984 *Huastec Maya Ethnobotany.* University of Texas Press, Austin.

Atran, Scott, and Edilberto Ucan Ek'

1999 Classification of Useful Plants by the Northern Petén Maya (Itzaj). In *Reconstructing Ancient Maya Diet,* ed. Christine D. White, 19–59. University of Utah Press, Salt Lake City.

Awe, Jaime J.

1998 *The Western Belize Regional Cave Project: A Report of the 1997 Field Season,* ed. Jaime J. Awe. Occasional Paper No.1. Department of Anthropology, University of New Hampshire, Durham.

Awe, Jaime J., and Christophe G.B. Helmke

1998 Preliminary Report on the Reconnaissance of Caha Uitz Na, Roaring Creek Valley, Cayo District. In *The Western Belize Regional Cave Project: A Report of the 1997 Field Season,* ed. Jaime J. Awe. Occasional Paper No. 1. Department of Anthropology, University of New Hampshire, Durham.

Balick, Michael J.

1990 Production of Coyol Wine From *Acrocomia mexicana* (Arecaceae) in Honduras. *Economic Botany* 44:84–93.

Barrera Marin, Alfredo, Alfredo Barrera Vazquez, and Rosa María López Franco

1976 *Nomenclatura Etnobotanica Maya: Una Interpretación Taxonómica.* Colección Científica 36. Instituto Nacional de Antropología e Historia, Mexico.

Berlin, Brent, Dennis E. Breedlove, and Peter H. Raven

1974 *Principles of Tzeltal Plant Classification: An Introduction to the Botanical Ethnography of a Mayan-Speaking People of Highland Chiapas.* Academic Press, New York.

Boremanse, Didier

1993 The Faith of the Real People: The Lacandon of Chiapas Rain Forest. In *South and Mesoamerican Spirituality: From the Cult of the Feathered Serpent to the Theology of Liberation,* ed. Gary H. Gossen, 324–351. Crossroad Publishing, New York.

Brady, James E.

1988 Sexual Connotation of Caves in Mesoamerican Ideology. *Mexicon* 10(3):51–55.

1989 An Investigation of Maya Ritual Cave Use With Special Reference to Naj Tunich, Guatemala. Ph.D. Dissertation. Archaeology Program, University of California, Los Angeles.

1995 A Reassessment of the Chronology and Function of Gordon's Cave #3, Copan, Honduras. *Ancient Mesoamerica* 6:29–38.

1997 Settlement Configuration and Cosmology: The Role of Caves at Dos Pilas. *American Anthropologist* 99:602–618.

Brady, James E., and Wendy Ashmore

1999 Mountains, Caves, Water: Ideational Landscapes of the Ancient Maya. In *Archaeologies of Landscape: Contemporary Perspectives,* eds. Wendy Ashmore and A. Bernard Knapp, 124–148. Blackwell Publishers, Oxford.

Brady, James E., Christopher Begley, John Fogarty, Donald J. Stierman, Barbara Luke, and Ann Scott

2000 Talgua Archaeological Project: A Preliminary Assessment. *Mexicon* 22(5):111–123.

Brady, James E., Ann Scott, Irma Rodas, John Fogarty, and Monica Urquizú Sánchez

1997a Glimpses of the Dark Side of the Petexbatun Project: The Petexbatun Regional Cave Survey. *Ancient Mesoamerica* 8:353–364.

Brady, James E., and Andrea Stone

1986 Naj Tunich: Entrance to the Maya Underworld. *Archaeology* 36(6):18–25.

Brady, James E., Gene A. Ware, Barbara Luke, Allan Cobb, John Fogarty, and Beverly Shade

1997b Preclassic Cave Utilization Near Cobanerita, San Benito. *Mexicon* 14(5):91–96.

Breedlove, Dennis E., and Robert M. Laughlin

1993 *The Flowering of Man: A Tzotzil Botany of Zinacantan.* 2 vols. Smithsonian Contributions to Anthropology, No. 35. Smithsonian Institution Press, Washington, D.C.

Camacho Uribe, Daniel

1988 *La Madera: estudio anatómico y catálogo de especies Mexicanas.* Colección Científica 168, Instituto Nacional de Antropología e Historia, Mexico.

Carreras, Raquel, and Roger Dechamps

1995 *Anatomía de la Madera de 157 especies forestales que Crecen en Cuba y sus usos tecnológicos, históricos y culturales.* Musée Royal de l'Afrique Centrale, Tervuren, Belgium.

Cliff, Maynrad B., and Cathy Crane

1989 Changing Maya Subsistence Economy at a Late Preclassic Maya Community. In *Prehistoric Maya Economies of Belize,* eds. Patricia A. McAnany and Barry L. Isaac, 295–324. Research in Economic Anthropology, Vol. 4. JAI Press, Greenwich.

Cruz Guzmán, Ausencio, Kathryn Josserand, and Nicholas A. Hopkins

1980 The Cave of Don Juan. In *Third Palenque Round Table,* ed. Merle Greene Robertson, 116–123. University of Texas Press, Austin.

DeMarrais, Elizabeth, Luis Jaime Castillo, and Timothy Earle

1996 Ideology, Materialization and Power Strategies. *Current Anthropology* 37:15–31.

Détienne, Pierre, and Paulette Jacquet

1983 *Atlas d'identification des Bois de l'Amazonie et des Régions Voisines.* Centre Technique Forestier Tropical, Nogent-sur-Marne, France.

Douglas, Mary, and Baron Isherwood
1979 *The World of Goods.* Basic Books, New York.

Earle, Timothy
1997 *How Chiefs Come to Power: The Political Economy in Prehistory.* Stanford University Press, Stanford.

Firth, Raymond
1973 *Symbols: Public and Private.* Cornell University Press, Ithaca.

Flores, José Salvador, and Jesús Kantún Balam
1997 Importance of Plants in the Ch'a Chaak Maya Ritual in the Peninsula of Yucatan. *Journal of Ethnobiology* 17:97–108.

Geertz, Clifford
1973 Ethos, Worldview, and the Analysis of Sacred Symbols. In *The Interpretation of Cultures: Selected Essays by Clifford Geertz,* ed. Clifford Geertz, 126–141. Basic Books, New York

Gómez-Pompa, Arturo, José Salvador Flores, and Mario Aliphat F.
1990 The Sacred Cacao Groves of the Maya. *Latin American Antiquity* 1:247–257.

Gossen, Gary H.
1974 *Chamulas in the World of the Sun: Time and Space in a Maya Oral Tradition.* Harvard University Press, Cambridge.

Halperin, Christina T.
2002 Caves, Ritual, and Power: Investigations at Actun Nak Beh, Cayo District, Belize. Master's Thesis. Department of Anthropology, Florida State University, Tallahassee.

Helmke, Christophe G.B.
1999 Molded-Carved Vases as Indicators of the Social Status of Cave Users in the Terminal Classic. Paper presented at the 64th Annual Meeting of the Society for American Archaeology, Chicago.

Lentz, David L.
1990 *Acrocomia mexicana:* Palm of the Ancient Mesoamericans. *Journal of Ethnobiology* 10:183–194.
1999 Plant Resources of the Ancient Maya: The Paleoethnobotanical Evidence. In *Reconstructing Ancient Maya Diet,* ed. Christine D. White, 3–18. University of Utah Press, Salt Lake City.

Lesure, Richard
1999 On the Genesis of Value in Early Hierarchical Societies. In *Material Symbols: Culture and Economy in Prehistory,* ed. Jon Robb, 23–55. Occasional paper No. 26. Center for Archaeological Investigations, Southern Illinois University, Carbondale.

Levi-Strauss, Claude
1969 *The Raw and the Cooked.* University of Chicago Press, Chicago.

MacLeod, Barbara, and Dennis Puleston
1978 Pathways Into Darkness: The Search for the Road to Xibalba. In *Tercera Mesa Redonda de Palenque,* Vol. 4, eds. Merle Greene Robertson and Donnan Call Jeffers, 71–77. Herald Press, Monterey.

Marcus, Joyce

1982 The Plant World of the Sixteenth and Seventeenth Century Lowland Maya. In *Maya Subsistence: Studies in Memory of Dennis E. Puleston,* ed. Kent V. Flannery. Academic Press, New York.

McAnany, Patricia A.

1995 *Living With the Ancestors: Kinship and Kingship in Ancient Maya Society.* University of Texas Press, Austin.

McGee, R. Jon

1990 *Life, Ritual, and Religion Among the Lacandon Maya.* Wadsworth Publications, Belmont.

McKillop, Heather I.

1994 Ancient Maya Tree Cropping: A Viable Subsistence Adaptation for the Island Maya. *Ancient Mesoamerica* 5:129–140.

1996 Prehistoric Maya Use of Native Palms: Archaeobotanical and Ethnobotanical Evidence. In *The Managed Mosaic: Ancient Maya Agriculture and Resource Use,* ed. Scott L. Fedick, 278–294. University of Utah Press, Salt Lake City.

McSweeney, Kendra

1995 The Cohune Palm (*Orbignya cohune,* Arecaceae) in Belize: A Survey of Uses. *Economic Botany* 49:162–171.

Miksicek, Charles H.

1991 The Economy and Ecology of Cuello. In *Cuello: An Early Maya Community in Belize,* ed. Norman Hammond, 70–97. Cambridge University Press, Cambridge.

Miksicek, Charles H., Robert M. Bird, Barbara Pickersgill, Sara Donaghey, Juliette Cartwright, and Norman Hammond

1981 Preclassic Lowland Maize From Cuello, Belize. *Nature* 289:56–59.

Morehart, Christopher T.

2001 Plants of the Underworld: Ritual Plant Use in Ancient Maya Cave Ceremonies. Paper presented at the 100th Annual Meeting of the American Anthropological Association, Washington, D.C.

2002a A Paleoethnobotanical Perspective on Ancient Maya Cave Utilization. Paper presented at the 67th Annual Meeting of the Society for American Archaeology, Denver.

2002b Ancient Maya Ritual Cave Utilization: A Paleoethnobotanical Perspective. Master's Thesis. Department of Anthropology, Florida State University, Tallahassee.

2003 Paleoethnobotany at Avila. In *Belize Postclassic Project 2002: Investigation of the Shore Settlements of Progresso Lagoon and San Estevan,* eds. Josalyn M. Ferguson, Maxine H. Oland, and Marilyn Masson, 126–151. Occasional Publication No. 9. Institute of Mesoamerican Studies, University at Albany–SUNY, Albany

Morehart, Christopher T., Keith M. Prufer, and David L. Lentz

2003 Wood of the Gods: The Ritual Use of Pine in Ancient Maya Society. Paper presented at the 68th Annual Meeting of the Society for American Archaeology, Milwaukee, WI.

Moyes, Holley
2001 The Sweatbath in the Cave: A Modified Passage in Chechem Ha Cave, Belize. Paper presented at the 66th Annual Meeting of the Society for American Archaeology, New Orleans.

Pohl, Mary D.
1983 Maya Ritual Faunas: Vertebrate Remains From Burials, Caches, Caves, and Cenotes in the Maya Lowlands. In *Civilization in the Ancient Americas,* eds. Richard M. Levanthal and Allan L. Kolata, 55–103. University of New Mexico Press, Albuquerque.

Pohl, Mary D., and John D. Pohl
1983 Ancient Maya Cave Rituals. *Archaeology* 36(3):28–32, 50–51.

Prufer, Keith Malcolm
2002 Communities, Caves, and Ritual Specialists: A Study of Sacred Space in the Maya Mountains of Southern Belize. Ph.D. Dissertation. Department of Anthropology, Southern Illinois University, Carbondale.

Prufer, Keith M., and David J. Goldstein
1999 Report on Rockshelter Excavations at Mayahak Cab Pek and Mohibal Kanchi 1998 Field Season. In *Archaeological Research in the Southern Maya Mountains: Report of the 1997 and 1998 Field Season of the Maya Mountains Archaeological Project.* Report on file. Department of Archaeology, Government of Belize.

Puleston, Dennis E.
1982 The Role of Ramón in Maya Subsistence. In *Maya Subsistence: Studies in Memory of Dennis E. Puleston,* ed. Kent V. Flannery, 353–364. Academic Press, New York.

Redfield, Robert, and Alfonso Villa Rojas
1934 *Chan Kom: A Maya Village.* University of Chicago Press, Chicago.

Reichert, Edward T.
1913 *The Differentiation and Specificity of Starches in Relation to Genera, Species, etc.* Chapman, London.

Rissolo, Dominique A.
2001 Ancient Maya Cave Use in the Yalahau Region, Northern Quintana Roo, Mexico. Ph.D. Dissertation. Department of Anthropology, University of California, Riverside.

Robertson, Merle Greene
1983 *The Sculpture of Palenque, Volume 1: The Temple of the Inscriptions.* Princeton University Press, Princeton.

Roys, Ralph L.
1931 *The Ethno-Botany of the Maya.* University of Chicago Press, Chicago.

Rust, William F., and Barbara Leyden
1994 Evidence of Maize Use at Early and Middle Preclassic La Venta Olmec Sites. In *Corn and Culture in the Prehistoric New World,* eds. S. Johannessen and C. A. Hastorf, 181–201. Westview Press, Boulder, CO.

Schele, Linda, and Peter Mathews
1998 *The Code of Kings: The Language of Seven Sacred Maya Temples and Tombs.* Scribner, New York.

Stadelman, Raymond

1940 Maize Cultivation in Northwestern Guatemala. In *Contributions to American Anthropology and History,* Vol. 4, No. 33, pp. 83–265. Carnegie Institution, Washington, D.C.

Stone, Andrea J.

1995 *Images From the Underworld: Naj Tunich and the Tradition of Maya Cave Painting.* University of Texas Press, Austin.

1997 Precolumbian Cave Utilization in the Maya Area. In *Human Use of Caves,* eds. Clive Bonsall and Christopher Tolan-Smith, 201–206. BAR International Series No. 667. Archaeopress, Oxford.

Taube, Karl A.

1985 The Classic Maya Maize God: A Reappraisal. In *Fifth Palenque Roundtable, 1983,* ed. Virginia M. Fields, 171–181. Pre-Columbian Art Research Institute, San Francisco.

Tedlock, Barbara

1982 *Time and the Highland Maya.* University of New Mexico Press, Albuquerque.

Tedlock, Dennis

1985 *The Popol Vuh: The Mayan Book of the Dawn of Life.* Simon and Schuster, New York.

Thompson, J. Eric S.

1930 Ethnology of the Mayas of Southern and Central British Honduras. *Field Museum of Natural History, Anthropological Series* 17:23–213.

1970 *Maya History and Religion.* University of Oklahoma Press, Norman.

Tozzer, Alfred M.

1941 *Landa's Relación de las Cosas de Yucatan.* Papers of the Peabody Museum of American Archaeology and Ethnology, Vol. 18. Harvard University, Cambridge.

Turner, Victor

1969 *The Ritual Process: Structure and Anti-Structure.* Aldine, Chicago.

Vogt, Evon Z.

1969 *Zinacantan: A Maya Community in the Highlands of Chiapas.* Belknap Press of Harvard University, Cambridge.

1976 *Tortillas for the Gods: A Symbolic Analysis of Zinacantan Rituals.* Harvard University Press, Cambridge.

Wisdom, Charles

1940 *The Chorti Indians of Guatemala.* University of Chicago Press, Chicago.

Chapter Ten

The Sweatbath in the Cave

A Modified Passage in Chechem Ha Cave, Belize

by Holley Moyes

In Mesoamerica a cognitive link between sweatbaths and caves has been noted by scholars (Child 2002; Gossen 1999: 16; Groark 1997: 23; Heyden 1976: 19–20; Houston 1996: 142; Vogt and Stuart 2005; Webster 2001). The reasons both spaces are similarly conceptualized may be that they are dark, enclosed, and womblike. Using ethnohistoric, ethnographic, and archaeological examples, this chapter demonstrates that in the Mesoamerican mind, both caves and sweatbaths are associated with generation, regeneration, fertility, and birth. Evidence from Chechem Ha Cave, an ancient Maya ritual cave site located in western Belize near the Guatemala border, suggests that this association dates to the Late Preclassic period (120 B.C.–A.D. 250) or possibly earlier. At Chechem Ha, morphological modifications made to a crawl space in the dark zone of the cave resemble the architectural features of ancient Maya sweatbaths from surface sites and fit descriptions of modern sweatbaths from ethnographic reports. This is the first recognized instance of a ritual sweatbath deep within a cave.

This study begins with a brief review of ethnographic and ethnohistoric examples of the function and meaning of sweatbaths in Mesoamerica. To create expectations of the morphology and artifact assemblage of a sweatbath, examples from the archaeological record are presented. Finally, the sweatbath feature located inside Chechem Ha Cave and its contents are described. The fact that the sweatbath is located within an ancient Maya ritual cave suggests that it was designed for ritual use, which is not surprising considering that ethnographically, sweatbaths are often used for ceremonial purposes. I argue that it is likely that rituals performed within the sweatbath in the cave related to earth deities.

THE ETHNOGRAPHY OF SWEATBATHING IN MESOAMERICA

Sweatbathing is an ancient indigenous custom once present throughout most of Central America (Driver and Massey 1957: 314, figure 107; Groark 1997: 6; Lopatin 1960: 977–979). The ethnohistorian Francisco Clavijero (1945: 349) notes that sweatbaths were used for hygienic, therapeutic, and ritual purposes—traditions that have continued to the present. Sweatbathing is practiced today primarily among Maya people located in the highland regions of Chiapas and Guatemala (Cresson 1938: 101–102; Groark 1997: 8; Houston 1996: 138; Tedlock 1987: 1073–1074). Barbara Tedlock (1987: 1074) notes that in Momostenango, Guatemala, sweatbaths are used for hygiene, massage, ritual purification, and birthing. Gary Gossen (1999: 15–17) notes the similarity between sweatbaths and caves and provides ethnographic data from his own experiences in a Chamula sweatbath. Gossen describes the sweatbath as "a dark, low rectangular cave slightly longer than the human body," that could hold two or three people and had just enough headroom to allow occupants to sit up. Near the door was a stone-lined hearth. Once the space was heated, the fire was extinguished and the door closed, water was poured on the rocks to create steam, and participants laid down and beat themselves with leafy branches. Sometimes sweatbaths were used for routine bathing, but more typically they were used for ritual or therapeutic purposes such as postpartum or postmenstrual bathing. They could also be used for ritual cleansing of patients in preparation for curing ceremonies or for ceremonial purification of those about to assume ritual responsibilities.

The use of sweatbaths in birthing practices is common throughout Mesoamerica. In Central Mexico ethnohistorians describe the use of sweatbaths and their relationship to childbirth and fertility (Clavijero 1945: 349; Moedano 1977: 11). Both Diego Durán (1994: 41) and Clavijero (1804: 250) report that among the Aztecs, women sat in sweatbaths for five or six days following delivery. According to Fray Bernardino de Sahagún, steam bathing was associated with particular deities and rituals and was under the auspices of the creatrix goddesses Toci (Teteoinnan) or Yoalticitl but was sometimes related to another female goddess, Tlazolteotl (the filth eater) (Groark 1997: 17; Miller and Taube 1993: 160). Toci was associated with female fertility, pregnancy, and childbirth and was worshipped by midwives.

In the Maya area the use of sweatbaths by women during and after childbirth has been noted by a number of ethnographers (Groark 1997: 50–54; Laughlin 1969: 187; Tax and Hinshaw 1969: 81; Tedlock 1987: 1074; Villa Rojas 1969a: 207; 1969b: 242; Wagley 1969: 66). In his detailed study, Kevin Groark (1997: 50–54) reports that in the central highlands village of Santo Tomás Oxchuc, Chiapas, both mother and child are given postpartum steam baths to prevent illness as a result of cold. Many Oxchuqueros believe the ancestors created the steam bath specifically to protect women during high-risk periods such as those associated with childbirth. Groark suggests that physiological changes in temperature may have initiated the practice of sweatbathing, since women may experience chills and uncontrollable shivering soon after delivery.

Steven Houston (1996) suggests that among the ancient Maya the connection between birth and sweatbaths dates back to the Classic period. He argues that the small inner structures located in the interior of the temples of the Palenque Cross Group were symbolic sweatbaths that represented the birthplace or origin of the gods. His interpretation is based on the inscriptions associated with the temples that refer to the buildings as sweatbaths related to the births of the principal deities.

THE ASSOCIATIONS OF CAVES WITH SWEATBATHS

Direct associations between sweatbaths and caves are found in the ethnohistoric and ethnographic literature and in the archaeological record. For instance, in the Codex Nuttall, figure 16a illustrates a temple within a mountain that is entered through a cave portal (Nuttall 1903). Doris Heyden (1981: 19) interprets the figure as a steam bath inside a cave.

Gary Gossen (1999: 15–17) specifically notes the similarity between sweatbaths and caves in the highland Chiapas town of Chamula. One of the most well-known ethnographic examples of the association occurs at the community's Festival of Games (Bricker 1973: 114). As part of this yearly renewal festival, villagers visit a small cave with water emerging from it. The feature is referred to as a "sweatbath" because of its morphology, which is long and narrow like a steam bath. Those who participate in the festival deposit three stones or potsherds at the entrance as tribute to earth deities, for as Bricker notes, "if they do not offer three stones to the cave, they will die."

Mesoamerican caves are well-known mythological places of origin from which humans were thought to emerge (Brady 1989: 40; Heyden 1975; LaFarge 1947: 127–128; Nielson and Brady n.d.; Taube 1986; Thompson 1970: 314, 316; 1975: xxxiii; Vogt 1969: 375). This resonates with common beliefs about sweatbaths that relate to female fertility. Sahagún (1969: vi, 118, 151) reports that among the Aztecs, women referred to their vaginas as "caves," indicating that children were created in human caves. When a woman was about to give birth, the steam bath, or *temazcalli,* to which she was taken was referred to as *xochicalli,* or "house of flowers," since flowers were regarded as a sexual symbol related to the uterus. According to

Sahagún, because it was a place of birth, the sweatbath represented an artificial cave.

Working among the Mixe, Ralph Beals (1939: 431; 1945: 86) reported a mountain shrine barren women used to petition for children. The shrine was located in a cavity in a natural rock that morphologically resembled a sweatbath in miniature. A pile of rocks was used to resemble the fire chamber. Fires had been built in the chamber, and branches and shrubbery were laid on top. Cornhusks were located inside the structure, and evidence of turkey sacrifice was present around the entrance.

SEXUAL CONNOTATIONS

Both caves and sweatbaths have sexual connotations. James Brady (1988) has called attention to the eroticism associated with ancient caves throughout Mesoamerica. This is explicitly expressed in cave art, such as the painting of the copulating couple found in the ancient Maya cave site of Naj Tunich (Brady 1989: 47, figure 3.2; Stone 1995: 100, plate 12) and in the painting of a jaguar copulating with a human in the Olmec cave Oxtotitlan (Grove 1973: 133). Expressions of sexuality are also stated in modern mythology concerning caves. The Tzotzil H'ik'al, or Black-man (similar to the Central Mexican *pingo*), is a hypersexual being with a six-foot-long penis who resides in a cave. If impregnated by the Blackman, women die from over-menstruation or multiple births of offspring that come to term in three days (Blaffer 1972: 20,117). Among the Tzotzil Maya, the word for cave, *c'en*, is a humorous metaphor for the vagina (Bricker 1973: 65–66, 150–151; Laughlin 1975: 132).

Similarly, sweatbaths are also associated with sexuality and have served as discreet locations for illicit sex among the Mam (Wagley 1949: 35), the Quiché (Carmack 1979: 361–367), the Mixtec (Parsons 1936: note 40), the Tzeltal, and the Tzotzil (Groark 1996: 56, footnote 1). In a personal communication to Kevin Groark (1997: 16), J. Rus reported that "the Chamula Tzotzil tell a number of hilarious stories about old male curers (*j'ilol*) who prescribe the steambath for their nubile young patients, then take advantage of them as they swoon in the heat. It is even said that you can tell when a woman has lost her attractiveness, because the *j'ilol* no longer insists on accompanying her to the steambath."

Although sweatbaths are intimately associated with the female aspect in Central Mexico, J. Eric Thompson (1970: 246) argues that the earth goddess/patroness of childbirth cult was temporally sensitive. He believes it was widespread in the Preclassic period, but among the later Maya it gave way to cults of the Young Maize God as well as the god Itzamna, who was deified as the earth reptile. Groark (1997: 20–23) reports that in the Maya Highlands, the steam bath may fall under the auspices of either a male or a female deity. The Tzeltal and Tzotzil consider the steam bath to be "owned" by either the Earth Lord, described as a male agricultural deity, or the Holy Earth, a female agricultural/lunar deity. In Chamula, the Sun-Christ deity, possessing curative powers, is said to manifest as fire in the sweatbath. Two nearby caves are referred to as "steam bath cave," or *pus ch'en* and *pus ch'entik*. One is thought to have been used by the people of the previous creation, and the other is thought to be a representation of an underworld steam bath located in the belly of a turtle. To burn their sins away in the heat, souls must pass through the steam bath/cave after death.

As Groark (1997: 23) has suggested, sweatbaths are metaphorically associated with caves because both reference the generative powers residing in the interior of the earth. At Santiago Atitlán, Guatemala, the Mam or Maximón, an Earth Lord who is the old god of transformative power, is thought to live in an underground sweatbath (Tarn and Prechtel 1997: 283–284). The Mam works at night and has dominion over sexual affairs and love, causes crops to grow, and forms children in the womb. His heat is said to cook them into existence, and he is considered the "road-opener" during childbirth (Groark 1997: 26). At one time the Mam figure was kept in a high niche in the wall of the church at Santiago Atitlán, which was referred to as a cave containing a sweatbath. The cave was thought to be the entrance to a hole that led underground and through which his washing water was poured (Tarn and Prechtel 1986: 184). In his underworld steam bath the Mam was thought to cohabitate with a harem of hypersexual women. Atitecos believe prostitutes in Guatemala City keep an image of the Mam in their rooms and call him "their best friend." It is also said that women who sin ask the Mam to take them to his underworld sweatbath when they die.

SWEATBATH MORPHOLOGY

Sweatbaths with masonry construction (Figure 10.1) are found throughout the Maya area from the Preclassic (Andrews IV and Andrews V 1980: 30; Hammond and Bauer 2001) through the Late Postclassic periods (Ichon 1977). The best-preserved example is the Classic period sweatbath located at the site of Ceren in El Salvador (Sheets 1992: 97–102). Although Frank Cresson (1938: 101) believes sweatbaths were not present among the Maya of Belize, a rare example was excavated at the site of Buenavista (Ball 1993: 56, figure 48), located near Chechem Ha Cave, and an Early Preclassic example was discovered at Cuello (Hammond and Bauer 2001). Interestingly, subterranean sweatbaths, morphologically similar to caves, are located at the sites of San Antonio in Chiapas (Agrinier 1969: 16–27) and at Agua Tibia in the southeastern Guatemalan Highlands (Alcina Franch 1981; Alcina Franch, Ciudad Ruiz, and Ponce de León 1980: 93–98; Ciudad Ruiz 1984: 109–112).

In his survey of ancient sweatbaths, Houston (1996: 143) concluded that they all have basically the same dimensions, although they vary in shape, from roughly square or circular to long and narrow. In Houston's sample the average width is 3.14 m, length is 3.34 m, and height is 2 m. The smallest structure in the sample is found at Quiriqua and measures 55 cm in width by 3.04 m in length by 1 m in height (Morley 1935: 141–142, figure 38a; Satterthwaite 1952: 25). The largest is from the

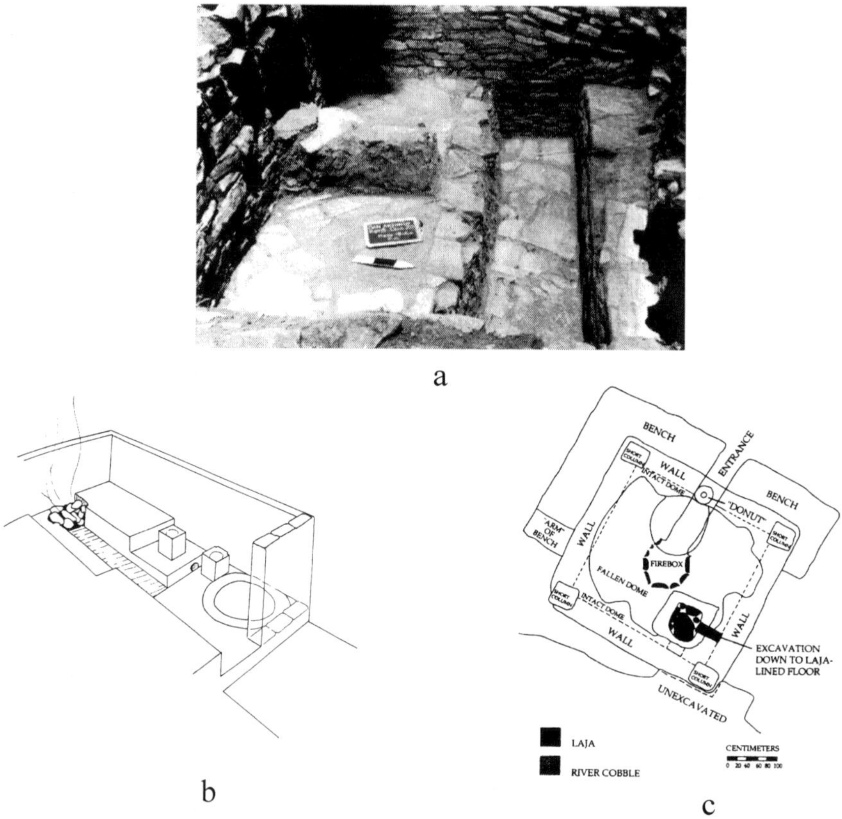

FIGURE 10.1. *Ancient sweatbaths with the bench/trench architectural feature. a. San Antonio Chiapas (Agrinier 1969: 22, figure 35), b. Los Cimientos–Chustum (redrawn from Ichon 1977: 207), and c. Cerén (Sheets 1992: 98, figure 6-7).*

site of San Antonio in Chiapas, Mexico, which measures 3 m by 10 m by 1.6 m (Agrinier 1966: 29–30).

Linton Satterthwaite (1952: 20) lists a number of architectural features common to ancient sweathouses. At a minimum, they can be expected to have small dimensions and low ceilings, a system of steam production such as a hearth or hot surface on which water will vaporize, and a draught hole. They may also feature a water drainage system or have benches running parallel to a sunken drain. In his ethnographic survey, Cresson (1938: 93) reported that the drains did not necessarily carry the water out the door but could form a sinkhole for the water. In their simplest form, the drains were made of dirt through which water could seep.

Benches lining the central drain are found not only at the Piedras Negras sweatbaths but also at Buenavista (Ball 1993: figure 48), San Antonio Chiapas

(Agrinier 1969: 22, figure 35), Los Cimientos–Chustum (Ichon 1977: 207), and Ceren (Sheets 1992: 98, figure 6-7). Although not every Mesoamerican sweatbath exhibits this feature, the bench/trench combination is a defining characteristic of sweatbath structures.

Although they are most commonly found at surface sites, at least one sweatbath feature has been located in a natural rural environment (Webster 2001). A small construction built into a rockshelter on the periphery of Piedras Negras, Guatemala, was identified as a sweatbath. The feature was small and rectangular, measuring 1.4 m by 1.9 m, and had a red-stained plaster floor. Three crudely built walls set in mud mortar bounded the rectangular feature, and the back of the shelter functioned as the fourth wall. The heating source appeared to be burned calcified rocks located in the corner. Hypothetically, water would be poured on the hot rocks to create steam. A circular mirror and five marine shells were found within the structure.

THE SWEATBATH IN THE CAVE

The Western Belize Regional Cave Project (WBRCP), under the direction of Dr. Jaime Awe, has been conducting investigations at Chechem Ha Cave since 1998.

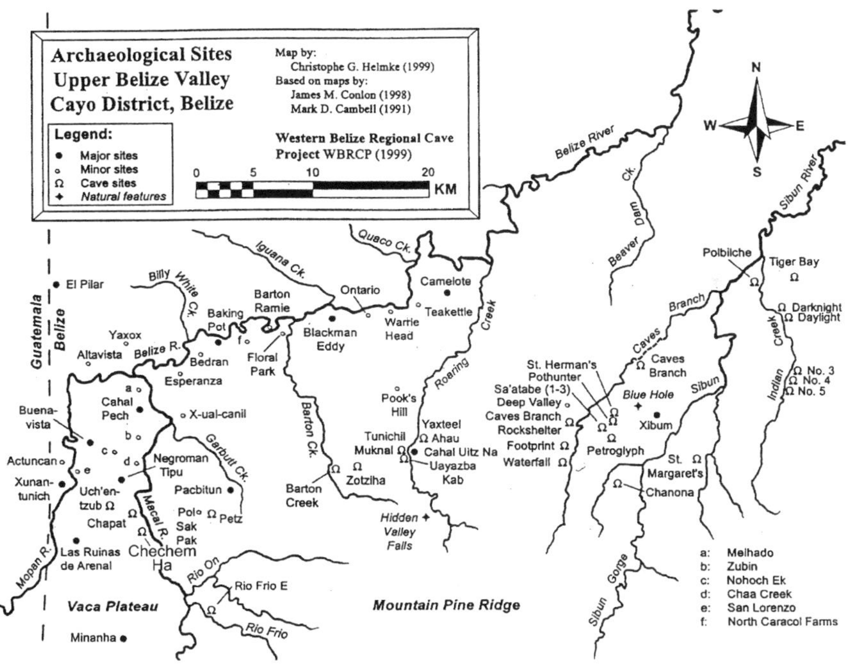

FIGURE 10.2. *Map of western Belize showing location of Chechem Ha Cave (courtesy of WBRCP).*

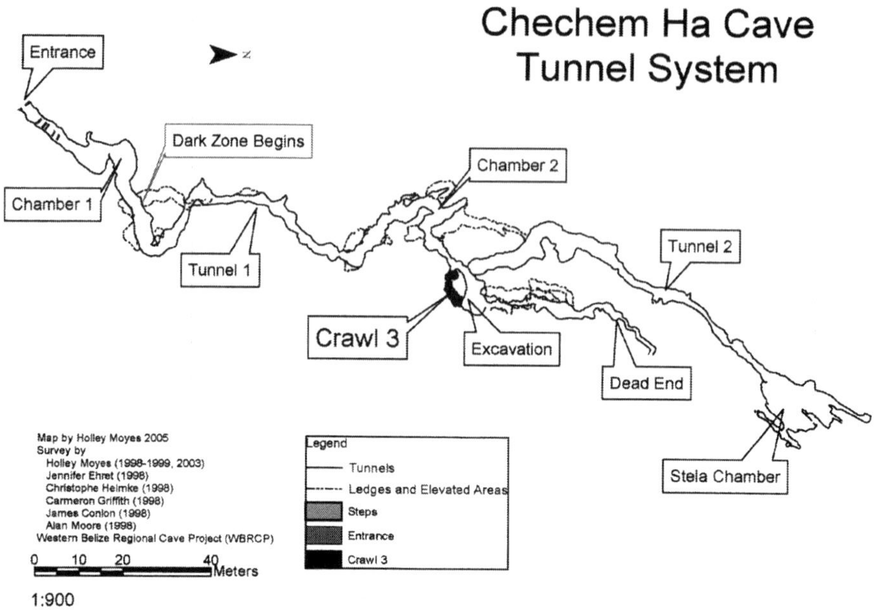

FIGURE 10.3. *Map of Chechem Ha Cave system illustrating location of Crawl 3.*

Chechem Ha (a.k.a. Vaca Falls Cave) is located in the Cayo District of western Belize on the western bank of the Macal River upstream from San Ignacio Town (Awe, Gibbs, and Griffith 2005; Figure 10.2). Positioned on a steep hill, the site can be classified as a dry cave because of the lack of an interior water source. The main tunnel is 237 m long and bifurcates 134 m from the cave entrance (Figure 10.3). One passage leads to a dead end, and the other descends to a large cathedral-like chamber designated the Stela Chamber because of the presence of a miniature stela (Awe, Gibbs, and Griffith 2005). Artifact deposits are located along the floor of the main tunnel and on eleven high ledges ranging from 3 to 7 m above the passage floor. Additionally, artifacts were found in six elevated side passages that branch off the main tunnel. Four of these passages are narrow and have low ceiling heights. These were designated as "crawls" because it is impossible to stand up in them. Crawl 3 is the focus of this chapter. It is unique in that it exhibits both morphological modifications and a hearth feature, which, coupled with the artifact assemblage, suggests that the area was used by the ancient Maya as a ritual sweatbath.

Crawl 3 is located deep within the dark zone of the cave, 154 m from the entrance. The crawl is 2.5 m above the tunnel floor. It is an L-shaped space oriented on an east/west axis, running roughly parallel to the main tunnel and opening into the tunnel system at both ends (Figure 10.4). The western end of the crawl makes a sharp turn and culminates in a vertical drop. The easiest access to the crawl is via

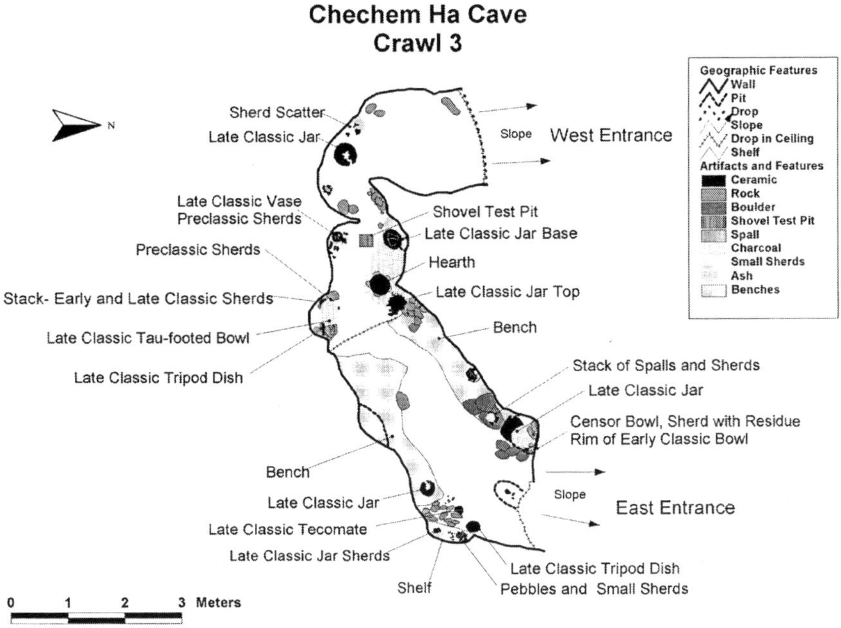

FIGURE 10.4. *Detail map of Crawl 3.*

the east entrance. The space measures 9 m in length, and its width ranges between 0.55 m and 2.75 m. The ceiling height is between 0.70 m and 1.2 m. These dimensions are most similar to the sweatbath at the site of San Antonio reported by Pierre Agrinier (1966: 29–30).

A 3-m-long area was modified by the Maya to produce low walls lining both sides of the Crawl 3 passage and a central trench. The width between the low walls of the trench is 0.50 m at its narrowest and 1 m at the widest point. The walls on both sides of the trench measure between 0.35 m and 1 m in width, with an average height of 0.45 m. The top surfaces are flat and resemble benches. The floor of the entire passage is covered with well-compacted brownish-yellow sediment, white marl, and charcoal. The walls consist of the same brownish-yellow sediment but are loosely compacted. Vertical cuts in the sediment matrix along the side of the walls are the result of the excavation of the central trench. A large pile of similarly colored sediment lies against the wall on the tunnel floor below the eastern entrance. An elemental analysis of sediments from Crawl 3 and the pile on the tunnel floor was carried out. Results suggested that the two are very similar sediments and confirmed that the pile was backdirt from the ancient excavation.

Crawl 3 is similar to sweatbaths found in other archaeological contexts, not only in size but also in morphology. Note the morphological similarity between the

FIGURE 10.5. *(Top) Modified area in Crawl 3 photographed from the east entrance (photo by the author). (Bottom) Reconstructed sweatbath from Piedras Negras (photo courtesy of Stephen Houston).*

low walls or benches in Crawl 3 as compared with the entrance to a Classic period sweatbath from the site of Piedras Negras (Figure 10.5). The low walls in Crawl 3 correspond to the benches present in the masonry structure in the Piedras Negras example, and the center trench is analogous to the central drain.

THE ARTIFACTS

Artifact concentrations are located at the eastern entrance and in the center of the passage. The portion of the tunnel lined with the low walls or benches previously discussed separates these two areas. Beginning on the north side of the crawl, adjacent to the eastern entrance, ceramic vessels and sherds are positioned in and around fist-sized stones arranged in a circle abutting the north wall. A Late Classic jar with a kill hole at the base and exhibiting exterior charring sits in the center of the circle. Charcoal flecks are present in the sediment matrix. Resting on top of the stones are a censor bowl with a heavily blackened interior, a jar sherd exhibiting a fire-blackened exterior surface, and a large potsherd. Adhering to the interior of the jar sherd is a caked, hardened, black greasy resin containing starch grains of *Zea mays* (maize) (Morehart 2002: 174). The large sherd was identified as an Early Classic deep-sided bowl (Joseph Ball 1998: personal communication). Several cobbles, small sherds, and a limestone spall are located against the wall. Spalls are chips or fragments removed from rock, usually by weathering and exfoliation (Gary, McFee, and Wolf 1972: 677). They are often found accompanying other offerings in caves and in many cases resemble potsherds in size and shape. Three charred jar sherds are stacked on a large rock on the east edge of the stone circle. To the east of the circle is a stack of spalls interspersed with sherds. This stacking creates a "sandwich-like" deposit.

On the south wall, adjacent to the east entrance, is a small natural shelf. Clustered at the eastern entrance are thirty pebbles and a number of small sherds (Figure 10.6a). The rocks are not limestone, are similar in size (2–3 cm), and are smoothed, which suggests that they were collected in a river or streambed. To the west of the stones are fifteen small sherds and a spall. Next to the cluster of sherds is a stack of seven Late Classic jar sherds sitting on top of a scatter of charcoal and ash. Adjacent to the shelf are half of a Late Classic, bichrome tecomate (gourd-shaped vessel) and a pile of fist-sized stones. A Late Classic jar in an inverted position with a kill hole and charring at the base sits next to the wall, along with a pile of cobbles and a spall. A Late Classic tripod dish (Ishihara 2000) sat below the shelf but was removed by the former Belize Department of Archaeology (now the Belize Institute of Archaeology). The geometric design on the interior of the vessel is faded, and all three feet are missing (Figure 10.6b).

In the midsection of the tunnel, adjacent to the western end of the low walls or benches, a dome in the ceiling creates an area with enough head room to allow visitors to sit upright. A hearth is situated on the north wall. It consists of a fully intact, Late Classic, wide-mouthed jar resting on five smoothed river cobbles (Figure

FIGURE 10.6. *a. Western entrance to Crawl 3. Black arrow points to water-worn pebbles and sherds on natural shelf on left. Tecomate sherd and pile of stones pictured in foreground. b. The tripod dish originally sat in the open space to the left of the north arrow (photos by the author).*

FIGURE 10.7. *(Top) View of hearth area facing east. Hearth is jar on far right behind north arrow. (Bottom) River cobbles located beneath jar surrounded by ash and charcoal (photos by the author).*

10.7). The exterior base of the jar is heavily charred, as are the cobbles on which it rests. The interior surface of the jar exhibits no apparent traces of residue. Beneath the vessel is a concentration of charcoal and ash 8 to 10 cm thick, which contained kernels of *Zea mays* (Morehart 2002: 174). The limestone floor of the cave is discolored, exhibiting a bluish cast, which is typical of the changes that occur when limestone is exposed to fire. The ceiling in the west area of the crawl is also heavily charred, which attests to the intense use of the hearth.

Next to the hearth is the top half of a charred, Late Classic, narrow-necked jar. Several jar sherds are located beneath the vessel. The base of the jar is located on the west side of the hearth. Three volleyball-sized stones with cobbles placed between them are stacked west of the jar. A scatter of twenty sherds and several cobbles lies between the vessel base and the wall.

On the south side of the midsection of the passage, at the western end of the bench, is a stack of five fist-sized stones. These stones are charred, and the artifacts in this area are surrounded by a heavy concentration of charcoal. Two polychrome vessels from the area were removed by the Department of Archaeology. Both are mostly intact, exhibit no signs of charring, and have been dated to the Late Classic period (Joseph Ball and Jennifer Taschek 2005: personal communication). Neither contained visible residues, suggesting that they either held perishable substances or functioned as offerings themselves. The first, a tripod dish with rattle feet, has a waterbird motif (Figure 10.8a). It was originally positioned on top of the stack of stones. The second vessel, a cylindrical, ash-tempered, tau-footed tripod bowl, displays a caiman motif (Figure 10.8b). It was positioned on the north side of the rocks. Adjacent to the tau-footed vessel is a stack of seven sherds. A sherd from an Early Classic dish is sandwiched between Late Classic jar sherds, and a large cobble sits on top of the stack. This stack is interesting because the Early Classic sherd sits between Late Classic examples, suggesting that it was stacked together in the later period. Although the practice of stacking sherds in caves is not well understood, in this instance it suggests repeated usage of the area, reminiscent of stacking sherds when cleaning shrine sites—a common practice among the Quiché in Guatemala (Tedlock 1992). Three sherds dating to the Late Preclassic period (Jaime Awe 1998: personal communication) sit adjacent to the stack.

To the west, adjacent to the south wall, is the bottom half of a Terminal Classic, flat-based, cylindrical, polychrome vase (Joseph Ball and Jennifer Taschek 2005: personal communication). It exhibits either fire clouding or light charring on both the interior and exterior surfaces. The polychrome design on the vessel is divided into three panels (Figure 10.9). Occupying each panel is a seated figure with its right arm extended. A birdlike creature hovers over an *akbal* vase in the center panel, and an oblong device lies on either side of each figure. Placed inside the vase were a spall and two sherds. One sherd was dated to the early part of the Late Preclassic period (Jaime Awe 1998: personal communication). Two additional Late Preclassic sherds (Joseph Ball 1998: personal communication) lie on the ground adjacent to the vase. At the elbow of the passage, also along the southern wall, is a stack of

FIGURE 10.8. *a. Tripod dish with rattle feet. b. Tripod cylindrical vessel displaying caiman motif (photos by the author).*

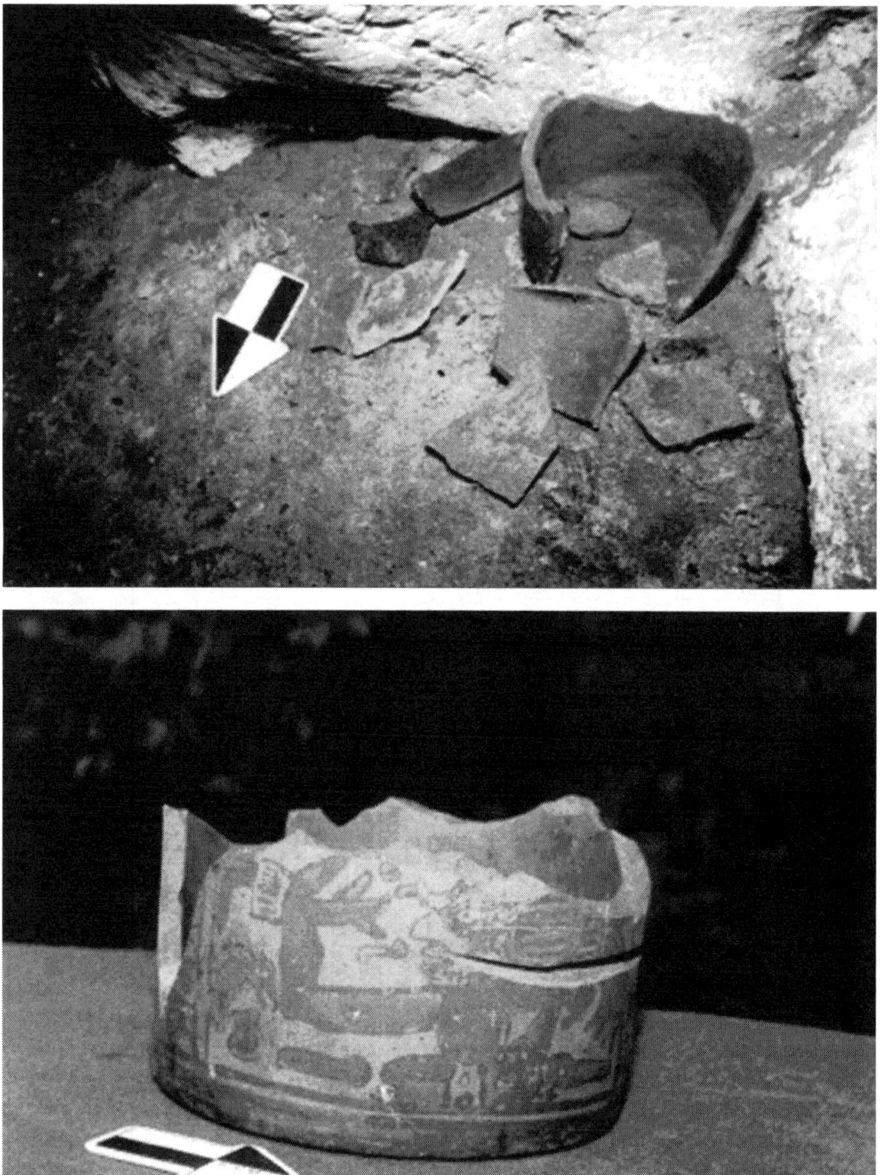

FIGURE 10.9. *Flat-based cylindrical vessel containing Late Preclassic sherd. (Top) Vessel in situ. (Bottom) Vase illustrates seated figure with elongated right arm (photos by the author).*

eight sherds positioned beneath a rock. West of the stack a Late Classic jar with a kill hole sits in an inverted position. A cluster of thirty-six small sherds sits next to the jar adjacent to the wall near the west opening.

CHRONOLOGY AND CHANGES OVER TIME

Chronology in caves is often difficult to establish. Ceramic chronologies provide adequate guidelines, but changes in ritual practice over time can obscure activities that do not require the use or deposition of ceramic vessels or sherds. As demonstrated in Crawl 3, artifacts and features are often surface deposits that become commingled, particularly in areas that are reused over long temporal spans. In the absence of stratigraphy, the palimpsest nature of these surface deposits can interfere with the interpretation of absolute dates from preserved or charred organic remains as well. To overcome these problems, it is necessary to utilize both absolute and relative dating techniques and to date material from subsurface contexts when possible.

Ceramic chronologies in Crawl 3 were determined by ceramic cross dating using James Gifford's type/variety method developed for Barton Ramie, Belize (1976). In Crawl 3, most of the ceramic assemblage was from the Spanish Lookout complex and dated to the later part of the Late Classic period (A.D. 700–950). The Late Classic assemblage was composed primarily of highly diagnostic whole or partial vessels. Only a few sherds dated to earlier periods. At least one sherd dated to the early part of the Late Preclassic (300–100 B.C.), two to the later part of the Late Preclassic (100 B.C.–A.D. 250), and one to the Early Classic (A.D. 250–600). Because of the paucity of ceramic sherds dating to the earlier periods, one would be tempted to assign a Late Classic date of usage to the area, but this is not the case.

To determine an absolute age for the initial use, a 25 by 25 cm test pit was excavated in the area of most intense activity. Bedrock was encountered at a depth of 7 cm, and a small sample of wood charcoal was collected from the base of the pit. The date obtained using ^{14}C AMS was 1944 ± 71 rcybp, calibrated using OxCal3 with a two-sigma range to 120 B.C.–A.D. 250, which falls at the end of the Late Preclassic period. An additional date obtained from a bulk sample of wood charcoal obtained from below the hearth vessel was 1696 ± 36 rcybp, calibrated using OxCal3 with a two-sigma range to A.D. 250–430, which falls within the Early Classic period. A third date that is perhaps less reliable but still of interest was collected from an excavation unit placed in the backdirt mound on the main tunnel floor. The sample of wood charcoal came from the interface of the backfill pile and the original floor surface. This date was 2432 ± 33 rcybp, calibrated using OxCal3 with a two-sigma range to 770–400 B.C., which correlates with the Middle Preclassic period. Caution is observed with this date because the charcoal fragment may have been resting on the tunnel floor for a long time before the sediment was piled on top. Also, because the subsurface sample from Crawl 3 suggests a later date for the modification of the space, it is safer to assign the Late Preclassic date to the initial use of the area. The

Early Classic date of the hearth material suggests continued usage of the area, and the large number of Late Classic vessels suggests a Late Classic date for the latest use.

There appears to be a change in ritual practice during the period of latest usage. Although the space underwent modification and intense utilization before this time, the number of ceramics deposited in the area increased dramatically during the Late Classic period (A.D. 700–950). A total of thirty-five partial and whole vessels were recorded in the crawl. Of these, thirty-two were diagnostic. Twenty-seven of the diagnostic examples were from the Spanish Lookout (Late Classic) complex. Additionally, all of the partially intact or whole vessels dated to this time period, and the rest of the assemblage consisted of small fragments. The Late Classic vessel and five river cobbles sitting on top of the pile of charcoal that dated to the Early Classic period suggest that the hearthstones and jar were a later addition.

DISCUSSION

The similarity in the size and morphology typical of masonry sweatbaths from archaeological sites and those of modern communities to the modifications in Crawl 3 illustrates that the passage was constructed as a sweatbath. The dimensions of Crawl 3 and its low ceiling height are within the ranges of sweatbaths found in other archaeological contexts and are most similar to the underground sweatbath located at San Antonio in Chiapas (Agrinier 1969: 16–27). The two low walls or benches in the passage bear a striking resemblance to the walls and central trenches of Classic period masonry sweatbaths. Additionally, the working hearth, which was used extensively, would have produced the environment appropriate to a functional sweatbath. The Late Classic wide-mouthed jar sitting on top the hearthstones showed no evidence of residue, which suggests that it contained water to create steam. In earlier times there may have been another jar, or steam may have been produced by throwing water on heated stones, as evidenced by the charred rock near the hearth.

Although the smoke produced in the crawl would have been suffocating, this was probably not unusual. Payson Sheets (1992: 101), describing the sweatbath at Ceren, noted that he was puzzled by the amount of charring on the inside of the roof. He later realized that in sweatbaths the firebox was often placed at the center of the room, and at least some of the smoke was probably let out via a small plugged hole in the roof before people entered the structure (McKee 2002: 91). Also, Frank Cresson (1938: 90–93) has reported that no ventilator holes were found in the sweatbath Structure N-1 at Piedras Negras, which suggests that the central chamber became filled with smoke. In his visit to a modern sweatbath at Milpa Alta, he observed that the steam room had no ventilator holes, and the smoke from the firebox escaped from the entrance door. Crawl 3 is well ventilated by comparison because its two access areas allow cross ventilation. Considering that the outside air from the cave's tunnel system remains cool year-round, it stands to reason that smoke would move into the tunnel. Interestingly, the hearth is placed roughly in the center of the crawl, similar to those found in sweatbaths such as the one at Ceren.

The artifacts within the area are commensurate with what might be expected in a ritual sweatbath. Of particular interest is the tau-footed vessel with the caiman motif found on the south side of the crawl across the passage from the hearth. The caiman motif, or Earth Monster, is also present on the Temple of the Cross at Palenque, previously discussed, identified by Houston (1996) as a cosmological sweatbath that functioned as a birthplace for the gods. Additionally, Mark Child (2005) reported a vessel with a similar motif from a Piedras Negras sweatbath.

Karl Taube (1989: 9) has suggested that among the Classic Maya there was an earth/caiman metaphor. He describes Itzam Cab, the earth caiman, as the *axis mundi* par excellence and has identified the creature as the god of creation and sustenance in both Highland Mexico and Postclassic Yucatán (1998: 437). Taube notes that in the iconography of Copan the deity is depicted with three stones in its mouth. This motif is identified as the *k'oben,* or kitchen hearth fire, which in *The Ritual of the Bacabs* is described by the term *pib,* or sweatbath (Roys 1965: 61). The mouth of the deity may also be symbolized as a cave. In architectural metaphor the mouth of the Witz Monster, a similar entity located on temple pyramids, is a symbolic cave opening (Gendrop 1980; Schavelzon 1980; Stuart 1997: 15–16).

Finally, a cluster of potsherds is located at the west entrance to Crawl 3, and a cluster of pebbles and sherds is found on the natural shelf on the south side of the eastern entrance. The pebbles in the later configuration are clearly waterworn. No other stones of this nature are found inside the cave, other than the river cobbles used to support the jar in the hearth feature. The arrangement and clustering of the pebbles, as well as their uniform size, suggest that they are a unique offering. The location of the clusters of sherds and pebbles near both the east and west entrances to the crawl suggests that these offerings are analogous to the pebbles and sherds offered as a tribute to earth deities at the entrance of the "sweatbath/cave" at the Festival of Games in Chamula, reported by Victoria Bricker (1973: 114). It is not unusual for pebbles to be used as payment or "money" intended for otherworld use. Bishop de Landa mentions that stones were placed in burials to be used for money by the deceased (in Tozzer 1941: 130). Among the Zapotec of Mitla, Oaxaca, in a ceremony performed on New Year's Eve, a ritual exchange takes place at a cross at the town boundary or in a cave. People bargain with each other for things they want in the upcoming year using pebbles for payment, which they call "the money of God" (Leslie 1960: 75).

CONCLUSION

This chapter has argued that Crawl 3, a modified passage within Chechem Ha Cave, served as a ritual sweatbath. The area has a number of shared characteristics with known sweatbaths in archaeological and ethnographic contexts that support this interpretation. Additionally, both caves and sweatbaths are strongly associated with aspects of fertility. Earth deities associated with creation and renewal are denizens of both of these dark enclosed spaces. The association of the sweatbath with earth deities among the Maya suggests that offerings to the cave/sweatbath propitiate these entities. Data presented in this chapter reinforce the cognitive association between sweatbaths and caves and suggest that this ancient concept developed as early as the Preclassic period.

ACKNOWLEDGMENTS

Work on this project was conducted with the Western Belize Regional Cave Project (WBRCP) under the direction of Jaime Awe. I am grateful to Dr. Awe, who has provided the opportunity and context for my research on ancient Maya caves. I would also like to thank members of the Institute of Archaeology in Belize: Alan Moore, George Thompson, Brian Woodeye, and John Morris. Appreciation is extended to Antonio Morales and Lea Plytez on whose property the cave lies and to their son, William. Thanks also to the 1998–1999 staff and students of the WBRCP, especially Cameron Griffith, Reiko Ishihara, Mike Mirro, and Paul Duffy; to Joseph Ball for identifying problematic ceramics; and to James Aimers for his work on the ceramics in 2003. This chapter benefited from editorial suggestions from Mark Aldenderfer, James Brady, and an anonymous reviewer. Appreciation goes to Stephen Houston for allowing me to use his photograph of the reconstructed sweatbath from Piedras Negras, to Payson Sheets for his drawing of the sweatbath at Ceren, and to the WBRCP for use of the project map. Special thanks to Karl Taube, who first suggested to me that the crawl was a ritual sweatbath and commented on early drafts of this chapter.

This chapter is based on work supported by National Science Foundation Grant DGE 9870668, "Integrative Graduate Education and Research Training in Geographic Information Science," awarded to the University at Buffalo.

REFERENCES CITED

Agrinier, Pierre

1966 La casa de baños de vapor de San Antonio. *Boletín del Instituto Nacional de Antropología* 25:29–32.

1969 Excavations at San Antonio, Chiapas, Mexico. *Papers of the New World Archaeological Foundation,* No. 24, 5–29. Brigham Young University, Provo, Utah.

Alcina Franch, José

1981 El baño de vapor entre los Mayas prehispánicos. *Scripta Ethnologica* (Buenos Aires) 6:41–47.

Alcina Franch, José, Andrés Ciudad Ruiz, and Josepha Iglesias Ponce de León

1980 El "temescal" en Mesoamérica: evolución, forma, y function. *Revista Española de Antropología Americana (Trobajos y Conferencias)* 10:93–132.

Andrews, E. Wyllis, IV, and E. Wyllis Andrews V

1980 *Excavations at Dzibilchaltun, Yucatan, Mexico.* Publication 48, Middle American Research Institute. Tulane University, New Orleans.

Awe, Jaime, Sherry Gibbs, and Cameron Griffith

2005 Stelae and Megalithic Monuments in the Caves of Western Belize. In *In the Maw of the Earth Monster: Mesoamerican Ritual Cave Use,* eds. James E. Brady and Keith M. Prufer, 223–248. University of Texas Press, Austin.

Ball, Joseph

1993 *Cahal Pech, the Ancient Maya and Modern Belize: The Story of an Archaeological Park.* San Diego State University Press, San Diego.

Beals, Ralph

1939 Sacrificial Rites of the Mixe. *Congreso Internacional de Americanistas* 27(2): 428–434.

1945 *Ethnology of the Western Mixe.* Publications in American Archaeology and Ethnology, Volume 42. University of California, Berkeley.

Blaffer, Sara C.

1972 *The Black-man of Zinacantan.* University of Texas Press, Austin.

Brady, James E.

1988 The Sexual Connotation of Caves in Mesoamerican Ideology. *Mexicon* 10(3):51–55.

1989 Investigation of Maya Ritual Cave Use With Special Reference to Naj Tunich, Peten, Guatemala. Ph.D. Dissertation. Archaeology Program, University of California, Los Angeles.

Bricker, Victoria Reifler

1973 *Ritual Humor in Highland Chiapas.* University of Texas Press, Austin.

Carmack, Robert

1979 *Historia social de los Quiches.* Seminario de Integración Social Guatemalteca No. 38, Editorial "José de Pineda Ibarra," Ministerio de Educación, Guatemala.

Child, Mark B.

2002 Ritual Purification and the Ancient Maya Sweatbath at Palenque. Paper presented at the 67th Annual Meeting of the Society for American Archaeology, Denver.

2005 The Archaeology of Religious Movements: The Evolution of the Sweatbath Cult in Ancient Maya Society. Paper presented at the 70th Annual Meeting of the Society for American Archaeology, Salt Lake City.

Ciudad Ruiz, Andrés

1984 *Arqueología de Agua Tibia, Totonicapán (Guatemala).* Instituto de Cooperación Iberoamericana, Madrid.

Clavijero, Francisco J.

1804 *The History of Mexico, Vol. II.* Trans. Charles Cullen, Esq. Budd and Bartrum, Philadelphia.

1945 *Historia Antiqua de México.* Editorial Porrúa, México D.F.

Cresson, Frank M., Jr.

1938 Maya and Mexican Sweathouses. *American Anthropologist* 40:88–104.

Driver, Harold, and William C. Massey

1957 *Comparative Studies of North American Indians.* Transactions of the American Philosophical Society, Philadelphia, 47, Part 2.

Durán, Diego
1994 *The History of the Indies of New Spain.* Trans. Doris Heyden. University of Oklahoma Press, Norman [original sixteenth century].

Gary, Margaret, Robert McFee Jr., and Carol L. Wolf
1972 *Glossary of Geology.* American Geological Institute, Washington, D.C.

Gendrop, Paul
1980 Dragon-Mouth Entrances: Zoomorphic Portals in the Architecture of Central Yucatan. In *Third Palenque Round Table, 1978, Part 2,* ed. Merle Greene Robertson, 138–150. University of Texas Press, Austin.

Gifford, James C.
1976 *Prehistoric Pottery Analysis and the Ceramics of Barton Ramie in the Belize Valley.* Memoirs of the Peabody Museum of Archaeology and Ethnology, Vol. 18. Harvard University, Cambridge, MA.

Gossen, Gary H.
1999 *Telling Tzotzil Maya Tales: Tzotzil Identities in Modern Mexico.* Routledge, New York.

Groark, Kevin P.
1996 *To Warm the Blood, To Warm the Flesh: The Role of the Steambath in Highland Maya (Tzeltzal-Tzotzil) Ethnomedicine.* M.A. Thesis. Department of Anthropology, University of California, Los Angeles.
1997 To Warm the Blood, To Warm the Flesh: The Role of the Steambath in Highland Maya (Tzeltzal-Tzotzil) Ethnomedicine. *Journal of Latin American Lore* 20(1):3–96.

Grove, David C.
1973 Olmec Altars and Myth. *Archaeology* 26(2):128–135.

Hammond, Norman, and Jeremy R. Bauer
2001 A Preclassic Sweatbath at Cuello, Belize. *Antiquity* 75:683–684.

Heyden, Doris
1975 An Interpretation of the Cave Underneath the Pyramid of the Sun in Teotihuacan, Mexico. *American Antiquity* 40:131–147.
1976 Los Ritos de paso en las Cuevas. *Boletín del Instituto Nacional de Antropología e Historia* 19:17–26.
1981 Caves, Gods, and Myths: World-View and Planning in Teotihuacan. In *Mesoamerican Sites and World Views,* ed. Elizabeth P. Benson, 1–39. Dumbarton Oaks Research Library and Collections, Washington, D.C.

Houston, Stephen D.
1996 Symbolic Sweatbaths of the Maya: Architectural Meaning in the Cross Group at Palenque, Mexico. *Latin American Antiquity* 7(2):132–151.

Ichon, Alain
1977 A Late Postclassic Sweathouse in the Highlands of Guatemala. *American Antiquity* 42:203–209.

Ishihara, Reiko
2000 An Investigation of the Ancient Maya Ritual Cave Activity at Actun Chechem Ha, Cayo District, Belize. Honors Thesis in Archaeology. University of Tsukuba, Japan.

LaFarge, Oliver
1947 *Santa Eulalia: The Religion of a Cuchumatan Indian Town.* University of Chicago Press, Chicago.

Laughlin, Robert M.
1969 The Tzotzil. In *Handbook of Middle American Indians, Vol. 7, Ethnology, Part 1,* ed. Evon Z. Vogt, 152–194. University of Texas Press, Austin.
1975 *The Great Tzotzil Dictionary of San Lorenzo Zinacantan.* Smithsonian Contributions to Anthropology, No. 19. Smithsonian Institution Press, Washington, D.C.

Leslie, Charles M.
1960 *Now We Are Civilized: A Study of the World View of the Zapotec Indians of Mitla, Oaxaca.* Wayne State University Press, Detroit.

Lopatin, Ivan A.
1960 Origin of the Native American Steambath. *American Anthropologist* 62:977–993.

McKee, Brian R.
2002 Structure 9: A Precolumbian Sweat Bath at Cerén. In *Before the Volcano Erupted: The Ancient Cerén Village in Central America,* ed. Payson Sheets, 89–96. University of Texas Press, Austin.

Miller, Mary, and Karl Taube
1993 *The Gods and Symbols of Ancient Mexico and the Maya.* Thames & Hudson, London.

Moedano, N. Gabriel
1977 El temazcal y su deidad protectora en la tradicion oral. *Boletín del Departamento de Investigación de las Tradiciones Populares* 4:5–32.

Morehart, Christopher T.
2002 Ancient Maya Ritual Cave Utilization: A Paleoethnobotanical Perspective. Master's Thesis, Department of Anthropology, Florida State University, Tallahassee.

Morley, Sylvanus G.
1935 *Guide to the Ruins of Quirigua.* Publication Supplement 16. Carnegie Institution of Washington, Washington, D.C.

Nielsen, Jesper, and James E. Brady
n.d. The Couple in the Cave: Origin Iconography on a Ceramic Vessel From Los Naranjos, Honduras. Unpublished manuscript in possession of author.

Nuttall, Zelia
1903 *The Book of Life of the Ancient Mexicans (Codex Magliabechiano).* University of California Press, Berkeley.

Parsons, Elsie C.
1936 *Mitla: Town of the Souls, and Other Zapoteco-Speaking Pueblos of Oaxaca, Mexico.* University of Chicago Press, Chicago.

Roys, Ralph L.
1965 *The Ritual of the Bacabs.* University of Oklahoma Press, Norman.

Sahagún, Fray Bernardino de
1969 *Florentine Codex, General History of the Things of New Spain.* Trans. Charles E. Dibble and Arthur J.O. Anderson. The School of American Research and the

University of Utah, Monographs of the School of American Research, Santa Fe, New Mexico [original sixteenth century].

Satterthwaite, Linton

1952 *Piedras Negras Archaeology: Architecture, Pt. V. Sweathouses.* University Museum Monograph. University of Pennsylvania, Philadelphia.

Schavelzon, Daniel

1980 Temples, Caves, or Monsters? Notes on Zoomorphic Facades in Pre-Hispanic Architecture. In *Third Palenque Round Table, 1978, Part 2,* ed. Merle Greene Robertson, 151–162. University of Texas Press, Austin.

Sheets, Payson D.

1992 *The Ceren Site: A Prehistoric Village Buried by Volcanic Ash in Central America.* Harcourt Brace College Publishers, San Diego.

Stone, Andrea J.

1995 *Images From the Underworld: Naj Tunich and the Tradition of Maya Cave Painting.* University of Texas Press, Austin.

Stuart, David S.

1997 The Hills Are Alive: Sacred Mountains in the Maya Cosmos. *Symbols,* Spring Issue, Peabody Museum, Cambridge, 13–17.

Tarn, Nathaniel, and Martín Prechtel

1986 Constant Inconstancy: The Feminine Aspect in Atiteco Mythology. In *Symbolism and Meaning Beyond the Closed Community: Essays in Mesoamerican Ideas,* ed. Gary H. Gossen, 173–184. Institute for American Studies, University of Albany, State University of New York, Albany.

1997 *Scandals in the House of Birds: Shamans and Priests on Lake Atitlan.* Marsilio Publishers, New York.

Taube, Karl A.

1986 The Teotihaucan Cave of Origin: The Iconography and Architecture of Emergence Mythology in Mesoamerica and the American Southwest. *RES: Anthropology and Aesthetics* 12:51–82.

1989 Itzam Cab Ain: Caimans, Cosmology, and Calendrics in Postcalssic Yucatán. *Research Reports on Ancient Maya Writing, No.26.* Center for Maya Research, Washington, D.C.

1998 The Jade Hearth: Centrality, Rulership, and the Classic Maya Temple. In *Function and Meaning in Classic Maya Architecture,* ed. Stephen D. Houston, 425–476. Dumbarton Oaks, Washington, D.C.

Tax, Sol, and Robert Hinshaw

1969 The Maya of the Midwestern Highlands. In *Handbook of Middle American Indians, Vol. 7, Ethnology, Part 1,* ed. Evon Z. Vogt, 69–100. University of Texas Press, Austin.

Tedlock, Barbara

1987 An Interpretive Solution to the Problem of Humoral Medicine in Latin America. *Social Science and Medicine* 24 (12):1069–1083.

1992 *Time and the Highland Maya,* Revised Edition. University of New Mexico Press, Albuquerque.

Thompson, J. Eric

1970 *Maya History and Religion.* University of Oklahoma Press, Norman.

1975 Introduction to the Reprint Edition. In *The Hill-Caves of Yucatan,* by Henry C. Mercer, vii–xliv. University of Oklahoma Press, Norman.

Tozzer, Alfred M.

1941 *Landa's Relacion de las Cosas de Yucatan.* Papers of the Peabody Museum of American Archaeology and Ethnology, Vol. 18. Harvard University, Cambridge.

Villa Rojas, Alfonso

1969a The Tzeltal. In *Handbook of Middle American Indians, Vol. 7, Ethnology, Part 1,* ed. Evon Z. Vogt, 195–225. University of Texas Press, Austin.

1969b Maya Lowlands: The Chontal, Chol, and Kekchi. In *Handbook of Middle American Indians, Vol. 7, Ethnology, Part 1,* ed. Evon Z. Vogt, 230–243. University of Texas Press, Austin.

Vogt, Evon Z.

1969 *Zinacantan, A Maya Community in the Highlands of Chiapas.* Belknap Press of Harvard University Press, Cambridge.

Vogt, Evon Z., and David Stuart

2005 Some Notes on Ritual Caves Among the Ancient and Modern Maya. In *In the Maw of the Earth Monster: Mesoamerican Ritual Cave Use,* eds. James E. Brady and Keith M. Prufer, 155–185. University of Texas Press, Austin.

Wagley, Charles

1949 *The Social and Religious Life of a Guatemalan Village.* Memoir No. 71. American Anthropological Association, Menasha, Wisconsin.

1969 The Maya of Northwestern Guatemala. In *Handbook of Middle American Indians, Vol. 7, Ethnology, Part 1,* ed. Evon Z. Vogt, 46–68. University of Texas Press, Austin.

Webster, David

2001 *A Rural Sweat Bath From Piedras Negras.* Paper presented at the 66th Annual Meeting of the Society for American Archaeology, New Orleans.

Chapter Eleven

An Analysis of Ancient Maya Stalactite Breakage at Balam Na Cave, Guatemala

by James E. Brady
Allan B. Cobb
Sergio Garza
Cesar Espinosa
Robert Burnett

Cave archaeology's increasing sophistication in dealing with cave environments is best exemplified in the documentation of a previously overlooked pattern of purposeful breakage of cave formations (speleothems) by the ancient Maya (Brady et al. 1997). Subsequent reports have verified the ubiquity of speleothem breakage (Prufer 2002; Rissolo 2001), and some limited attempts have been made to develop more detailed studies of the context, extent, and significance of this practice (Moyes 2001). This chapter describes initial attempts to assess the extent of breakage in a single cave, Balam Na Cave 1. The study assembled data on the amount of stalactite breakage from this single cave to provide some type of benchmark for estimating the quantity of material that left caves and was incorporated into surface deposits. In addition, the process of inventorying the stalactites aroused the curiosity of our Q'eqchi' Maya guide, who discussed the matter with Garza. In the discussion, Garza was able to collect important ethnographic data that significantly increase our understanding of the meaning of speleothems for the modern Maya.

BALAM NA CAVE 1

In the spring of 2001, California State University, Los Angeles, working in conjunction with the Atlas Arqueológico de Guatemala, conducted a survey of a small hill called Balam Na, located approximately 16 km northwest of the town of Poptun in southeastern Petén (Figure 11.1). The hill was selected for investigation because it contained a cave that had received a good deal of visitation in the past. Cave 1 was first mentioned by Michel Siffre (1979: 39–41), who visited the cave in December 1978 and noted the presence of rock art. It was revisited independently by Danish explorer Christian Christensen in August 1998. Christensen photographically recorded part of the corpus of rock art and brought it to the attention of Brady, then a visiting professor at the University of Copenhagen. The Atlas Arqueológico de Guatemala surveyed the cave and collected ceramics from the surface. Most of this material dated to the Late Preclassic (Valdizón Burmester 1995: 77–80). The California State University, Los Angeles, survey in March 2001 relocated Cave 1 and mapped and investigated three other caves in the same hill. Initial work in Cave 1 concentrated on recording the speleothem rock art, which was more extensive than previous investigators had realized (Brady et al. 2003).

The search for all of the rock art elements led to a detailed examination of the speleothems in the cave. It was noted that speleothem breakage in Cave 1, as in other Maya caves, was extensive. It was also recognized that because no detailed speleothem inventory had ever been published for a Maya cave, the field had little idea in quantitative terms what *extensive* meant. The decision was made to conduct an inventory in 2001 to establish some quantitative measure of speleothem modification. Cave 1 was selected for the inventory for a number of reasons. The cave is only 40 m in length, so the task was manageable with our relatively small staff and limited time.

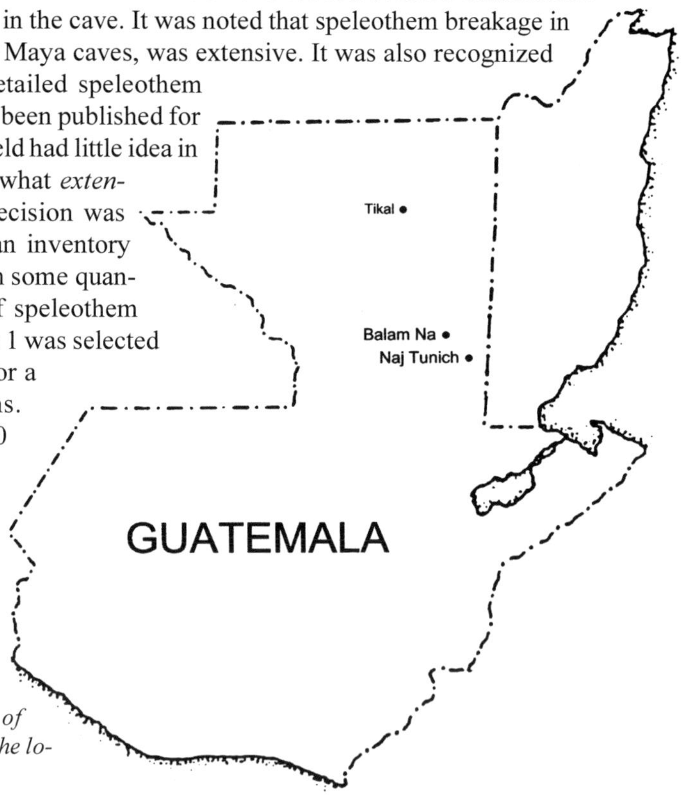

FIGURE 11.1. *Map of Guatemala showing the location of Balam Na.*

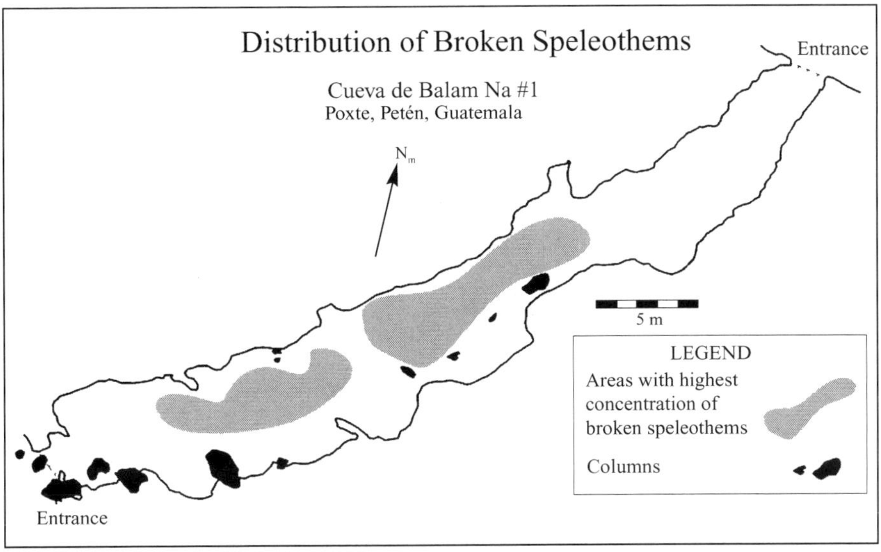

FIGURE 11.2. *Map of Balam Na Cave 1 showing the position of the stalactite curtains.*

On the other hand, the dense formation growth ensured that the sample would be large enough to be meaningful. On initial inspection, Cobb and Brady also felt the amount of breakage was rather typical, so an inventory would not provide data that were excessively high or low. The simple morphology of the cave—a single, relatively straight passage with a relatively low ceiling—also aided in data recording (Figure 11.2). The majority of stalactites are concentrated in two principal curtains, one running along the northern cave wall and the other in the center of the chamber. Enough stalactite regrowth is present to indicate that the bulk of the breakage is ancient, and there are few obviously fresh breaks that would suggest recent vandalism (Figure 11.3). At the same time, the cave is clearly dryer than in the past with relatively few active formations, so regrowth does not threaten to obscure past breakage.

The survey was limited to stalactites because the floor of the cave had been so badly disturbed by previous visitation that stalagmites had been uprooted or pushed from their original positions. Since so much of this disturbance was recent, it was clearly not possible to obtain any reliable estimate of ancient stalagmite modification. The study, therefore, was forced to focus exclusively on stalactite breakage.

Burnett was asked to conduct the 2001 stalactite inventory, but no specific methodology had been developed. A total of 601 broken formations were recorded. Given the small size of the cave, the number was larger than had been estimated before conducting the inventory. A host of methodological problems, however, limited the utility of the data collected, so the cave was resurveyed in 2002.

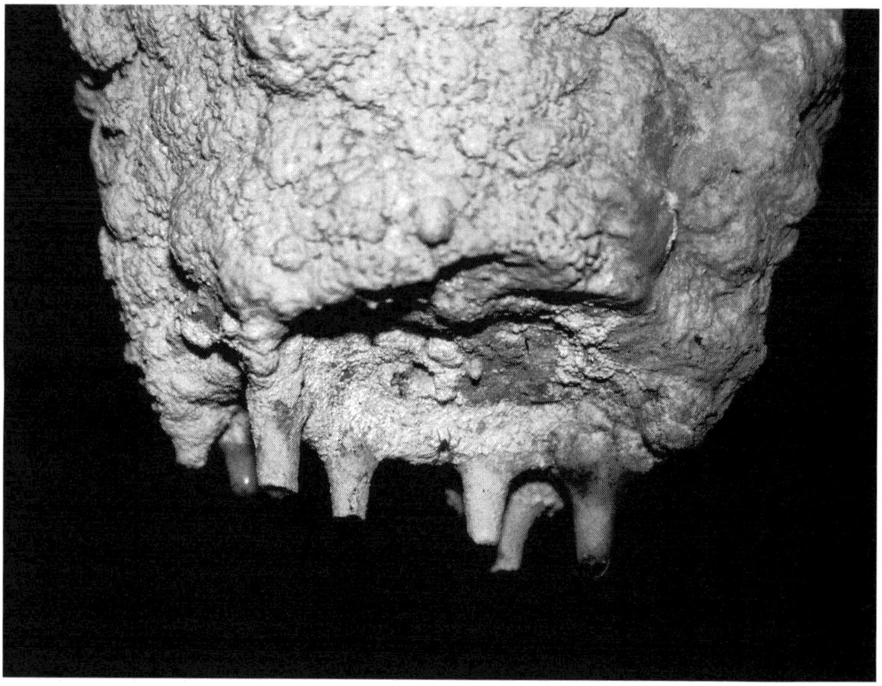

FIGURE 11.3. *The stump of the broken stalactite shows regrowth over the ancient break.*

METHODOLOGY

The stalactites were systematically inventoried in 2002 by moving from the western to the eastern entrance and recording all formations, shafts, and stumps on a map of the cave. The recording differed in several ways from the 2001 survey. First, both broken and unbroken stalactites were recorded to give some idea of the percentage of breakage. Second, the cave was broken into smaller units so that the number of stalactites in each unit was more manageable. This allowed for a more intensive, systematic, and accurate count. Third, for added precision, the size of each stalactite was also estimated based on formation diameter. Four sizes were defined: small, less than 3 cm; medium, ranging between 3 and 7 cm; large, varying between 7 and 15 cm; and finally, those greater than 15 cm. Fourth, the actual counting was done by Brady and Cobb, who alternated between units to reduce fatigue. In the first sections, there was considerable consultation to establish interobserver reliability in handling problematic cases. Fifth, Garza and Espinosa, one responsible for broken and the other for unbroken formations, recorded the data while Brady or Cobb called out the counts. This permitted the counter to move over an area without taking his eyes off the ceiling. In conducting the inventory, formations were counted as broken only if they were clearly fractured. Thus the figures will tend to err on the conservative side, and this error was most noticeable with the smallest formations.

RESULTS

The more intensive, systematic, and detailed manner in which the 2002 stalactite inventory was conducted is clear in the fact that 1,660 broken stalactites were recorded, nearly two and a half times the number counted in 2001. A total of 2,803 formations were noted overall, indicating that 59 percent of all the stalactites had been broken. The percentages across formation size were quite consistent, with differences explainable by the methodology adopted. Problematic formations without clear evidence of having been deliberately broken were counted as unbroken. Since this occurs most frequently with the smallest stalactites, it is not surprising that only 56 percent of the stalactites with diameters less than 3 cm were recorded as broken. The formations with diameters of 3 to 7 cm and 7 to 15 cm showed breakage rates of 60 percent and 61 percent, respectively, whereas the stalactites greater than 15 cm in diameter—those with the least equivocal evidence—were broken at a rate of 69 percent. The large numbers of stalactites overall and the high rate of breakage brought home forcefully that the harvesting of speleothems had occurred on a large scale. The implications of the patterns of breakage will be discussed later.

After the stalactite inventory was completed, a check of other types of speleothems was made and breakage of stalagmites, draperies, and flowstone was also noted. The one exception, which will be discussed later, was that no columns were broken. It is also clear from our study that most broken formations had been removed from the cave.

Dean Arnold (1971: 33) suggests that a rock called *Hi'* is mined from a cave around Ticul in Yucatán for use as ceramic temper. *Hi'* is not specifically identified as a cave formation, but the possibility exists. The pattern of breakage noted in this study does not support mining consistent with this type of utilitarian use because there was no evidence of systematic removal, such as from front to back, that one would expect from such exploitation. Instead, broken and unbroken stalactites are interspersed within clusters of formations and throughout the cave (Figure 11.4). This pattern is consistent with individuals knocking off single stalactites. If the stalactites had been harvested for temper, one would expect all the formations in a given cluster to have been systematically broken. Second, there appears to be no deliberate selection of formations by size, such as the smallest, which would be easiest to break, or the largest, which would yield the greatest amount of stone. Third, the actual breakage appears to be the result of a sharp rap that detached the ends while leaving most of the formation. There is no evidence of hammering near the top of stalactites to dislodge additional sections or the whole formation. Finally, some stalactites were left on the floor, which would have been the easiest material to harvest. This speleothem inventory is important, therefore, because it represents

FIGURE 11.4. *This cluster of stalactites shows broken formations interspersed with unbroken ones, indicating a nonsystematic pattern of removal.*

the first attempt to test Arnold's hypothesis generated by ethnographic analogy. Archaeologists in general seem to feel that economic/utilitarian explanations for behavior are more "scientific." It is distressing, however, to see how seldom these economic explanations are actually tested against the archaeological record. At least at Balam Na, the evidence does not appear to support systematic speleothem mining. We suggest that the nonsystematic pattern of removal noted here is related to their use in ritual.

ETHNOGRAPHIC MODELS OF SPELEOTHEM USE

As mentioned, the stalactite inventory drew the attention of our guide and provided an opportunity for Garza to gather ethnographic data on Q'eqchi' Maya beliefs about speleothems. The forty-one-year-old native of Alta Verapaz states, "They [stalactites and stalagmites] are part of Mother Earth. The rocks are also alive, they grow and sweat water. They are sacred because they sweat Mother Earth's water; they themselves are water. When the rocks from the ceiling grow downward, they eventually join together with the rocks from the floor and establish a sacred connection with Mother Earth." Interestingly, the Codemex Dictionary also records the fact that in Yukatek these formations are called *ch'ak xix* and are thought to be distilled or coagulated water (Barrera Vásquez 1980: 123, 946, 961). We are not aware, however, of previous data establishing a relationship with the sacred earth or with the description of the water as sweat of the earth. The explicit statement that the formations are living entities is also new but completely consistent with the Mesoamerican view of the landscape as animate.

The connection of speleothems with water, earth, and fertility makes formations sacred and powerful. As noted previously, the amount of broken speleothems on the floor of the cave cannot begin to account for all the stalactites that were broken. This suggests that broken formations were removed from the cave. Garza's informant tells us, "Sometimes, people take pieces of these rocks from the caves. These rocks are sacred because they only grow in caves and they belong to Mother Earth. These rocks are alive and they have a spirit. People have altars in their houses, and they place these rocks on their altars. People do ceremonies for them, and the entire family can make offerings to these rocks." This information is once again important in confirming Michael Deal's (1988: 74) observation that speleothems are used on native altars in Chiapas. J. Eric Thompson (1970: 183) also lists stalagmites as one type of offering in rituals. The fact that these observations come from the opposite ends of the Maya area also suggests that this pattern of use is widespread.

In addition, Garza's ethnographic data suggest that differences between the types of speleothems are both recognized and important. The connection with water has profound implications because it is associated with fertility. In Mesoamerica, anything that is fertile tends to be sexual. The exchange of fluid between formations also suggests the sexual complementarily so fundamental to Maya thinking (Tarn and Prechtel 1986: 173). This was especially true of stalagmites and stalactites, which have definite sexual connotations. The informant said,

> Stalactites, some people call them *chi-chis* [breasts] because they come out and grow from the body of the earth, just like women's breasts. Also, when water drips from them to the ground they feed the earth, just like when a mother breastfeeds her baby. Stalagmites are different. Men call them *picos* [penises] because they look like a man's thing and like our things grow when we want our women. They also grow upward because they want to touch and be with the female from whom the *chi-chis* are growing. When they grow big and reach them it is like a man and a woman mating, and the two are one because now they are just one column or wall [*muro*] that touches the ceiling and the earth.

The sexual nature of the speleothems for the Maya is not altogether surprising in that the cavers working with Brady have referred to stalagmites as "dickoliths" for years (Figure 11.5). Robert Ravicz and A. Kimball Romney also call attention to the phallic quality of speleothems, along with the connection to fertility in Oaxaca. They note:

> At marriage in the Alta, stones representing the bride and groom are taken from a natural formation or from a cave and set up outside of the dwelling of those just married. Considered to bring good fortune, health, and many children, the stones are phallic and have a fertility function. (Ravicz and Romney 1969: 394)

Their description sounds close enough to Garza's Q'eqchi' data that one must suspect that the stones are not simply phallic but rather that they form a complementary male and female set. The presence of such similar ideas in both areas suggests that this may be a widely distributed Mesoamerican concept. Furthermore, this information suggests that columns might have also held a particularly sacred meaning for the ancient Maya because of their close identification with fertility. At the conclusion of the 2002 stalactite inventory, this possibility was tested by individually examining all the columns and checking for scars that might indicate a column had been broken. Our inspection found that virtually all of the columns had been left intact. These findings need to be checked in future studies, but the data suggest that the ancient Maya also observed special respect for columns.

Although the column as a symbol of fertility does hold great importance, we suspect there may be additional meanings and associations. When Q'eqchi' settlers in the area began to conduct pilgrimages to Naj Tunich, they performed their ceremonies directly in front of a huge ribbed column over 15 m high. An informant near the cave at La Compuerta told Garza that the deity resides within the column. This is interesting in relation to data collected in Yucatán. John Sosa (1985: 414) notes that his informant referred to the formations at the entrance to a cave as "his bench." At Balankanche, a Maya priest identified an indentation in the central column as "the throne of the Balam" (Andrews 1971: 260). These data suggest that the column is of central importance because it is the place of residence where people can communicate with the deity.

There are also indications that formations are more than simply places of residence. Jamis Alcorn (1984: 237) notes that the Huastec will first pay respects to the central stalagmite, after which they petition lesser stalagmites, which have control over specific matters. Incense is burned to the formations, and if *aguardiente* is present it will be offered to the stalagmite as well (Alcorn 1984: 200). Thus, the formations are very closely identified with deities. In Oaxaca, offerings are made before stalagmites that represent the rain god (Ravicz and Romney 1969: 394), and in one community the stalagmite was identified as "The Archbishop" and was said to talk (Pohl 1984: 88). Bishop Francisco de Burgoa records that a stalagmite destroyed by Padre Geronimo Abrego was actually the deity (in Hoppe and Weitlaner 1969: 506). In a cave ritual observed by Marion Oettinger in Guerrero, "[S]talactites and stalagmites were revered as deities" (in Heyden 1987: 129). At Tila in Chiapas, a large stalagmite is worshiped as a representation of Christ (Schuster 1997: 50). We suspect that the formations are actually thought to be the deities because of the nature of speleothems. Western archaeologists have been slow to recognize the animate nature of the indigenous universe. To the Maya the evidence is clear: "The rocks are alive—they have a spirit. They grow and sweat water." Thus, the Maya

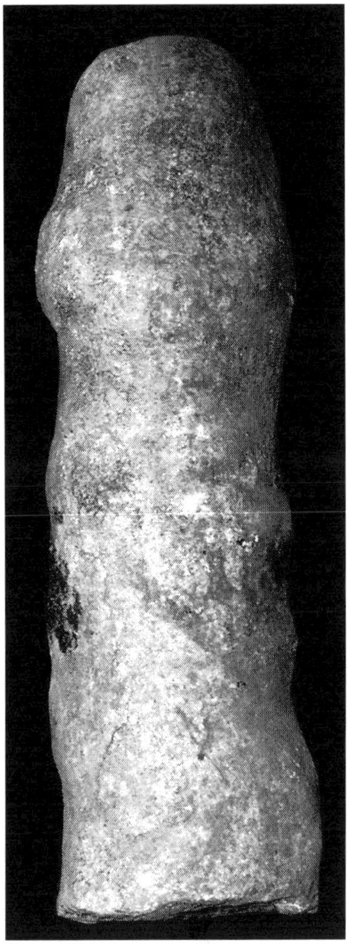

FIGURE 11.5. *The phallic quality of many stalagmites is clear in this broken speleothem.*

are not addressing a "representation" of the deity but instead an animate entity.

Finally, Garza's informant provided information on what we have considered to be one of the more unconventional ideas about speleothem use in the field. Dennis Puleston (MacLeod and Puleston 1978: 75) championed the notion that speleothems could have been beaten like a drum to produce music. Although every cave archaeologist has probably tried this and produced a variety of sounds, Puleston's theory has won few supporters. Garza's informant, however, states:

> When the spirits of the hill get together and play music they use stalactites and stalagmites in the cave as their instruments. Most are used as drums, but others make different sounds. At night they play for many hours, and people from far away hear their music. Their music sometimes reminds us that we need to give thanks to them.

Another informant added:

> About 5 kilometers from Nueva Esperanza, in Don Mario's *parcela*, there is a cave whose name is the Cave of Friendship. The people of this area say that at night the owner of the hill and other spirits get together in the cave to play drums and to play the music of the hill. These spirits conduct ceremonies when they play their music and nobody can see them; they can only be heard. Also, with their music the spirits establish contact; they communicate with spirits of other hills and, therefore, these caves are alive.

The informants' accounts do not appear to be either unique or idiosyncratic. Although this is the first identification of speleothems as the drums of the hill spirits, Richard Wilson (1995: 81) also mentions a belief in drums being played within mountains among the Q'eqchi' of Alta Verapaz. The informant's description is significant because it indicates that there is an indigenous awareness of the acoustical properties of speleothems and caves.

Since speleothem drums are used for communication between the gods, it seems reasonable that speleothems could also be used by humans for communication with the supernatural. This is suggested by ethnographic data on drums in general. Charles Wisdom (1952: 127) notes the close association of musical instruments to saint worship and says, "The *tun* drum of Guatemala is the best example, since it is used only ceremonially, and since each has a unique origin and history." The deep significance of the *tun* is especially clear for the Jalkaltek Maya. The *Alcaldes Rezadores* (elder cargo holders) kept three objects as symbols of their authority: the *Santa Vara* (sacred staff) from the Founding Father, the *Caja Real* (royal box) that contained documents and land titles, and the *tun* (Delgado Montejo 2005: 78). The *tun* was thought to be the voice of the earth. Arnulfo Delgado states, "In general, the *tun* represents the earth mother. The *tun* was also used at feasts. When the *tun* was played, it signified that the earth mother was asking her children to come together to celebrate the feast" (Delgado Montejo 2005: 86). Humans do use drums to communicate with the supernatural. After being persuaded to burn his idol, a shaman played his drum all night to console the idol's spirit (Beals 1933: 23).

CONCLUSIONS

This study is important in providing quantitative data for the first time on the actual extent of speleothem breakage. The high percentage of breakage (nearly 60 percent of all stalactites) obviously makes this a major form of cultural modification of the cave. Although it was not possible to inventory and classify the broken formations on the floor, it is clear that a large percentage of the broken formations had been removed from the cave.

Ethnographic data gathered in the course of the study are part of an ongoing process of attempting to understand the "emic" significance of the patterns observed archaeologically. These data suggest that speleothems may have been broken and pieces removed for use on household altars. The pieces were taken because they are animate and powerful. Speleothems appear to be particularly associated with water, rain, and fertility. The data on the sexual connotation of stalagmites and stalactites suggest that surface archaeologists need to observe whether speleothems are found in complementary pairs. Finally, data indicate that columns are considered particularly potent symbols of fertility. In addition, ethnographic data from Naj Tunich and elsewhere suggest that large columns are considered to be residences or even manifestations of deities. This may explain why none of the columns in Balam Na Cave 1 had been broken. Finally, speleothems may have been used as drums, and the sound produced may have been considered to be the voice of the earth.

ACKNOWLEDGMENTS

This study was carried out while the authors were working under the Atlas Arqueológico de Guatemala. The authors wish to thank the director, Dr. Juan Pedro Laporte, for his support and assistance. Funding for the project is gratefully acknowledged from DR1, Danish Public Television, and from the Danish newspaper the *Jyllands Posten*. Special thanks to Christian Christensen for bringing the cave to our attention and leading us back to it and for his dedication as field director of the 2001 project. This chapter has benefited from comments made by Keith Prufer.

REFERENCES CITED

Alcorn, Janis B.
1984 *Huastec Mayan Ethnobotony.* University of Texas Press, Austin.

Andrews, E. Wyllys, IV
1971 Balankanche—Throne of the Tiger Priest. *Explorers Journal* 49(4):254–262.

Arnold, Dean E.
1971 Ethnominerology of Ticul Yucatan Potters: Etics and Emics. *American Antiquity* 36:20–40.

Barrera Vásquez, Alfredo
1980 *Diccionario Maya Cordemex.* Ediciones Cordemex, Merida.

Beals, Ralph L.
1933 *The Acaxee: A Mountain Tribe of Durango and Sinaloa.* Ibero-Americana 6. University of California Press, Berkeley.

Brady, James E., Allan Cobb, Sergio Garza, and Robert Burnett
2003 Balam Na: Reporte preliminar de la investigación de una Cueva Asociada al Río Poxte, Poptun. *Atlas Arqueológico de Guatemala Reporte 17,* ed. Juan Pedro Laporte, 131–157. Ministerio de Cultura y Deportes, Dirección General del Patrimonio Cultural y Natural, Universidad de San Carlos de Guatemala, Escuela de Historia, Area de Arqueología, Guatemala.

Brady, James E., Ann Scott, Hector Neff, and Michael Glascock
1997 Speleothem Breakage, Movement, Removal and Caching: An Unreported Aspect of Ancient Maya Cave Utilization. *Geoarchaeology* 12(3):725–750.

Deal, Michael
1988 Recognition of Ritual Pottery in Residential Units: An Ethnohistorical Model of the Maya Family Altar Tradition. In *Ethnoarchaeology Among the Highland Maya of Chiapas, Mexico,* eds. Thomas A. Lee Jr. and Brian Hayden, 61–89. Papers of the New World Archaeological Foundation, No. 56. Brigham Young University, Provo.

Delgado Montejo, Arnulfo
2005 Jacaltenango: A Restudy. M.A. Thesis. Department of Anthropology, California State University, Los Angeles.

Heyden, Doris
1987 Caves. In *The Encyclopedia of Religion,* ed. Mircea Eliade, Vol. 3:127–133. Macmillan, New York.

Hoppe, Walter, and Roberto J. Weitlaner
1969 The Chocho. In *Handbook of Middle American Indians, Vol. 7: Ethnology,* ed. Evon Z. Vogt, 506–515. University of Texas Press, Austin.

MacLeod, Barbara, and Dennis E. Puleston
1978 Pathways Into Darkness: The Search for the Road to Xibalbá. In *Tercera Mesa Redonda de Palenque,* Vol. 4, eds. Merle Greene Robertson and Donnan Call Jeffers, 71–77. Hearld Peters, Monterey.

Moyes, Holley

2001 The Cave as a Cosmogram: The Use of GIS in an Intrasite Spatial Analysis of the Main Chamber of Actun Tunichil Muknal, A Maya Ceremonial Cave in Western Belize. M.A. Thesis. Department of Anthropology, Florida Atlantic University, Boca Raton.

Pohl, John M.D.

1984 The Earth Lords: Politics and Symbolism of the Mixtec Codices. Ph.D. Dissertation. Department of Anthropology, University of California, Los Angeles.

Prufer, Keith Malcolm

2002 Communities, Caves and Ritual Specialists: A Study of Sacred Space in the Maya Mountains of Southern Belize. Ph.D. Dissertation. Department of Anthropology, Southern Illinois University, Carbondale.

Ravicz, Robert, and A. Kimball Romney

1969 The Mixtec. In *Handbook of Middle American Indians, Vol. 7: Ethnology, Pt. 1,* ed. Evon Z. Vogt, 367–399. University of Texas Press, Austin.

Rissolo, Dominique A.

2001 Ancient Maya Cave Use in the Yalahau Region, Northern Quintana Roo, Mexico. Ph.D. Dissertation. Department of Anthropology, University of California, Riverside.

Schuster, Angela M.H.

1997 Rituals of the Modern Maya. *Archaeology* 50(4):50–53.

Siffre, Michel

1979 *A la Recherche de l'Art des Cavernes du Pays Maya*. Editions Alain Lefeuvre, Nice.

Sosa, John Robert

1985 The Maya Sky, the Maya World: A Symbolic Analysis of Yucatec Maya Cosmology. Ph.D. Dissertation. Department of Anthropology, State University of New York, Albany.

Tarn, Nathaniel, and Martin Prechtel

1986 Constant Inconstancy: The Feminine Principal in Atiteco Mythology. In *Symbol and Meaning Beyond the Closed Community: Essays in Mesoamerican Ideas,* ed. Gary H. Gossen, 173–184. Institute of Mesoamerican Studies, Studies in Culture and Society, Vol. 1. State University of New York, Albany.

Thompson, J. Eric

1970 *Maya History and Religion*. University of Oklahoma Press, Norman.

Valdizón Burmester, Wanda Mariana

1995 Reconocimiento en la cuenca del Río Poxte, Petén: un aceramiento a la organización política del area. Tesis de Licenciatura. Área de Arqueología, Universidad de San Carlos, Guatemala.

Wilson, Richard

1995 *Maya Resurgence in Guatemala: Q'eqchi' Experiences.* University of Oklahoma Press, Norman.

Wisdom, Charles

1952 The Supernatural World and Curing. In *Heritage of Conquest: The Ethnology of Middle America,* ed. Sol Tax, 119–141. Free Press, Glencoe, IL.

Chapter Twelve

De-fanging the Earth Monster

Speleothem Transport to Surface Sites in the Sibun Valley

by Polly A. Peterson
Patricia A. McAnany
Allan B. Cobb

As cave research has matured, the breakage and movement of cave formations—or speleothems—have come to be recognized as ubiquitous forms of cave modification (Brady et al. 1997). Most research, however, has been cave focused, although it is generally suggested that a substantial amount of the broken material has been removed from caves (Burnett et al. 2002; Espinosa et al. 2003). The recent integration of cave studies into larger archaeological projects provides an unparalleled opportunity to test that assumption and to recover data on how speleothems were actually used. This chapter reports on attempts by the Xibun Archaeological Research Project (XARP) to document speleothem utilization in surface archaeological contexts. The most serious problem faced by the study was the inability of archaeologists to recognize speleothems. XARP developed a speleothem typology with specific identification criteria that was presented to all project personnel and is reproduced in the next section. As a result of this specialized training, XARP amassed the most extensive data on the surface utilization of speleothems, with thousands purposely incorporated into Maya surface architecture.

A TYPOLOGY OF SPELEOTHEMS

Whereas other aspects of ancient Maya cave use have received attention in the literature, the transport of speleothems from caves and their deposition in burials and architectural features at surface sites have been largely overlooked (Brady et al. 1997: 725). A primary reason for this oversight has been the failure to recognize speleothems. None had been found at Dos Pilas until James Brady and members of the cave subproject discussed speleothems with the project archaeologists (Brady et al. 1997: 737). Examples were recovered the very next day. In the Sibun Valley, once Cobb explained to project members how to identify speleothems, they were soon discovered in excavations at surface sites. Additionally, field school students were trained in both caves and settlements in the Sibun Valley; thus, their firsthand familiarity with speleothems growing in their natural state facilitated the identification of speleothems in other contexts. The following typology of speleothems developed by XARP is based on the classification system presented by Coral Hill and Paulo Forti (1997) and includes speleothems that commonly are found in caves and have been observed in archaeological contexts.

Speleothem is a general term that denotes any secondary mineral deposit resulting from chemical precipitation of groundwater that has entered a cave. As water percolates through the limestone/dolomite bedrock, minerals (primarily calcite, aragonite, and gypsum) dissolved by acids in the water are redeposited as secondary crystal growth, or speleothems. Speleothems form in a wide variety of shapes and sizes depending on the minerals involved and the depositional environment. The rate of growth varies widely; thus, it is not possible to make any kind of assumption about the age of speleothems based on their size, even if found within the same cave. Speleothem growth depends on factors such as water source, water quantity, water composition, carbon dioxide content, and temperature. All of these conditions vary both seasonally and over longer periods of time. A general rule is that speleothems grow faster in areas with higher annual rainfall than in drier areas. Some speleothems may be tens or hundreds of thousands of years old. Conversely, a stalagmite over a meter tall has been observed growing out of a Maya vessel—less than 2,000 years old—at Actun Kabal in the Chiquibul cave system of Belize (McNatt 1996: 86, figure 1; Stone 1995: 19, figure 2-5).

A *stalactite* is a cylindrical or conical speleothem that hangs from a cave ceiling or ledge and resembles an icicle. Stalactites are formed from the mineral calcite and are one of the most easily recognizable types of speleothems, ranging in size from a few centimeters to tens of meters in length. Stalactites vary widely in color, from white to yellow or brown and tan, although color may be altered by postdepositional processes (e.g., burning). Stalactites form by water dripping from the ceiling of a cave. Calcite is deposited on a stalactite as water flows down its

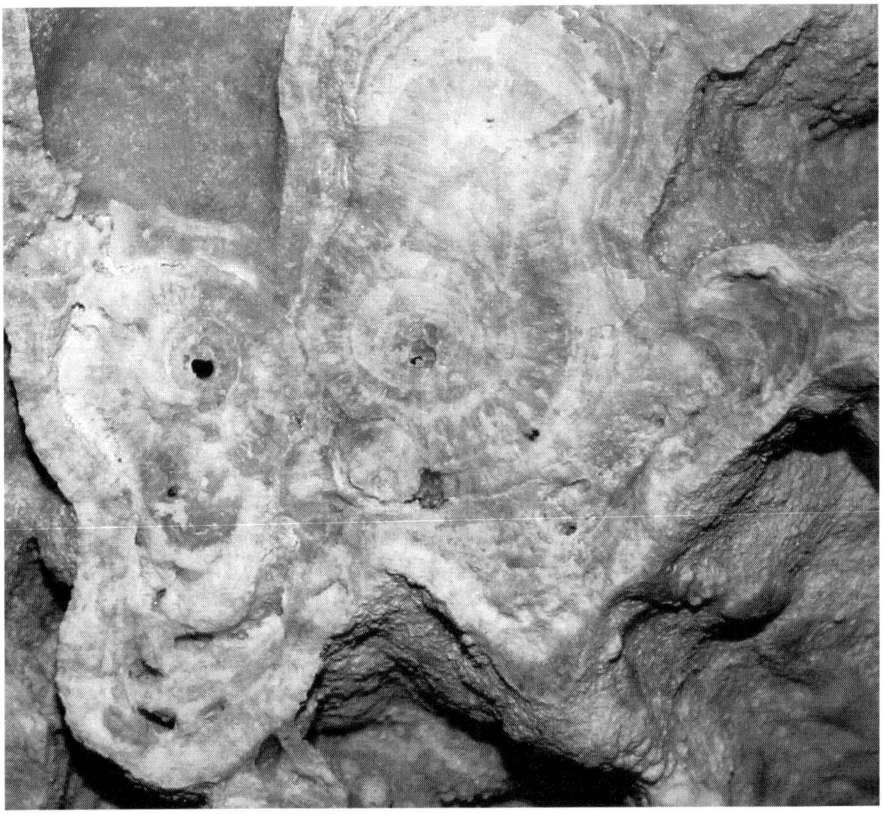

FIGURE 12.1. *Cross section of a stalactite (photo by Allan B. Cobb).*

surface; therefore, a cross section of a stalactite reveals growth rings similar to those of a tree and often has a canal at the core (Figure 12.1). Broken stalactites are readily identified by their pointed tips. When only a fragment of the body is found, its cylindrical shape, central canal, and growth rings are identifying characteristics.

A *soda straw* is a stalactite in the beginning stage of formation. As the name implies, they are morphologically similar to a straw, with thin walls and a hollow interior. Common in tropical caves, soda straws generally are no longer than 60 cm, although lengths of up to 14 m have been recorded. Soda straws are delicate and easily broken. Once their thin walls dry out, they become fragile and quickly turn to calcite dust. In our experience, most speleothems excavated in archaeological surface sites become fragile and powdery as they dry out; thus, care should be taken in their conservation and analysis.

Draperies, also known as "curtains," are another common calcite speleothem. Draperies form as water trickles down inclined cave ceilings or walls. They may be flat or highly furled and contain calcite crystals that form perpendicular to the cave wall. Impurities in the water may result in colored bands, and it is common to see draperies with red, yellow, and white stripes like bacon. The lower edge may have fringes or serrations resembling the teeth of a saw. Draperies may be very thin and translucent or several centimeters thick. When fragments are found, draperies are readily identifiable by their banding, two growth surfaces, and serrated edge.

A *stalagmite* (Figure 12.2) is a calcite speleothem of cylindrical or conical shape that grows up from the floor of a cave as a result of water dripping from the ceiling or from a stalactite. When found in association with a paired stalactite, a stalagmite will typically have a larger diameter. Usually rounded on top, stalagmites in cross section do not show growth rings as stalactites do. Stalagmites range in size from a few centimeters to tens of meters in height. They may be as thin as a broomstick or tens of meters in diameter. When fragments are found, stalagmites are readily identified by their cylindrical shape, rounded ends, and solid crystalline structure without growth rings or a central canal.

Flowstone, or *travertine*, is one of the most common types of speleothems. Flowstone forms in layers as water deposits calcite across a surface. Flowstone exhibits rippled surface textures that range between smooth and very rough. Color also varies widely, from white to yellow, red, brown, and tan. Usually composed of calcite, flowstone crystals form perpendicular to the growth surface. In cross section, flowstone shows distinct layers that may appear as multicolored bands. Fragments of flowstone are easily identified by their relatively flat but slightly rippled surface (Figure 12.3) and banded or layered cross section. Because of the manner in which flowstone forms, it is easily broken into slabs that often exhibit one smooth surface. When travertine is formed not in a cave but on the surface, in a river, for example, it is referred to as *tufa* (Jennings 1985: 103–106) to distinguish it from cave travertine, which is referred to as a speleothem.

Dogtooth spars are large crystals that form very slowly in standing water (Figure 12.4). It is not uncommon to find such large crystals of calcite or other minerals within caves.

Coralloids, commonly called "popcorn" or "cave coral," cover a broad category of common speleothems. Coralloids grow on cave walls, floors, ceilings, and even on other speleothems. Their shape may be globular, nodular, like a bunch of grapes, or coral-like. Their color varies widely among shades of white, brown, and red. Outside of the cave environment, the smaller and more delicate coralloids are likely to dry out and become fragile. It is not uncommon to see coralloids growing on the surface of artifacts deposited in caves.

INVESTIGATION OF CAVES AND SETTLEMENTS IN THE SIBUN VALLEY

The study of cave use and speleothem transport is a component of the Xibun Archaeological Research Project, which receives its name from Early Colonial pe-

FIGURE 12.2. *Stalagmite (photo by Polly A. Peterson).*

riod spellings of the river and a seventeenth-century *visita* reputed to have been established among Xibun Maya. XARP is a multidisciplinary project designed to integrate settlement with landscape use in a karst-rich region of central Belize (Figure 12.5). XARP is one of several archaeological projects that combine investiga-

FIGURE 12.3. *Cut flowstone slab (photo courtesy of Sandra López-Varela).*

FIGURE 12.4. *Dogtooth spar (photo by Patricia A. McAnany).*

tion of settlement patterns with cave studies in an effort to understand how Maya people of the past perceived their natural landscape and materialized those perceptions. More specifically, the ideological significance of caves and other natural features of a landscape is increasingly recognized as an integral part of understanding the ancient Maya built environment (Awe 1998; Brady 1997; Brady and Ashmore 1999; Hammond 1981: 176–177; McAnany 1998; Prufer 2002; Rissolo 2001). Nowhere is this more apparent than in the Sibun Valley of central Belize where the inhabitants of valley settlements traveled to the surrounding karstic landscape to deposit cultural material in caves, most of which are located directly across the river from settlements. This study builds on previous cave surveys conducted by Juan Luis Bonor Villarejo (1989) at Oxkintok, Ann Scott (1992) at Copan, James Brady (1997) at Dos Pilas, Philip Reeder (Reeder, Brady, and Webster 1998) on the Vaca Plateau, Dominique Rissolo (2001) in the Yalahau region, Keith Prufer (2002) on the Maya Mountains Archaeological Project, and Reiko Ishihara (2003) at Caracol, but it has stressed the reciprocal nature of cave/settlement interaction to a greater extent than past work. The Maya did not simply deposit offerings in caves, but they also took items from this subterranean world back to their settlements. Speleothems incorporated into architectural features such as shrines, burials, ball courts, and residences represent the materialization of this reciprocal relationship at surface sites.

Within the Sibun drainage, most caves in our investigation are located in the Sibun-Manatee karst. One important exception is Actun Chanona, a large cave

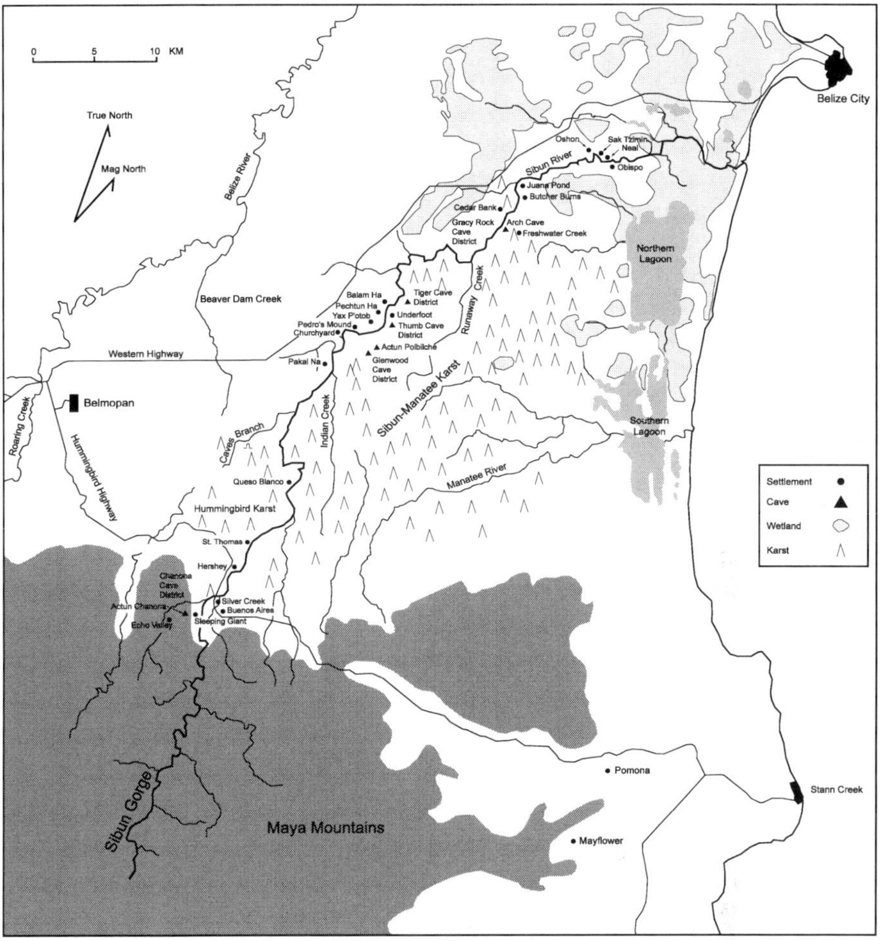

FIGURE 12.5. *Location of settlements relative to cave districts (map courtesy of Ben Thomas).*

situated near the base of the Sibun Gorge in the majestic Hummingbird karst on the northeastern flank of the Maya Mountains. The Sibun-Manatee karst is one of eight karst regions that, taken together, cover about half of the surface area of Belize (Miller 1996: 103). It is characterized by towers (steep-sided hills of erosion-resistant Cretaceous limestone and dolomite) that rise up to 200 m, with dramatically contrasting interior solution valleys (or cockpits) that plunge to sea level (Boles 1999: 9; Miller 1996: 113). The landscape resembles an egg carton. The Tiger Cave District, for instance, is a series of isolated interior valleys interconnected by small caves like Pottery Cave, which, despite its diminutive size, contained thirteen pottery vessels. This cone karst dominates the landscape on the southeastern side of the Sibun River and extends roughly 30 km eastward toward the shores of the Northern and Southern Lagoons. In addition to hundreds of small caves, large caverns, like Glenwood Cave, are found in some of the larger, more isolated hills of the Sibun-Manatee karst. Flat pine savannah and riparian forest characterize the northern side of the river in the midreaches. Today, citrus and cacao groves cover river terraces on which Late Terminal Classic Maya settlements, such as Pechtun Ha and Pakal Na, are located. Downstream near the settlement of Cedar Bank and Arch Cave, the karst ends at Gracy Rock. The settlements of Samuel Oshon and Augustine Obispo are located east of the karst zone on the edge of the mangrove swamps that characterize the Sibun Valley before the river empties into the Caribbean Sea.

The Hummingbird karst is part of the same central Belize limestone belt as the Sibun-Manatee karst but is located farther to the southwest. The Hummingbird karst is positioned at a boundary fault line that divides the upthrust, granitic Maya Mountains from a zone of Cretaceous limestone pocketed with Paleocene-Eocene chert-bearing limestone (Boles 1999: 9). The limestone is brecciated in the Hummingbird area and contains metamorphics from the adjacent Maya Mountains (Day, Neal, and Rosen 1987: 22). Cockpit valleys are not common in the Hummingbird karst; rather, it is characterized by freestanding hills with pointed peaks and open valleys, suggesting paleodrainage into the Belize Valley and Roaring Creek (Day, Neal, and Rosen 1987: 22, 24). Actun Chanona, the largest of the Xibun caves and the only one to contain monumental architecture, is situated high on a hill within the Hummingbird karst. Down on the floodplain is the Hershey site, which contains the largest mass of monumental architecture within the Sibun Valley.

Since 1997, XARP teams have investigated ancient Maya settlements and caves in this environmental context (McAnany 1998, 2002; McAnany and Thomas 2003; McAnany et al. 2002). A total of eighteen caves utilized by the ancient Maya have been located and mapped; these data complement parallel data sets collected from the twenty-two settlements documented by XARP, each located within 1 km of a cave. Plan view maps of cave floors were created to document the location of artifacts and cultural modifications to cave interiors, such as rock art (Rowe et al. 2002) and architecture (Cobb 2003; Kenward 2002; Kenward, this volume). Surface collections recovered well-preserved artifacts, including polychrome vessels, marine shell, wooden torches, and obsidian blades (Peterson 2002, 2003a, 2003b). Although Xibun caves were the loci of ritual activity from the Formative through the Colonial period, the majority of identifiable ceramic types date to the Late and Terminal Classic periods, when data from settlement excavations suggest that the population maximum was reached in the valley.

CONTEXTUALIZING SPELEOTHEM TRANSPORT

Large numbers of speleothems were noted on the surface and in tumbled construction material atop structures at the Hershey, Samuel Oshon, Augustine Obispo, and Pechtun Ha sites. The enormous work entailed in documenting the thousands of speleothems on the surface of structures would have monopolized too large a percentage of the project personnel, so the decision was made to limit the sample to speleothems found within excavation units. In total, 162 speleothems were collected from excavations at the Samuel Oshon, Cedar Bank, Pechtun Ha, Pakal Na, and Hershey sites. Analysis of the 98 speleothems documented during the XARP 1999 and 2001 seasons is presented in Table 12.1. During the 2003 field season, an additional 64 speleothems were collected from three locales at the Hershey site—most notably a ball court (Structures 508 and 509)—and from a circular shrine (Structure 479) at the Augustine Obispo site. Although these data are not presented in Table 12.1, their salient characteristics are included in the following discussion. The specimens collected from the XARP 1999 and 2001 excavations ranged widely in mass (from 0.2 g up to the hefty weight of 3.6 kg and from 1.6 to 23 cm in length), although larger speleothems—such as a 58-cm-long drapery found in front of the main pyramid at the Hershey site—were noted on the surface. The contexts of the analyzed sample are summarized in Table 12.1.

Sixty-seven percent of the speleothems collected during the XARP 1999 and 2001 seasons came from the construction fill of shrines and monumental architecture. Although tufa can be found along the banks of the Sibun and the sides of the karst hills, the sample from construction fill includes unambiguous speleothems—namely, six soda straws, two stalactites, one stalagmite, four dogtooth spars, and two coralloids. These speleothems likely originated in the caves located directly across the river from the settlements. Construction materials may have been mined from caves, but the breakage of speleothems would have been deliberate.

Six of the seven dogtooth spars, or cave crystals, collected by XARP were found in the largest platform (Structure 351) at the site of Cedar Bank. Significantly, this residence contained associated Colonial period Maya and Spanish materials (Morandi 2003).

Xibun Maya incorporated speleothems into ritual architecture. For example, a flowstone slab (found covered with mortar) along with thirty-four additional speleothems were used in the construction of the terraced walls and alley of the ball court at the Hershey site. Also, speleothems were integrated into circular shrines at the sites of Pechtun Ha (Structure 100), Samuel Oshon (Structure 402), and Augustine Obispo (Structure 479). At Pechtun Ha, a large stalactite (Figure 12.6) was found atop the walls of the shrine. This structure is the only circular building at the site, as well as the only platform built entirely out of stone, in contrast to the earthen mounds with limestone retaining walls that characterize the site (Harrison and Acone 2002: 134). In addition to the presence of speleothems, these shrines contained the majority of unworked marine and riverine shells recovered from the sites (Harrison 2003: 180–181). Conch shells and speleothems were used in the construction of the doorway of the circular shrine at the Augustine Obispo site (Harrison-Buck 2004: 22, figure 3.3).

Surface association of speleothems with architecture was also noted along Caves Branch, a tributary of the Sibun River that contains some of the best-known

TABLE 12.1. Speleothems collected from excavations at Sibun Valley sites

	Speleothem type							
	stalactite	*stalagmite*	*soda straw*	*flowstone*	*dogtooth spar/crystal*	*coralloid/ popcorn*	*unidentified*	*total number collected*
Excavation Context								
Collected from modern ground surface	1	—	—	—	—	—	—	1
Construction tumble	2	—	—	4	—	—	4	10
Top zone	—	—	—	2	—	—	—	2
Ancient surface (not plaster floor)	—	—	1	2	1	—	3	7
Midden	—	—	1	1	—	—	1	3
Construction fill	2	1	6	34	4	2	17	66
Burial	1	1	—	1	—	—	—	3
Earthen layer	—	—	—	4	2	—	—	6
Total number collected	6	2	8	48	7	2	25	98

Xibun Archaeological Research Project 1999 and 2001

FIGURE 12.6. *Stalactite found atop the circular shrine at Pechtun Ha (photo by Patricia A. McAnany).*

caves in the Maya Lowlands (Bonor Villarejo 1995; Reents 1980). Although documentation of surface sites within Caves Branch Valley has yet to be undertaken, McAnany and Cobb visited a large hilltop center, locally called Deep Valley. Surface reconnaissance revealed a cut flowstone slab that had been used in architectural construction as well as a stalactite, measuring almost 90 cm in length, that was found in a courtyard. In southern Belize, Peterson observed speleothems on the surface of structures located in the main plazas of Uxbenka and Nim Li Punit. Travertine was also noted in several contexts at Lubaantun, where the nearest cave is located less than 2 km upstream (Norman Hammond 2001: personal communication).

The presence of speleothems in settlement contexts is complemented by evidence of speleothem mining within all of the Xibun caves. Some breakage resulted in movement of speleothems within caves (Parks 2003: 210–211) and use in cave architecture (see Kenward, this volume); however, the large amount of speleothem breakage cannot be accounted for by redeposition within caves alone. The broken materials have resurfaced at settlement contexts in far greater quantities than within caves themselves.

UNDERSTANDING SPELEOTHEM USE

The Xibun data have important implications for our understanding of speleothem use among the ancient Maya. Brady and colleagues' (1997) proposal that large numbers of broken speleothems had been removed from caves has received scant attention from settlement archaeologists in the absence of a theory of ritual use that could account for their removal. XARP has found that the use of speleothems as symbolic adjuncts to construction at surface contexts was extensive enough to account for the bulk of breakage and removal evident in Xibun caves. It is noteworthy that the first project in which personnel were trained in the identification of speleothems should document transport and utilization on a previously unimagined scale. This suggests that the failure of previous projects to collect comparable data is a reflection of their inability to recognize speleothems.

These data are relevant to related debates. Dean Arnold (1971: 33) has recorded an ethnographic example of the use of crushed speleothems as temper for ceramic production in the Yucatán. Brady and colleagues (1997: 727) tend to dismiss this use in ancient times because ceramic production would have rapidly exhausted the finite supply of speleothems and because the pattern of breakage and removal does not resemble what one would expect from systematic mining. Arnold's suggested function, however, still has appeal to archaeologists who are more comfortable with a utilitarian explanation, especially where a ritual use could not be recognized. The XARP team has now documented the incorporation of speleothems in surface architecture, which reduces the tenability of the temper hypothesis, particularly in the absence of any recorded use in ancient ceramics.

The incorporation of speleothems into architecture in the Sibun Valley is not unique. At the northern Yucatecan site of Naranjál, a large stalactite was discovered in the collapse of a Late Postclassic shrine built on the top of Structure 2 (Lorenzen 1999: 102). Burned speleothems were also found with *incensario* fragments around basal altars (Karl Lorenzen 2000: personal communication). The presence of conch shells and speleothems in the doorway of the circular shrine at the Augustine Obispo site is a particularly interesting example. Throughout Mesoamerica, round temples are associated with water, wind, fertility, and the underworld (Ringle, Gallareta Negrón, and Bey 1998: 185–186; Taube 2000), which may also be symbolized by shells and speleothems. The inclusion of speleothems in the construction of shrines, along with the deposition of marine shells, may have been used to strengthen and accentuate these associations.

The question remains as to why speleothems have been associated with public architecture in such large numbers. The answer appears to lie in Maya cosmology, particularly as it relates to architecture and its place in the cultural landscape. At the most basic level, Maya cosmology shares the general Amerindian concern with earth as a sacred entity. Human settlements are referred to as "*chan ch'een*" (sky cave) (Martin 2001: 178; Vogt and Stuart 2005: 160, 162). Although the significance of this is not fully understood, it appears analogous to the Nahuatl use of the term *altepetl* (water-filled mountain) to refer to settlements. In both cases human settlement is identified with these important landscape features, and Brady (1997: 603) argues that mountains and caves are part of the same complex that represents earth. This is important because architecture is intimately associated with landscape. In Yucatán during the sixteenth century, the Maya used the word *aktun* to refer to both a cave and a stone building, suggesting to J. Eric Thompson (1959: 124) that the two were closely linked conceptually. David Stuart and Stephen Houston (1994: 86) note that architectural features are often referred to by some metaphor for "hill." It may be that in identifying architectural features with hills and caves, it was the incorporation of speleothems that made it so. At the least, this type of importation makes it clear that caves possessed a power that could be infused into surface architecture.

Speleothems also appear to be associated with burials. A stalactite, a stalagmite (Figure 12.7), and a piece of flowstone were deposited in the fill of a burial pit prepared for an elite male at the site of Pakal Na (Harrison and Acone 2003: 107–108). The speleothems found in this burial appear to be part of a larger pattern. Speleothems have been reported from mortuary deposits at other Maya sites, such as Burial E-54/9 at Altun Ha (Pendergast 1990: 150), Burials 5 and 6 at Piedras Negras (Coe 1959: figure 64), and Tomb 6 at Copan (Longyear 1952: 43). A ground speleothem celt from an Early Middle Formative midden containing burials was discovered at Colha (Buttles 2002: 314). In southern Belize, Nim Li Punit Tomb 2 contained stalagmites, an Early Classic polychrome dish, and marine shells but no human remains (Juan Luis Bonor Villarejo 2004: personal communication). More speleothem fragments have been reported from a tomb at Muklebal Tzul in the Maya Mountains (Peter Dunham 2004: personal communication). Keith Prufer (2002: 434) reported that many natural caves located below structures at Muklebal Tzul were used for mortuary purposes. Caches containing stalagmites and stalactites were found in front of and within eastern buildings interpreted as charnel houses at Caracol (Chase and Chase 1994: 59; 1998: 311). These offerings were probably obtained locally, as broken speleothems and architecture have been recorded by Cobb in caves surrounding Caracol. The ideology behind the inclusion of speleothems as burial offerings is unclear. It may be that they were related to tombs seen as symbolic caves. Richard Adams and Hubert Robichaux (1992: 416) describe the Rio Azul tombs as "cave-like" and remark that "[t]he use of such artificial caves

FIGURE 12.7. *A stalactite and a stalagmite excavated from a burial of an elite male at Pakal Na (photo by Patricia A. McAnany).*

[tombs] for burial is consistent with ancient and modern Maya beliefs in which caves are and were a holy abode where the Earth God resides."

Brady and colleagues (1997: 733) note that the fabrication of idols constitutes the most frequently reported use of speleothems, but this may simply reflect the fact that the Spanish ecclesiastical sources were particularly sensitive to such things. Within the Sibun-Manatee karst, a single anthropomorphic figurine carved from a speleothem was discovered in Pottery Cave (Figure 12.8). Although eventually deposited in a cave, the figurine likely enjoyed a long life history, including initial removal and transport from a cave for shaping and use in a surface context, with eventual return to a cave as an offering. An almost identical figurine was recovered from Terminal Classic construction at Colha (Buttles 2002: 278–279, figure 8.7). Although identified by Palma Buttles as made of "limestone," the Colha figurine is likely a carved speleothem. Although such deity representations may have played a culturally important role, the Xibun data suggest that this function was probably relatively unimportant in the explanation of the bulk of speleothem breakage.

A more numerically significant practice may have been associated with pilgrimage. Speleothems may have been used as a material link between ritual performers and the practices that transpired within caves. Just as offerings are left in caves as evidence of a ritual event, visitors to sacred places also carry away tokens that

FIGURE 12.8. *An anthropomorphic figurine carved from a speleothem discovered in Pottery Cave (photo courtesy of Jaime Awe).*

embody the power of the locale to which a pilgrimage has been made (Morinis 1992: 6). Obtaining objects imbued with the power of a particular sacred landmark may have been one of the primary reasons for speleothem use.

CONCLUSIONS

The integration of cave investigations into Maya settlement pattern studies has allowed XARP to make two significant contributions. First, Brady and colleagues (1997) asserted that a significant amount of the material resulting from speleothem breakage noted in caves had been removed, although only meager support for this could be found in the archaeological literature. Excavation in the Sibun region produced evidence on an unprecedented scale for the removal of speleothems from caves. Second, the data clearly show that the majority of the speleothems were incorporated into site architecture. Although a number of uses for speleothems had been proposed, this was not mentioned, but it clearly accounts for the bulk of surface speleothems. These discoveries place this entire area of cave research on a firm evidential basis that can no longer be ignored by settlement archaeology.

In the recently discovered Formative period mural at San Bartolo (Figure 12.9a), a stalactite has been depicted as the fang of the Earth Monster (Saturno, Taube, and Stuart 2005), and cave entrances often assume a distinct resemblance to an open maw (Figure 12.9b) in Maya iconography. Yukatek Maya continue to associate speleothems with the fangs of the serpent deity, *yum baalam* (Sosa 1985: 414); thus, speleothems are emblems of the animate earth. Whereas modern practices may inform us of the symbolic meaning of speleothems, a contextual analysis of speleothems at surface archaeological sites suggests that in the past the fangs of the Earth Monster were extracted and transported from caves for a range of uses. Archaeologically, the recovery of speleothems in surface sites indicates their significance in mortuary assemblages, to structure dedication, and in general public architecture. These examples of speleothems recovered at surface sites indicate that our interpretive narratives of ancient Maya sites will be greatly enhanced by the recognition and recording of these transported pieces of the landscape. Moreover, increased attention to contextual analyses—not only of artifacts deposited within caves but also of speleothems that were extracted from caves and deposited within ritually charged settlement contexts—will refine our understanding of both landscape cognition and the built environment. The interplay between rituals conducted in caves and those practiced within settlements is crucial to the refinement of anthropological theories of ritual practice. The transport of speleothems from caves to surface sites provides a window into both worlds.

ACKNOWLEDGMENTS

The cave research reported herein is a component of the Xibun Archaeological Research Project, which has received funding from the National Science Founda-

FIGURE 12.9a. *Fangs of the Earth Monster. Woman inside an anthropomorphic cave with a stalactite "fang." Detail from a Formative period mural at San Bartolo, Guatemala (art by Heather Hurst, courtesy of William A. Saturno, Proyecto San Bartolo).*

tion (BCS-0096603), the Division of International Programs at Boston University, and the Ahau Foundation. Numerous field school students, graduate students, specialists, support staff, and volunteers contributed to XARP, which was conducted under permits issued by the Department of Archaeology, Belmopan, Belize. We would especially like to thank James Brady for thoughtful comments on this work and the opportunity to present an earlier version of this chapter in the symposium, "In the Maw of the Earth Monster: Recent Advances in Cave Archaeology," at the 2003 meeting of the Society for American Archaeology in Milwaukee, Wisconsin.

FIGURE 12.9b. *Fangs of the Earth Monster. The mawlike entrance of Actun Chanona (photo courtesy of David McLain/Aurora).*

REFERENCES CITED

Adams, Richard E.W., and Hubert Robichaux

1992 Tombs of Rio Azul, Guatemala. *National Geographic Research and Exploration* 8:412–427.

Arnold, Dean E.

1971 Ethnominerology of Ticul Yucatan Potters: Etics and Emics. *American Antiquity* 36:20–40.

Awe, Jaime J.

1998 *The Western Belize Regional Cave Project: A Report of the 1997 Field Season,* ed. Jaime J. Awe. Occasional Paper No. 1. Department of Anthropology, University of New Hampshire, Durham.

Boles, Ed

1999 *The Sibun River Watershed Atlas.* Sibun Watershed Association and the Government Printer, Belmopan, Belize.

Bonor Villarejo, Juan Luis

1989 *Las cuevas Mayas: simbolismo y ritual.* Universidad Complutense de Madrid, Madrid.

1995 Excavación de Salvamento en "Caves Branch Rock Shelter," Cayo District, Belize, *IV Encuento Internacional Investigadores de la Cultura Maya* 1:46–70.

Brady, James E.

1997 Settlement Configuration and Cosmology: The Role of Caves at Dos Pilas. *American Anthropologist* 99(3):602–618.

Brady, James E., and Wendy Ashmore

1999 Mountains, Caves, Water: Ideational Landscapes of the Ancient Maya. In *Archaeologies of Landscape: Contemporary Perspectives,* eds. Wendy Ashmore and A. Bernard Knapp, 124–145. Blackwell Publishers, Malden, MA.

Brady, James E., Ann Scott, Hector Neff, and Michael D. Glascock

1997 Speleothem Breakage, Movement, Removal, and Caching: An Aspect of Ancient Maya Cave Modification. *Geoarchaeology* 12(6):725–750.

Burnett, Robert, Sergio Garza, James E. Brady, and Allan Cobb

2002 An Assessment of Ancient Maya Stalactite Breakage From Balam Na Cave 1, Peten, Guatemala. Paper presented at the 67th Annual Meeting of the Society for American Archaeology, Denver.

Buttles, Palma J.

2002 Material and Meaning: A Contextual Examination of Select Portable Material Culture From Colha, Belize. Ph.D. Dissertation. Department of Anthropology, University of Texas, Austin.

Chase, Arlen F., and Diane Z. Chase

1994 Maya Veneration of the Dead at Caracol, Belize. In *Seventh Palenque Round Table, 1989,* eds. Merle Greene Robertson and Virginia M. Fields, 55–62. Pre-Columbian Art Research Institute, San Francisco.

Chase, Diane Z., and Arlen F. Chase

1998 The Architectural Context of Caches, Burials, and Other Ritual Activities for the Classic Period Maya (as Reflected at Caracol, Belize). In *Function and*

Meaning in Classic Maya Architecture, ed. Stephen D. Houston, 299–332. Dumbarton Oaks, Washington, D.C.

Cobb, Allan B.
2003 Caves as Modified and Constructed Space for Ritual Practice: The Case of Actun Chanona. In *Between the Gorge and the Estuary: Archaeological Investigations of the 2001 Season of the Xibun Archaeological Research Project,* eds. Patricia A. McAnany and Ben Thomas, 35–49. www.bu.edu/tricia/reports.shtml (access date 9/28/05).

Coe, William R.
1959 *Piedras Negras Archaeology: Artifacts, Caches, and Burials.* The University Museum, University of Pennsylvania, Philadelphia.

Day, Michael J., Michael Neal, and Carol Rosen
1987 Physical Geography: An Introduction. In *Environment and Resources in the Hummingbird Karst,* Occasional Paper No. 2, ed. Michael J. Day, 21–31. Department of Geography, University of Wisconsin, Milwaukee.

Espinosa, Cesar, James E. Brady, Sergio Garza, and Allan Cobb
2003 Quantifying Speleothem Breakage: An Example From Balam Na Cave 1. Paper presented at the 68th Annual Meeting of the Society for American Archaeology, Milwaukee.

Hammond, Norman
1981 Settlement Patterns in Belize. In *Lowland Maya Settlement Patterns,* ed. Wendy Ashmore, 157–186. University of New Mexico Press, Albuquerque.

Harrison, Eleanor
2003 A Circular Shrine and Repositioned Stelae at the Oshon Site (Operation 24). In *Between the Gorge and the Estuary: Archaeological Investigations of the 2001 Season of the Xibun Archaeological Research Project,* eds. Patricia A. McAnany and Ben Thomas, 165–185. www.bu.edu/tricia/reports.shtml (access date 9/28/05).

Harrison, Eleanor, and Kevin Acone
2002 Further Investigations at Pechtun Ha: Feasting and Mass Importation of Cave Speleothems. In *Sacred Landscape and Settlement in the Sibun River Valley,* ed. Patricia A. McAnany, 123–147. Institute of Mesoamerican Studies, Occasional Publication No. 8. University at Albany, State University of New York, Albany.
2003 Revisiting the Mortuary Deposits of Structure 130 at Pakal Na (Operation 22). In *Between the Gorge and the Estuary: Archaeological Investigations of the 2001 Season of the Xibun Archaeological Research Project,* eds. Patricia A. McAnany and Ben Thomas, 99–121. www.bu.edu/tricia/reports.shtml (access date 9/28/05).

Harrison-Buck, Eleanor
2004 Circular Shrine at the Augustine Obispo Site (Operation 32). In *Sibun Valley From Late Classic Through Colonial Times: Investigations of the 2003 Season of the Xibun Archaeological Research Project,* eds. Patricia A. McAnany, Eleanor Harrison-Buck, and Steven Morandi, 19–39. www.bu.edu/tricia/reports.shtml (access date 9/28/05).

Hill, Carol, and Paulo Forti

1997 *Cave Minerals of the World*, Second Edition, eds. Carol Hill and Paulo Forti. National Speleological Society, Huntsville, AL.

Ishihara, Reiko

2003 Are There Any Holes Around Here? A Preliminary Report on the Caracol Regional Cave Survey. Paper presented at the 68th Annual Meeting of the Society for American Archaeology, Milwaukee.

Jennings, Joseph N.

1985 *Karst Geomorphology*. Basil Blackwell, Oxford.

Kenward, Amalia

2002 Ritual Pathways and the Alteration of Cave Features. In *Sacred Landscape and Settlement in the Sibun River Valley,* ed. Patricia A. McAnany, 59–70. Institute of Mesoamerican Studies, Occasional Publication No. 8. University at Albany, State University of New York, Albany.

Longyear, John M., III

1952 *Copan Ceramics: A Study of Southeastern Maya Pottery,* Publication 597. Carnegie Institution of Washington, Washington, D.C.

Lorenzen, Karl J.

1999 New Discoveries at Tumben-Naranjál: Late Postclassic Reuse and the Ritual Recycling of Cultural Geography. *Mexicon* 21:98–107.

Martin, Simon

2001 Under a Deadly Star: Warfare Among the Classic Maya. In *Maya: Divine Kings of the Rainforest,* English Edition, ed. Nikolai Grube, 174–185. Könemann, Cologne, Germany.

McAnany, Patricia A.

1998 The Xibun Archaeological Research Project. In *Caves and Settlements of the Sibun River Valley, Belize: 1997 Archaeological Survey and Excavation,* ed. Patricia A. McAnany, 1–12. www.bu.edu/tricia/reports.shtml (access date 9/28/05).

2002 *Sacred Landscape and Settlement in the Sibun River Valley,* ed. Patricia A. McAnany. Institute of Mesoamerican Studies, Occasional Publication No. 8. University at Albany, State University of New York, Albany.

McAnany, Patricia A., and Ben Thomas

2003 *Between the Gorge and the Estuary: Archaeological Investigations of the 2001 Season of the Xibun Archaeological Research Project,* eds. Patricia A. McAnany and Ben Thomas. www.bu.edu/tricia/reports.shtml (access date 9/28/05).

McAnany, Patricia A., Ben S. Thomas, Steven Morandi, Polly A. Peterson, and Eleanor Harrison

2002 Praise the Ajaw and Pass the Kakaw: Xibun Maya and the Political Economy. In *Ancient Maya Political Economies,* eds. Marilyn A. Masson and David A. Freidel, 123–139. Altamira Press, Walnut Creek, CA.

McNatt, Logan

1996 Cave Archaeology of Belize. *Journal of Cave and Karst Studies* 58(2):81–99.

Miller, Thomas E.
1996 Geologic and Hydrologic Controls on Karst and Cave Development in Belize. *Journal of Cave and Karst Studies* 58(2):100–120.

Morandi, Steven
2003 Colonial-Period Occupational Debris at Cedar Bank (Operation 40). In *Between the Gorge and the Estuary: Archaeological Investigations of the 2001 Season of the Xibun Archaeological Research Project,* eds. Patricia A. McAnany and Ben Thomas, 153–157. www.bu.edu/tricia/reports.shtml (access date 9/28/05).

Morinis, Alan
1992 Introduction: The Territory of the Anthropology of Pilgrimage. In *Sacred Journeys: The Anthropology of Pilgrimage,* ed. Alan Morinis, 1–28. Greenwood Press, Westport, CT.

Parks, Shoshaunna
2003 Modification and Transport of Speleothems in the Sibun River Valley. In *Between the Gorge and the Estuary: Archaeological Investigations of the 2001 Season of the Xibun Archaeological Research Project,* eds. Patricia A. McAnany and Ben Thomas, 209–217. www.bu.edu/tricia/reports.shtml (access date 9/28/05).

Pendergast, David M.
1990 *Excavations at Altun Ha, Belize, 1964–1970, Vol. 3.* Royal Ontario Museum, Toronto.

Peterson, Polly A.
2002 Shedding Light on Xibalba Through Cave Survey and Surface Collection. In *Sacred Landscape and Settlement in the Sibun River Valley,* ed. Patricia A. McAnany, 37–57. Institute of Mesoamerican Studies, Occasional Publication No. 8. University at Albany, State University of New York, Albany.
2003a Actun Chanona: The Steep Ascent to the Largest Cave in the Valley. In *Between the Gorge and the Estuary: Archaeological Investigations of the 2001 Season of the Xibun Archaeological Research Project,* eds. Patricia A. McAnany and Ben Thomas, 23–33. www.bu.edu/tricia/reports.shtml (access date 9/28/05).
2003b Caves of the Sibun-Manatee Karst. In *Between the Gorge and the Estuary: Archaeological Investigations of the 2001 Season of the Xibun Archaeological Research Project,* eds. Patricia A. McAnany and Ben Thomas, 83–98. www.bu.edu/tricia/reports.shtml (access date 9/28/05).

Prufer, Keith M.
2002 Communities, Caves, and Ritual Specialists: A Study of Sacred Space in the Maya Mountains of Southern Belize. Ph.D. Dissertation. Department of Anthropology, Southern Illinois University, Carbondale.

Reeder, Philip, James E. Brady, and James Webster
1998 Geoarchaeological Investigations on the Northern Vaca Plateau, Belize. *Mexicon* 10:37–41.

Reents, Dorie J.
1980 The Prehistoric Pottery From Petroglyph Cave, Caves Branch Valley, El Cayo District, Belize, Central America. M.A. Thesis. Department of Anthropology, University of Texas, Austin.

Ringle, William M., Tomás Gallareta Negrón, and George J. Bey III

1998 The Return of Quetzalcoatl: Evidence for the Spread of a World Religion During the Epiclassic Period. *Ancient Mesoamerica* 9:183–232.

Rissolo, Dominique A.

2001 Ancient Maya Cave Use in the Yalahau Region, Northern Quintana Roo, Mexico. Ph.D. Dissertation. Department of Anthropology, University of California, Riverside.

Rowe, Marvin, Allan B. Cobb, Polly A. Peterson, and Patricia A. McAnany

2002 Terminal Classic Pictographs From Actun Ik. In *Sacred Landscape and Settlement in the Sibun River Valley,* ed. Patricia A. McAnany, 71–77. Institute of Mesoamerican Studies, Occasional Publication No. 8. University at Albany, State University of New York, Albany.

Saturno, William A., Karl A. Taube, and David Stuart

2005 The Murals of San Bartolo, El Petén, Guatemala, Part 1: The North Wall. *Ancient America* 7. The Boundary End Archaeology Research Center, Barnardsville, NC.

Scott, Ann M.

1992 Cave Reconnaissance in the Copan Valley. Manuscript on file, Instituto Hondureño de Antropología e Historia, Tegucigalpa.

Sosa, John R.

1985 *The Maya Sky, The Maya World: A Symbolic Analysis of Yucatec Maya Cosmology.* Ph.D. Dissertation. Department of Anthropology, University at Albany, State University of New York, Albany.

Stone, Andrea J.

1995 *Images From the Underworld: Naj Tunich and the Tradition of Maya Cave Painting.* University of Texas Press, Austin.

Stuart, David, and Stephen D. Houston

1994 *Classic Maya Place Names.* Dumbarton Oaks Studies in Pre-Colombian Art and Archaeology 33, Washington, D.C.

Taube, Karl

2000 The Breath of Life: The Symbolism of Wind in Mesoamerica and the American Southwest. In *The Road to Aztlan: Art From a Mythic Homeland,* eds. Virginia M. Fields and Victor Zamudio-Taylor, 102–122. Los Angeles County Museum of Art, Los Angeles.

Thompson, J. Eric S.

1959 The Role of Caves in Maya Culture. *Mitteilungen aus dem Museum für Völkerkunde im Hamburg* 25:122–129.

Vogt, Evon Z., and David Stuart

2005 Some Notes on Ritual Caves Among the Ancient and Modern Maya. In *In the Maw of the Earth Monster: Mesoamerican Ritual Cave Use,* eds. James E. Brady and Keith M. Prufer, 155–185. University of Texas Press, Austin.

Chapter Thirteen

Showing the Way

by Amalia Kenward

The Function of Three Small Caves in the Sibun-Manatee Karst

There is growing acceptance of the fact that caves were important features in the sacred landscape of the Maya (Bonor Villarejo 1989; Brady 1989; Thompson 1975). Intensive investigation over the past twenty years has increased our appreciation of the number of functions in which caves are involved. Some of these functions appear to be related to cave morphology. J. Eric Thompson (1975: xxxix–xli) recognized that some caves were used as "depositories of ceremonially discarded utensils," and James Brady and Irma Rodas (1995) refined this category to show that this occurred in caves with steep vertical chimneys near the entrance or where the chimney opened on the surface. Brady (1997) also argued that cave size appeared to be an issue in elite appropriation of caves at Dos Pilas. Very small caves at the site may have been limited to household utilization. In Quintana Roo, Dominique Rissolo (2003: 132–133) found that large collapse domes appeared to have been appropriated for elite elaboration, and she contrasts this with another morphological type, the rockshelter. In the southern Maya Lowlands, a number of investigators have proposed that rockshelters served as cemeteries (Bonor 1995; Bonor and Glassman 1999; Glassman and Bonor Villarejo, this volume; Prufer 2002; Saul, Prufer, and Saul, this volume; Scott and Brady, this volume). While a member of the Xibun Archaeological Research Project (XARP) directed by Patricia McAnany, I noted a previously unrecorded function related to cave morphology. This study proposes that a particular type of cave was used as a conduit for pedestrian traffic in the Sibun region.

THE SIBUN CAVES

The caves discussed in this study formed in the Sibun-Manatee karst (Miller 1996: 103), which is bounded by the middle reaches of the Sibun and Manatee rivers in south-central Belize. Data presented in this chapter were collected in 1997 and 1999 when I was a XARP member. The thirteen caves and one rockshelter mapped during the two field seasons were divided into three different cave districts: the Tiger Cave District, the Thumb District, and the Glenwood Cave District. The Tiger Cave District (Figure 13.1) was the most extensively documented, as it was the focus of intensive research over the two field seasons. In total, five valleys and eleven caverns within the district were investigated, representing only a sample of caves in the area. The karst hills of this area form small valleys. The majority of the valleys can be reached either through caves that link adjacent valleys or by climbing over the karst hills. Of the eleven caves investigated in the district, three appear to have served a special function in the movement of traffic between valleys.

Actun Yax Tun

Actun Yax Tun (Figure 13.2) is a short, open cave with a high ceiling, running roughly northeast to southwest from Just Two Valley into Yax Valley. Actun Yax Tun is entered from Just Two Valley via a gradual 5-m descent into the cave's nearly 15-m-wide entrance. The cave itself measures 30 m in length and averages 8 to 9 m in width. The ceiling is generally around 8 m high, except in the center where a fissure in the cave roof rises into a dome 10 m above the floor. Once in the cave, light from both entrances can be seen at all times, and the darkest portions of the center of the cave would still be considered to be in the twilight zone.

The route through Actun Yax Tun is fairly unimpeded until near the center, where the cave constricts to 7 m in width and several large chunks (1.5 by 2.0 m and measuring 3 by 4 m) of ceiling collapse, 2 m high, further restrict the passage. Two multicourse rubble walls, 1.0 to 1.5 m high, block sections of the passage. The first, 3 m long, stretches from the northern cave wall to the larger of the boulders (Figure 13.3). The second wall, also about 3 m in length, runs from the southern cave wall and restricts access to a narrow gap in the middle of the passage. Both walls were constructed from limestone cobbles and broken cave formations, some as large as 1 m in length. Similar walls have been documented elsewhere, such as in Cueva de

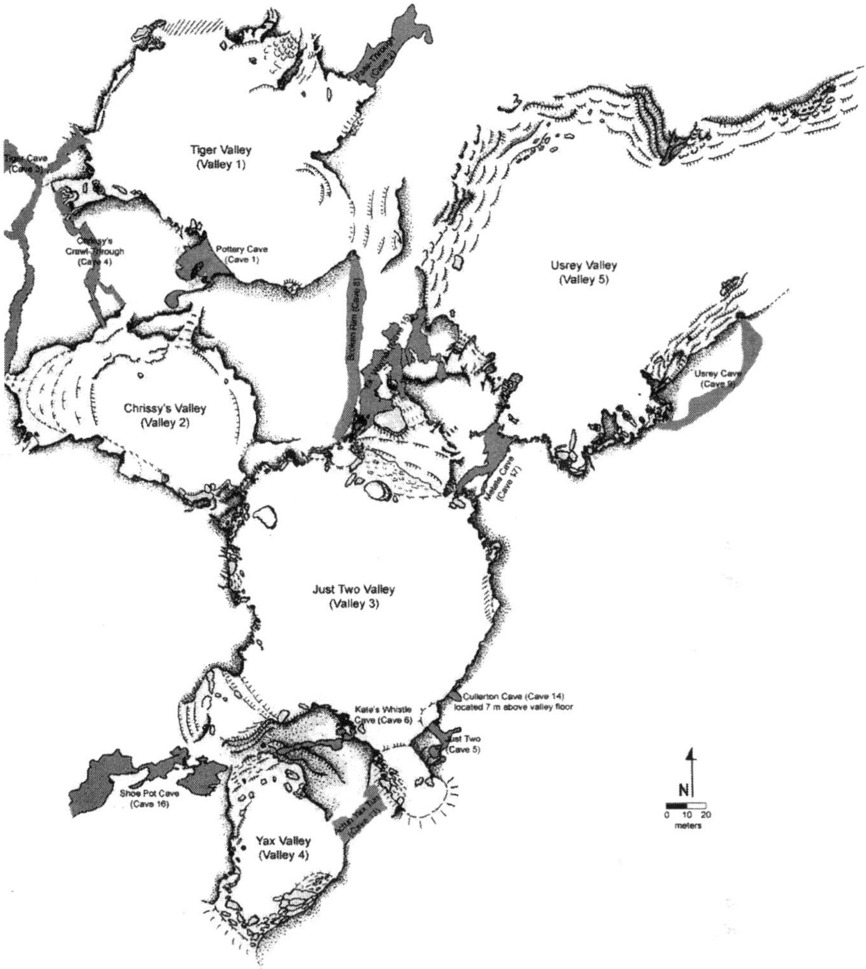

FIGURE 13.1. *Map of the interior cockpit valleys of the Tiger Cave District (paced map, cave locations approximate; for more exact locations see McAnany 2002, map sheet 7).*

los Chiches in Guatemala (Woodfill et al. 2002) and Actun Balam in the Cayo District of Belize (Pendergast 1969: 8).

Beyond this wall, the passage widens to 12 m for the remaining 7 m of the cave. The southwestern entrance is nearly 15 m wide. Near the northern cave wall five broken speleothems were laid end to end to make an arc 3.5 m long and 0.5 to 1.0 m wide. A polished green stone *hacha* (Peterson 2002: 45) was found within 2 m of this arc. Other surface artifacts were rare, but several calcite-encrusted sherds were noted near a speleothem in the central portion of the cave.

FIGURE 13.2. *Map of Actun Yax Tun (courtesy of the Xibun Archaeological Research Project).*

Broken Rim Cave

Broken Rim Cave is a 90-m-long passage that connects Tiger Valley to Just Two Valley. The cave runs roughly northeast to southwest and varies between 5 and 8 m in width throughout. Both entrances measure about 5 m in width. The cave floor is fairly even, and a direct path, deviating only in the central portion to avoid a flowstone column, runs through the cave.

Despite its considerable length, Broken Rim could be traversed without a light if need be. The cave was the preferred transportation corridor between Tiger Valley and Just Two Valley for the XARP team, and a number of ancient modifications suggest that it may have been for the ancient Maya as well. Near the northern entrance, small cobbles were used to fill rimstone dams. A number of holes in the

FIGURE 13.3. *Artificial wall in Actun Yax Tun (photo by Patricia A. McAnany).*

floor near a flowstone column in the middle of the cave had also been filled with gravel and cobbles. The use of cobbles to fill pits and crevices in the passage created a level walkway that could be navigated without light. The few surface artifacts recovered were found near the cave entrances (Isaza, Kenward, and Berry 1998: 73).

Pass-Through Cave

Pass-Through Cave runs northeast to southwest, linking Tiger Valley with the agricultural land of the Sibun floodplain. The cave measures approximately 46 m in length and ranges in width from 8 to 20 m. Pass-Through Cave is the most morphologically complex of the three caves. It would have been quite easy to go astray in the cave if it were not for walls built from speleothems and rubble. The southwestern (Tiger Valley) entrance to the cave is fairly wide, approximately 8 m, although not particularly high. A long wall bisects the southern entrance and runs half the length of the passage. It extends floor to ceiling at the southern entrance and had been cemented in place by calcite from active drips. The ceiling rises above the level of the wall as one moves north. A second, shorter wall bisects the first wall and blocks passage down the eastern side of the cave. The widest point in the cave is in the northeast and terminates in an alcove. Together, these walls direct traffic down the more open western section of the room along a pathway that averages about 10 m wide. Diverting traffic from the dark areas and sections of lower roof facilitates the movement of individuals through the cave.

Although the architectural modifications mentioned previously appear to be designed to direct traffic through the cave, an anomalous feature is a stone wall that almost entirely closes off the 4-m-wide northern entrance. A small opening at the top of the wall currently allows access, but this may not have been present in antiquity. Brady and Pierre Colas (2004, this volume) have recently proposed that some caves have been blocked off as a form of termination after a military defeat. This possibility could easily be checked at Pass-Through Cave by seeing if a hard-packed use-floor runs under the stone wall. If one exists, it would indicate that the northern entrance had been unobstructed during much of the use of the cave.

Few artifacts were recorded in the cave. These were limited to a few sherds at the southern entrance and near the artificial walls. The ceramics consisted of a broken *olla* and fragments of a shallow dish. The fact that the ceramic was covered in calcite suggests that it had been moved from near the wall, the only area of actively dripping water (Isaza, Kenward, and Berry 1998: 60–61).

MORPHOLOGY OF THE SIBUN PEDESTRIAN CAVES

The morphology of the caves described previously is strikingly similar. All three caves have two entrances that terminate in different valleys. All are relatively short. The floors of all three are fairly level throughout, and the passages are fairly straight. The ceilings are also high enough to permit walking without ducking or crawling. Where natural obstructions occur, architectural modifications were constructed to increase accessibility. Areas that could have been dangerous or have allowed travelers to lose their way were blocked with access-altering and access-limiting modifications. It is clear that they were purposely constructed to guide individuals to the opposite end. Although Pass-Through Cave and Broken Rim Cave do have dark zone areas, all three caves can be traversed without a source of light—even Broken Rim Cave, where sight of both entrances is lost en route.

DISCUSSION

Evidence suggests that the three small caves were used by the Xibun Maya as passages between valleys that saved travelers from a longer and more arduous climb over the karst hills that separated those valleys. The use of caves for pedestrian travel appears at first glance to be a utilitarian function, similar to the use of caves as "sources of drinking water" described by Thompson (1975: xiv). Brady (1997: 604) has noted, however, that even caves used as sources of drinking water are marked by crosses (Redfield and Villa Rojas 1962: 114), are named in prayers (Góngora Cámara and Preuss 1990: 144; Redfield 1941: 117; Redfield and Villa Rojas 1962: 343–344), and are the recipients of ritual offerings (Redfield 1941: 118–119; Redfield and Villa Rojas 1962: 176), indicating that they also function as sacred landmarks.

For a number of reasons, I believe a very similar situation occurs with these small caves. The topography of this area is similar to what is found in the highlands, with very well-defined valleys surrounded by hills. Barbara Tedlock (1992: 454) has noted that the name for the principal indigenous deity in most Maya languages translates as "hill-valley." These deities, often referred to as the Earth Lords, are the owners of land and animals within their hill-valley (Gordon 1915). The wide distribution of this figure suggests that it was ancient and probably found in the lowlands as well. Thus, these pedestrian caves would have marked the boundaries between the domains of two Earth Lords. Among modern Maya, these are the types of places where one asks permission to leave one valley, to use the cave, and to enter the other valley (Wilson 1995: 68).

I also argue that pedestrian caves were sacred, not simply because caves are sacred landmarks but because this type of movement appears to be associated with the Earth Lords. Abigail Adams and Brady (2005: 306–307), speaking of the Q'eqchi' Earth Lord, say:

> The term, *Tzuultaq'a,* has another deep meaning in everyday life. The word indicates journeys across the region: people talk of their experience traveling from community to community as *xo-nume chiru tzuultaq'a* (English: We passed through these hills and valleys). People also say that in dreams the *Tzuultaq'a* may appear in the form of or "like a road."

They note that roads and crossroads are also places where offerings are made. Ann Scott and Walter Little (2003) note that the Kaqchikel never approach a cave empty-handed but always have some type of offering. Thus, I would expect that these pedestrian caves would have been places where the Maya paused to make an offering or a prayer.

The archaeological evidence to support this is meager. The caves had few surface artifacts, generally only a small number of sherds. Artifacts tended not to be found within the central portions of the passages but were concentrated in the entrance areas. Part of the problem lay in the fact that so many caves were discovered and the project simply did not have the resources to study them all. Because these caves were small and had few surface artifacts, they were not prime candidates for excavation or intensive investigation. Although the function of these caves was implicitly recognized by project members who were using the caves as tunnels between valleys, the proposal was only formally articulated after an analysis of the architecture suggested a deliberate program of cave modification to enhance accessibility. Since this occurred after the 1999 season, I did not have an opportunity to gather additional data.

I suspect that large numbers of surface artifacts were not found because these caves were regularly cleaned so the offerings did not diminish accessibility. Such ritual maintenance has been documented by Evon Vogt (1976: 102) for the waterholes at Zinacantan. Thus, the large number of small offerings left by the Maya would have been swept up and perhaps deposed nearby.

Modifications were documented in all three caves. In fact, every cave documented within the Tiger Cave District had been modified (Kenward 2002), be it by the construction of multicourse walls made of limestone rubble, the resetting of cave formations, or the removal of speleothems to surface sites (Peterson, McAnany, and Cobb, this volume). Architecture documented in these caves includes a variety of walls, altars, rubble piles, paving, and ramps. The architecture can be viewed as access-altering modifications or focal modifications (Kenward 2002). Focal modifications include altars and rubble piles and are the focus of ritual activity. Access-altering modifications can facilitate, restrict, or obstruct accessibility. The eight other caves documented in the Tiger Cave District had modifications dominated by imposing walls designed to restrict traffic into the caves and impede access to certain areas. Meanwhile, passage to focal areas in these caves was facilitated by the addition of modifications such as paving or walls that indicated the flow of traffic. The modification strategies used in the eight other caves are complex and likely served to facilitate a variety of ritual functions. However, the presence, with one exception, of only modifications that facilitated traffic through the three caves considered here appears to be a key to understanding their function. The one exception, the wall blocking the northern entrance to Pass-Through Cave, may not have been added until near the end of Maya utilization of the area.

CONCLUSION

Actun Yax Tun, Broken Rim, and Pass-Through Caves appear to have functioned as conduits for pedestrian traffic between valleys in the Tiger Cave District of the Sibun-Manatee karst of Belize. The three caves are morphologically similar. They are relatively short and have two entrances that open on different valleys. They have a generally simple morphology that makes navigating them possible without the use of a torch. The function of the three caves was identified through modifications that appear to have been designed to facilitate passage between valleys. The paucity of artifacts may reflect regular sweeping as part of ritual maintenance. It has been argued that offerings may have been left at the cave entrances, as documented in modern Maya rituals, but that the caves would have been periodically cleared of offerings so as not to diminish accessibility. The function of Actun Yax Tun, Broken Rim, and Pass-Through caves as passages between valleys has not been previously suggested in the literature, but, so far as I know, no caves with similar morphology have been investigated archaeologically.

ACKNOWLEDGMENTS

I would like to thank Patricia A. McAnany, for her advice and encouragement, both in the field and in the classroom; Polly Peterson, for her perseverance and inspiration; Brent Woodfill and the 2001 Vanderbilt Upper Pasión Archaeological Cave Survey crew for a chance to get perspective from the Alta Verapaz and the Candelaria cave system; and James Brady for his patience, thoughtful advice, and careful editing, as well as for the opportunity to present an earlier version of this chapter at the symposium "New Light on Ancient Mesoamerican Cave Use," at the 2001 meeting of the Society for American Archaeology in New Orleans, Louisiana. The cave research reported herein is a component of the Xibun Archaeological Research Project (XARP), which has received funding from the National Science Foundation (BCS-0096603), the Division of International Programs at Boston University, and the Ahau Foundation. Numerous field school students, graduate students, specialists, support staff, and volunteers contributed to XARP, which was conducted under permits issued by the Department of Archaeology, Belmopan, Belize.

REFERENCES CITED

Adams, Abigail E., and James E. Brady

2005 Q'eqchi' Pilgrimage and Cave Ritual: Implications for Archaeological Interpretation. In *In the Maw of the Earth Monster: Mesoamerican Ritual Cave Use,* eds. James E. Brady and Keith M. Prufer, 301–327. University of Texas Press, Austin.

Bonor Villarejo, Juan Luis

1989 *Las Cuevas Mayas: Simbolismo y Ritual.* Universidad Compultense de Madrid, Madrid.

1995 Excavación de Salvamento en "Caves Branch Rock Shelter," Cayo District, Belize. *IV Encuento Internacional Investigadores de la Cultura Maya* 1:46–70.

Bonor, Juan Luis, and David M. Glassman

1999 La arqueología y el estudio de los restos humanos en "Caves Branch Rock Shelter," distrito de El Cayo, Belice. *Mayab* 12:18–30.

Brady, James E.

1989 An Investigation of Maya Ritual Cave Use With Special Reference to Naj Tunich, Peten, Guatemala. Ph.D. Dissertation. Archaeology Program, University of California, Los Angeles.

1997 Settlement Configuration and Cosmology: The Role of Caves at Dos Pilas. *American Anthropologist* 99(3):602–618.

Brady, James E., and Pierre R. Colas

2004 Nikte Mo' Scattered Fire in the Cave of K'ab Chante: Epigraphic and Archaeological Evidence for Cave Desecration in Ancient Maya Warfare. Paper presented at the 69th Annual Meeting of the Society for American Archaeology, Montreal.

Brady, James E., and Irma Rodas

1995 Maya Ritual Cave Deposits: Recent Insights From the Cueva de los Quetzales. *Institute of Maya Studies Journal* 1(1):17–25.

Góngora Cámara, José, and Mary H. Preuss

1990 A Yucatec-Mayan Prayer for Rain From the Ch'aa Chaac Ritual. *Latin American Indian Literatures Journal* 6:130–144.

Gordon, George Byron
1915 Sucaneb. *The Museum Journal* 6(4):180–183.

Isaza, Ilean, Amalia Kenward, and Kimberley Berry
1998 Ritual Use of the Sibun-Manatee Karst System. In *Caves and Settlement of the Sibun River Valley, Belize: 1997 Archaeological Survey and Excavation,* ed. Patricia A. McAnany, 55–75. Manuscript on file, Department of Archaeology, Belmopan, Belize, and Boston University Department of Archaeology, Boston.

Kenward, Amalia
2002 Ritual Pathways and the Alteration of Cave Features. In *Sacred Landscape and Settlement in the Sibun River Valley: XARP 1999 Archaeological Survey and Excavation,* ed. Patricia A. McAnany, 59–70. Institute for Mesoamerican Studies Occasional Publication No. 8. University at Albany, State University of New York, Albany.

McAnany, Patricia A.
2002 *Sacred Landscape and Settlement in the Sibun River Valley: XARP 1999 Archaeological Survey and Excavation.* Institute for Mesoamerican Studies Occasional Publication No. 8. University at Albany, State University of New York, Albany.

Miller, Thomas E.
1996 Geologic and Hydrologic Controls on Karst and Cave Development in Belize. *Journal of Cave and Karst Studies* 58(2):100–120.

Pendergast, David M.
1969 *The Prehistory of Actun Balam, British Honduras.* Art and Archaeology Occasional Paper No. 16. Royal Ontario Museum, Ontario, Canada.

Peterson, Polly A.
2002 Shedding Light on Xibalba Through Cave Survey and Surface Collection. In *Sacred Landscape and Settlement in the Sibun River Valley: XARP 1999 Archaeological Survey and Excavation,* ed. Patricia A. McAnany, 37–57. Institute for Mesoamerican Studies Occasional Publication No. 8. University at Albany, State University of New York, Albany.

Prufer, Keith Malcolm
2002 Communities, Caves and Ritual Specialists: A Study of Sacred Space in the Maya Mountains of Southern Belize. Ph.D. Dissertation. Department of Anthropology, Southern Illinois University, Carbondale.

Redfield, Robert
1941 *The Folk Culture of Yucatan.* University of Chicago Press, Chicago.

Redfield, Robert, and Alfonso Villa Rojas
1962 *Chan Kom: A Maya Village.* University of Chicago Press, Chicago.

Rissolo, Dominique A.
2003 *Ancient Maya Cave Use in the Yalahau Region, Northern Quintana Roo, Mexico.* Association for Mexican Cave Studies, Bulletin 12. Association for Mexican Cave Studies, Austin.

Scott, Ann, and Walter Little
2003 Contemporary Maya Beliefs and Cave Utilization: Implications for Archaeological Interpretation. Paper presented at the 68th Annual Meeting of the Society for American Archaeology, Milwaukee.

Tedlock, Barbara
1992 The Role of Dreams and Visionary Narratives in Mayan Cultural Survivals. *Ethnos* 20:453–476.

Thompson, J. Eric
1975 Introduction to the Reprint Edition. In *The Hill-Caves of Yucatan,* by Henry C. Mercer, vii–xliv. University of Oklahoma Press, Norman.

Vogt, Evon Z.
1976 *Tortillas for the Gods: A Symbolic Analysis of Zinacanteco Rituals.* Harvard University Press, Cambridge.

Wilson, Richard
1995 *Maya Resurgence in Guatemala: Q'eqchi' Experiences.* University of Oklahoma Press, Norman.

Woodfill, Brent, Nic Miller, Margaret Tarpley, and Amalia Kenward
2002 Reconocimientos espeleo-arqueológicos en la region del Alto Pasión. Paper presented at the XVI Simposio de Investigaciones Arqueológicos en Guatemala, Guatemala City.

III

Interpretations of Human Skeletal Material in Caves

Chapter Fourteen

Human Remains in Lowland Maya Caves

Problems of Interpretation

by Ann M. Scott
James E. Brady

Human skeletal material is some of the most commonly encountered evidence of cultural utilization found in Maya Lowland caves (Brady 1989: 343–344; Scott 1997). Interestingly, more so than other types of evidence, human remains have played an important role in archaeologists' interpretation of cave use from the earliest investigations. For that reason, human skeletal material is the only aspect of Maya cave archaeology for which there are early attempts at explanation, synthesis, and debate, although until recently the actual advances in our understanding have been rather meager.

HISTORICAL BACKGROUND

In perhaps the first formal study of Maya caves, Henry Mercer explored a number of Yucatecan caves in 1895, looking for evidence of Paleolithic age occupation. Twenty-nine caves were investigated, and excavations were carried out in thirteen (J. E. Thompson 1975: vii). Human remains were recovered both on the surface and in excavation.

Human bone "split as if for marrow" (Mercer 1975: 159), found in what was considered habitational refuse, led Mercer (1975: 161) to propose that "the old inhabitants of Yucatan practiced cannibalism."

George Gordon (1898) investigated five caves located just north of the Maya site of Copan, Honduras. In Cave 5 the remains of an individual were found. He discovered a skeleton in Cave 3 that had originally been placed in a seated position with a single vessel left as an offering. In Chamber 3, a room approximately 25 m long by 6 m wide had been filled with burned bone from a large number of cremations. Two ceramic jars found in the chamber contained bones of children (Gordon 1898: 147). The sheer quantity of bone found in this chamber was unique, and no other cave had reported finding human remains in such large numbers. Gordon (1898: 146) concluded that this was a mortuary chamber of a cult group such as the Nagualists described by Daniel Brinton (1894). This is noteworthy because it is one of the few early reports that interpreted cave use as essentially ceremonial.

This was not the only case in which the presence of human remains led researchers to consider a ritual function for a cave. In 1929, Thomas Joyce found the remains of five individuals in a cave deposit he excavated at Pusilha. Although he considered the cave in general to be "a convenient dump for broken and discarded pots," he also remarked (Joyce 1929: 443), "Yet it is quite possible that the cave was also, in a sense, a sacred place, because traces of five burials were found there." Linton Satterthwaite (cited in Butler 1934: 223) was also inclined to believe that a cave at Piedras Negras had a religious association because of a burial found there.

Oliver Ricketson (1925: 392–394), in discussing Maya burial practices, concluded that caves were not a usual burial place because human remains were relatively uncommon in the caves explored by Mercer and Edward Thompson. He concluded, "But on the whole, the evidence is strongly against the use of caves in Yucatan as a usual burial place. Had it been so, the dense population which must have existed when the Maya were at their height would probably have rendered these caves archaeological treasure houses" (Ricketson 1925: 394). His point is well-taken and raises several questions. If caves were not normal burial places, who were the individuals who were buried there, and what were the circumstances that led to their being interred in a cave?

Mary Butler's "note" on Maya cave burials specifically disputed Gordon's idea that cave burials were related to a Nagualist cult. The concept of the Nagual among modern Indians, she pointed out, is quite different than what is described by Brinton, and if such a cult existed it was a later, colonial response to Spanish persecution. Although Butler (1934: 223) did not offer an explanation of cave burials, she rejected the idea that they were the result of cave habitation, saying that the Maya "used caves sporadically at special times or for special purposes."

Frans Blom (1954) provided data on several types of cave burial in Chiapas. At Cieneguilla, Chiptic, and Rosario Trabajo caves, ceramic vessels containing human cremations were discovered. Based on associated artifacts (O'Neale 1942; Wauchope

1942), these appear to date to the Late Postclassic to Early Colonial periods, and Blom (1954: 130–131) felt they are restricted for the most part to the area inhabited by the Tojolabal Maya. The cave cremation burials are interesting because they appear to relate to urn cremation burials in a formal cruciform tomb discovered by Blom, which suggests this was a regular form of burial. At Huxjal, Moxviquil, San Felipe, and the Lake Lacandon caves, secondary burials were found on the surface of the cave floors. Blom pointed out that at the site of Moxviquil only secondary burials had been located, so this may also be a regular burial practice. Blom did not speculate on why certain individuals may have been selected for burial in a cave rather than in a tomb at a site.

In his survey of Maya burial customs, Alberto Ruz Lhuillier (1965, 1968) noted a large number of burials in caves, which he attributed to a desire by the Maya to provide shelter for the dead (Ruz Lhuillier 1968: 151). His explanation is unconvincing because it lacks supporting data to suggest that this was a Maya concern and it ignores the ritual importance of caves. Ruz (1968: 165) also suggested that the custom was late (Postclassic) and restricted to the Puuc Hills in Yucatán and the area between the Usumacinta and Grijalva rivers. Neither contention is well supported. Ruz seemed to have overlooked many cave burials in other areas of Yucatán (Smith 1953: 71–72) and Belize (Anderson 1962; Gann 1894–1895, 1928, 1929; Joyce 1929; Joyce et al. 1928; Mason 1928, 1940; Pendergast 1964; J. E. Thompson 1939, 1959). The Belizean material in general dated to the Classic period, and the ceramics from the Copan caves were known to date to the Preclassic (Porter 1953: 54; J. E. Thompson 1965: 337). Only when skeletal material was found immersed in *cenotes* did Ruz attribute this to sacrifice.

As part of his general synthesis, J. Eric Thompson (1959, 1975) presented a detailed discussion of human remains under the heading of caves as places for "Burials, Ossuaries, and Cremations." He did not pretend to have a clear idea of what was occurring in commenting that "[i]nhumations occur fairly frequently in caves, but no pattern to govern their relationships to the other contents of the cave emerges; in most cases they appear to be casual" (J. E. Thompson 1975: xxxiii). Instead, he summarized the studies by Mercer, Gordon, and Blom and suggested a number of circumstances that may account for human remains in caves. Over the centuries, individuals who died while performing religious rituals may have been buried in "hallowed ground" (J. E. Thompson 1975: xxxiii). More space is devoted to the possibility of the remains relating to ancestor worship or lineage cults than to any other explanation. This is proposed at Zopo Cave, where a skull appears to have been among the objects that were the focus of ritual. Thompson (1975: xxxiii) sees this to be analogous to an ethnohistoric example where "[a]ccording to Bishop Núñez de la Vega, the bones of the supposed founders of the group . . . were objects of veneration 'as though they had been saints,' and the people [were] taking flowers and copal to them in their caves."

In his analysis of Classic Lowland Maya burials, Bruce Welsh excludes cave burials from consideration because few good descriptions are available. He feels cave "burials may have had a different role and purpose from site burials and should therefore be considered separately" (Welsh 1988: 3). He fails, however, to provide any suggestions as to what that role and purpose might have been.

Finally, in his analysis of the Naj Tunich skeletal remains, James Brady (1989) attempted the first problem-oriented discussion by posing the question, who ends up in caves and why? Models of different practices, ranging from elite burial to lineage burial to disposal of sacrificial victims, were discussed. Ethnographic and ethnohistoric data supporting each model were presented and compared with all of the cave material then available. Elite burial and sacrifice accounted for most of the remains at Naj Tunich.

Despite 100 years of study, the most noteworthy features of the investigation of human osteological remains in caves are the paucity of explanations for the material, the lack of consensus over its meaning, and the near absence of research questions dealing with skeletal material. The scarcity of cave data has contributed to the problem. The most systematic studies have cast the widest possible net, but in doing so, control over space and time has been lost. These writers tend to pull examples from the highlands, the southern lowlands, and the northern lowlands, with too few examples available in any one area to discern possible regional patterns. At the same time, the cursory nature of most early cave investigation and reporting has meant that chronological data are rarely provided. In recent years, the situation has improved markedly. In this chapter we will attempt to build a bridge to those earlier studies by discussing cave data from all parts of the Maya area and will attempt to place these in a regional and temporal perspective where possible. Our primary interest, however, is in clarifying the situation in the southern lowlands (Figure 14.1). We attempt to isolate categories of functionally different behaviors in dealing with human remains in the hopes of illuminating some possible explanations for osteological material in caves. At a minimum, we would distinguish among burials, special and problematic deposits, and the remains of sacrificial victims.

Individual Cave Burial

For our purposes, *burial* will be used to refer to the deliberate and intentional interment of the remains of a community member. Burials may be primary or secondary and can be found on the surface or in the ground. Thus, the body does not need to have been buried to be a burial. As noted, most early writers simply assumed that human remains represented burials, so detailed descriptions of body position, immediate cave environment where the bones had been left, and even presence or absence of burial furniture were often omitted. With the advent of multiple models for the deposition of osteological material, the lack of good contextual data makes these earlier interpretations problematic at best. This was apparent in Brady's (1989) survey of the literature in which definitive evidence of cave burial was difficult to find. During the 1990s the quality of reporting improved, so it is now possible to discern a number of patterns of cave burial.

FIGURE 14.1. *Map of the Maya area showing the location of the major cave sites.*

Elite Cave Burial. Not surprisingly, elite burials, because of their location or formal elaboration, are more easily recognized than non-elite situations. The first example of elite cave burial recognized was the High Priest's Grave at Chichén Itzá (E. H. Thompson 1938). The presence of grave offerings and the placement directly under a major structure suggest that the individuals may have been community founders or early leaders (Headrick 1991). At this point, however, the High Priest's Grave is unique.

In the southern lowlands, elite burials were first recognized at Naj Tunich. A highly modified natural rise in the entrance chamber called the "Balcony" contains four elaborate masonry structures (Brady 1989). The earliest, Structure 1, is unusual in having a doorway and is thought to have originally been used in connection with religious rituals. During the Early Classic a rich burial was placed in the main room, the doorway was sealed, and a wall was built across the front of the structure to conceal the presence of the doorway (Figure 14.2). Structures 2, 3, and 4 all appear to have been constructed as tombs during the Late Classic (Figure 14.3). Elite

FIGURE 14.2. *Photograph of the exterior of Structure 1 at Naj Tunich* (top), *with the doorway as seen from the inside* (bottom) *(photo by George Veni).*

status is proposed based on the remains of rich furnishing and the presence of a text on sherds from a ceramic vessel in Structure 2 that refers to royal succession (Brady and Stone 1986). Naj Tunich is the only cave site to report such elaborate formal tombs.

FIGURE 14.3. *Photograph of Structure 3, a semisubterranean tomb at Naj Tunich.*

Three other Naj Tunich structures, if that term can be used loosely to refer to alcoves blocked by a single stone wall, were more difficult to interpret (Figure 14.4). All had been extensively looted and so produced no elite artifacts, but the situation was complicated in that these features appeared to be somewhat earlier than the masonry structures (Brady 1989: 354). Investigations at Balam Na Cave 4 in southeastern Petén uncovered evidence of very similar blocked-alcove tombs. All the ceramic dated to the Late Preclassic, reinforcing the suggestion that the Naj Tunich alcove-tombs were also Preclassic. Although looted in antiquity, jade, pyrite, and other stone beads were recovered, suggesting that at one time the burials had contained rich offerings (Garza, Brady, and Christensen 2001). Thus, it appears that a pattern of elite burial in alcove-tombs can be defined that dates at least as early as the Late Preclassic. At Naj Tunich, this may have evolved into elaborate masonry tombs during the Classic period. At present, this burial form has only been documented in southeastern Petén.

Within the limited corpus of cave burial data, a few clear examples of elite burial have been documented to show that the practice occurred in both the southern and northern lowlands. Nevertheless, it appears that this was rather rare. Sergio Garza and colleagues (2001: 20) suggest that elite cave burial may have been more common during the Preclassic but was discontinued in the Classic period, as the caves became too susceptible to sacking after a military defeat. More data are needed to confirm this suggestion, however.

FIGURE 14.4. *Structure 5 at Naj Tunich, a blocked alcove used as a tomb.*

Non-Elite Cave Burial. Individual, non-elite, nontomb remains in caves are some of the most difficult to interpret. The presence of associated offerings would provide fairly compelling evidence of burial, but this appears to be relatively rare because of (1) the lack of original grave goods, (2) looting, or (3) the failure to note and report their presence. A. H. Anderson appears to have excavated a burial accompanied by at least one and possibly two ceramic vessels and several bone pins from Chamber 5 in Eduardo Quiroz Cave (in Pendergast 1971: 11). David Pendergast (1971: 15–18) interpreted the badly preserved remains of four of the five individuals (one infant, two children, and two adults) found in Chamber 1 as burials, although no offerings were present and body positions varied widely. Interestingly the best-preserved body, that of a child three to five years of age, was accompanied by several bone beads but was classified as a possible sacrificial victim because of evidence of trauma to the skull and the association with construction (Pendergast 1971: 18).

Brady was shown a small cave near Naj Tunich that contained the body of an adult neatly laid out on the surface against one wall. A pile of unshaped stone had blocked the entrance before being removed by looters. Because of the looting it is not known if offerings had accompanied the individual, but the body was neatly arranged—faceup in an extended position parallel to the cave wall—suggesting a deliberate burial.

Deliberate burial is also likely in cases of secondary burial. Osteological material has often been discovered in small crevices where an intact body would not fit, indicating a secondary placement after the flesh was gone. This practice has been reported from Belize (MacLeod and Puleston 1978: 72; Pendergast 1971: 15), the lowland area of Chiapas (Blom 1954: 132), and the Yucatán (Márquez de González, Benavides Castillo, and Schmidt 1982), indicating that this practice is widely distributed in the lowlands. At Xcan and in Belize the practice dates to the Late Classic. In addition, George Brainerd (1958: 21) excavated an Early Classic bowl containing remains from the Cenote Chen Mul at Mayapán.

Cave Ossuaries

Another fairly clear burial type is the formal ossuary cave, in which a main function of the cave or at least one of its chambers is to hold burials. Ossuary caves are known to exist in other areas of Mesoamerica. They appear to be particularly important in Oaxaca. Francisco de Burgoa (1934: I: 338, II: 115) stated that kings and chiefs were buried in caves. The practice seems to have extended to the lesser elite as well and even to the wives of the elite (Dahlgren de Jordan 1966: 295). Christopher Moser (1975, 1976, 1983) has investigated one such cave that contained over forty masonry tombs. The tombs are quite different from those at Naj Tunich, varying in form from rectangular to circular, and are made with adobe mortar and roughly squared blocks of stone. The rectangular tombs use the natural cave wall or the walls of previous tombs for one or more sides of the construction. The circular tombs are freestanding in clusters of two to five, and they vary in diameter from 1 to 2.5 m. The body or mummy was probably set vertically in the tombs, which were 3 to 4 m high (Moser 1975: 30).

In the Maya area, most discussions of ossuary burials begin with Gordon's Cave 3 at Copan, in part because the find is so unusual and Gordon's description is so dramatic. He says of the ossuary chamber:

> The walls are black, the air close and foul, and altogether it is as repulsive a hole as could be found in the face of nature. The floor seemed more uneven than in either of the other chambers, and gave way still more to the pressure of the feet, and with a crushing sound. I soon discovered that I was walking upon the dust and crumbling bones of decomposed human bodies, mingled with ashes and lime. A mass of charred and calcined bones occupied the entire floor to a depth of about two feet. (Gordon 1898: 143)

Limited test excavation suggests that there may be 600 to 700 burials in the third chamber (Rue, Freter, and Ballinger 1989: 398). Although there is disagreement over the chronology of the site because no remains have ever been radiocarbon dated (Brady 1995), it is generally agreed that the initial use of ossuary dates to the Middle/Early Preclassic. Although Copan is generally considered a Lowland Maya site, this clearly predates the lowland influence. More recently, our work in the Talgua region of eastern Honduras has led to the investigation of a series of cave ossuaries in the Talgua, Arañas, and Piedra Blanca caves (Brady, Hasemann, and Fogarty 1995; Brady et al. 2000; Dixon et al. 1998). These have been securely dated to between 1400 and 800 B.C. The investigation also made it clear that the Talgua caves were part of a larger Honduran tradition. Many years ago, Doris Stone (1957: 56) proposed that there was a Honduran pattern of cave burial that included other sites, such as Cuyamel (Healy 1974), El Sitio, Guanizale, Cueva del Diablo, and perhaps Guapinole (Stone 1957). Gordon's Cave appears to be part of this Honduras tradition that may extend into the Guatemalan highlands, but this has not been documented (Brady 1997: 27). At present, there is no evidence that the pattern extends into the lowlands, so we strongly argue that it is inappropriate to consider Gordon's Cave 3 as an example of Lowland Maya cave burial practices.

Although Blom (1954) appears to consider all caves in which skeletal material is found to be ossuaries, in point of fact the ossuary cave is not a well-documented form. It does appear that many of the cases identified by Blom as containing cremation in urns do qualify as ossuary caves. The cases, however, appear to be restricted to the highlands and date to the Postclassic based on a few cases that have produced diagnostic artifacts (O'Neale 1942; Wauchope 1942).

The caves with large quantities of uncremated bones investigated by Blom are for the most part also located in the highlands, although the distribution does extend into the Lake Lacandon area. Ethnographers who have visited the Lacandon caves of Tsibaná (Petryshyn 1969) and Mensäbak (Boremanse 1993: 327–328; McGee 1990: 58–59) have commented on the human skeletal material on the surface. Several authors (McGee 1990: 58–59; Petryshyn 1969: 173) noted the presence of skulls exhibiting cranial deformation, indicating that they are probably pre-Hispanic in date. The ethnographers considered the material to have been unearthed by looters digging in the caves, but the bones do not show signs of having been buried. It is also interesting that when Gertrude Duby visited the cave of Mensäbak in 1943, she commented on the presence of the skeletal material but did not mention any looters' pits (Blom and Duby 1955: 350). Thus, it would appear that there was a cave ossuary tradition in the western lowlands in which bodies or bones were simply deposited on the floors of caves. It is possible that cave ossuaries were more widely distributed. E. H. Thompson (1904: 7) described a cave near Oxkutzcab containing large quantities of skeletal material but did not provide enough information to determine what was occurring.

Rockshelter Cemetaries/Ossuaries

The most dramatic revision of our thinking concerning cave ossuary burial has come with the discovery that rockshelters were regularly utilized as places of interment. The first important discovery in this regard was made by Juan Luis Bonor (1995; Bonor and Martínez Klemm 1995; Glassman and Bonor Villarejo, this volume), who recovered thirty-two burials and the commingled remains of at least 42 additional individuals in the Caves Branch Rock Shelter, Belize. It is estimated that the ossuary contains the remains of over 150 individuals and dates from the Middle Preclassic to the Postclassic.

Shortly after Bonor's discovery, Keith Prufer, working on the Maya Mountains Archaeological Project, excavated three rockshelters containing numerous burials. These discoveries, together with the Caves Branch Rock Shelter, led Prufer (1997, 2002; Saul, Prufer, and Saul, this volume) to propose that there was a larger pattern of rockshelter burial that included several previously reported cases from Chiapas (Lee and Clark 1988; Lee and Hayden 1988).

Recent work indicates that the burial function is not limited to rockshelters but also includes the light zone areas of small caves. This has been found at Actun Nak Beh (Halperin, this volume) and Handprint Cave, excavated by the Western Belize Regional Cave Project. The shallow caves at Piedras Negras also appear to fall into this pattern. William Coe (1959: 125) reported one such cave burial uncovered by the University of Pennsylvania Project. As part of a cave survey organized for the Brigham Young University Piedras Negras Project in 1999, Pierre Colas discovered a burial in a second small cave (Veni 2000: 16–17), suggesting that burials may be a regular feature of the shallow caves in this area.

Special Deposits

Archaeologists have not given a great deal of consideration to the possibility that some human remains may have been curated, perhaps as artifacts in active use in cave ceremonies. The remains of important ancestors, as Bishop Núñez de Vega's description suggests, could have been the focus of indigenous worship for centuries after the individual's death. It is possible that over time single, disarticulated bones, rather than bundles of bone, became the focus of devotion. Certainly, the presence of skulls on altars or in association with areas of intense ritual activity could reflect a function as a curated object of veneration (J. E. Thompson 1975: xxxiii). Another possible case of curation could be a single tibia placed inside an altar at Naj Tunich (Brady 1989: 353).

Another type of curation consists of trophies of carved human femurs or skull cups found in surface archaeology but rarely reported from cave sites. A plaque carved from a human mandible was reported from a cave at Pusilha (Joyce 1929: 446–447). A "Human Skull Incense Burner," which had the cranial vault modified, painted, and stuccoed for burning copal and rubber, was recovered from the Cenote of Sacrifice at Chichén Itzá (Coggins and Shane 1984: 155). A necklace of human teeth and a carved human bone were also recovered from the *cenote* (Tozzer 1957: XI: 197). Trophy remains are not of direct concern here because the motive behind their deposition appears different from other human remains. These "artifacts" appear more related to other objects of value like carved jade that are ultimately made as an offering to the deities.

The deposition of single, disarticulated human bones has been suggested as a pattern by a discovery in the Cueva de Sangre, Dos Pilas. The proximal end of a human tibia was found beneath approximately one-third of a Late Classic tripod vessel lying facedown with the other vessel fragments nearby. The bone was clearly associated with the vessel. A calcite encrustation encasing the surface of the bowl was carefully removed in the laboratory, revealing a scene painted on the vessel interior depicting the lower body of a fallen or reclining individual (Figure 14.5). A spear is shown piercing the left leg at approximately the point where the recovered tibia is broken, and blood is depicted as flowing from the wound. A reasonable interpretation is that the scene shows a warrior wounded and then captured during one of Dos Pilas's many wars. It is likely that the captive was later sacrificed and a portion of the victim was offered in a vessel commissioned to celebrate the victory. Frequently, such capture scenes include a short hieroglyphic text identifying the victor and his site, as well as the name and site of his captive. Unfortunately, the two other large sherds belonging to the plate had their entire painted surfaces gnawed away by large rodents, so the identities of the individuals depicted may never be known. Nevertheless, this example is important because if the practice of leaving some part of the sacrificial victim in the cave were common, it would explain why isolated human bones are so frequently encountered.

OSTELOGICAL REMAINS AS EVIDENCE OF HUMAN SACRIFICE

In reviewing the history of archaeologists' dealings with osteological material in caves, it is interesting to see how few suggestions have been made that the remains may represent victims of human sacrifice, despite the fact that the practice is well

FIGURE 14.5. *A fragment of a ceramic plate from the Cueva de Sangre, Dos Pilas, depicting an individual being wounded with a spear thrust. The human leg bone was found beneath the plate.*

documented in pre-contact Maya art. A number of ethnohistorical accounts suggest that human sacrifice to the gods most closely associated with caves was widespread. In many instances the sacrifice occurred in a cave or the victim's body was disposed of in a cave. The sacrifice of children is particularly prevalent in the ethnohistorical works dealing with Yucatán. Alfred Tozzer (1941: 117n) notes that in the records of testimony given at Sotuta and Homun, the age of the victims was repeatedly between five and six years. France Scholes and Ralph Roys (1938: 611) note that the prevalence of child sacrifice resulted in part from the lack of war captives and adult slaves after the conquest, but they also suggest the possibility that children formed the majority of sacrificial victims in pre-conquest times.

The sacrifice of victims, particularly children, by throwing them into the Cenote of Sacrifice at Chichén Itzá is documented by both ethnohistorical sources (Tozzer 1941: 44n) and archaeology (see Tiesler, this volume). This practice, however, was not limited to the *cenote* at Chichén Itzá and seems to have been widespread (Scholes and Roys 1938: 615). As part of the *cenote* cult, children were often publicly sacrificed and the body was disposed of in a *cenote*/cave (Scholes and Roys 1938: 615; Tozzer 1941: 44n, 116n). The disposal of the bodies in the *cenote* was not simply a way of hiding the remains. At Yaxleuea three children were sacrificed and the bodies were thrown into a deep cave, after which a large stone was used to seal the mouth. Scholes and Roys (1938: 615) feel the sealing of the cave mouth was part of the ritual performance. Support for this position is provided by Toribio Motolinía (1971: 50), who records a similar rite performed in Central Mexico in honor of Tlaloc. Children were sacrificed and their bodies were placed in a cave, which was sealed until the rite was performed the following year. It would appear that this form of ceremony was widely distributed in Mesoamerica.

A similar association of human sacrifice with cave rituals can be documented throughout Mesoamerica. In the Guatemalan Highlands, children were sacrificed in a cave near Mixco Viejo as part of a ceremony designed to bring rain (Fuentes y Guzmán 1932: 336). In Oaxaca, the sacrifice of children appears to have been common (Spores 1967: 26), especially to the rain god (Zilbermann 1966: 122). In Central Mexico, the sacrifice of children to the rain god was well established (Heyden 1981: 19–20; Nicholson 1971: table 4; Sahagún 1981: 1–2, 5, 8, 42–44, 192). At Chalma, Oztoteotl, the god of caves and an aspect of Tlaloc, received sacrifices of children (Brundage 1979: 231n).

Dennis Tedlock (1994) has given a valuable warning not to uncritically accept Landa's accounts of human sacrifice, which were extracted under torture, but his suggestion that the idea of human sacrifice was a concept in the minds of the Spanish rather than the Maya is weak and unconvincing. Human sacrifice is frequently depicted in Maya vase painting, a form of native document unsullied by contact with the Spanish. Accounts by Landa and others concerning the disposal of bodies in *cenotes* could easily be tested by examining the results of the three expeditions to the Cenote of Sacrifice (Ediger 1971; Hooton 1940; Piña Chán 1970: 51; Tiesler, this volume), which recovered human skeletal material each time; and osteological material has been recovered from *cenotes* at Mayapán and elsewhere (Ruz Lhuillier 1965: 457; 1968: 135). This suggests that the argument is not over *if* but *how much* human sacrifice occurred.

A number of controversies surround the interpretation of osteological remains as reflecting human sacrifice. Pendergast (1971: 18) argued that without clear indications of a violent death, the cause of death could not be attributed to human sacrifice. There are a number of problems with this position. First, it assumes that all sacrifice leaves an osteological signature that can be recovered. Such practices as strangulation, disembowelment, or imprisonment in a cave leave little or no signature. On strictly osteological grounds, one would have to conclude that the individuals recovered from the Cenote of Sacrifice died of natural causes. Second, Pendergast's suggestion is also reductionistic in limiting the argument to the osteological artifact and ignoring the far richer information often found in archaeological context. Last, osteologists' practice of assuming that an individual died of natural causes if no good case can be made to the contrary is probably not applicable to caves. Their assumption is valid in normal burial contexts, which are expected to reflect the fact that the overwhelming percentage of the population dies of natural causes. As Oliver Ricketson (1925) pointed out so cogently eighty years ago, caves are not normal burial contexts, so there is every reason to assume that a special context will contain a special population. This puts both archaeologists and osteologists in the uncomfortable position of not being able to assume anything and of being forced to justify whatever interpretation is made.

A number of remains of children are the best candidates for being sacrificial victims. Pendergast (1971: 16–18) raises this possibility for the skeleton of a child, three to five years of age, found under a plaster floor at Eduardo Quiroz Cave. The child had two unhealed holes in its skull and may have been sacrificed in connection with the construction of the floor. Brady (1989: 351) interpreted the body of a five- to six-year-old child found in a shallow grave at Naj Tunich as that of a sacrificial offering based on three unhealed holes in the parietals. Petroglyph Cave (Reents-Budet and MacLeod 1986: 41–45, 80–81) produced remains of at least twenty-two individuals, nine adults and thirteen children, that Dorie Reents-Budet and Barbara MacLeod (1986: 80–81) suggest were sacrificial victims based on context. At Copan, Brady (1995: 35) raised the possibility that the children in Gordon's Cave 3 were sacrificed based on the fact that the burial treatment was different than that of the adults. In one of the burials excavated, the skull of a child accompanied the body of an adult, and at least some portion of a child's skull had been placed in a leather bag found with the burial.

The recovery of children's bodies in caves is noteworthy because children appear to be favored sacrificial victims throughout Mesoamerica (see Brady 1989: 359–361 for a review of the sources) to the cults most closely associated with caves. Alfred Tozzer (1941: 117n) notes that the sources frequently mention the children being five or six years of age. Diana Ballinger (1986: 58), in analyzing an excavation unit with several children in this age range, comments that mortality is generally not high in this age group (also see Tiesler, this volume). The finding of a significant number of children of this age therefore suggests something other than natural causes.

There is often far more ambiguity with skeletal remains of adults, but the archaeological context can frequently make a compelling case for sacrifice. In the Cueva de Sangre at Dos Pilas, the first 200 m of passage can be characterized as a muddy trench, 2 to 4 m wide, with a rock shelf on one or both sides where people could stand or walk above the trench. Much of the length of the passage could be traversed on these shelves, and stepping stones had been placed across the trench in places where it was necessary to cross from one side to the other. These may have been placed as steps when water puddled on the floor after rains. The trench was completely carpeted along its entire length with artifacts, including ceramics, bone, shell, chipped stone, and jade. It appears that all of the ceramic vessels had been broken in place, probably at the conclusion of ceremonies. Human skeletal material was also found among the offerings in the sticky mud. The context, a wet, muddy passage that seasonally floods and that may have been periodically disturbed by pedestrian traffic, is hardly one where the Maya normally chose to place the body of a loved one. The presence of innumerable offerings, clearly unassociated with the burials, suggests that the human skeletal material should be viewed as an offering as well. Thus, the several dozen individuals in the trench are tentatively considered sacrificial victims.

CONCLUSION

In reviewing the literature on human osteological material found in caves, several observations need to be made. First, previous studies tended to provide too little data on context to permit convincing interpretations. The quality of recent work has improved markedly, and, as a result, the complexity of the questions asked of the data has increased. Far more attention is now paid to issues of social status and social meaning. Second, most early interpretations treated all human remains as burials and have only recently begun to investigate the possibility that some remains may represent the bodies of sacrificial victims. Caves were the scene of religious rituals, and human sacrifice at least occasionally accompanied such rites, so the presence of sacrificial victims should not be surprising. Recent archaeological work appears to document cases of sacrifice (see Owen, this volume). The expansion of interpretive models of human remains is certain to impact our interpretations of larger issues of cave utilization. Third, the paucity of data forced previous attempts at synthesis to move across geographic areas in their search for patterns. As more information becomes available, we expect to see greater refinement in our understanding of regional and temporal differences in the use of caves for the deposition of human skeletal material. This may be important in addressing larger issues of detecting regional boundaries in the lowlands. Finally, the recent recognition that rockshelters appear to have been regularly used as cemeteries has drawn attention to these previously ignored features in the landscape and has documented their importance as sacred landmarks.

REFERENCES CITED

Anderson, A. H.

1962 Cave Sites in British Honduras. In *Akten des XXXIV Internationale Amerikanisten-Kongresses,* 326–331. Verlag Ernest Berger, Horn, Vienna.

Ballinger, Diana A.

1986 Ossuary Burial of Cremated Human Remains From Copan, Honduras. M.A. Thesis. Department of Anthropology, University of Houston, Houston.

Blom, Frans
1954 Ossuaries, Cremation and Secondary Burials Among the Maya of Chiapas, Mexico. *Journal de la Société des Américanistes* 43:123–135.

Blom, Frans, and Gertrude Duby
1955 *La Selva Lacadona.* Editorial Cultura, Mexico.

Bonor, Juan Luis
1995 Excavación de salvamento en "Caves Branch Rock Shelter," Cayo District, Belize. *IV Encuento Internacional Investigadores de la Cultura Maya* 1:46–70.

Bonor, Juan Luis, and Carolina Martínez Klemm
1995 Trabajos recientes en la región de Caves Branch, distrito de el Cayo, Belice. *V Encuento Internacional Investigadores de la Cultura Maya* 4:250–267.

Boremanse, Dider
1993 The Faith of the Real People: The Lacandon of the Chiapas Rain Forest. In *South and Meso-American Native Spirituality,* eds. Gary H. Gossen and Miguel León-Portilla, 325–351. Crossroads Publishing, New York.

Brady, James E.
1989 An Investigation of Maya Ritual Cave Use With Special Reference to Naj Tunich, Peten, Guatemala. Ph.D. Dissertation. Archaeology Program, University of California, Los Angeles.
1995 A Reassessment of the Chronology and Function of Gordon's Cave 3, Copan, Honduras. *Ancient Mesoamerica* 6:29–38.
1997 Palaces of the Dead: Glimpses of the Afterlife From a Middle Preclassic Cave Ossuary. In *Proceedings of the 1995 and 1996 Latin American Symposia,* eds. Alana Cordy-Collins and Grace Johnson, 21–32. San Diego Museum Papers No. 34. San Diego Museum of Man, San Diego.

Brady, James E., Christopher Begley, John Fogarty, Donald J. Stierman, Barbara Luke, and Ann Scott
2000 Talgua Archaeological Project: A Preliminary Assessment. *Mexicon* 22(5):111–118.

Brady, James E., George Hasemann, and John Fogarty
1995 Harvest of Skulls and Bones. *Archaeology* 48(3):36–40.

Brady, James E., and Andrea Stone
1986 Naj Tunich: Entrance to the Maya Underworld. *Archaeology* 39(6):18–25.

Brainerd, George W.
1958 *The Archaeological Ceramics of Yucatan.* Anthropological Records 19. University of California Press, Berkeley.

Brinton, Daniel
1894 Nagualism: A Study of Native American Folk-lore and History. *Proceedings of the American Philosophical Society* 33:11–73.

Brundage, Burr Cartwright
1979 *The Fifth Sun: Aztec Gods, Aztec World.* University of Texas Press, Austin.

Burgoa, Francisco de
1934 *Geográfica descripción.* Talleres Graficos de la Nación, Mexico [original 1674].

Butler, Mary
1934 A Note on Maya Cave Burials. *American Anthropologist* 36:223–225.

Coe, William R.
1959 *Piedras Negras Archaeology: Artifacts, Caches, and Burials.* University Museum Monograph, University of Pennsylvania, Philadelphia.

Coggins, Clemency Chase, and Orrin C. Shane III
1984 *Cenote of Sacrifice: Maya Treasures From the Sacred Well at Chichén Itzá.* University of Texas Press, Austin.

Dahlgren de Jordan, Barbro
1966 *La Mixteca: Su Cultura e Historia Prehispanica.* Imprenta Universitaria, México.

Dixon, Boyd, George Hasemann, James Brady, Pastor Gomez, and Marilyn Beaudry-Corbett
1998 Multi-Ethnicity or Multiple Enigma: Archaeological Survey in the Rio Talgua Drainage, Department of Olancho, Honduras. *Ancient Mesoamerica* 9:327–340.

Ediger, Donald
1971 *The Well of Sacrifice.* Doubleday, Garden City.

Fuentes y Guzmán, Francisco Antonio de
1932 *Recordación Florida: Discurso Historical y Demostración Natural, Material, Militar y Politica del Reyno de Goathemala.* Biblioteca Goathemala Vols. 6–8. Guatemala.

Gann, Thomas W.F.
1894–1895 On Exploration of Two Mounds in British Honduras. *Proceedings of the Society of Antiquaries of London,* n.s., 15:430–434.
1928 Recently Discovered Maya City in the Southwest of British Honduras. *Proceedings of the XXIII International Congress of Americanists,* 1:188–192. N.p., New York.
1929 *Discoveries and Adventures in Central America.* Charles Scribner's Sons, New York.

Garza, Sergio, James E. Brady, and Christian Christensen
2001 Balam Na Cave 4: Implications for Understanding Preclassic Cave Mortuary Practices. *California Anthropologist* 28(1):15–21.

Gordon, George Byron
1898 Caverns of Copan, Honduras. *Peabody Museum of Archaeology and Ethnology Memoirs* 1:137–148.

Headrick, Annabeth
1991 The Chicomoztoc of Chichen Itza. M.A. Thesis. Department of Art, University of Texas, Austin.

Healy, Paul F.
1974 The Cuyamel Caves: Preclassic Sites in Northeast Honduras. *American Antiquity* 39:435–447.

Heyden, Doris
1981 Caves, Gods and Myths: World-View and Planning in Teotihuacan. In *Mesoamerican Sites and World-Views,* ed. Elizabeth P. Benson, 1–39. Dumbarton Oaks Research Library and Collection, Washington, D.C.

Hooten, Earnest A.
1940 Skeletons From the Cenote of Sacrifice at Chichén Itzá. In *The Maya and Their Neighbors: Essays on Middle American Anthropology and Archaeology,* eds. Clarence L. Hays et al., 272–280. D. Appleton-Century Company, New York.

Joyce, T. A.
1929 Report on the British Museum Expedition to British Honduras, 1929. *Journal of the Royal Anthropological Institute* 59:439–459.

Joyce, T. A., T. Gann, E. L. Gruning, and R.C.E. Long
1928 Report on the British Museum Expedition to British Honduras, 1928. *Journal of the Royal Anthropological Society* 58:323–349.

Lee, Thomas A., Jr., and John E. Clark
1988 Oro, Tela y Xute: Investigaciones Arqueológicas en la Región Cancum, Colonia Las Delicias, Chiapas. *Arqueología* 4:7–46. Instituto Nacional de Antropología e Historia, Mexico.

Lee, Thomas A., Jr., and Brian Hayden
1988 *San Pablo Cave and El Cayo on the Usumacinta River, Chiapas, Mexico.* Papers of the New World Archaeological Foundation No. 53. Brigham Young University, Provo.

MacLeod, Barbara, and Dennis E. Puleston
1978 Pathways Into Darkness: The Search for the Road to Xibalbá. In *Tercera Mesa Redonda de Palenque, Vol. 4,* eds. Merle Greene Robertson and Donnan Call Jeffers, 71–77. Herald Peters, Monterey.

Márquez de González, Lourdes, Antonio Benavides Castillo, and Peter J. Schmidt
1982 *Exploración en la Gruta de Xcan, Yucatán.* Instituto National de Antropología e Historia, Merida.

Mason, Gregory
1928 *Pottery and Other Artifacts From Caves in British Honduras and Guatemala.* Indian Notes and Monographs No. 47. Museum of the American Indian, New York.
1940 *South of Yesterday.* Henry Holt, New York.

McGee, R. Jon
1990 *Life, Ritual, and Religion Among the Lacandon Maya.* Wadsworth Publishing, Belmont, CA.

Mercer, Henry C.
1975 *The Hill-Caves of Yucatan.* University of Oklahoma Press, Norman [original 1896].

Moser, Christopher L.
1975 Cueva de Ejutla: ¿una cueva funeraria postclásica? *Boletín del Instituto Nacional de Antropología e Historia* 14 (Época II, Julio/Sept):25–36.
1976 Cueva de Ejutla: A Postclassic Burial Cave? *Katunob* 9(1):22–27.
1983 A Postclassic Burial Cave in the Southern Cañada. In *The Cloud People,* eds. Kent V. Flannery and Joyce Marcus, 270–272. Academic Press, New York.

Motolinía, Toribio de Benavente
1971 *Memoriales o Libro de las Cosas de la Nueva España y de los Naturales de ella.* Universidad Nacional Autónoma de México, Mexico [original 1555].

Nicholson, H. B.
1971 Religion in Pre-Hispanic Central Mexico. In *Handbook of Middle American Indians, Vol. 10: Archaeology of Northern Mesoamerica, Part 1,* eds. Gordon F. Ekholm and Ignacio Bernal, 395–446. University of Texas Press, Austin.

O'Neale, Lila M.
1942 Early Textiles From Chiapas, Mexico. *Middle American Research Records* 1(1):1–6. Middle American Research Institute, New Orleans.

Pendergast, David M.
1964 Excavaciones en la Cueva Eduardo Quiroz, Distrito Cayo, Honduras Britanica. *Estudios de Cultura Maya* 4:119–139.
1971 *Excavations at Eduardo Quiroz Cave, British Honduras (Belize).* Art and Archaeology Occasional Paper No. 21. Royal Ontario Museum, Toronto.

Petryshyn, Jaroslaw T.
1969 Ein Lakandonischer Gottesdienst in der Höhle des Gottes Tsibaná am Heiligen See von Mensabok in den Tropischen Urwäldern von Chiapas. *Archiv fur Völkerkunde* 23:169–176. Vienna.

Piña Chán, Román
1970 *Informe preliminar de la reciente exploración del cenote sagrado de Chichén Itzá.* Investigaciones, No. 24. Instituto Nacional de Antropología e Historia, Mexico.

Porter, Muriel N.
1953 *Tlatilco and the Preclassic Cultures of the New World.* Viking Fund Publications in Anthropology, No. 19. Wenner-Gren Foundation for Anthropological Research, New York.

Prufer, Keith Malcolm
1997 Pilgrimages for the Dead: Early Classic Mortuary Caves in Southwestern Belize. Paper presented at the 62nd Annual Meeting of the Society for American Archaeology, Nashville.
2002 Communities, Caves and Ritual Specialists: A Study of Sacred Space in the Maya Mountains of Southern Belize. Ph.D. Dissertation. Department of Anthropology, Southern Illinois University, Carbondale.

Reents-Budet, Dorie, and Barbara MacLeod
1986 The Archaeology of Petroglyph Cave, Belize. Unpublished manuscript.

Ricketson, Oliver
1925 Burials in the Maya Area. *American Anthropologist* 27:381– 401.

Rue, David J., AnnCorinne Freter, and Diane A. Ballinger
1989 The Caverns of Copan Revisited: Preclassic Sites in the Sesesmil River Valley, Copan, Honduras. *Journal of Field Archaeology* 16:395–404.

Ruz Lhuillier, Alberto
1965 Tombs and Funerary Practices of the Lowland Maya. In *Handbook of Middle American Indians, Volume 2: Archaeology of Southern Mesoamerica, Part 1,* ed. Gordon R. Willey, 441–461. University of Texas Press, Austin.
1968 *Costumbres Funerarias de los Antiguos Mayas.* Universidad Nacional Autónoma de México, Mexico.

Sahagún, Bernardino de
1981 *General History of the Things of New Spain, Book 2: The Ceremonies,* trans. Arthur J.O. Anderson and Charles E. Dibble. University of Utah Press, Salt Lake City.

Scholes, France V., and Ralph L. Roys
1938 Fray Diego de Landa and the Problem of Idolatry in Yucatan. In *Cooperation in Research,* 585–620. Carnegie Institution of Washington Publication 501. Washington, D.C.

Scott, Ann
1997 Human Remains in Mesoamerican Caves: Problems of Interpretation. Paper presented at the 62nd Annual Meeting of the Society for American Archaeology, Nashville.

Smith, Robert E.
1953 Cenote X-Coton at Mayapan. Department of Archaeology. *Current Report* 5:67–81. Carnegie Institution of Washington, Washington, D.C.

Spores, Ronald
1967 *The Mixtec Kings and Their People.* University of Oklahoma Press, Norman.

Stone, Doris
1957 *The Archaeology of Central and Southern Honduras.* Papers of the Peabody Museum of American Archaeology and Ethnology, Vol. 49, No. 3. Harvard University, Cambridge.

Tedlock, Dennis
1994 Torture in the Archives: Mayans Meet Europeans. *American Anthropologist* 95:139–152.

Thompson, Edward H.
1904 *Archaeological Researches in Yucatan.* Memoirs of the Peabody Museum of American Archaeology and Ethnology, Volume 3, No. 2. Harvard University, Cambridge.
1938 *The High Priest's Grave, Chichen Itza, Yucatan, Mexico.* Prepared for publication, with notes and introduction by J. Eric Thompson. Field Museum of Natural History, Anthropology Series 27, No. 1.

Thompson, J. Eric
1939 *Excavations at San Jose, British Honduras.* Carnegie Institution of Washington, Washington, D.C.
1959 The Role of Caves in Maya Culture. *Mitteilungen aus dem Museum für Völkerkunde in Hamburg* 25:122–129.
1965 Archaeological Synthesis of the Southern Maya Lowlands. In *Handbook of Middle American Indians, Volume 2: Archaeology of Southern Mesoamerica, Part 1,* ed. Gordon R. Willey, 331–359. University of Texas Press, Austin.
1975 Introduction to the Reprint Edition. In *The Hill-Caves of Yucatan,* by Henry C. Mercer, vii–xliv. University of Oklahoma Press, Norman.

Tozzer, Alfred M.
1941 *Landa's Relación de las Cosas de Yucatán.* Papers of the Peabody Museum of American Archaeology and Ethnology, Vol. 18. Peabody Museum, Cambridge.
1957 *Chichen Itza and Its Cenote of Sacrifice: A Comparative Study of Contemporaneous Maya and Toltec.* Memoirs of the Peabody Museum of American Archaeology and Ethnology, Vols. 11–12. Peabody Museum, Cambridge

Veni, George
2000 In Search of Xibalbá: An Archaeological Expedition to the Caves of Piedras Negras, Peten, Guatemala. *International Caver 2000,* 14–18.

Wauchope, Robert
1942 Notes on the Age of the Cineguilla Cave Textiles From Chiapas. Middle American Research Institute, New Orleans. *Middle American Research Records* 1(2):7–8.

Welsh, W. Bruce M.
1988 *An Analysis of Classic Lowland Maya Burials.* BAR International Series 409, Oxford.

Zilbermann, Maria Cristina
1966 Idolatries de Oaxaca en el Siglo XVIII. *XXXVI Congreso Internacional de Americanistas* 2:111–123. Spain.

Chapter Fifteen

Mortuary Practices of the Prehistoric Maya From Caves Branch Rock Shelter, Belize

Problems of Interpretation

by David M. Glassman
Juan Luis Bonor Villarejo

Archaeological surveys of the Caves Branch region conducted during the early 1990s by the Belize Department of Archaeology located a rockshelter with the presence of a substantial concentration of human bone, lithic materials, and ceramic sherds on its surface. Periodic monitoring of the rockshelter revealed that movement and destruction of cultural and faunal materials were occurring at a rapid rate as a result of natural erosion, looting, and animal activity. The continued disturbance of the site necessitated a systematic project to identify the prehistoric cultural use of the rockshelter and a biological description of its inhabitants. The rockshelter became designated the Caves Branch Rock Shelter (CBRS) site.

During 1994 and 1995, excavations were conducted at CBRS with the assistance of the Belize Valley Archaeological Reconnaissance Project and the Belizean Department of Archaeology (Bonor Villarejo 1995, 1997; Bonor and Glassman 1999; Bonor and Martínez Klemm 1996). All excavations and the analysis of cultural materials occurred under the direction of Juan L. Bonor Villarejo. David Glassman was responsible for directing analyses of the skeletal remains. With no more than approximately fifty Maya rockshelters and caves that have yielded burials, CBRS is assumed to rank among the most important given the number of interments, its clear burial patterns, its sole use as an ossuary, and the comprehensive study of its skeletal remains.

Until now, few archaeological investigations have been done in the many caves that occupy the Caves Branch region. The most comprehensive work has been conducted at Petroglyph Cave by Dorie Reents-Budet and Barbara MacLeod (Reents 1980, 1981; Reents-Budet and MacLeod 1986). In addition, Elizabeth Graham, Logan McNatt, and Mark Gutchen (1980) have described Footprint Cave, and other investigators have focused their attention on the geology and morphology of other caves in the region. These few studies aside, extensive investigations have not been done during the past twenty years.

THE SITE

Caves Branch Rock Shelter is located close to the Caves Branch River in central Belize (Figure 15.1). In front of the shelter are five mounds in good condition. Evidence suggests that between ten and fifteen additional mounds may have been present in the past but were destroyed by current bulldozing activities. The rockshelter is 35 m long, 15.20 m in height, and a maximum depth of 10 m from the drip line. A cave is located just above CBRS. It, like the shelter, had been looted. Near CBRS are other caves that were used by the ancient Maya, including Te Tun Cave and Pottery Cave (Bonor and Martínez Klemm 1996).

EXCAVATION

Excavations of CBRS were controlled within nine units and revealed its use as an ancient ossuary estimated to include the remains of over 150 individuals. Skeletal remains were found throughout the site and in each excavation unit. Although a paucity of artifacts was recovered in association with the remains, those that were recovered indicated that the site had been used by local communities for burial activities over several hundred years. During excavation, thirty-two burials and the commingled remains of at least an additional 42 individuals were exposed in an area of approximately 10 m^2. The concentration of burials was most dense in Unit 6, which contained the remains of at least 7 different individuals within an excavated volume of 1 m^3. Site locations of the units are illustrated in Figure 15.2.

Over 1,000 pieces of lithic material were recovered from the CBRS, including obsidian blades, small pieces of quartz, granite, chert cores, a single biface identified as a fish tail point, and debitage. Three sources have been identified for the twenty-eight obsidian blades recovered at the site. Twenty-two of the blades were manufactured from obsidian of El Chayal, five from Ixtepeque, and one from Jilotepeque.

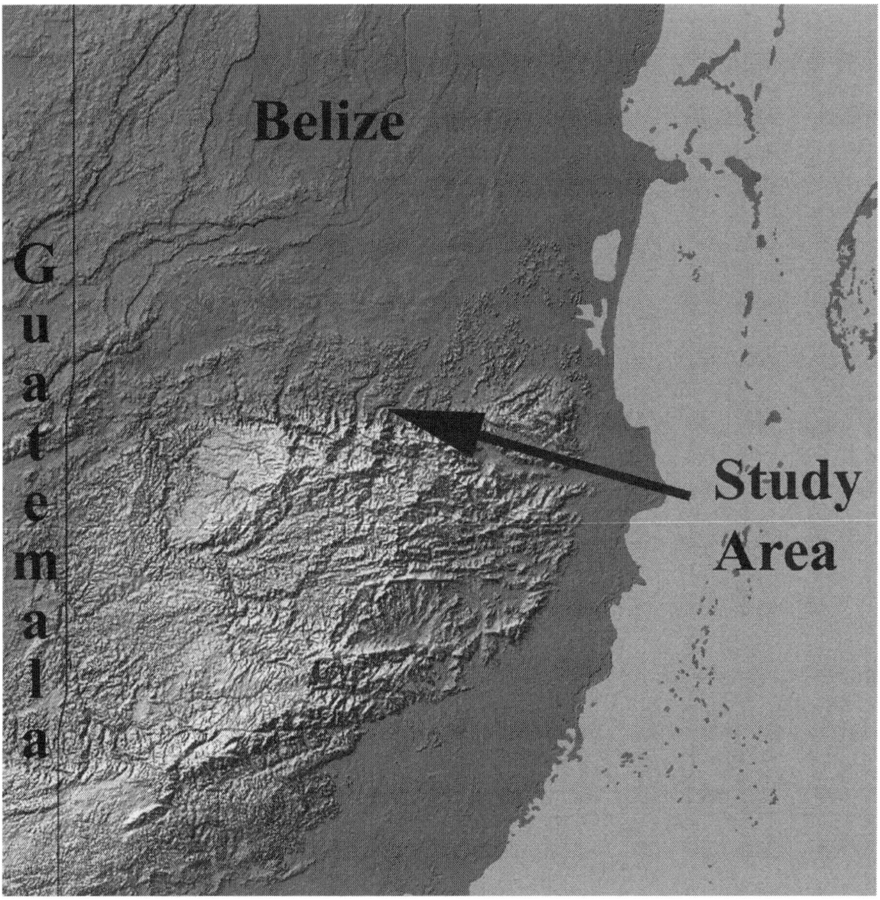

FIGURE 15.1. *Map of the Maya area including the Caves Branch Rock Shelter region (modified by Keith Prufer, base map courtesy of NASA/JPL).*

Shell materials were also common among the cultural assemblage associated with the burials at CBRS. Thousands of "Jute" shells (*Pachichylus indioum* and *Pachichylus glaphyrus*) were recovered, similar to reports of other caves in Belize used by the ancient Maya at Actun Balam (Pendergast 1969) and Eduardo Quiroz (Pendergast 1971) and also at major archaeological centers such as Xunantunich (Zeleznik 1993), Lubaantun (Hammond 1975), and Pacbictun (Healy, Emery, and Wright 1990), among others. In addition to the "Jute" varieties, a collection of shells (*Oliva reticularis* Lamarck) was recovered that exhibited cultural modification whereby a hole had been cut into the body. Similar worked shells have been reported from other caves such as Actun Balam (Pendergast 1969).

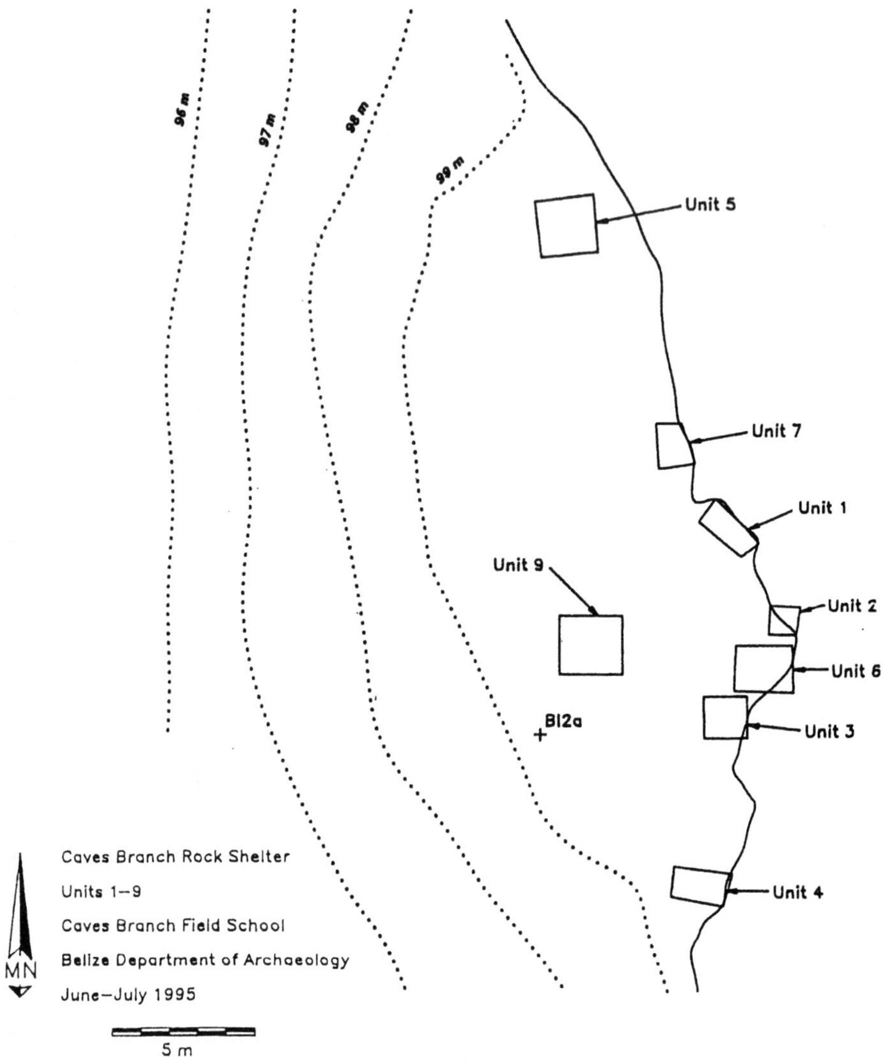

FIGURE 15.2. *Site map of the Caves Branch Rock Shelter (drawing by Cameron S. Griffith).*

The ceramic materials obtained during excavations at CBRS span temporally from the Middle Preclassic period (*Jocote Orange-Brown* and *Joventud Red*), the early phase of the Jenny Creek complex (900–600 B.C.) (Gifford 1976), through the Classic period, and into the Postclassic period (*Rio Juan Unslipped*) New Town complex, A.D. 900.

The cultural assemblage of the CBRS is unexceptional in its object types, design, material source, and quantity and by itself would not suggest that the site function was ritual. However, taken in context with the numerous burials intentionally interred in this location, the site interpretation becomes one of ritual use, and the artifacts placed in association with these burials can be considered ritual items as well. These "culturally ritual" items differ dramatically in style and quantity from the types found at ritual mass burial sites and tombs of upper-caste prehistoric Maya. Therefore, the CBRS is considered to be a ritual burial site used by lower-caste farming members of the neighboring areas.

BURIALS OF THE CAVES BRANCH ROCK SHELTER

Evidence that the CBRS represents ritual use comes from the many burials consciously placed at this location. At the time of excavation, most of the remains were fragmentary, disarticulated, and commingled. The pattern of disarticulation appears to have been the result of disturbance to "older" primary burials during interment activities associated with burying the more recently deceased. This may also be taken to imply that the location of the burials at CBRS may have been more important to the culture of the local population than the long-term care of the physical remains of past generations. Grave offerings would have also been disturbed and perhaps destroyed by the grave renewal activities. The removal and disturbance of older interments to make space for new burials is not unique to rockshelter and cave ossuaries but has also been noted within tombs at ceremonial centers. Bonor Villarejo noted that at the site of Nim Li Punit, the multiple burials in Tomb 3 were found stacked in corners and up against the walls, making space for someone else to be buried there.

Further evidence of ritual behavior having taken place at CBRS was attributed to the cultural patterning found among the CBRS burials in body position and orientation. Each of the CBRS burials that was complete enough to provide position and orientation information was found in a flexed position. All burials were oriented in a north-south orientation with the exception of Burial 17. And all skeletons were positioned with their faces toward the east, in the direction of the cave's entrance.

The analysis of the 32 individuals whose skeletal remains were recovered during excavation indicated that both males and females and individuals of all ages, from newborn to old age, were buried at the site (Table 15.1). Of the 13 individuals whose sex could be determined, 5 (38.5%) were males and 8 (61.5%) were females. Using 18 years of age as a subadult/adult cutoff point, 9 (28.1%) individuals were subadults and 23 (71.9%) individuals were adults. The data further indicated that male and female adults shared a similar life expectancy profile. This is in contrast to a pattern observed in a Late Classic Maya population on Ambergris Caye, Belize, which indicated females averaged a younger age at death than males (Glassman 1995).

Although a common practice among the prehistoric Maya, no cranial deformation was identified among the CBRS burials, and only one individual exhibited

Table 15.1. Age[1] and sex composition of the Caves Branch Rock Shelter Prehistoric Maya Burials

	B–2	*2–6*	*6–18*	*30–40*	*40+*	*Adult*[2]	*Indet.*[3]	*Total*	*%*
Male	—	—	—	1	3	1	—	5	15.6
Female	—	—	—	2	4	2	—	8	25.0
Subadult	3	5	1	—	—	—	—	9	28.1
Sex (?)	—	—	—	1	2	7	—	10	31.3
Total	3	5	1	4	9	10	—	32	100.0
%	9.4	15.6	3.1	12.5	28.1	31.3	0.0	100.0	

[1]Age in years.
[2]Age unknown.
[3]Indeterminate.

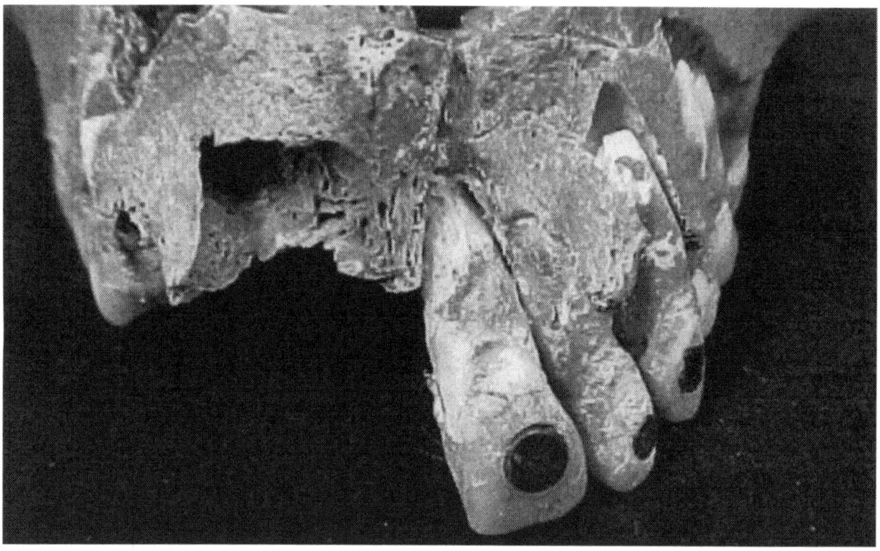

FIGURE 15.3. *Hematite inlays in the anterior teeth of Burial 11.*

intentional dental modification. This individual, Burial 11, exhibited circular hematite inlays on the labial surfaces of the maxillary left-central and lateral incisors and a more "square-shaped" hematite inlay in the maxillary left canine (Figure 15.3).

Health status and the incidence of disease among the CBRS sample were similar to findings from pathological studies of other prehistoric Maya groups (Glassman, Harris, and Bonor 2001). The most common skeletal pathology of the CBRS sample was vertebral osteoarthritis, observed in almost all adult individuals. Healed fractures accounted for the next most common pathology with twelve cases identified (for example, see Figure 15.4). During their lives, several CBRS individu-

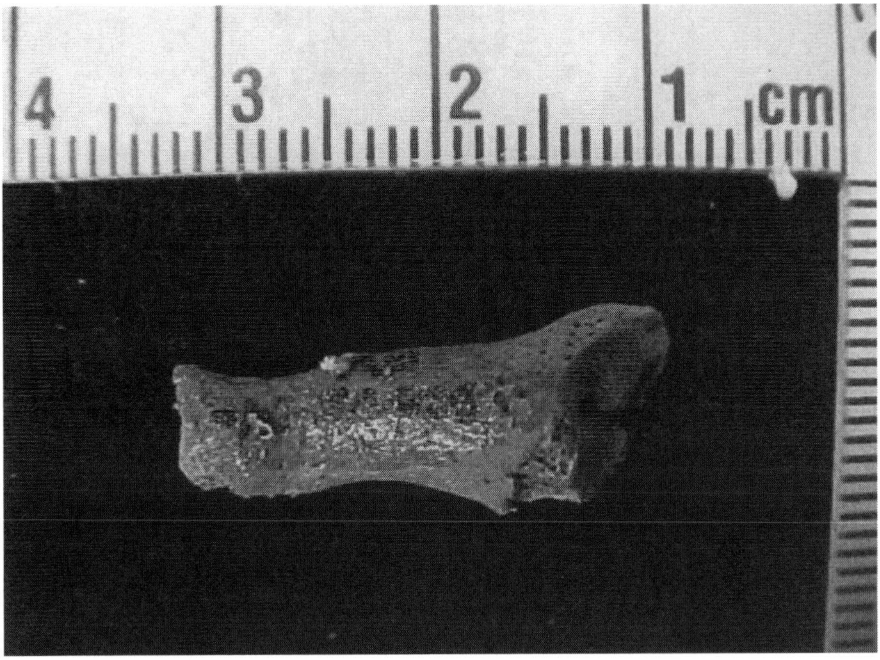

FIGURE 15.4. *Healed fracture at the midshaft of a proximal hand phalanx of Burial 11.*

als had been subjected to pathogenic organisms that caused inflammation of the bone. As many as seven individuals presented periostitic morphology (Figure 15.5), and a similar number exhibited areas of abscessed bone. Evidence of metabolic disturbances, although present, was limited to one case of porotic hyperostosis of the cranium and one case of hypercurvature of a right tibia.

RELATIONSHIP OF BURIALS AND THE ROCKSHELTER

Clearly, the CBRS represents a significant funerary site that was used over an extensive period by members of a local community. The data from the rockshelter show an important difference between the rituals practiced by the ruling elite of powerful and large sites and the rituals practiced by smaller communities lacking elite residents. These differences reflect two different ways of envisioning the world and of living in that world. Ritualism, exemplified at the rockshelter and other areas of the Caves Branch region, is conducted on a more "domestic-type" basis than what is regularly identified for elite-dwelling communities. There are thousands of caves and rockshelters in the Maya area with clear indications that they were used for ritual and other activities. However, no more than fifty of these caves and rockshelters have yielded human skeletal remains. The occupants who used

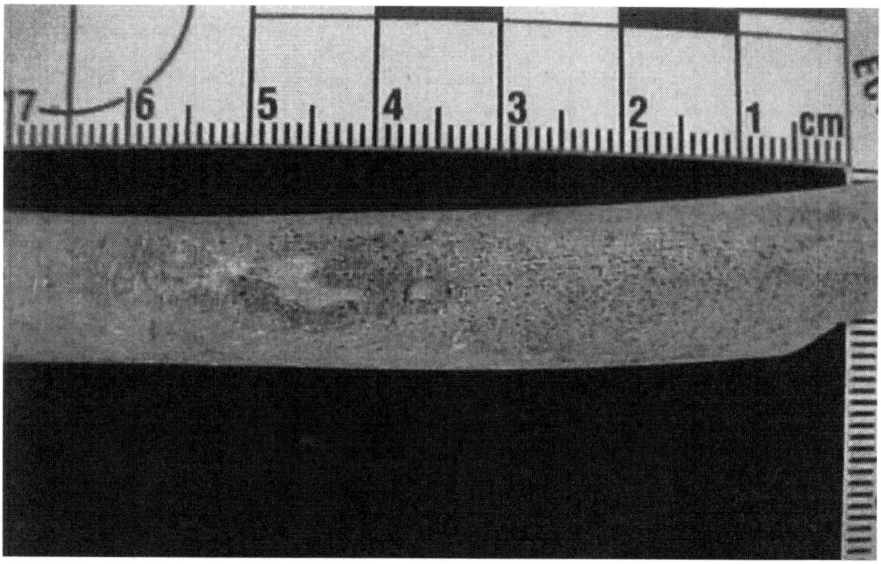

FIGURE 15.5. *Periostitis of the left tibia on Burial 23b.*

these caves—whether Maya elite, lower-caste groups within the social stratum, or both—are still debated. We contend that the archaeological and burial data recovered from the CBRS reveal the latter use, that of rural non-elites, for this particular site.

It is clear that the evidence outlining the religious beliefs of the ancient Maya inhabiting the rural areas is poorly documented and understood. This paucity of information mirrors the traditional study of Maya prehistory that has concentrated primarily on the dominant elite. Regardless of the intrigue, vast and beautiful material wealth, elaborate architecture, and complex interpretation and practices of ritual, religion, and cosmology that celebrate the life of the elite, they are not a representative sample of the culture and beliefs of the majority of the ancient Maya population. It is evident that compared to the great centers such as Tikal, Palenque, and Caracol, there were many more settlements that were smaller in size and would have possessed a similar social strata as the major centers but that lacked the power, influence, armed force, and command over the natural resources.

We disagree with the long-standing view that the numerous complex ideological concepts of the Maya were held exclusively by the governing elite of the great centers and did not reach the lower class. Consistent with this view is the fact that the majority of data that have become available to decipher the religion and ideology of the ancient Maya stems from the archaeological remains left behind by these elite groups and not from excavations of smaller settlements. This, however, should not indicate that the groups that were both socially and economically inferior to the truly elite were not in reach of, or did not have knowledge of, the religious practices and symbolism of the elite-defined ceremonies. We argue that all settlements, large and small, shared the Maya ideology of the elite but expressed and celebrated it in different ways and utilized different resources for symbolism.

To demonstrate our position, evidence is needed to show that the lower-caste or rural Maya were not only aware of and participated in the practices of the elite rituals but also understood the symbolism and traditional iconographic elements associated with these rituals. We believe a portion of this evidence can be found in the interpretation of the role of rockshelters in Maya culture, and we use our data from the CBRS to support this hypothesis.

Caves and rockshelters have played an important role in Maya culture and have been used for water sources, storage, and burials. They also serve an extremely important role in the development of Maya religion, whereby they have been considered the source of origin for the various Mesoamerican tribes (Bonor Villarejo 1989). Nevertheless, only a few rockshelter and cave sites exist that have documented use for religious practices by the elite. It would appear, then, that the religious use of rockshelters and caves falls more often to those who do not have enough economic resources to build sumptuous tombs that could be used for the same ritual purposes.

The lower-caste Maya may have used rockshelters, caves, and *chultuns* in the manner that the elite used their tombs. Although they did not have craftsmen to carve the basic and indispensable concepts of their religious ideology on altars and stelea, they engraved drawings on the walls of their rockshelters and caves that depicted the religious concepts, events, and symbolism embraced by the elite. We suggest that CBRS adequately demonstrates that communities with less political, religious, and economic power were adapting to Maya religious concepts, traditionally associated only with the ruling elite. That is, the group in the area of Caves Branch took advantage not only of this rockshelter but also of several caves in the surrounding areas. In these associated caves, they exhibited their perfect knowledge of the religious principles and ideology but altered them to be more consistent with their socioeconomic stratum by utilizing a more simplified and domestic form.

According to our excavation data, the CBRS was a place where males and females of all ages were equally buried. Although many of the burials were incomplete, no evidence suggests that these individuals died traumatic deaths, such as from human sacrifice or warfare. We suggest that the rockshelter was used by the common people who lived in nearby communities for purposes of burying their dead in sacred, ceremonial space.

The questions yet unanswered include, why do rockshelters represent sacred space for burial among the lower-caste communities, and what are their homologues in ritual and ideology among the elite? Rockshelters and caves have always been sacred spaces among the Maya, and they have played a major role in Maya cosmology as interpreted from iconographic materials and writings such as the Popol Vuh. We infer that it is the use of tombs by the elite to symbolize the sacred caverns that represents the more recent adaptation. The growing power of the elite resulted in their ability to construct their own burial "cave." The substitution of the natural cavern for magnificent and imposing constructions of their own design would more greatly reinforce their undeniable power and high social and political status.

The tombs themselves were often further enhanced to symbolize natural caves. For example, a series of stalactites was recently discovered in Tomb 2 of Nim Li Punit. The archaeological levels of Tomb 2 were perfectly defined, and we suggest that the stalactites were placed within the tomb with a definite purpose and intention—to increase the symbolism of the tomb as a cave. The retrieval activities of the stalactites from surrounding caves would have required significant time and manpower. Thus, the importance of "creating" a cave would have been substantial. An additional example can be seen at Palenque. Here, on a slab that covered the tomb of Pacal, is the image of the seven caverns originally mentioned in the Popol Vuh.

The substitution of the natural cavern for zoomorphic facades—such as jaws of serpents, jaguars, or the so-called Earth Monster—is very symbolic. The facades are absorbed ideologically by elites for the day of their death and subsequent rebirth. The "burial cavern" of the elite is no ordinary cave but is representative of the seven caves from which humans originated and to which the elite, such as Pacal, wanted to return.

New evidence on Maya cave and rockshelter research can be interpreted to suggest that rockshelters and caves may have had differing functions relative to ancient burial practices. Rockshelters, it seems, may have been used by the rural communities (non-elite) for burying their dead at the "portal" or gate of the "creation cave." In contrast, caves appear to have been used for the burial of elites, as if their status accorded direct privilege and permission to enter the "creation cave."

The Caves Branch site is not a unique example of a rockshelter used as sacred burial space among the Maya. During the past few years, the Maya Mountains Archaeological Project (Peter Dunham and Keith Prufer 1999: personal communication) discovered various shelters in southern Belize—larger than CBRS—that share similar characteristics, including burial density, pattern of burial position, and sex/age composition. We believe further investigations of rockshelters in the Maya region will undoubtedly provide a greater understanding of the funeral rites and rituals associated with the notion of death among the ancient Maya, both the elite and non-elite, and even perhaps more fully explain the nature of elite tomb construction and its symbolism.

ACKNOWLEDGMENTS

Archaeological excavations and skeletal research depend on the assistance of many individuals in both the field and the laboratory. Without their valuable contributions, the information contained in this chapter could not have been accumulated and presented. We thank Jaime Awe, David Cheetam, David Lee, Rhan-Ju Song, David Iguaz, Terry Powis, Bobby Hohman, Carolina Martinez, David Goldstein, and Cameron Griffith for their contributions to the archaeological component of the Caves Branch Rock Shelter Project. In addition, we thank Jennifer Harris, James Tyler, Jason Wiersema, Julie Mathis, Robin Cordero, Iris Korus, Dale Norton, and all the other volunteers at the Osteology Laboratory at Texas State University. Finally, we are grateful to the Belize Department of Archaeology for issuing the excavation permit and to its former archaeological commissioner, Dr. Harriot Topsey, who recognized the great importance of saving the archaeological information at CBRS from looter destruction.

REFERENCES CITED

Bonor Villarejo, Juan Luis

1989 *Las cuevas Mayas: simbolismo y ritual.* Universidad Complutense–Instituto de Cooperación Iberoamericana, Madrid.

1995 Excavacion de salvamento en Caves Branch Rock Shelter, Cayo District, Belize. In *Investigadores de la cultura Maya,* 3(1): 45–70. Universidad Autónoma de Campeche, Campeche.

1997 Current Problems at Mesoamerica Caves Investigations: Underground Archaeologist and Surface Archaeologist. Presentation at the Annual Meeting of the Society for American Archaeology, Nashville.

Bonor, Juan Luis, and David M. Glassman

1999 La arqueología y el estudio de los restos humanos en "Caves Branch Rock Shelter," distrito de El Cayo, Belice. *Mayab* 12:18–30.

Bonor, Juan Luis, and Carolina Martínez Klemm

1996 Trabajos reciented efectuados en la region de Caves Branch, distrito de El Cayo, Belice. *Investigadores de la Cultura Maya,* 4:249–267. Universidad Autónoma de Campeche, Campeche.

Gifford, James C.

1976 *Prehistoric Pottery Analysis and the Ceramics of Barton Ramie in the Belize Valley*. Memoirs of the Peabody Museum of Archaeology and Ethnology, Vol. 18. Harvard University, Cambridge.

Glassman, David M.

1995 Skeletal Biology of the Prehistoric Maya of Northern Ambergris Cay. In *Maya Maritime Trade, Settlement, and Populations of Ambergris Cay, Belize,* eds. Thomas H. Guderjan and James F. Garber, 73–93. Labyrinthos, Lancaster, CA.

Glassman, David M., Jennifer A.K. Harris, and Juan Luis Bonor

2001 Paleopathology of the Prehistoric Maya From Caves Branch Rock Shelter, Belize. *American Journal of Physical Anthropology,* Supplement 32:70.

Graham, Elizabeth, Logan McNatt, and Mark A. Gutchen

1980 Excavations in Footprint Cave, Caves Branch, Belize. *Journal of Field Archaeology* 7:153–172.

Hammond, Norman

1975 *Lubaantun: A Classic Maya Realm.* Monograph of the Peabody Museum of Archaeology and Ethnology. Harvard University, Cambridge.

Healy, Paul F., Kitty Emery, and Lori E. Wright
1990 Ancient and Modern Maya Exploitation of the Jute Snail (*Pachichylus*). *Latin American Antiquity* 1(2):170–183.

Pendergast, David M.
1969 *The Prehistory of Actun Balam, British Honduras.* Occasional Paper, 16. Royal Ontario Museum, Ontario.
1971 *Excavations at Eduardo Quiroz Cave, British Honduras (Belize).* Occasional Paper, 21. Royal Ontario Museum, Ontario.

Reents, Dorie Jane
1980 The Prehistoric Pottery From Petroglyph Cave, Caves Branch Valley, El Cayo District, Belize, Central America. M.A. Thesis. Department of Anthropology, University of Texas, Austin.
1981 The 1978 Caves Branch Cave Archaeological Project: Ceramic Analysis. Department of Archaeology, Belmopan.

Reents-Budet, Dorie, and Barbara MacLeod
1986 The Archaeology of Petroglyph Cave, Belize. Department of Archaeology, Belmopan.

Zeleznik, Scott
1993 Excavations and Consolidation A-1. In *Xunantunich Archaeological Project, 1993 Field Season.* Department of Archaeology, Belize–UCLA.

Chapter Sixteen

Nearer to the Gods

Rockshelter Burials From the Ek Xux Valley, Belize

by Julie Mather Saul
Keith M. Prufer
Frank P. Saul

In the Maya Mountains of southern Belize, near the ancient Maya community Ek Xux (Figure 16.1), three natural rockshelters have produced extremely well-preserved burials in both primary and secondary contexts. These rockshelters—Saki Tzul, Mohibal Kanchi, and Mayahak Cab Pek—appear to have been used as cemeteries before and during the Late Preclassic to Late Classic (A.D. 200–750) occupation of the site.

For those who study caves, it is becoming apparent that burials in rockshelters are not uncommon, although they remain vastly understudied and poorly discussed. Most ancient Maya burial sites are associated with surface architecture. However, at Ek Xux there is no evidence that any of the surface structures had mortuary functions, an anomaly for Maya communities. Excavations in both large and small residential buildings have failed to uncover any evidence of burials. This may result in part from the availability or choice of building materials at the site. Most buildings are small (< 3 m), single episode constructions, consisting of rounded river cobble facades overlaying dirt

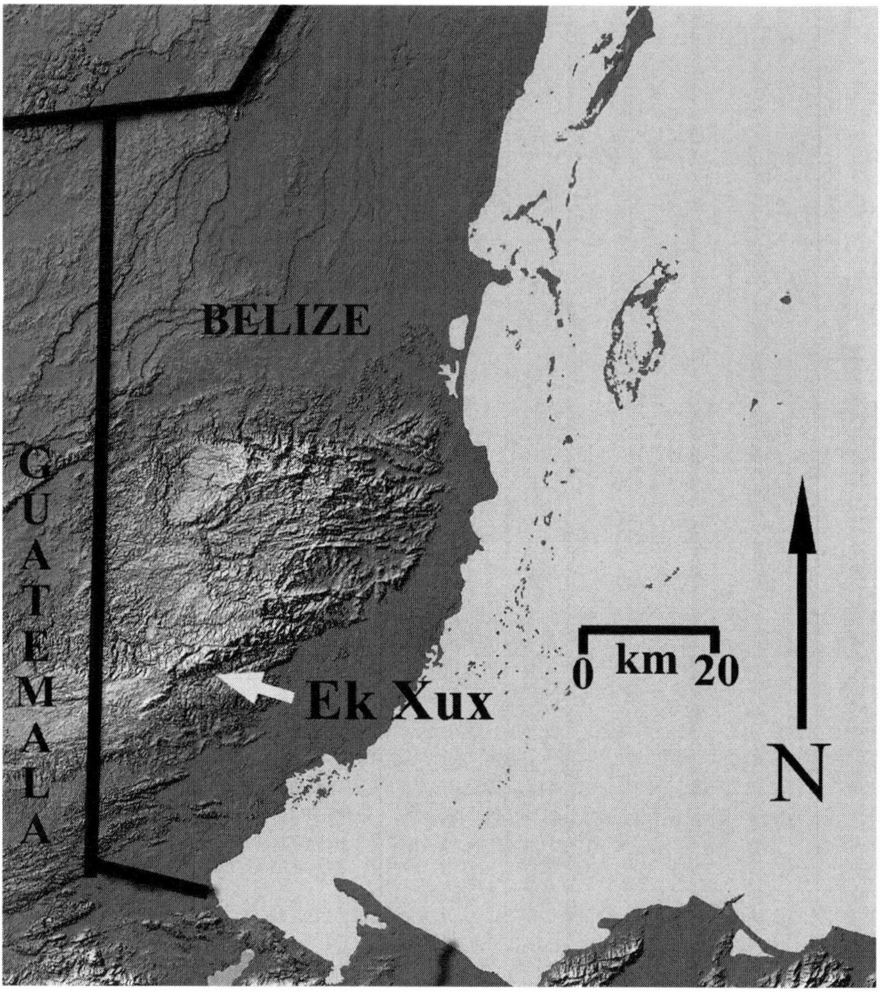

FIGURE 16.1. *Map of the Maya Mountains in southern Belize showing the location of the site Ek Xux. The southern Maya Mountains are largely derived from limestone overlying earlier volcanics (modified after base image courtesy of NASA/JPL/Caltech).*

and debris cores. Regardless of the apparent absence of mortuary activity at the site (additional sampling may yet reveal burials), it seems that nearby rockshelters were favored burial areas. Excellent preservation of the skeletal material has allowed us to reconstruct the life histories of many of the individuals. There is no evidence that any of them were of elite status, by way of either noticeable health disparities or associated grave furniture. Here, we present our findings concerning the mortuary treatment of these individuals and the results of analyses of the excavated remains. Our primary goal is to demonstrate how these relatively undisturbed rockshelter contexts can provide a wealth of information related to burial treatment and osteobiographical reconstruction.

ROCKSHELTERS IN THE EK XUX VALLEY

The real estate axiom "location, location, location" comes to mind inasmuch as these open-air cave sites combine two sacred elements: proximity to the sky and the entrance to the underworld. Limited data from elsewhere in Belize (see Awe, Helmke, and Griffith 1998; Gibbs 1997; Glassman and Bonor Villarejo, this volume) and from elsewhere in the Maya area (also see Lee 1967, 1969, 1985; MacNeish and Peterson 1962; Scott and Brady, this volume) indicate that rockshelters commonly have mortuary functions. However, little is known about rockshelters in general or how the Maya perceived them as features in their geography. Rockshelters likely fall into a general class of places in the landscape that include dark zone caves, grottos, springs, wells, and mountain-shrines in that they represent places in nature made sacred by the Maya based on their relationship to terrestrial deities and connections to revered ancestors (Prufer 2002).

Our three rockshelters surround the site of Ek Xux (Figure 16.2). All three are overhangs located at the bases of large cliffs that circumscribe the alluvial valley where the site is located. Mayahak Cab Pek is located approximately 1.2 km from the site core and below a ridge that defines the western boundary of the settlement area. Mohibal Kanchi is located 200 m from the site core and less than 50 m from the nearest settlement. Saki Tzul is perched above the site, 400 m southeast of the site core. Both Mayahak Cab Pek and Mohibal Kanchi were partially looted. At Mayahak Cab Pek the damage was minor and confined to a 1- by 2-m area. Damage at Mohibal Kanchi was more significant, and contexts of several shallow burials were disturbed (several deeper interments were left intact).

Burials at surface sites are affected by varying degrees of exposure to vegetation roots, architectural decay, and environmental conditions unfavorable to preservation of human remains. Our natural rockshelters, however, offer unparalleled conditions for the recovery of skeletal data. The rockshelter soils remained dry even during occasional deluges. Their locations, adjacent to but sheltered from steep to vertical hillsides, were free of flooding from runoff. Additionally, there were few intrusions of the plant and tree roots that in most other Maya burials produce major bone damage. Aside from looting, disturbances to mortuary contexts were attributed to settling of soft unconsolidated soils, animal burrowing, and the Maya proclivity for placing interments near or above earlier burials, which may have been unmarked in antiquity. Since our investigation consisted of limited excavations at each rockshelter, these results only describe a portion of the population interred. With the exception of one "ossuary pit," we largely limit our discussion to the analysis of complete, partial, and commingled individuals, excluding from the discussion random skeletal fragments found in excavations and looter's backdirt.

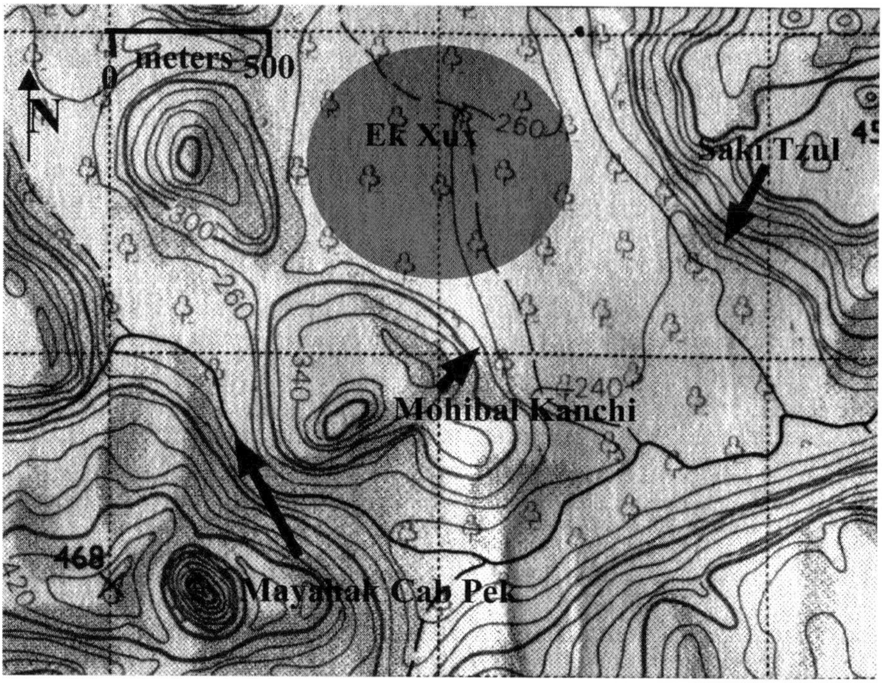

FIGURE 16.2. *Ek Xux and the three rockshelters discussed in this chapter. The rockshelters are all along the valley floor at the same level as the site (modified after DGMS 1993).*

POPULATION COMPOSITION

To date, thirteen intact or mostly intact individuals, as well as a number of commingled and fragmentary remains, have been excavated at these three sites. Eight are adults, evenly divided between male and female (although one is a "probable" male). Five are immature. Within each of the three sites, males and females are evenly divided and immature remains were found. Sex of the adults was based on pelvic and cranial morphology, with the exception of the one incomplete probable male whose sex could be based only on less reliable metric analysis. The females are slightly younger than the males, with two females in their late teens to early twenties, one 20–30 years old, and one who can be referred to only as "adult." The males consist of one 20–30 years old, one 20–35 years old, and two middle adults (35–50 years). Excellent preservation enabled us to determine most ages using many of the preferred indicators, including degree of long bone epiphyseal union, union of annular epiphyses to vertebral bodies, iliac crest fusion, sternal rib end and pubic symphysis stages, dental attrition, and cranial suture closure. Ages of children could be determined in all but one case by development and eruption of the denti-

FIGURE 16.3. *Mohibal Kanchi, showing the looters' trench and excavation units. Burials were found in the looted trench, but in levels below the disturbance.*

tion in combination with long bone diaphyseal length: one child of 9–11 years and four infants (8–12 months, 6–18 months, 12–16 months, and 6–30 months). Because of lack of dentition, the age of the 6–30-month-old child was based only on long bone diaphyseal length.

Fragments of other individuals were found in association with four burials. At Saki Tzul a portion of immature metatarsal was found in the fragmentary male burial. At Mayahak Cab Pek a fragment of an adult temporal bone was excavated among the bones of a 12–16-month-old infant, a fragment of a young child's tibia shaft (with rodent gnawing) was included with a late teen to early twenty-year-old female, and two fragments of adult femur, a tooth, a pelvic fragment, three hand phalanges, and two metatarsals were associated with the 20–30-year-old male. It is unknown whether these fragments were deliberately placed in context with these burials or were simply present in the grave fill. None of these "extra" remains could be linked to nearby burials.

Mohibal Kanchi had been visited by looters before we discovered it (Figure 16.3), and examination of surface scatter produced by their quest for salable items (it is hoped unsuccessful) yielded fragments of a minimum of four individuals: three adults and an infant of 6–18 months. Again, none of these could be linked to any of the burials excavated nearby.

STATUS

The population composition of occupants of these three rockshelters suggests that, although interred in a "prime" location, these may be "ordinary" citizens rather than the elite populations of ceremonial centers such as the Guatemalan sites of Altar de Sacrificios and Rio Azul, which were heavily biased toward adults and males. (The adult:subadult ratio for Altar de Sacrificios is 63:27 and adult male:female:undetermined ratio is 31:21:11 [Saul 1972]. The adult:subadult ratio for Rio Azul is 52:13 and adult male:female:undetermined ratio is 20:12:21 [F. Saul and J. Saul 2000].)

Accompanying grave goods and burial arrangements are also suggestive of non-elite individuals interred away from settlement architecture. Burial fill was in all cases dense with jute shells, burned and unburned, making excavation difficult. In some cases, jute comprised up to 30 percent of the matrix surrounding interments. Jute shells are common offerings in caves and other religious contexts, and these deposits are associated with Earth Lords and earthly fertility (Halperin et al. 2003; Prufer 2002).

Grave goods at Mohibal Kanchi consisted of fragments of carved marine shell and shell beads, a crude anthropomorphic figurine carved from a jaguar (*Panthera* onca) canine, two unmodified feline canines, several stingray spines, a bone perforator or needle, several fragmentary obsidian blades, and numerous modified calcite crystals. Crystals have recently been discussed as a common finding in cave contexts associated with the activities of Mesoamerican religious specialists (Brady and Prufer 1999). Burned wood accompanied all the burials, although skeletal material was not charred. Ceramics recovered indicate a Late Classic date for the Mohibal Kanchi burials, along with a single radiocarbon date of A.D. 660–860 (CAL two-sigma deviation, AA40693).

At Saki Tzul, burned resins (possibly incense) were found at two locations in the same level as the female burial. Arranged above these resins, moving upward, were found a "long bead," burned armadillo scutes, a fragment of burned animal canine tooth, a cluster of fragmentary ceramics, and a pocket of seeds. A grinding stone fragment was located about 5 cm from her right ankle. Like Mohibal Kanchi, ceramics indicate Late Classic use, supported by a Late to Terminal Classic radiocarbon date of A.D. 780–1000 (CAL two-sigma deviation, AA40691).

Mayahak Cab Pek presents a much more complex picture. There, ceramic and radiocarbon evidence indicates use during the Middle Preclassic through the Late Classic. A stone-lined ossuary pit filled with highly mixed and disarticulated skeletal material provided a date of 360 to 50 B.C. (CAL two-sigma deviation, AA40679) and also contained Protoclassic to Late Classic ceramics. A date associated with the extended burial of a young adult male places it between A.D. 240 and 440 (CAL two-sigma deviation, AA40678). This individual's head was resting in a Protoclassic Caribal Red dish (see Brady 1989: 173 for type description). Although the bulk of the ceramics from the site date from the Late Classic, several contexts contained Protoclassic and Early Classic sherds (Prufer 2002: 388). The Protoclassic burial coincides with the earliest known settlement in the Ek Xux Valley, possibly indicating that mortuary use of the rockshelter was part of the burial strategies of the earliest settlers in the region.

BURIAL POSITIONS

Five individuals were buried in flexed positions (three adult females, two immatures) and four in extended positions (one female, one male, and one immature—all faceup), including one 20–30-year-old Mayahak Cab Pek male who was placed facedown with his head resting in an Early Classic vessel that also contained an eggshell of unknown species (Figure 16.4). The positions of two individuals could not be determined, and a 9–11-year-old child is neither flexed nor extended but part of the unique and initially confusing arrangement described below (J. Saul and F. Saul 2002).

At Mohibal Kanchi a fully articulated 20–35-year-old male lies in an extended supine position, head to the south, with the postcranial remains of a child of 9–11 years carefully arranged across his knees. The skull and mandible of this child are located on the right shoulder of the adult male, beside his own skull. Kneeling over these two, tightly flexed and with her head pointing north, is a fully articulated female (20–30 years). This arrangement is noteworthy not only for the unusual positioning involved but also because it implies that the local population kept track of the remains of at least one or perhaps two individuals after death. Using our knowledge of taphonomy (what happens to the body after death) and powers of observation (and imagination?), we have attempted to sequence these deaths as follows.

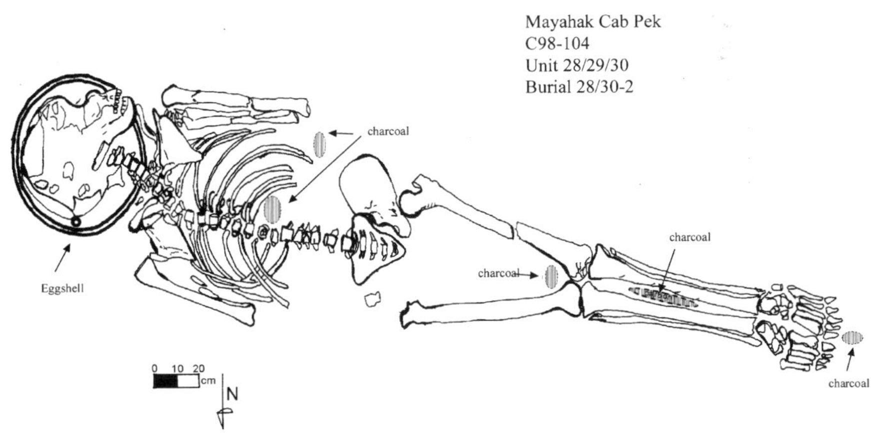

FIGURE 16.4. *Male (20–30-year-old) from Mayahak Cab Pek, buried facedown with his head resting in an Early Classic bowl.*

Her head rests on a flat, pillow-like stone lying on the upper chest of the male, with her face turned to her right shoulder (east). She was deliberately placed with her right knee resting on the skull of the child and her left knee resting on the skull (or head) of the adult male. That the remains of the child had been placed in the grave after skeletonization became obvious with careful examination of the exact positions of bones. For instance, the left radius and ulna were placed close together and parallel, as they would be in life, but one bone had been turned end-for-end so that its distal end rested alongside the proximal end of the other. Also, the distal (elbow) end of the right humerus was placed as if in articulation with the glenoid fossa of the right scapula—again a physical impossibility if covered with flesh. The clincher was that although the first cervical vertebra was placed on top of the second cervical vertebra, each of these vertebrae was turned upside down. If the first cervical vertebra and the second cervical vertebra are properly articulated, turning them upside down as a unit will put the second cervical vertebra on top.

Our resulting interpretation is that the child was the first to die. Sometime later, after this child had become skeletonized, the male died. The male was placed in the grave while still "fleshed" (all bones retained their proper anatomical relationships), and the bones of the child were carefully moved from their original resting place to join the male adult, with the child's skull and mandible positioned on the right shoulder of the male, perhaps in a place of honor. When the female died she was placed (while also in a "fleshed" condition) in the same grave, kneeling over them in a seemingly protective manner (Figure 16.5). Although we could not determine the

FIGURE 16.5. *Artist's reconstruction of the possible family unit from Mohibal Kanchi (M. J. Naujock, artist).*

time interval between the burials of the adults, the exact positioning of the female relative to the other two individuals suggests that either she was placed into the grave at (or very close to) the time of the male's burial or the location of the double burial was so precisely marked on the ground surface that she could be inserted at a later time in relation to, but without disturbing, the other two.

The question of the "pillow stone" remains. Was it placed on the chest of the male upon his burial as a future marker, indicating to the grave diggers that the desired level and location for the burial of the female had been reached? This suggests that the arrangement had been planned in advance. Or was the stone put in place at the time of her burial to facilitate her kneeling position?

Nearby are the articulated remains of an 8–12-month-old infant, buried in an extended supine position with the head to the south. This infant may or may not be part of this possible nuclear family (DNA analysis of all four is ongoing). One way or the other, this is a unique group burial.

One other deliberate grouping, possibly a mother with her child, was found at Mayahak Cab Pek—a flexed adult female with the flexed body of an 8–12-month-old infant held to her chest (Figure 16.6).

At least some of the rockshelter burials were probably not marked on the ground surface, producing unintentional groupings, as suggested by the 18–24-year-old female in Saki Tzul who was severely disturbed through the midsection (no animal burrows were evident) and at Mayahak Cab Pek, where a flexed female (16–24 years) appeared to have been placed "into" the much earlier burial of a 35–50-year-old male who was thereby so thoroughly disturbed that his burial position could not be determined.

Heads of individuals pointed to three of the four cardinal directions, with south and north perhaps preferred; among the immature, three pointed to the south (two flexed, one extended) and one to the east (flexed), whereas adult heads pointed two to the north (both flexed females, one prone, one supine), three south (two extended males, one prone, one supine, and a flexed female), and one east (extended supine female). No heads pointed west.

HEALTH AND NUTRITION

Differential diagnosis of health conditions is difficult in living people where soft tissues and fluids are available for testing, symptoms can be discussed, and a health history can be obtained from the patient. Relatively few conditions leave visible clues of their presence in life in bone, even if all skeletal elements are present in a good state of preservation (Ortner and Putschar 1985).

As a result of skeletal and dental preservation problems in the Maya area, we think in terms of "evaluable individuals" when looking at the prevalence or incidence of a particular lesion or trait. An individual is considered "evaluable" for a specific lesion/trait if the element in which the condition would normally appear is completely present or at least present in sufficient quantity and quality for us to be

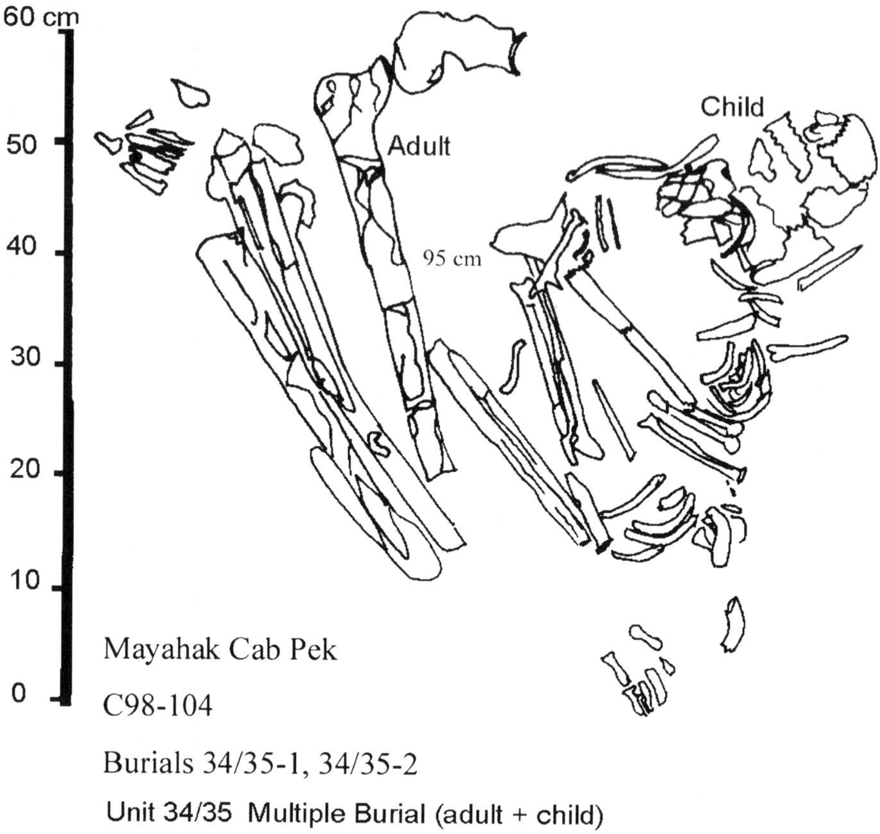

FIGURE 16.6. *Female and 8–12-month-old child burial from Mayahak Cab Pek. These two individuals were interred in a 1.5-m-deep circular pit.*

assured that its absence can be determined (Saul 1972; F. Saul and J. Saul 1989, 1991; J. Saul and F. Saul 1997b). Unlike most of our previous research populations, these rockshelter burials represent one of the best-preserved collections of evaluable individuals found in the Maya area.

Caries, Periodontoclasia, and Antemortem Tooth Loss

As caries cavities are a common finding in the Maya area, the noncarious dentitions of one male (twenty-three teeth recovered) and one female (twenty-seven teeth recovered) were a surprise. However, antemortem tooth loss, also a very common finding among the Maya, was present in all of the five evaluable adults, including the noncarious young adult male. Antemortem tooth loss may be a result of carious destruction, or it may be the end result of periodontoclasia, a common form of alveolar soft tissue inflammation resulting in degeneration of tooth sockets, with consequent tooth loss followed by root socket resorption. Periodontoclasia can be produced by a variety of interacting factors such as mechanical irritation, infection and tissue fragility, and breakdown (Saul 1972; F. Saul and J. Saul 1984a, 1984b, 1991; J. Saul and F. Saul 1997b). Antemortem tooth loss and periodontoclasia are not limited to older individuals and have been found in young adults. In fragmentary and incomplete remains, presence can be more definitely determined than absence, which requires access to complete alveoli of both jaws. Decorated teeth may suffer premature loss because of the interaction of decay and attrition with the modification procedures involved in the decorative process. Trauma is also a remote causative factor in individual tooth loss.

Linear Enamel Hypoplasia

Linear enamel hypoplasia represents a systemic developmental arrest during the process of tooth crown formation, resulting in horizontal grooves in the dental enamel. This nonspecific marker may be caused by malnutrition, fever, illness, and other factors, operating singly or in combination. The location of the permanent defect on the tooth crown indicates the approximate age of the individual when normal enamel formation was disrupted. In ancient Maya populations, linear enamel hypoplasia is frequently found in permanent tooth crowns at locations on the crowns that indicate problems at around three or four years of age, which perhaps not coincidentally happens to be about the age of weaning among the Maya as recorded by de Landa (in Tozzer 1941: 125) at the time of European contact. Weaning is a critical time, with greater risk for malnutrition and infectious disease as the child loses the nutritional benefits and anti-infectious disease agents present in mother's milk and is put on a maize-dependent, probably protein-deficient diet. The switch to a maize-based and less easily digested diet is often a time of illness (Saul 1972, 1982; F. Saul and J. Saul 1984a, 1984b, 1991, 2000; J. Saul and F. Saul 1997b; Saul, Saul, and Muñoz 1995).

These linear defects are present on the permanent tooth crowns of three of the five evaluable individuals (65 percent). Linear enamel hypoplasia is present in both evaluable females (the female at Saki Tzul and the female with an infant at Mayahak Cab Pek) and one of the two evaluable children (present in the 9–11-year-old at Mohibal Kanchi, absent in the 8–12-month-old infant with the female at Mayahak Cab Pek) but is absent in both evaluable males (the male at Mohibal Kanchi and the extended male with his head in a bowl at Mayahak Cab Pek). In two cases (the female from Saki Tzul and the 9–11-year-old child at Mohibal Kanchi) multiple grooves on a single permanent crown indicate multiple episodes of growth arrest. Linear enamel hypoplasia is present in 80 percent of the evaluable individuals at Rio Azul (F. Saul and J. Saul 2000; J. Saul and F. Saul 1998) and 95 percent at Altar de Sacrificios (Saul 1972; F. Saul and J. Saul 1984a, 1984b).

Nonlinear Dental Defects and Staining, and Osteological Defects

Horizontal staining and small enamel defects on deciduous tooth crowns indicate nutritional or other health problems or both during the late fetal period through soon after birth in two of the three very young children for whom dentition was recovered (present in the infant from Mohibal Kanchi and the 12–16-month-old from Mayahak Cab Pek, absent in the 8–12-month-old from Mayahak Cab Pek buried with the female). The presence of these fetal nutritional and other health problems in turn suggests that the mother may also have been suffering from malnutrition—perhaps complicated by disease.

Patches of porous and striated reactive bone on long bone shafts and on the internal surface of cranial bones (especially occipital bones) of two of the three evaluable children are also suggestive of nutritional difficulties. Both the 9–11-year-old child from Mohibal Kanchi and the 12–16-month-old infant from Mayahak Cab Pek had indications suggestive of malnutrition, disease, or both on both bones and teeth. None of these indicators were present on the teeth or bones of the infant found cradled in its (probable) mother's arms at Mayahak Cab Pek.

Parity

The presence of pronounced preauricular sulci ("scars" of pregnancy produced by the late-term interaction of the hormone relaxin with mechanical factors) on pelvic fragments of the female holding an infant hints that she had probably had at least one late-stage pregnancy, as is also true of the female kneeling over the male and child at Mohibal Kanchi. The maternal status of the young female from Saki Tzul is indicated by both preauricular sulci and parturition pits (the latter are associated with difficult births as a result of cephalopelvic disproportionism) (F. Saul and J. Saul 1989). Pubic bones, on whose dorsal surfaces parturition pits would be located if present, were not recovered for the other two females.

Spongy or Porotic Hyperostosis Cranii

Porosities can be seen on occipital bone and orbital roof fragments of the 9–11-year-old child from Mohibal Kanchi, who was arranged across the adult male's knees, in addition to linear enamel hypoplasia and patches of reactive bone on long bones and the internal surface of cranial (occipital) bone fragments. In spongy or porotic hyperostosis, the expansion of marrow tissue within the diploe between the inner and outer tables of cranial bones is accompanied by a vertical reorientation of diploe, thereby producing erosion of the outer table, resulting in a sievelike pattern of porosities. This lesion may be associated with several varieties of anemia, especially iron-deficiency anemia, perhaps in association with protein-deficiency anemia. Underlying factors in the Maya area include nutritional deficiencies, blood loss caused by intestinal and other parasites, iron-deficient soils, and a high-carbohydrate, low-protein, maize-dependent diet complete with iron absorption problems related to the introduction of chelating agents in maize preparation. In addition, there is an increased iron requirement in the tropics because of sweating, and an anemic mother will produce an infant with low iron stores (Saul 1972, 1977, 1982; F. Saul and J. Saul 1984a, 1984b, 1991; J. Saul and F. Saul 1997b, 1998, 2001). Spongy or porotic hyperostosis, suggestive of nutritional deficiencies, is a common finding at some Maya sites (89 percent at Altar de Sacrificios [Saul 1972; F. Saul and J. Saul 1984a, 1984b] and 50 percent at Rio Azul [F. Saul and J. Saul 2000; J. Saul and F. Saul 1998]) but was found in only two of the six evaluable individuals (30 percent) in these rockshelters—the other was the prone adult male. Cranial remains of only one of the eight evaluable individuals in the Programme for Belize region of northwestern Belize showed signs of spongy or porotic hyperostosis (J. Saul and F. Saul 1997a, 1998, n.d.; Saul, Saul, and Muñoz 1995). Clearly, some of these Maya Mountains people had nutritional problems, but perhaps not to the degree of some other Maya populations. However, as the children present in this population did not survive childhood, malnutrition may be considered at least an underlying factor.

Periostitis or Treponemal Disease?

The right tibia of the kneeling female from Mohibal Kanchi appears normal whereas the left tibia is curved, anterior-posterior, like a cavalry saber. The interosseous crest is straight, but the anterior crest of the left tibia is blunted and swollen by cortical expansion with periosteal reaction striations. This is suggestive of possible treponemal disease (syphilis is one of the treponemal diseases), and bony indications suggestive of pre-Columbian treponemal disease have been found in the Maya area, in particular at the Guatemalan sites of Altar de Sacrificios (Saul 1972; F. Saul and J. Saul 1984a, 1984b) and Seibal (F. Saul and J. Saul 1989), as well as in the Preclassic (as early as 950 B.C.) population of Cuello in northern Belize (F. Saul and J. Saul 1991; J. Saul and F. Saul 1997b, 1998). However, the anterior crest of the tibia is also vulnerable to injury and subsequent infection (leading to periostitis), and conclusions based on just one tibia would be unwise and premature. No other indications of treponemal disease were found on this individual or in any other individuals from the rockshelters. Since no definite indications of treponemal disease have been found in the rockshelter population, at Rio Azul, or at any of the sites in the Programme for Belize region (F. Saul and J. Saul 2000; J. Saul and F. Saul 1997b, 1998, n.d.; Saul, Saul, and Muñoz 1995), it may be that treponemal disease was present only in localized areas of the ancient Maya world.

CULTURAL MODIFICATIONS

Intentional cranial shaping and dental decoration are commonly found among the Maya, sometimes in combination. These modifications can be found in both males and females and their presence or absence is not necessarily an indication of elevated status. For instance, the skull of the elite female within Tomb 25 at Rio Azul was not shaped and her teeth were not decorated (F. Saul and J. Saul 2000). The elite male occupant of the tomb at La Milpa (within the Programme for Belize region) also had an unshaped skull; however, the presence or absence of dental decoration is unknown, as no teeth were recovered for this individual (J. Saul and F. Saul 1997a).

Cranial Shaping

We prefer to use the neutral term *shaping* rather than the often used but pejorative term *deformation* in discussing the cranial modifications commonly practiced by the Maya and other groups (Saul 1972, 1982; F. Saul and J. Saul 2001; J. Saul and F. Saul 1997b, 1998). Some varieties of shaping were probably unintentional, as, for instance, that resulting from the use of a cradleboard or other infant carrier (producing flattening on the back of the head) or the use of a tumpline to carry burdens in later years (slightly modifying the upper forehead). Other shapes could only have been intentionally created.

In 1938, José Imbelloni and Adolfo Dembo introduced a classification of shaping "styles" that was presented in Juan Comas (1960). Although other classifications exist, this one is used most frequently in Latin America, and therefore we use it because of its congruity with Latin American scholarship.

"Tabular" shaping is produced by fronto-occipital compression and "orbicular" or "annular" shaping by the use of bands that compress the head circumferentially. These two basic categories are further subdivided into the "erect" variety (the direction of pressure resulting in an essentially vertical or anteriorly tilted orientation of the occipital bone) and the "oblique" variety (the entire occipital flattened and tilted posteriorly).

Only one skull suggestive of cranial shaping has been found thus far in the rockshelters—that of the 8–12-month-old infant at Mohibal Kanchi. The parietals appear foreshortened and bulging and the occipital bone is flattened, suggestive of Imbelloni and Dembo's tabular style. If it is indeed intentionally shaped, the exact style cannot be determined because of incompleteness, although the "erect" style seems more likely.

Dental Decoration

Here again, we prefer to use a neutral term (*decoration*) instead of the more negative but often used term *mutilation.* We suspect that within the Maya culture the intent was to "decorate" rather than to "mutilate" (Saul 1972, 1982; F. Saul and J. Saul 2001; J. Saul and F. Saul 1997b, 1998). People of various cultures in both the Old and New Worlds have been known to decorate anterior tooth crowns by filing the incisal edges, engraving labial surfaces, and inserting substances such as jade or hematite into shallow holes drilled into the labial surfaces. The types (or "styles") found in Mexico and Central America have been classified by Javier Romero Molina (1970).

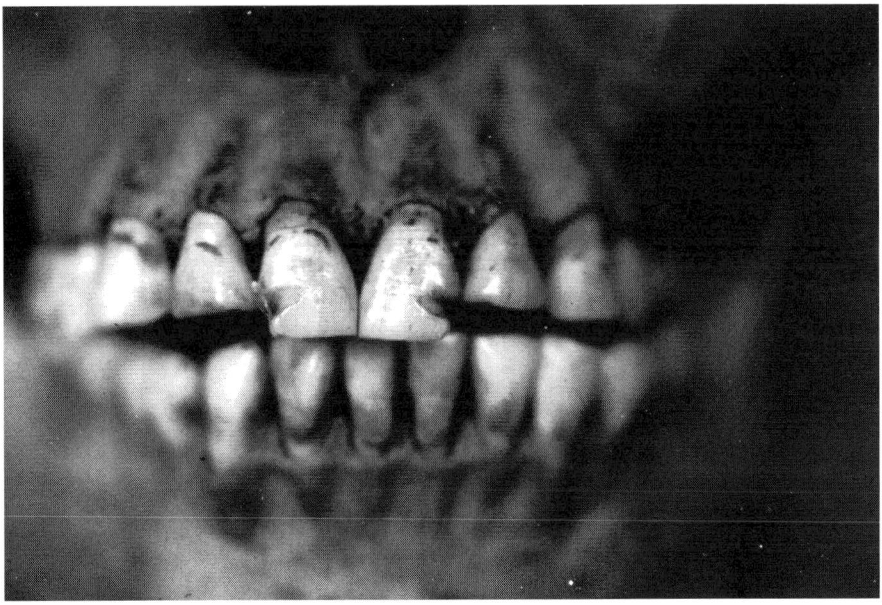

FIGURE 16.7. *Teeth of the 18–24-year-old female from Saki Tzul showing Romero B 5 (medial incisors) and A 4 (lateral incisors and canines) dental decoration.*

The only decorated teeth found so far are those of the female at Saki Tzul (Figure 16.7). The lateral edges of her maxillary central incisors are notched in Romero's B 5 decoration style, and the maxillary canines and lateral incisors are examples of Romero type A 4 (incisal edges shortened horizontally).

ACTIVITY INDICATORS

Some of the most interesting information we have acquired is a consequence of the excellent preservation of these Maya skeletons. Usually, vertebrae, articular ends of long bones, and bones of the hand, wrist, ankle, and foot do not survive the rigors of burial in the tropics as a result of damage by plant roots and alternating wet and dry seasons. However, many of these skeletal regions are preserved in our rockshelter people, giving us information not usually obtainable (Capasso, Kennedy, and Wilczak 1999; Kennedy 1983, 1989; Merbs 1983).

Moving about in the rugged terrain of this part of the Maya Mountains puts strains on all joints, particularly those of the lower limbs, as seen in the slightly lipped and markedly sharp borders of articular surfaces of the legs, ankles, and feet of all evaluable adults.

The vertebrae of all evaluable adults also show signs of one or more of the following: osteoarthritic lipping on bodies and posterior joints, osteophyte formation, laminal spurs, body compression, and in one case (the prone male from Mayahak Cab Pek) herniation of the intervertebral disc into the body (a Schmorl's node). These are all indicators of spinal stress such as would be involved in carrying heavy loads, particularly over uneven terrain. Sacroiliac and lumbosacral joints are also strongly affected. Compression and lipping of cervical bodies, along with deformed posterior joints, suggest the use of a tumpline or otherwise carrying heavy burdens using the head and muscles of the neck.

The male from Mayahak Cab Pek (found extended with his head resting in a bowl) also has an extra articular facet on one side of his sacrum. Usually, these extra posterior or dorsal facets are on both sides (bilateral) and are thought to be caused by carrying heavy loads on the back. We were puzzling over this when we noticed some of our Maya workers carrying heavy burdens slung over one shoulder. The resulting spinal asymmetry gave us a possible explanation.

Articular extensions onto the anterior femoral neck, known as Poirier's facets, are present in one male and two females. These may indicate habitual extreme leg flexion and extension as in squatting or climbing up and down steep hills, as suggested by J. Lawrence Angel (1946), who noted it on ancient Greek skeletons. Erosions on femoral heads and irregularities on the distal condylar surfaces are combined with these articular extensions in the female from Saki Tzul, who also has squatting facets (Figure 16.8). "Squatting facets" are anterior extensions of the distal articulation of the tibia caused by extreme and habitual dorsiflexion of the foot, such as might result from hunkering, squatting, or frequently climbing up and down steep hillsides—a likely activity here. Habitual knee flexion, as in squatting or climbing, is also suggested by the presence of an incisure or groove on the superolateral surface of the evaluable left patella of the male with the Poirier's facet.

Vigorous arm activity, such as lifting and carrying heavy loads or grinding material such as maize with mano and metate, is suggested in all evaluable adults of both sexes by marked deltoid tuberosities plus flattening of humeral shafts, lipping of proximal and distal articulations of the radii and ulnae, plus marked interosseous crests. Markedly roughened and gouged out insertions of brachialis are present on the ulnae of one female and one male, indicative of heavy lifting. Activity involving forearm rotation is suggested by enlarged and sharply marked supinator crests on ulnae.

Dental wear, or attrition, is a normal consequence of chewing gritty foods. However, the presence of marked oblique lingual surface attrition of the maxillary anterior teeth (LSAMAT) with lower anterior teeth showing "normal" horizontal wear was described by Christy Turner and Lilia Machado (1983), as seen in an Archaic Brazilian site, and by Joel Irish and Turner (1987) in prehistoric Panamanians. Found in combination with a high incidence of caries, Turner, Irish, and Machado theorize that the use of the maxillary incisors and tongue to manipulate a high-carbohydrate, gritty food might account for this unusual wear. We first noted LSAMAT in the dentitions of the Preclassic population of Cuello and subsequently at Rio Azul and several sites in the Programme for Belize region (F. Saul and J. Saul

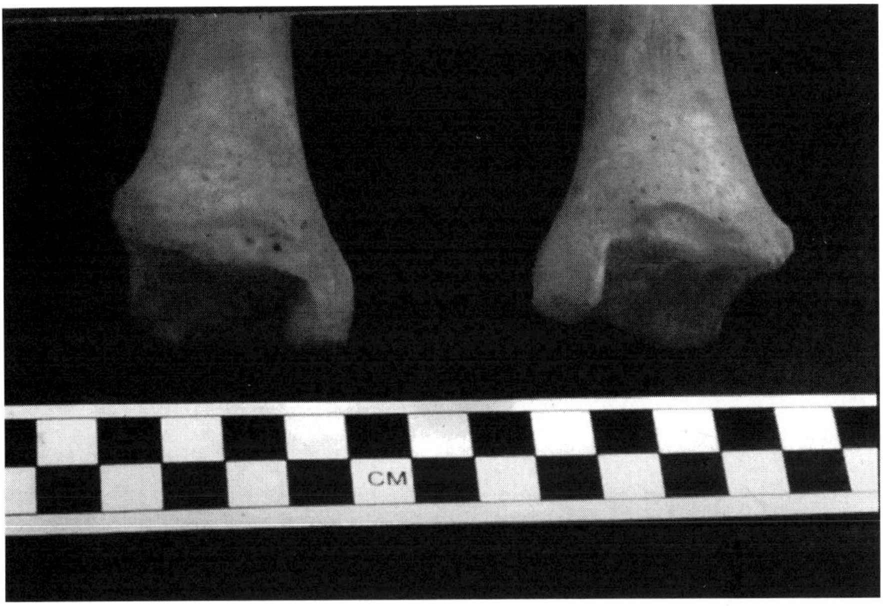

FIGURE 16.8. *Squatting facets on distal tibiae of the female at Saki Tzul.*

1989, 1991, 2000; J. Saul and F. Saul 1997b, 1998, n.d.; Saul, Saul, and Muñoz 1995). This dental wear is present in two of the three evaluable individuals (one male, one female) from the Maya Mountain rockshelter burials. Its specific etiology in the Maya area is still unclear.

HEALED TRAUMA

The hazards inherent in living and moving about in this rugged terrain can also be seen in healed trauma. A left rib of the kneeling female from Mohibal Kanchi was fractured well before death (Figure 16.9). Unfortunately, as ribs are very difficult to immobilize, continuing movement caused healing with non-union. A second healed fracture is apparent near the anterior end of another of her ribs. Perhaps she fell, striking her chest on one of the ever-present rocks. Her left fifth metacarpal (the bone on the outside of her right palm) is twisted and deformed, probably as a result of a healed but poorly aligned fracture. This location is also easily injured when falling. In the Maya Mountains, footing is treacherous and falling a continuing threat. An alternate scenario might be a deliberately inflicted blow, including a defense injury to the hand.

The male member of the possible family group at Mohibal Kanchi appears to have led an interesting life, beginning with osteoarthritis, or degenerative joint disease, indicated by lipping on posterior joints of cervical and upper thoracic

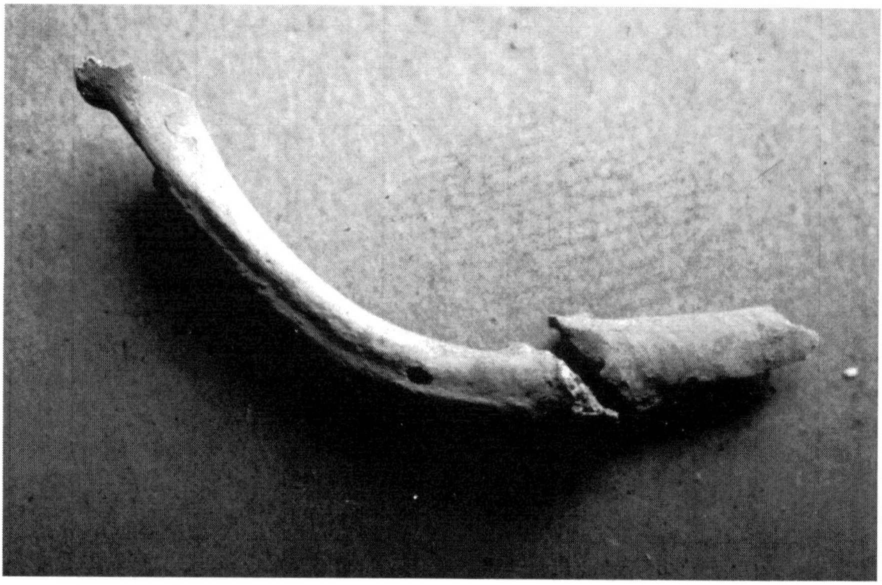

FIGURE 16.9. *Healed rib fracture with non-union from the 20–30-year-old female found in the possible family group at Mohibal Kanchi.*

vertebrae (especially on the right side), healed compression fractures of cervical vertebral bodies four and five, lipping of all long bone articular surfaces present, and strongly marked gluteal tuberosities of both femora—indicative of lifting and carrying burdens over steep terrain. A healed but probably still draining wound on the back of the olecranon process of his left ulna (elbow) may be a puncture that became infected. This is not surprising in an area that is full of vegetation containing sharp spines. Infections resulting from puncture by these spines, often accompanied by retention of the broken-off tip, are common today. He may also have suffered a nonfatal blow to the head in the past. A shallow depression or "dent," with signs of healing on the left side of the upper frontal bone, may represent a healed osseous reaction secondary to traumatic injury to the periosteum. Similar "cranial erosions" were ascribed to relatively minor blunt force trauma by the Spanish neurosurgeon Domingo Campillo (1977), based on his clinical practice. (Similar lesions were found in two males at Cuello [F. Saul and J. Saul 1991; J. Saul and F. Saul 1997b] and one male at Altar de Sacrificios [Saul 1972].) Whether this blow was dealt by another person in battle or was the result of a fall or misadventure in a cave is unknown. The location (upper left forehead) lends itself to many interpretations.

In addition, a small nodule of bone partially obscures his auditory canal. Known as auditory exostoses, these nodules are associated with divers and others who submerge themselves and their unprotected ear canals in cold water (Figure 16.10). One does not expect to find these ear canal changes in tropical or inland popula-

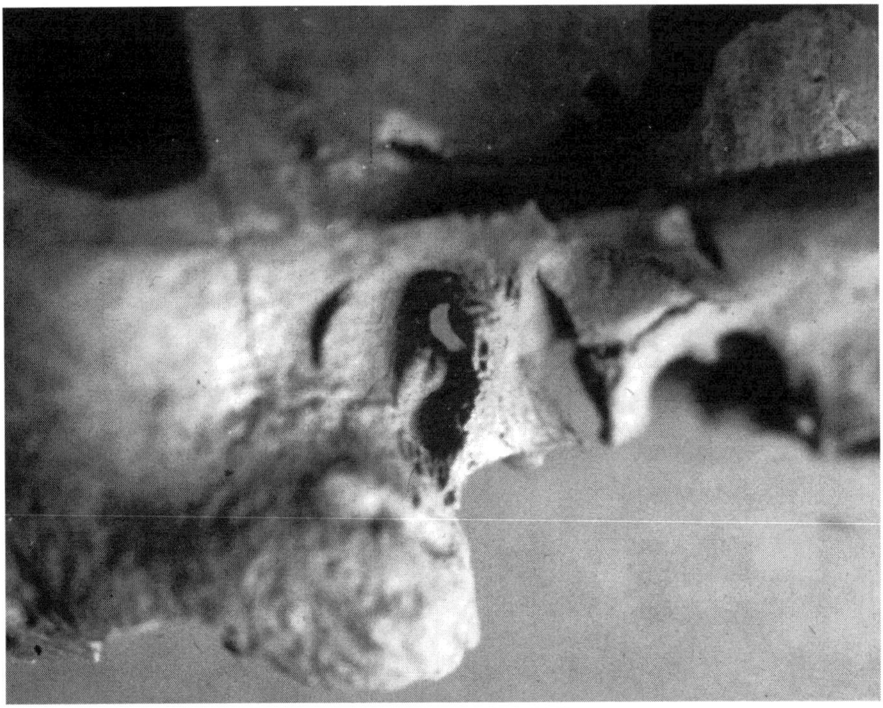

FIGURE 16.10. *Auditory exostosis projecting into the right ear canal of the 20–35-year-old male from the possible family grouping at Mohibal Kanchi.*

tions and certainly not in the middle of the tropical rain forest, far from the sea (Capasso, Kennedy, and Wilczak 1999; Kennedy 1989). At first this mystified us. Then we remembered the caves. The Bladen River flows out of the largest of these caves. It can only be entered by swimming. Most of this huge cave is flooded even during the dry season, and the water is extremely cold. This cave, as were all caves in this area, was used for ritual activities. Might this male be one of those chosen to enter this cave regularly, perhaps in a ritual context? And in that case, perhaps that dent came from hitting his head in a cave?

As an intriguing sidelight, this same male has a diastema (gap between the mesial, or central, maxillary incisors). The presence of similar diastemas in two high-status individuals at Rio Azul (male in Tomb 23 and female in Tomb 25) raises questions of genetic linkage between the two sites (F. Saul and J. Saul 1991, 2000).

STATURE

Stature is important because it is a polygenic and multifactorial trait that can be affected by nutrition and disease in both an ontogenetic (life cycle) and phylogenetic (generation to generation) context. It can also provide clues to gene flow and population change. Stature estimates were derived using formulas developed by Santiago Genovés (1964), who based his formulas on data obtained from individuals without Spanish surnames in a cadaveral population from the National School of Medicine of Mexico.

Stature estimates for three females could be obtained from long bone lengths. The mean stature for Maya Mountain rockshelter females is 153.6 cm, which is above the mean but within the range for Classic period females at Altar de Sacrificios (mean 152.3 cm) and below the mean but within the range for Classic females so far in the Programme for Belize region (mean 158.2 cm). The long bones of two males give us an estimated mean stature of 166.2 cm. This is just above the range (156–165 cm) for Classic males at Altar, Rio Azul, Seibal, Tancah (Yucatán Peninsula of Mexico), Programme for Belize sites, and Cuello (Saul 1972, 1982; F. Saul and J. Saul 1989, 1991, 2000; J. Saul and F. Saul 1997a, 1997b, 1998; Saul, Saul, and Muñoz 1995).

THE MIDDLE PRECLASSIC OSSUARY PIT AT MAYAHAK CAB PEK

The Middle Preclassic ossuary pit is treated here as a separate unit because of both its possible different time period and its unique nature (Figure 16.11). Faunal and human bones and teeth (and fragments) were found commingled at all levels throughout the pit, with all individuals apparently scattered at all levels as well. Although fragmentary and incomplete, all regions of the skeleton are present in a good state of preservation, and the individuals represented in the ossuary pit appear to have activity markers and dental findings consistent with those of the individuals from the other burials.

Adults

A minimum of two adults are represented by both bones and teeth. One of these adults is a probable male (large right mastoid process, everted gonial angles, large and robust postcranial bones). One adult is smaller and less robust (long, slender long bones with less marked muscle attachments, including metacarpals, phalanges, and metatarsals) and may be either a smaller male or a female. Degree of dental attrition plus relative recency of annular epiphyseal union and lack of osteoarthritic lipping on vertebrae and lack of osteoarthritic lipping on other articulations suggest that the adults are young adults (20–35 years). The epiphysis on the medial clavicle of one individual has recently fused.

All articular surface borders are sharply defined, especially those of the hands and feet, as was the case with the other burials in the rockshelters. The bones of the larger individual have more strongly marked muscle attachments, including a fragment of right humerus with very prominent deltoid tuberosities. Marked lateral ridges on the palmar surfaces of hand phalanges belonging to the larger individual

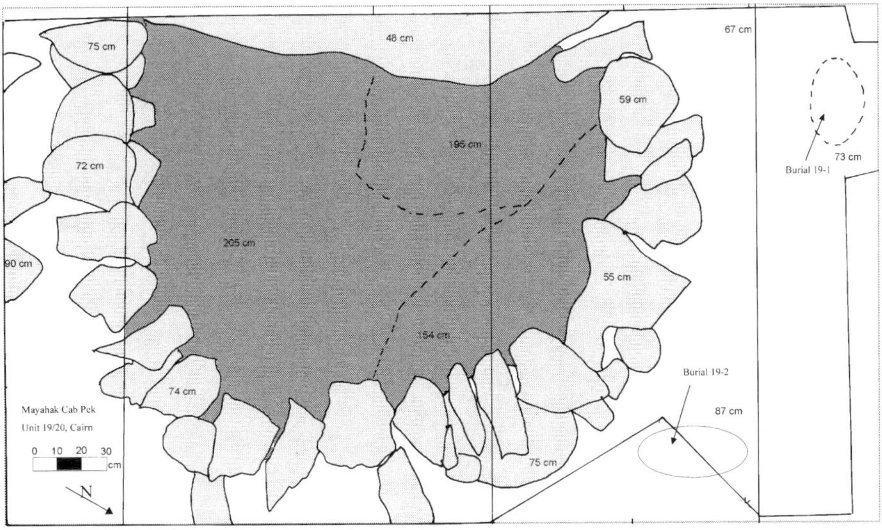

FIGURE 16.11. *Plan view of the stone-lined ossuary pit at Mayahak Cab Pek. The lower levels of the pit date to the Middle Preclassic, and there are also mixed materials from the Late and Terminal Classic periods.*

suggest use of the hands in a strong gripping motion. These ridges are not prominent on the smaller, more slender hand phalanges of the other individual.

Only one caries cavity is apparent on the nine adult teeth recovered from the pit. No teeth are duplicated, and the variation in the degree of dental attrition suggests that either two people are represented dentally (one a little older than the other) or the differential wear is a result of use of the teeth as tools. Linear enamel hypoplasia is present on three teeth, with one stressful episode occurring between the ages 1–1.5 years and another episode from 3.5–4.5 years. None of the teeth shows indications of dental decoration. Cranial shaping could not be evaluated.

Subadults

At least three young children (one 2–3 years old and two 2–4 years old) are represented by dentition (three maxillary right lateral incisors are present). Ages were determined by the degree of dental development. Linear staining similar to that seen on other young children at the rockshelter sites is present on the teeth of the 2–3-year-old child, indicating that the fetus was negatively impacted twice (at 3–7 months and 5–9 months postfertilization). This suggests health problems for the pregnant mother at these times.

Cranial and postcranial bone fragments of at least one very young child and at least one older child were recovered. These fragments represent all regions of the body and are present in all levels of the pit.

Discussion

Although fragmentation and incompleteness of the remains limited analysis, the individuals in the ossuary pit appear similar in population composition, health, and activity markers to the other burials found in the rockshelters. It also appears that, if this is a secondary burial, care was taken in moving the remains, as loose single-rooted teeth were recovered. On the other hand, if this pit was the place of primary interment, it is interesting that the remains are so fragmentary, incomplete, and mixed up within the pit. Bone preservation is excellent, and there are few indications of animal gnawing, although faunal remains are present.

CONCLUSION

How do the people of the Maya Mountains rockshelters compare with other Classic Maya? From what we have seen so far, the people of the rockshelters, although showing some signs of probable nutritional deficiencies, may have been somewhat healthier in terms of infectious disease and nutrition than those of Altar, Rio Azul, and Seibal but perhaps not quite as healthy and well nourished as those in the Programme for Belize region. They were very strong and physically very active within an extremely rugged and even hostile environment. Their bones show it. The life expectancy—at least for these few people—was low, particularly for women, and infancy was a perilous time. Survival in the Maya Mountains was not easy.

The repeated and long-term use of rockshelters as mortuary sites, although the site proper seems devoid of burials, is intriguing. We do not know what demographic of the universe of the local population our sample represents, nor do we know with certainty if it is representative of the local population as a whole. Our preliminary investigations indicate that we have literally just touched the "base of the mountain" in our investigations of these shelters. To date, every excavated test unit in a rockshelter, save one (a small 1- by 1-m excavation at the margin of Mayahak Cab Pek), has produced evidence of either articulated human burials or large deposits of disarticulated skeletal material. We have tested less than 3 percent of the total surface area of these three shelters, indicating that the vast majority of burials are still unstudied.

Although most of the burials can be temporally associated with the surface site Ek Xux, mortuary activity at Mayahak Cab Pek may predate any known settlement in the southern Maya Mountains. It is possible that it was a pilgrimage site or that there were small settlements in the area that have so far evaded archaeological detection. There is no reason to doubt that the area was part of early pilgrimage circuits. Three other cave sites within 5 km of Mayahak Cab Pek have deposits that date to before 600 B.C. (Prufer 2002). Certainly, the rockshelters' proximity to the giant cave where the Bladen River emerges from the underworld would have made it a prominent feature in the landscape, and the significance of the region's caves would not have been lost on early travelers.

In 1999, modern Q'eqchi' Maya priests who trekked up into this region of the Maya Mountains to bless our work in the rockshelters spoke of the sacredness of the area, with its caves and rockshelters high in the mountains. Their sense of being in a sacred place strengthened as they moved through Ek Xux, performing several ceremonies before climbing up to one of the rockshelters. In this most sacred spot, a final dramatic ceremony was held. The black smoke of their ritual fire billowed upward to the sky, further darkening the smoke stains on the white cliff face above the rockshelter, left behind by ancient fires. And here in these rockshelters, in the mouths of caves at the edge of the sky—a truly coveted location—these people were buried.

ACKNOWLEDGMENTS

The Sauls acknowledge with gratitude the encouragement, support, and research opportunities provided by Maya archaeologists R.E.W. Adams, Norman Hammond, Fred Valdez, Brandon Lewis, Peter Dunham, and especially our coauthor, Keith Prufer.

REFERENCES CITED

Angel, J. Lawrence

1946 Skeletal Change in Ancient Greece. *American Journal of Physical Anthropology* 4(1):69–97.

Awe, Jaime J., Christophe G.B. Helmke, and Cameron S. Griffith

1998 Archaeological Reconnaissance in the Roaring Creek Valley: Caves, Rockshelters, and Settlements. In *The Western Belize Regional Cave Project: A Report of the 1997 Field Season,* 216–236. Department of Anthropology Occasional Paper No. 1. University of New Hampshire, Durham.

Brady, James E.

1989 An Investigation of Maya Ritual Cave Use With Special Reference to Naj Tunich, Peten Guatemala. Ph.D. Dissertation. Archaeology Program, University of California at Los Angeles.

Brady, James E., and Keith M. Prufer

1999 Caves and Crystalmancy: Evidence for the Use of Crystals in Ancient Maya Religion. *Journal of Anthropological Research* 55(1):129–144.

Campillo, Domingo

1977 *Paleopatología del Craneo en Cataluña, Valencia y Baleares.* Editorial Montblanc-Martín, Barcelona, Spain.

Capasso, Luigi, Kenneth A.R. Kennedy, and Cynthia A. Wilczak

1999 *Atlas of Occupational Markers on Human Remains.* Edigrafital S.P.A., Teramo, Italy.

Comas, Juan

1960 *Manual of Physical Anthropology.* Charles C. Thomas Press, Springfield, IL.

DGMS
1993 1:50,000 Topographic Map of Belize (Series E 775-MIL, Edition 5-GSGS). Director General of the Military Survey, Surrey, UK.

Genovés, Santiago
1964 Introdución al estudio de la proporción entre los huesos largos y la reconstrución de la estatura en restos Mesoamericanos. *Anales de Antropología* 1:47–62. Instituto de Investigaciones Históricas, Universidad Nacional Autónoma de México, México.

Gibbs, Sherry A.
1997 Human Skeletal Remains From Actun Tunichil Muknal and Actun Uayazab Kab. In *The Western Belize Regional Cave Project: A Report of the 1997 Field Season,* 71–92. Department of Anthropology Occasional Paper No. 1. University of New Hampshire, Durham.

Halperin, Christina, Sergio Garza, Keith M. Prufer, and James E. Brady
2003 Caves and the Ritual Use of Jute. *Latin American Antiquity* 14(2):207–220.

Irish, Joel D., and Christy G. Turner II
1987 More Lingual Surface Attrition of the Maxillary Anterior Teeth in American Indians: Prehistoric Panamanians. *American Journal of Physical Anthropology* 73:209–213.

Kennedy, Kenneth A.R.
1983 Morphological Variations in Ulnar Supinator Crests and Fossae, as Identifying Markers of Occupational Stress. *Journal of Forensic Science* 28 (4):871–876.
1989 Skeletal Markers of Occupational Stress. In *Reconstruction of Life From the Skeleton,* eds. Mehmet Y. Iscan and Kenneth A.R. Kennedy, 129–160. Alan R. Liss, New York.

Lee, Thomas A.
1967 Excavation of a Rockshelter in Chiapas. *Katunob* 6(3):4.
1969 Cuevas secas del Río la Venta, Chiapas: informe preliminar. *Antropología e Historia de Guatemala* 21:23–38.
1985 Cuevas secas del Río la Venta, Chiapas: informe preliminar. *Revista de la Universidad Autónoma de Chiapas,* Segunda Época, No. 1, 20–42.

MacNeish, Richard S., and Fredrick A. Peterson
1962 *The Santa Marta Rockshelter Ocozoaulta, Chiapas, Mexico.* Papers of the New World Archaeological Foundation 14, Provo, Utah.

Merbs, Charles C.
1983 *Patterns of Activity-Induced Pathology in a Canadian Inuit Population.* National Museum of Man Mercury Series, Archaeological Survey of Canada Paper No. 119, National Museums of Canada, Ottawa, Canada.

Ortner, Donald J., and Walter G.J. Putschar
1985 *Identification of Pathological Conditions in Human Skeletal Remains.* Smithsonian Institution Press, Washington, D.C.

Prufer, Keith M.
2002 Cave, Communities, and Ritual Specialists: A Study of Sacred Space in the Maya Mountains of Southern Belize. Ph.D. Dissertation, Department of Anthropology, Southern Illinois University.

Romero Molina, Javier
1970 Dental Mutilation, Trephination and Cranial Deformation. In *Handbook of Middle American Indians: Physical Anthropology,* ed. T. Dale Stewart, 50–67. University of Texas Press, Austin.

Saul, Frank P.
1972 *The Human Skeletal Remains of Altar de Sacrificios: An Osteobiographic Analysis.* Papers of the Peabody Museum of Archaeology and Ethnology, vol. 63, no. 2. Harvard University, Cambridge, MA.
1977 The Paleopathology of Anemia in Mexico and Guatemala. In *Porotic Hyperostosis: An Enquiry,* ed. Eve Cockburn, 10–15, 18, cover. Monograph 2. Paleopathology Association, Detroit, MI.
1982 Appendix II—The Human Skeletal Remains From Tancah, Mexico. In *On the Edge of the Sea: Mural Paintings at Tancah-Tulum,* ed. Arthur G. Miller, 115–128. Dumbarton Oaks Trustees for Harvard University, Washington, D.C.

Saul, Frank P., and Julie M. Saul
1984a Paleobiología en la zona Maya. In *Investigaciones recientes en el area Maya, tomo 1. Memorias de la XVII Mesa Redonda,* 23–42. Sociedad Mexicana de Antropología, San Cristobal de las Casas, Mexico.
1984b Osteopatología de los Mayas de las tierras bajas del sur. In *Mexico Antiguo, Tomo I of Historia General de la Medicina en Mexico,* eds. A. López Austin and C. Viesca Trevino, 313–321. Universidad Nacional Autónoma de México, Facultad de Medicina, and the Academia Nacional de Medicina, Mexico, D.F.
1989 Osteobiography: A Maya Example. In *Reconstruction of Life From the Skeleton,* eds. Mehmet Y. Iscan and Kenneth A.R. Kennedy, 297–302. Alan R. Liss, New York.
1991 The Preclassic Population of Cuello. In *Cuello: An Early Maya Community in Belize,* ed. Norman Hammond, 134–158. Cambridge University Press, Cambridge.
2000 The People of Rio Azul. In *Rio Azul Reports, Number 5, The 1987 Season,* ed. Richard E.W. Adams, 240–254. Mesoamerican Archaeological Research Laboratory, University of Texas, San Antonio.
2001 Cosmetic Alterations of the Face and Body. In *The Archaeology of Ancient Mexico and Central America: An Encyclopedia,* eds. Susan Toby Evans and David L. Webster, 291–295. Garland Publishing, New York.

Saul, Julie M., and Frank P. Saul
1997a The Skeletal Remains From a Maya Royal Tomb at La Milpa, Northwest Belize. In *Abstracts of the 62nd Annual Meeting of the Society for American Archaeology,* Nashville, TN. Society for American Archaeology, Washington, D.C.
1997b The Preclassic Skeletons From Cuello. In *Bones of the Maya: Recent Studies of Ancient Skeletons,* eds. Stephen L. Whittington and David M. Reed, 28–50. Smithsonian Institution Press, Washington, D.C.
1998 From Cuello to Rio Azul and La Milpa: Common (and Uncommon) Threads From the Preclassic to the Classic. In *Abstracts of the 14th International Congress of Anthropological and Ethnological Sciences,* International Union of Anthropological and Ethnological Sciences, Williamsburg, VA. Society for American Archaeology, Washington, D.C.

2001 Together in Death: A Maya Family Plot? *Abstracts of the 65th Annual Meeting of the Society for American Archaeology,* New Orleans, LA. Society for American Archaeology, Washington, D.C.

2002 Forensics, Archaeology and Taphonomy: The Symbiotic Relationship. In *Advances in Forensic Taphonomy: Method, Theory and Archaeological Perspectives,* eds. William G. Haglund and Marcella H. Sorg, 71–97. CRC Press, Boca Raton, FL.

n.d. Unpublished Data From Sites in the Programme for Belize Region in Northwestern Belize.

Saul, Julie M., Frank P. Saul, and A. René Muñoz

1995 Osteological Analysis of Burials From a Small, Non-elite Site (RB-11, Programme for Belize). In *Abstracts of the 60th Annual Meeting of the Society for American Archaeology,* Minneapolis, MN. Society for American Archaeology, Washington, D.C.

Tozzer, Alfred M.

1941 *Landa's Relacion de las Cosas de Yucatan.* Papers of the Peabody Museum of Archaeology and Ethnology, vol. 18. Harvard University, Cambridge, MA.

Turner, Christy G., II, and Lilia M. Cheuiche Machado

1983 New Dental Wear Pattern and Evidence for High Carbohydrate Consumption in a Brazilian Archaic Skeletal Population. *American Journal of Physical Anthropology* 61:125–130.

Chapter Seventeen

A Question of Sacrifice

by Vanessa A. Owen

Classic Maya Cave Mortuary Practices at Barton Creek Cave, Belize

Archaeological research has documented abundant human remains in Maya caves (Brady 1989: 343–344), which clearly indicates that subterranean features were important places to the ancient Maya for the final deposition of human bodies, although little is known regarding the mortuary practices that took place at these sacred sites. Some remains represent formal burials, whereas others appear to have been deposited hastily or haphazardly. Although Oliver Ricketson (1925: 394) noted early on that caves were not the usual repository for the deceased, no theories were put forth to explain why the Maya would inter certain individuals in caves rather than under the floors of their houses. Cave investigators in recent years have suggested that mortuary practices such as human sacrifice, ancestor worship, or lineage burials may account for the presence of human remains in caves (Brady 1989; Gibbs 2000; Prufer and Hurst 2006 [in press]; Reents-Budet and MacLeod 1986; Scott and Brady, this volume).

This study analyzes the Classic Lowland Maya mortuary remains recovered from Barton Creek Cave in the

Cayo District of Belize to determine why these individuals may have been deposited in the cave. Using a bioarchaeological approach, it is suggested that sacrifice played a primary role in the osteological deposition at Barton Creek Cave based on mortuary treatment and contextual information.

HUMAN SACRIFICE IN MESOAMERICA

Current discussions of human sacrifice rely heavily on ethnohistoric and iconographic sources, with little contribution from archaeological evidence (Welsh 1988a, 1988b). This is the case because determination of sacrifice based on osteological evidence alone is difficult, so it is necessary to look for other clues.

Osteological remains provide the only direct evidence of human sacrifice recoverable archaeologically. Skeletal mutilation is often indicative of a violent death and thus can be linked to sacrifice. Skeletal mutilation includes decapitation, severed limbs, throat slashing, and heart extraction. In addition, cut marks on the crania and elsewhere may suggest flaying of the skin, which, according to ethnohistoric and iconographic sources, was common following sacrifice (Mock 1998). Although such evidence may imply sacrifice, other lines of evidence must also be brought to bear to make a convincing argument. For instance, burial position may provide one line of evidence. William Fowler (1984) noted that the majority of the extended burials at Chalchuapa, El Salvador, had right and left carpals or right and left tarsals touching, suggesting that the individuals had been bound at the wrists and ankles. The "prone," or facedown, position may be an indication that one is dealing with sacrificial victims in pre-Hispanic Mesoamerica. At Kaminaljuyu, a Preclassic lord was buried in the standard "supine," or faceup, position, and a number of retainers were interred in the "prone" position, suggesting that they had been sacrificed (Shook and Kidder 1952).

Burial context may also provide clues as to whether sacrifice should be suspected as the cause of death. Martha Sempowski and Michael Spence (1994: 256) argue that commingled individuals within a single burial context (i.e., grave, tomb) suggests that death may have taken place at a single point in time for the interred. W.B.M. Welsh (1988b: 144) suggests that burials containing the commingled remains of two adults and children may represent the parents who had died accompanied by sacrificed slave children, orphans, or related offspring. However, Patricia McAnany (1995: 63) cautions that based on ethnographic and ethnohistoric descriptions of ritual behavior associated with the deposition of dead ancestors, all of these burials could equally well be the result of reverential rather than sacrificial behavior. She suggests that evidence for opening and resealing a tomb containing partial remains would have indicated ancestor veneration rather than sacrifice. Thus, it may be necessary to draw on additional evidence to support one's claim.

CAVES AND HUMAN SACRIFICE

Ethnohistoric sources discuss human sacrifice in caves and caves serving as repositories for sacrificial victims (Tozzer 1941). Typically, children and young adults were favored as sacrificial victims in Mesoamerican societies (Ballinger 1986: 58; Hooton 1940; Scholes and Roys 1938). Despite abundant ethnohistoric evidence, archaeologists appear to have been extremely reluctant to suggest sacrifice as a cause of death for individuals interred in caves. The first to actually make such an interpretation was David Pendergast (1971: 18), who discovered the remains of a child under the floor of a structure in Eduardo Quiroz Cave. Unhealed holes in the skull led Pendergast to suggest that this child may have been sacrificed. In Actun Tunichil Muknal the articulated skeleton of a young woman was cemented to the cave floor by the deposition of calcite in what appears to be the position in which the Maya left her over a thousand years ago. The body position is atypical, with one arm stretched above the head and the legs apart (Roberts 1990). The individual has been interpreted as a victim of sacrifice based on burial position (Gibbs 2000). In their investigation of Petroglyph Cave, Dorie Reents-Budet and Barbara MacLeod (1986: 81) suggest that the remains in the cave fit the pattern of sacrificial victims; that is, they exhibit no clear relationship to other cave artifacts, skeletal remains are found in disordered piles or stuffed in crevices, and they typically lack grave goods.

James Brady (1989: 362–363) has investigated a number of caves containing the remains of possible sacrificial victims. For instance, at Naj Tunich in Guatemala, eight of the nineteen individuals interred within the cave are believed to be victims of sacrifice because of their age, mortuary contexts, and overall lack of grave goods.

THE BARTON CREEK CAVE SITE

Archaeological investigations were conducted at Barton Creek Cave from 1998 to 2000 by the Western Belize Regional Cave Project. The cave (Figure 17.1) is a large subterranean riverine system with evidence of ancient Maya usage. Over 10 km of passage have been surveyed to date, but the total length has yet to be determined. Cultural material, however, is found only in the first 450 m on ten ledges located above the river.

A cluster of residential mounds representing a small settlement was documented on the floodplain within 300 m of the cave entrance. Excavations of three mounds suggest that occupation spanned the Preclassic/Early Classic into the Late Classic. No burials were encountered in the mounds.

A bioarchaeological approach, the study of human remains within their archaeological context, was used to investigate the mortuary remains in the cave. This approach focused on reconstructing the behavioral aspects of mortuary practices from associated artifacts, contextual information, and the demographic profiles of the individuals interred within the cave.

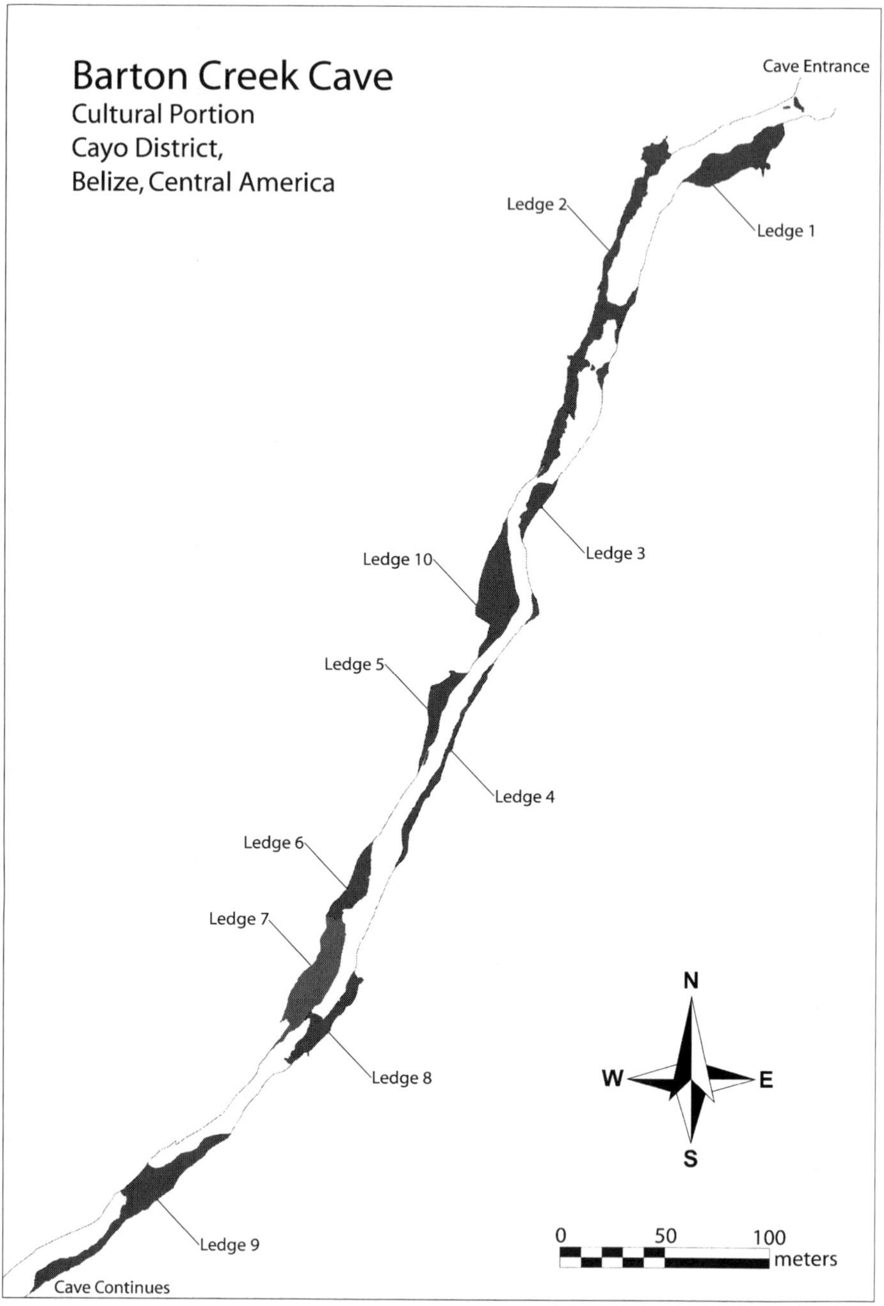

FIGURE 17.1. *Map of the ledges exhibiting Maya use in Barton Creek Cave.*

TABLE 17.1. Contextual and mortuary variables

Contextual and Mortuary Data Considered	*Examples*
Location of bones within the cave	Daylight zone versus dark zone
Location of bones relative to a feature	Bones clustered near a large formation
Presence and patterns of grave offerings	High frequency of ceramics with deceased
Interment type	Primary versus secondary
Position of the individual	Flexed, extended, prone, supine
Orientation of the individual	Head to the north, head to the south, etc.
Single versus multiple interments	Isolated individuals or possible ossuaries

An osteological analysis was conducted to determine the age, sex, and health status of the interred, as well as to establish a basic MNI (minimum number of individuals). Clusters of bone and discrete individuals were systematically recorded, mapped, and photographed. For the purpose of this study, bone clusters are defined as anything from a few, isolated skeletal elements to large concentrations of bone in a natural feature.

Age, sex, and pathological conditions were determined using methodological procedures summarized by Donald Ortner and Walter Putschar (1981), Douglas Ubelaker (1989), Tim White (1991, 2000), Jane Buikstra and Ubelaker (1994), Jeffery Schwartz (1995), William Bass (1987), and Louise Scheuer and colleagues (2000). When possible, individuals were assigned specific age categories (infant, 0–3 years; child, 3–12 years; adolescent, 12–18 years or eruption of the third molars; young adult, 18–34 years; middle adult, 35–54 years; and old adult, 55 years and older), as outlined in Buikstra and Ubelaker (1994). In cases where age could not be definitively assigned to one of these categories, more general categories of subadult (0–18 years) and adult (18 years and older) were assigned.

Contextual and mortuary information was recorded. The variables considered are summarized in Table 17.1.

DESCRIPTION OF SAMPLE

Human remains were encountered on six of the ten ledges in Barton Creek Cave, with evidence of ancient activity. Analysis of the skeletal material indicates that at least thirty-one individuals were interred in the cave. Given that much of the material is fragmentary and disturbed, the number interred is likely higher than is described here.

Interment Location

All individuals were found in fairly inaccessible areas. In addition, all of the individuals were found in naturally circumscribed features such as depressions, pits, alcoves, or crevasses. Several of the features are rimstone pools that seasonally flood or were filled with water in the past. There are at least three cases in Barton Creek Cave where individuals were placed in an area of high pedestrian traffic (in past and present times), which resulted in significant damage to the skeletal material. For instance, two young adult males were placed in an area of actively dripping water, which is thus muddy, on pathways that access other sections of the ledge. Brady (1989: 262) argued that deposition in extremely wet and muddy locations is inconsistent with the interment of a relative and thus suggests sacrifice.

Burial Type

A basic analysis attempted to establish if the individuals represented (1) primary or secondary interments and (2) single or multiple interments. The degree of disturbance to many of the skeletal deposits made the assessment of burial type impossible. Five individuals are primary interments, eighteen individuals are classified as most likely primary interments, and the rest were too disturbed to assess. There were no clear cases of secondary burial.

There are nine single and four multiple interments. No obvious relationship exists between age or sex and interment type. However, all three infants were found in multiple interments with at least one adult individual. The multiple interments in Barton Creek Cave typically contain a combination of adults and subadults. Details on both single and multiple interments are summarized in Table 17.2.

Burial Position

Because of disturbances, burial positions could not be established in most instances. Burial position could be established for only four of the thirty-one individuals. Of these, one appears to have been placed in an extended supine position. The other three individuals (two children and one adolescent) exhibit "atypical" positions. Here, atypical refers to positions that deviate from those most commonly

TABLE 17.2. Age and sex distribution based on burial type

Single Interments	*Multiple Interments*
Child (BC22, Ledge 2)	Infant, child, four young adults (one male, two female?, one ?), middle adult female (BC1–4, Ledge 8)
Young adult male (BC24, Ledge 2)	Infant, child, adult (35+) female (BC9–10, Ledge 8)
Child (BC25, Ledge 2)	Infant, adolescent (BC11, Ledge 8)
Young adult male (BC26, Ledge 3)	Three children, one adolescent, five young adults (three male, two female), middle adult (BC15–21, 23)
Child (BC27, Ledge 3)	
Middle adult female (BC13, Ledge 6)	
Adult (BC14, Ledge 7)	
Adult (BC5–7, Ledge 8)	
Child (BC8, Ledge 8)	

observed for Maya burials (extended, supine, or flexed). Perhaps the best example of "atypical" positions in the sample is the child from Ledge 3 (Barton Creek [BC]27), who was laid to rest in an awkward, sprawled, prone position with one leg bent at the knee. The adolescent from Ledge 8, based on the position of the radius and ulnae relative to the rest of the body, may have had his/her arms bound behind the back. The individual appears to have been lying on the right side in a flexed position.

Orientation. In mortuary archaeology the conventional method for determining burial orientation is to use either cardinal directions or orientation relative to an architectural structure. Body orientation showed no correlation with cardinal directions. It should be noted, however, that in that the cave context and in the complete darkness, cardinal directions would have been difficult to determine without a compass. When in a cave, orientation is quickly made relative to natural features, especially the direction of the passage or cave wall. Some individuals may have been oriented with their heads toward the back of the cave and others with their heads toward the entrance. Whether this phenomenon is ritually significant is unclear, and further investigation at other cave sites is needed. Unfortunately, taphonomic and looting disturbance prevents a complete assessment of interment orientation. Of thirty-one individuals, orientation of only eight could be established: four were oriented with their heads toward the interior of the cave, two were oriented with their heads toward the entrance, and the other two were oriented with their heads toward the wall and the river, respectively. In short, there does not appear to be a consistent pattern of orientation.

Demographic Profile. Assessment of the age and sex distribution for the Barton Creek Cave sample is compromised as a result of small sample sizes and the fact that many of the bones and teeth were fragmented or entirely absent. However, the data suggest that males and females, at least among adults, are more or less equally represented in the sample. Of the seventeen adults, five are female and six are male.

The age distribution reveals a high proportion of young adults (18–34 years) and children under age 12, with a low percentage of adolescents and adults over age 35. The demographic profile is summarized in Table 17.3.

Grave Goods

Grave goods were largely absent in the cave assemblage. The most common artifacts found near human remains were small ceramic sherds, and these materials have little to no direct association with the skeletal remains. In one instance a ceramic vessel is found in close proximity to human skeletal material (Figure 17.2)—the relatively undisturbed remains of a child (BC27, Ledge 3). However, the vessel does not appear to be directly associated with the child. Rather, the child and the

TABLE 17.3. Demographic profile of the Barton Creek Cave sample

Age Category	*# Individuals*	*Sex*
Infant (0–3)	3	N/A
Child (3–12)	9	N/A
Adolescent (12–18)	2	N/A
Young Adult (18–34)	11	6 male, 2 female, 2 female?, 1 unknown
Middle Adult (35–54)	3	2 female, 1 unknown
Old Adult (55+)	0	N/A
Adult (age unknown, 18+)	3	2 unknown, 1 female
Total	31	6 male, 5 female, 2 female?, 3 unknown

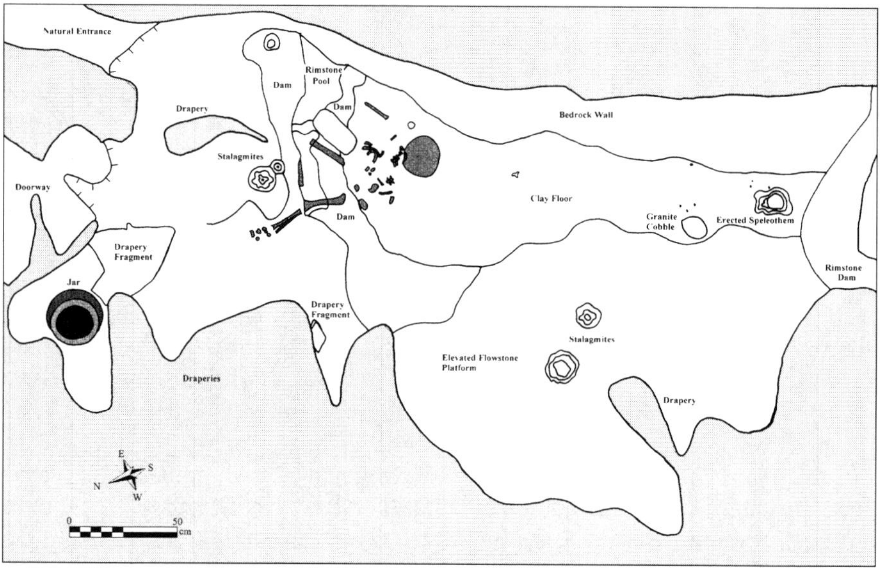

FIGURE 17.2. *Plan of BC27.*

vessel appear to be part of a larger ceremonial deposit. Other materials that may be classified as possible grave goods include personal adornments, such as a bone hairpin found with a young adult male and a drilled bead found with a young child. However, these may have been worn by the individuals at time of death and therefore are not necessarily grave goods.

Grave goods are often perishable and so are not preserved in the archaeological record. Items such as plants, wood, and textiles have been documented in ethnographic and ethnohistoric reports as interred with the dead but are rarely encountered in an archaeological context. In Barton Creek Cave, however, plant remains and textile fragments were recovered. They were associated with cultural features, and only a single charred seed was in any way associated with human bone (Christopher Morehart 2002: personal communication).

Associated Features

A variety of cultural features are associated with interments in the cave. One of the most common is the modification of cave formations near or directly associated with interments. On Ledge 3, drapery formations were broken to provide access to areas. Other modifications include blocking drainages in pools with rocks and speleothems. It is not clear whether the purpose was to block water from draining or if drainages were inadvertently blocked to complete enclosures. Nevertheless, blocked drainages were documented in at least two pools.

Ash and charcoal lenses were found under five burial deposits. They suggest that burning occurred before the placement of the deceased. Generally, the skeletal remains exhibit no sign of burning. This suggests that either the bone was fleshed or that the ashes and charcoal had cooled before the placement of the body. Although ash lens, charcoal, and other forms of burning are common features in caves in the Maya area (Brady and Prufer 1999: 135), their association with cave interments has rarely been reported elsewhere.

DISCUSSION

Grave goods equip the deceased for the afterlife and are generally placed with the body as part of a burial ritual. The presence of grave goods suggests that interment was accompanied by some type of ritual that reflected the individual's social status in life (Binford 1971; Gillespie 2001; Parker Pearson 2001; Tainter 1975). The lack of grave goods may suggest that the individual occupied some marginal status in the community, such as orphan, criminal, or sacrificial victim. Other factors may account for the lack of grave goods, such as perishable items not being preserved or nonperishable items being looted. However, the lack of grave goods has been observed at so many cave sites, such as Petroglyph Cave (Reents-Budet and MacLeod 1986), Cueva de los Muertos (Rushin-Bell 1982), Aktun Tunichil Muknal (Gibbs 2000), and Aktun Yaxteel Ahau (Owen and Gibbs 1999), that it suggests a cultural pattern. C. J. Rushin-Bell (1982: 13), in her investigation of Cueva de los Muertos, states, "[E]xquisite items of jade, bone, and crystal, often encountered in temple burials, have not been found in the caves." The absence of grave goods accompanying the Barton Creek interments suggests that these individuals held a marginal status.

Burial position offers another clue to the treatment of the body after death. Typical Maya burial positions are extended supine and flexed. An atypical position might suggest that the individual was not deliberately interred. Only one of the Barton Creek Cave individuals appears to have been interred in a normal burial position. One individual is in a dramatic "sprawled" posture, another is in a prone position, and a third appeared to be bound at the time of death—all of which supports the idea that these individuals were sacrificial victims.

Atypical burial positions appear common at cave sites. There are a number of reports that individuals in caves may have been bound at the time of death, including one individual at Barton Creek Cave. At Petroglyph Cave, two individuals were found in small "piles," leading Reents-Budet and MacLeod (1986) to suggest that the individuals were originally situated in a "seated position." At Aktun Tunichil Muknal, Sheryl Ann Gibbs (2000: 110, 113) reports that one individual appears to be "bound in a flexed position with the hands tied behind the back and in a kneeling position facing the wall." Another individual in the same chamber in the cave was found in a supine position, with the right arm raised and the legs sprawled. One of the most dramatic examples of this "sprawled" position is that from Ch'en K'iin, a cave in the Cayo District, Belize. The skeleton's position is described as "laying on its back with its legs drawn upward, knees spread, and feet drawn together. The left arm is extended along the side of the body. The right arm is thrown back such that the upper arm and hand are above the head" (Webster and Reeder 2000: 102).

Atypical body postures are seen in depictions of captives in Maya iconography (Marcus 1992). Joyce Marcus comments that captives were often depicted with arms tied behind their backs with rope rather than in the formal postures of various elites. These captives were portrayed "in unnatural and awkward, contorted body positioning" in an effort to humiliate them (Marcus 1992: 229). The contorted burial positions observed among the cave interments may have resulted from the manner of death. Most of the reconstructable burial positions of the Barton Creek Cave individuals are incompatible with normal burial practices.

The placement of the individuals relative to cave features also supplies important bioarchaeological data. At other cave sites, human remains are often found within depressions in the cave floor, stuffed in crevasses, or placed in rimstone pools (Brady 1989; Gibbs 2000; Owen and Gibbs 1999; Rushin-Bell 1982; Thompson 1975: xxxi). MacLeod and Dennis Puleston (1978: 72) have linked the placement of skeletal material in cracks or in ancient evaporated pools with sacrificial rites based on their observations of cave interments. Brady has argued that the deposition of bodies in a muddy trench that may have seen some pedestrian traffic also indicated sacrifice at the Cueva de Sangre at Dos Pilas (Scott and Brady, this volume). At Naj Tunich, Brady states that "the wet, muddy conditions are . . . conditions, however, that one might expect to be chosen for rituals directed to the gods who control rain and water" (Brady 1989: 362). At Barton Creek Cave, interments have been placed in areas of pedestrian traffic, in muddy areas, and around actively dripping formations. The burial contexts are therefore unlikely places for deliberate burial.

Demographic information derived from the human skeletal remains at Barton Creek Cave found an unusually high proportion of infants and children (ages 0–12 years) relative to older adult individuals (ages 35 and more years). In addition, a

TABLE 17.4. Distribution of age groups from caves in West-Central Belize

Age Category	*Barton Creek Cave* (%) N=31	*Tunichil Muknal* (Gibbs 2000) (%) N=14	*Petroglyph* (Reents-Budet and MacLeod 1986) (%) N=23	*Yaxteel Ahau* (Owen and Gibbs 1999) (%) N=13	TOTAL (%) N=81
Infant (0–3)	9.7	42.8	30.4	23.1	23.5
Child (3–12)	29.0	7.1	26.1	15.4	22.2
Adolescent (12–18)	6.4	7.1	0.0	0.0	3.7
Young Adult (18–34)	35.5	7.1	21.7	7.6	22.2
Middle Adult (35–54)	9.7	28.6	0.0	15.4	11.1
Old Adult (55+)	0.0	0.0	0.0	7.6	1.2
Adult (age unknown, 18+)	9.6	7.1	21.7	30.8	16.0

significant number of young adults (ages 18–34 years) are found in caves. When the age distribution of Barton Creek individuals is compared to the age distribution of individuals recovered from three other caves in west-central Belize, it is clear that the skewed age distribution is not the result of a sampling problem (Figure 17.3 and Table 17.4). These caves are similar with regard to cave size and morphology, geographical location, and temporal use (i.e., Classic period). Most of the infants in the sample are at least 6 months of age and do not represent perinatal infants.

The high proportion of infant/child skeletons in caves has been pointed out by MacLeod and Puleston (1978: 72), who suggest that "children about five years of age are common, though the bones of young adults are also occasionally found." Similarly, Logan McNatt reports that a large river cave in Belize yielded the remains of twenty-six burials, sixteen of which are infant/child. This led McNatt to suggest that they may represent "special offerings" (McNatt 1996: 88). In Cenote Sagrado at Chichén Itzá, Vera Tiesler reports a predominance of subadults in the sample and proposes that the osteological age profile mirrors colonial testimonies of the sacrifice of children at the Sacred Cenote (Tiesler, this volume).

In the cave samples reported here, age at death seems more likely to be a result of factors other than general population mortality. Mortality curves for four different countries are shown in Figure 17.4. The graphs indicate a generally low mortality rate of children over age one until age thirty-five, after which mortality rate increases, with rather high mortality rates after age fifty-five. The curve for the combined cave sample (Figure 17.3) is almost the inverse of those curves. Why should this curve be so different? The overall health status of the sample may be a factor. Health status is indicated by general nutrition, pathological load, and coping ability to combat stress. Alan Goodman and colleagues (1984: 17) state that "age-at-death stands as perhaps the most important single indicator of stress. If other stress indicators are associated with decreased ages at death, then this supports their validity as indicators of stress."

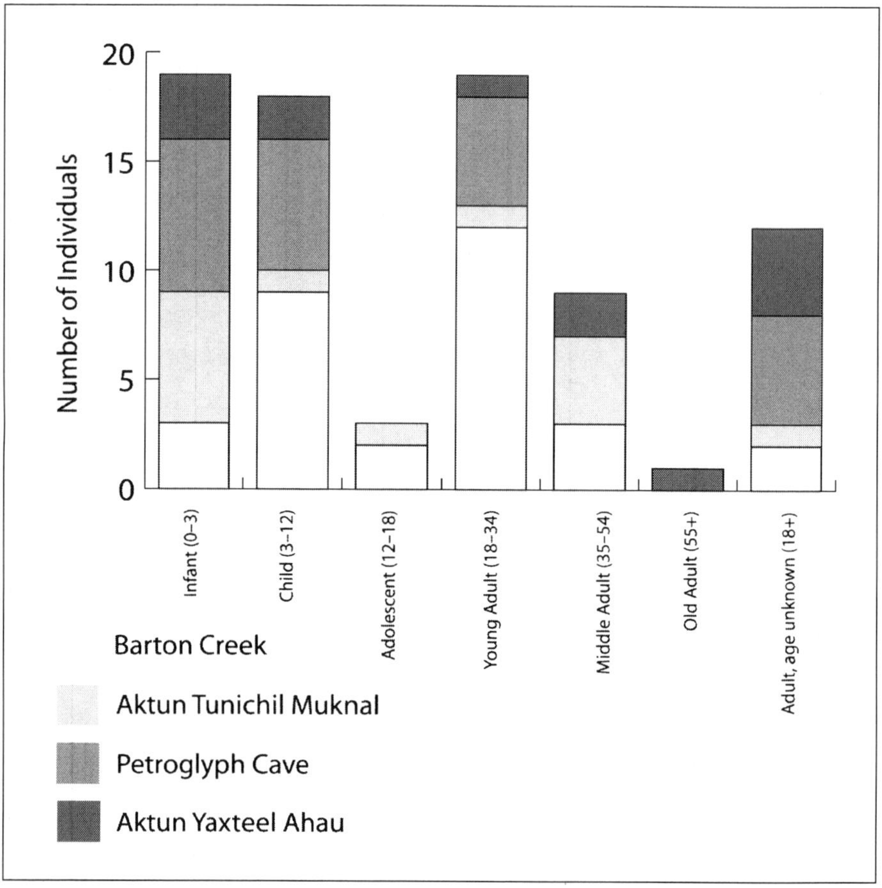

FIGURE 17.3. *Distribution of age groups in caves of west-central Belize.*

Other ways of measuring stress are through the presence/absence of enamel hypoplasias and porotic hyperostosis. Porotic hyperostosis can result from a number of diseases such as malaria and hemoglobin-derived anemias (Goodman, Martin, and Armelagos 1984: 31). In the New World, however, cases of porotic hyperostosis are more likely to be a result of nutritional stress and parasitism rather than hemaglobinopathies (Goodman, Martin, and Armelagos 1984: 31; Wright and Chew 1998: 932). Porotic hyperostosis was a common condition among the Classic Lowland Maya (Hooton 1940; Saul 1977: 14).

Pathological information was not available for all of the individuals shown in Table 17.4. At Aktun Tunichil Muknal, much of the bone was covered with calcite; however, at least one case of cribra orbitalia was observed (Gibbs 2000: 115; Roberts 1990: 126). In the Barton Creek Cave sample, at least seven of the thirty-one

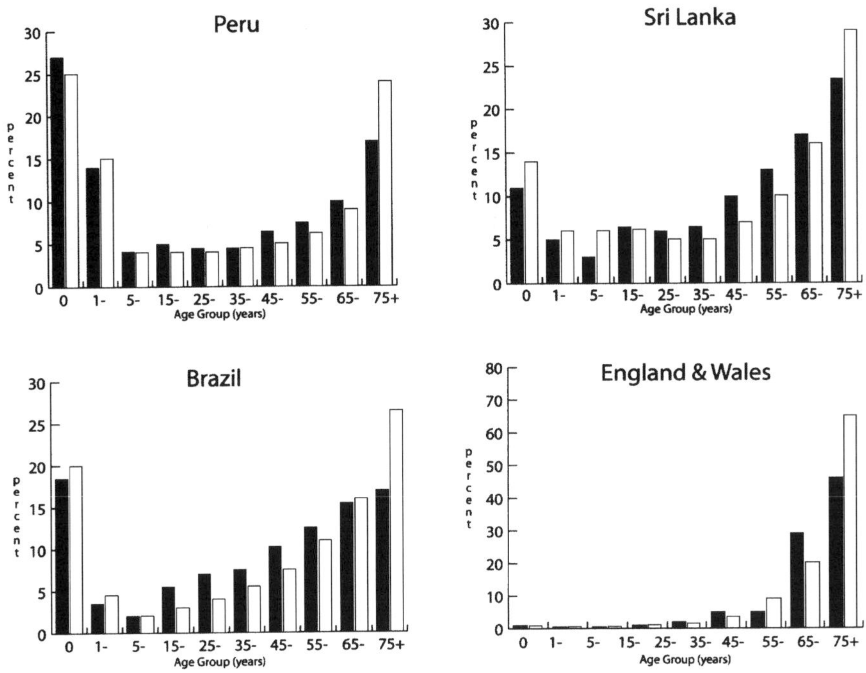

FIGURE 17.4. *Age-at-death distributions for four contemporary populations. Black bars represent males, gray bars represent females (Waldron 1994; reproduced with permission).*

individuals displayed porotic hyperostosis (both remodeled and unremodeled lesions) ranging in density from sparse to severe. A minimum of two individuals from the sample exhibited enamel hypoplasia. Pathological manifestations in the Barton Creek Cave sample suggest that the individuals were exposed to varying degrees of environmental stress, as evidenced by porotic hyperostosis. The incidence, however, is not high for a Maya population, so health status did not appear to contribute to the age-at-death distribution for Barton Creek Cave and the others in Table 17.4. Pathological manifestations in the sample do not adequately explain the high percentage of infants, children, and young adults relative to adolescents and middle- to old-age adults. Therefore, factors independent of morbidity and mortality influenced the age distribution of cave interments in west-central Belize.

As noted at the beginning of the chapter, a number of cultural practices have been suggested to explain the presence of human skeletal material in caves—among them, lineage burial (Villa Rojas 1969: 215) and ancestor worship (Thompson 1975: xxxiii). The high frequency of infants, children, and young adults in caves does not support either ancestor worship or lineage burial. The role of the ancestor is usually reserved for leaders and prominent lineage members, which therefore makes infants and children unlikely candidates (McAnany 1995: 60).

A consideration of mortality and morbidity rates during the Classic period in the Maya Lowlands, as well as the high frequency of infants, children, and young adults, supports a theory of sacrifice. In addition, the archaeological data from Barton Creek Cave that include the lack of grave goods, body posture, and cave context all support this position. The association between child sacrifice and caves has been documented elsewhere. In Highland Guatemala, Francisco Fuentes y Guzman reported that children marched in a solemn procession to a spring inside a cave where it is said they were sacrificed to the *madre del agua* (Fuentes y Guzman 1932). In Yucatán, Bishop de Landa recorded the practice of child sacrifice to the rain god, Chaak, who was believed to reside in caves (Tozzer 1941: 44, 119–120). Similar rites have been reported for Central Mexico, where children were sacrificed to Tlaloc, the rain god, and then their bodies were deposited in a cave (Motolinia 1941, cited in Brady 1989: 360).

CONCLUSION

A consideration of the mortuary, contextual, and osteological data supports the hypothesis of sacrifice for the individuals interred in Barton Creek Cave and possibly a number of other caves in the Maya Lowlands. Multiple lines of evidence supporting sacrifice include lack of grave goods with interments, atypical burial positions observed, burial context, and age-at-death distribution.

The primary goal of this study was to better understand the mortuary use of caves by the ancient Maya and to establish whether the thirty-one individuals interred within Barton Creek Cave were sacrificial victims. An analysis of the skeletal, contextual, and mortuary data, combined with a review of ethnohistoric, ethnographic, and archaeological sources, suggests that the majority of the interments were victims of sacrifice.

Archaeologists have long understood that caves were not the usual place for interment of the deceased in Maya society. This realization has prompted a series of investigations attempting to understand who these individuals were and why they were "laid to rest" in such a dark and watery realm (Gibbs 1997). Systematic studies such as these will enable us to take a step further in investigating broader questions relating to such things as Maya cosmology, collapse theories, and agricultural rituals. We are now realizing that Maya cave ritual was not so much about death, as was once believed, but had more to do with life, rain, and fertility.

REFERENCES CITED

Ballinger, Diana A.

1986 Ossuary Burial of Cremated Human Remains From Copan, Honduras. M.A. Thesis. Department of Anthropology, University of Houston, Houston.

Bass, William M.
1987 *Human Osteology: A Laboratory and Field Manual,* Third Edition. Special Publication No. 2. Missouri Archaeological Society, Columbia.

Binford, Lewis
1971 Mortuary Practices: Their Study and Their Potential. *Memoirs of the Society for American Archaeology* 25:6–29.

Brady, James E.
1989 An Investigation of Maya Ritual Cave Use With Special Reference to Naj Tunich, Peten, Guatemala. Ph.D. Dissertation. Archaeology Program, University of California, Los Angeles.

Brady, James E., and Keith Prufer
1999 Caves and Crystalmancy: Evidence for the Use of Crystals in Ancient Maya Religion. *Journal of Anthropological Research* 55:129–144.

Buikstra, Jane, and Douglas Ubelaker
1994 *Standards for Data Collection From Human Skeletal Remains,* eds. Jane Buikstra and Douglas Ubelaker. Proceedings of a Seminar at the Field Museum of Natural History, Arkansas Archaeological Survey Research Series No. 44, Fayetteville, AR.

Fowler, William R.
1984 Late Preclassic Mortuary Patterns and Evidence for Human Sacrifice at Chalchuapa, El Salvador. *American Antiquity* 49(3):603–618.

Fuentes y Guzman, Francisco Antonio de
1932 *Recordación Florida: discurso historical y demostración natural, material, militar y politica del reyno de Goathemala.* Biblioteca Goathemala Vols. 6–8. Guatemala.

Gibbs, Sheryl Ann
1997 Those Laid to Rest: Skeletal Remains From Actun Tunichil Muknal, Belize. In *Belize Valley Archaeological Reconnaissance Progress Report of the 1996 Field Season,* eds. J. Awe and J. Conlon, 105–114. Department of Anthropology, Trent University, Peterborough, Ontario.
2000 An Interpretation of the Significance of Human Remains From the Caves of the Southern Maya Lowlands. Master's Thesis. Department of Anthropology, Trent University, Peterborough, Ontario.

Gillespie, Susan D.
2001 Personhood, Agency, and Mortuary Ritual: A Case Study From the Ancient Maya. *Journal of Anthropological Archaeology* 20:73–112.

Goodman, Alan H., Debra L. Martin, and George J. Armelagos
1984 Indications of Stress From Bone and Teeth. In *Paleopathology at the Origins of Agriculture,* eds. Mark N. Cohen and George J. Armelagos, 13–49. Academic Press, Orlando.

Hooton, Earnest A.
1940 Skeletons From the Cenote of Sacrifice at Chichen Itza. In *The Maya and Their Neighbors,* eds. Clarence L. Hay, et al., 272–280. Dover Publications, New York.

MacLeod, Barbara, and Dennis E. Puleston
1978 Pathways Into Darkness: The Search for the Road to Xibalba. In *Tercera Mesa Redonda de Palenque,* Vol. 4, eds. Merle Greene Robertson and Donnan Call Jeffers, 71–77. Hearld Peters, Monterey.

Marcus, Joyce
1992 Royal Families, Royal Texts: Examples From the Zapotec and From the Maya. In *Mesoamerican Elites: An Archaeological Assessment,* eds. Diane Z. Chase and Arlen F. Chase, 221–241. University of Oklahoma Press, Norman.

McAnany, Patricia
1995 *Living With the Ancestors.* University of Texas Press, Austin.

McNatt, Logan
1996 Cave Archaeology of Belize. *Journal of Cave and Karst Studies* 58(2):81–99.

Mock, Shirley B.
1998 The Defaced and the Forgotten: Decapitation and Flaying/Mutilation as a Termination Event at Colha, Belize. In *The Sowing and the Dawning: Termination, Dedication, and Transformation in the Archaeological and Ethnographic Record of Mesoamerica,* ed. Shirley Boteler Mock, 113–123. University of New Mexico Press, Albuquerque.

Ortner, Donald J., and Walter G.J. Putschar
1981 *Identification of Pathological Conditions in Human Skeletal Remains.* Smithsonian Institute Press, Washington, D.C.

Owen, Vanessa, and Sheryl Gibbs
1999 A Preliminary Report on Ledge 2, Aktun Yaxteel Ahau. In *The Western Belize Regional Cave Project: Progress Report of the 1998 Field Season,* eds. Jaime Awe and David Lee, 186–204. Department of Sociology and Anthropology, Occasional Paper No. 2, University of New Hampshire, Durham.

Parker Pearson, Michael
2001 *The Archaeology of Death and Burial.* Texas A&M University Press, College Station.

Pendergast, David M.
1971 *Excavations at Eduardo Quiroz Cave, British Honduras (Belize).* Art and Archaeology Occasional Papers No. 21. Royal Ontario Museum, Toronto.

Prufer, Keith M., and Jeffrey Hurst
2006 Chocolate and the Underworld Space of Death. *Ethnohistory* (in press).

Reents-Budet, Dorie, and Barbara MacLeod
1986 Archaeology of Petroglyph Cave, Belize. Unpublished manuscript housed at the Department of Archaeology, Belize.

Ricketson, Oliver
1925 Burials in the Maya Area. *American Anthropologist* 27:381–401.

Roberts, Charlotte
1990 Observations of Mayan Cave Archaeology in Belize. *Cave Science* 17(3):123–129.

Rushin-Bell, C. J.
1982 The Living Caves of the Dead. *Caving International* 14:12–18.

Saul, Frank P.

1977 Paleopathology of Anemia in Mexico and Guatemala. In *Porotic Hyperostosis: An Enquiry,* ed. Eve Cockburn, 10–15. Monograph No. 2. Harvard University Press, Cambridge.

Scheuer, Louise, Sue Black, and Angela Christie

2000 *Developmental Juvenile Osteology.* Academic Press, San Diego.

Scholes, France V., and Ralph L. Roys

1938 Fray Diego de Landa and the Problem of Idolatry in Yucatan. In *Cooperation in Research,* 585–620. Publication 501. Carnegie Institute of Washington, Washington, D.C.

Schwartz, Jeffery H.

1995 *Skeleton Keys: An Introduction to Human Skeletal Morphology, Development and Analysis.* Oxford University Press, New York.

Sempowski, Martha L., and Michael W. Spence

1994 *Mortuary Practices and Skeletal Remains at Teotihuacan.* University of Utah Press, Salt Lake City.

Shook, Edwin M., and Alfred V. Kidder

1952 *Mound E-III-3, Kaminaljuyu, Guatemala. Carnegie Institution of Washington, Contributions to American Anthropology and History* 11(53):33–127, Publication 596. Carnegie Institute of Washington, Washington, D.C.

Tainter, Joseph

1975 Social Inferences and Mortuary Practices: An Experiment in Numerical Classification. *World Archaeology* 7:1–15.

Thompson, J. Eric S.

1975 Introduction to the Reprint Edition. In *The Hill-Caves of Yucatan,* by Henry Mercer, vii–xliv. University of Oklahoma Press, Norman.

Tozzer, Alfred M.

1941 *Landa's Relación de las Cosas de Yucatan.* Papers of the Peabody Museum of American Archaeology and Ethnology, Vol. 18. Cambridge.

Ubelaker, Douglas

1989 The Estimation of Age at Death From Immature Human Bone. In *Age Markers of the Human Skeleton,* ed. Mehmet Yasar Iscan, 55–70. Charles C. Thomas, Springfield.

Villa Rojas, Alfonso

1969 The Tzeltal. In *Handbook of Middle American Indians, Vol. 7: Ethnology,* ed. Evon Z. Vogt, 195–225. University of Texas Press, Austin.

Waldron, Tony

1994 *Counting the Dead: The Epidemiology of Skeletal Populations.* John Wiley and Sons, New York.

Webster, James, and Philip Reeder

2000 Vaca Plateau Geoarchaeological Project Celebrates Its Tenth Year. *NSS News* 58(4):100–105.

Welsh, W.B.M.

1988a *An Analysis of Classic Lowland Maya Burials.* BAR International Series 409, British Archaeological Reports, Oxford.

1988b A Case for the Practice of Human Sacrifice Among the Classic Lowland Maya. In *Recent Studies in Precolumbian Archaeology,* eds. Nicholas J. Saunders and Olivier de Montmollin, 143–165. International Series 421. British Archaeological Reports, Oxford.

White, Tim D.

1991 *Human Osteology,* First Edition. Academic Press, San Diego.

2000 *Human Osteology,* Second Edition. Academic Press, San Diego.

Wright, Lori R., and Francisco Chew

1998 Porotic Hyperostosis and Paleoepidemiology: A Forensic Perspective on Anemia Among the Ancient Maya. *American Anthropologist* 100(4):924–939.

Chapter Eighteen

What Can the Bones Really Tell Us?

by Vera Tiesler

The Study of Human Skeletal Remains From Cenotes

There are inherent difficulties in the reconstruction and interpretation of skeletal assemblages from waterlogged contexts such as *cenotes*, and they have limited our understanding of an important aspect of ancient Maya ritual mortuary behavior. This is true despite the generally good preservation of remains recovered from *cenotes* and their potential for addressing questions of funerary treatment and sacrifice. The complex taphonomic processes involved in the underwater decay of human bodies pose multiple challenges for both bioarchaeological and forensic investigations, as their decomposition usually results in the loss of articulation and anatomical relationships, leading to commingling of bone assemblages.

The aims of this chapter are twofold. First, I wish to provide a methodological contribution to aid in the assessment of human remains from underwater contexts, a source of information that so far has only been marginally employed in the archaeology of the Yucatán Peninsula.[1] Second, the analytical potential of skeletal analysis is highlighted by two case studies in the second part of the chapter. These cases emphasize the need for multidisciplinary approaches to better understand the formation and transformation of bone assemblages in *cenotes* and the cultural processes that result in their deposition.

HISTORICAL AND ARCHAEOLOGICAL BACKGROUND

The use of *cenotes*[2] as resting places for human remains is amply documented in the historical records. According to H. C. Yarrow (1881), the islander Itzas placed their dead in lakes for lack of other appropriate spaces. Diego de Landa (1982: 114) asserts that the residents of Chichén Itzá would habitually "push people alive [into the water] as a sacrifice to the gods during dry seasons, believing they would not die even though they were no longer to be seen." Pedro Sánchez de Aguilar (1937), in his report on Yucatecan idolatry, relates that after being sacrificed, bodies were discarded in dry wells, *cenotes*, and caves. He describes the use of weights and wrappings to prevent bodies from floating. Other colonial testimonies identify the victims as mostly subadults and fringe members of local society (Nájera 1987: 122–129, 187–192; Scholes and Adams 1938: 71–76). Some victims were pushed into the water alive, from where they could later be retrieved if still living (Landa 1982: 51; Scholes and Adams 1938: 156; Tozzer 1957). In other cases submersion followed heart removal or other forms of ritual sacrifice (Scholes and Adams 1938: 71–129). Numerous *cenotes* are reported to have served as aqueous depositories of sacrificial victims during colonial times. Prosecution records of the Indian idolatry of 1562 testify to the fact that *cenotes* were used in Maya ritual immolations. C*enotes* like those at Chichén Itzá, Tepopox, Mopila, Tecon, Tibolon, Usil, Yaxcaba, and Mani figure as depositories in an astounding 80 percent of prosecutors' references to postsacrificial placements, underscoring their crucial role in human sacrifice during the second half of the sixteenth century (De Anda, Tiesler, and Zabala 2004; Scholes and Adams 1938: 71–129, 149, 155–158). Following France Scholes and Eleanor Adams's transcriptions, *Ah Kinob,* high priests, guided the transports of the sacrificed victims up to 70 km to *cenotes* destined as ritual depositories (De Anda et al. 2004).

Historic accounts, supported by recent studies (Bonor Villarejo 1989; Brady 1989; Evia Cervantes 2000; Nájera 1987; Ruz Lhuillier 1991), attribute ceremonial functions to caves and rockshelters in Yucatán. C*enotes* were, and are, considered sacred spaces where sacrificial acts were performed. These activities relate to procuring virgin water, climatic augury rites, and the yearly renewal ceremonies. The presence of human remains and associated ritual objects recovered during archaeological research in the *cenotes* of Chinkultic in Chiapas (Borhegyi 1968; Gallegos Ruiz 1976), Dzibilchaltún (Andrews IV and Andrews V 1980),[3] and Chichén Itzá in northern Yucatán corroborates their ancient function as depositories of human bone.

Extensive archaeological investigations of the Cenote Sagrado (Cenote of Sacrifice) at Chichén Itzá have contributed to our understandings of ancient Maya

FIGURE 18.1. *Cenote of Sacrifice at Chichén Itzá (photograph by author).*

ritual (Coggins 1992; Coggins and Shane 1989; Folan 1968; Piña Chan 1970; Proskouriakoff 1974; Sievert 1992; Tozzer 1957) (Figure 18.1). Relatively less is known about the rituals related to the deposition of the faunal and human assemblages recovered during the explorations (Álvarez 1976; Hooton 1940). Scientific efforts peaked during the 1960s with massive excavations conducted by the Mexican Instituto Nacional de Antropología e Historia (INAH). In the beginning, heavy pumps were employed to lower the water level and then pull the mud-laden offerings from the bottom (Folan 1968; Piña Chan 1970). Along with other objects, eighty well-preserved skulls and other human skeletal parts were retrieved, mostly from the *cenote's* western quadrant.[4] Román Piña Chan (1970) mentions that during the final stages of extraction, objects dating to the Classic period started to appear from the lower levels of sediments.

Whereas the *cenotes'* function as ritual depositories is well documented, much less is known about their role as receptacles of primary burials or ossuaries. Considering the broad range of funerary practices in the Maya area and the documented practice of deposing of the dead inside caves (Brady 1989, 1995; Ruz Lhuillier 1991; Scott and Brady, this volume), the nonsacrificial underwater placement of the dead as a form of burial needs closer consideration. Caves, like *cenotes,* had their place in the ancient weltanschauung as entrances to the underworld.

Despite having made important contributions to archaeology and osteology, *cenote* researchers have yet to provide a synthetic interpretation of the ritual activities that led to human skeletal remains being placed in watery environs. There is still no agreement among researchers regarding circumstances surrounding death and mortuary treatment, whether the rituals were funerary or sacrificial, and whether placement was the cause of death or occurred after it. Unfortunately, research designed specifically to answer these questions has not yet been conducted and discussions concerning the type of rituals have been lacking. At the least, we need to determine whether complete skeletons or simply parts of cadavers were deposited in *cenote*s and to ascertain the number of individuals represented in the assemblages, their depositional sequence, and osteobiographic profiles.

DECOMPOSITION AND PERTURBATION OF SKELETAL REMAINS IN AQUATIC ENVIRONMENTS

Answering these questions will require drawing on studies of the taphonomic processes involved in underwater corpse decomposition. The methods used for this chapter derive mainly from the field of forensic taphonomy (Behrensmeyer and Hill 1980; Binford 1981; Boulestin 1999; Gifford 1981; Haglund and Sorg 1997, 2002a; Martin 2000; Micozzi 1991). Documentary procedures were drawn from the French *anthropologie de terrain* (Duday 1987, 1997; Duday and Sellier 1990; Duday et al. 1990; Leclerc 1990) and personal observations from the Maya area (Tiesler 1999b, 2004).

The changes that occur during the decay process can be viewed as a complex interaction of processes of deterioration and preservation, driven by intrinsic and extrinsic agents (Boddington, Garland, and Janaway 1987: 4, table 1; Miccozi 1991). The latter denote the biochemical and physical phenomena involved in decomposition up to skeletonization, fossilization, or complete disintegration. The sequence of changes is determined by the body's intrinsic organic properties as well as individual characteristics such as age, sex, pathologies, and physical constitution.

In most aerobic environments, human soft tissue decay follows a broad sequence in which early cadaveric signs are followed by active putrefaction of soft tissue (bloating, liquefaction, dehydration) and finally skeletonization. In aquatic environments this general pattern is conditioned by the alternating movements of the body between the bottom and the water's surface (Haglund and Sorg 2002b; Rodríguez 1997). After the initial introduction into the water, the lungs fill with liquid and the body usually sinks to the bottom. Since body fat content affects buoyancy, bodies with a relatively high fat proportion have a greater tendency to float (females more than males, obese bodies more than lean ones). A similar effect is produced by bulky or impermeable clothes, which can trap air, causing the body to float.

Once at the bottom, the corpse is exposed to a set of extrinsic decay agents such as underwater currents, fish, and crustaceans, along with the substrate's surface properties, which may cover and hold the body on the floor. The gases produced during the initial stages of putrefaction remain partly trapped in the body cavities and may cause its ascent to the water surface. Low temperatures and water depth, which increase hydraulic pressure, reduce or inhibit the accumulation of gases, thus reducing buoyancy. In warm water and shallow depths[5] the body tends to emerge to the surface within a few days and floats facedown until advanced decomposition and disarticulation. Compared to fully submerged carcasses, the decompositional rate in floating bodies tends to be accelerated by exposure to the aereous environment and additional biotic agents, like insects and scavenging birds.

Skeletal disarticulation sets in relatively late in this process, resulting from the progressive decay of connective and cartilaginous tissues. In floating carcasses the bones of hands and feet are observed to be the first to sink, followed by the mandible, the skull, then the upper and lower extremities (Haglund and Sorg 2002b; Rodríguez 1997). The last to give way is the trunk, starting with the disassembly of the pelvic girdle and what remains of the thoracic cage. The final result of disarticulation, therefore, is extremely variable. It can result in the separation of entire body segments with joints still in anatomical connection or in the complete dispersal of bones.

Once on the floor, the skeletal remains undergo long-term biochemical and mechanical changes (Table 18.1). The expression of taphonomic factors on or in the muddy substrate now depends on the properties of each bone and tooth segment, such as its weight, volume, size, density, and morphology. M. Voorhies (1969) describes three mobility groups according to the disturbance patterns observed in isolated bones, whereas Noel Boaz and Anna Behrensmeyer (1976) distinguish sliding, slipping, and rolling as different movement patterns. Based on the results of their studies, rounded and short bones (from hands and feet) tend to slide more than long and irregular bones (Boaz and Behrensmeyer 1976; Haglund and Sorg 2002b). Skulls tend to be relatively stable when covered by sediments but are particularly prone to rolling down slopes or to being transported by underwater currents. Teeth and small bone fragments are generally less mobile (Boaz and Behrensmeyer 1976). Despite discrepancies in some of the outcomes, these experiments provide useful patterns that are also applicable to the reconstruction of taphonomic behavior of remains in karstic lake environments.

Long-term extrinsic factors cause skeletal deterioration at different levels, depending on the agents involved. Some factors degrade the bony surface by covering or destroying it through erosion, encrustation, or abrasion (Figure 18.2). Other factors result in the fracture or disintegration of the entire bone unit. A third group of agents changes the original position or orientation of the skeletal segments, engendering the loss of primary relationships and increasing the disturbance of the skeletal assemblage as a whole (Table 18.1).

In bone assemblages from *cenotes,* taphonomic changes are determined by prevailing karstic geophysical conditions, coupled with water pressure, water and air temperature, water pH, minerals, and oxygen concentrations. *Cenotes* are relatively homogeneous in terms of mineral content, surface temperature (> 20°C), and slight alkalinity. Variation is introduced by their volume, morphology, and water

TABLE 18.1. Cadaveric and skeletal phenomena in aqueous environments

INTRINSIC CHANGES
Sequence of cadaveric phenomena
· Putrefaction (formation of *adipocira*)
· Skeletal reduction
Sequence of disarticulation
· Loose vs. persistent articulations
· Axial vs. appendicular skeleton
Sequence of transport and dispersal
· Formal properties of bone, teeth, and fragments
EXTRINSIC CHANGES
Degradation of the bony external surface
· Incrustation (bivalves)
· Mechanical abrasion and polishing
· Formation of patina
· Diagenetic substitution and congestion
· Chemical erosion, dissolution, and bioerosion
· Decoloration (algae)
Fractures and disintegration of bones and teeth
· Perforation of thin portions
· Fractures
· Crushing
· Splintering
Changes in position
· Loss of anatomic relation
· Perturbation, differential movements of the parts

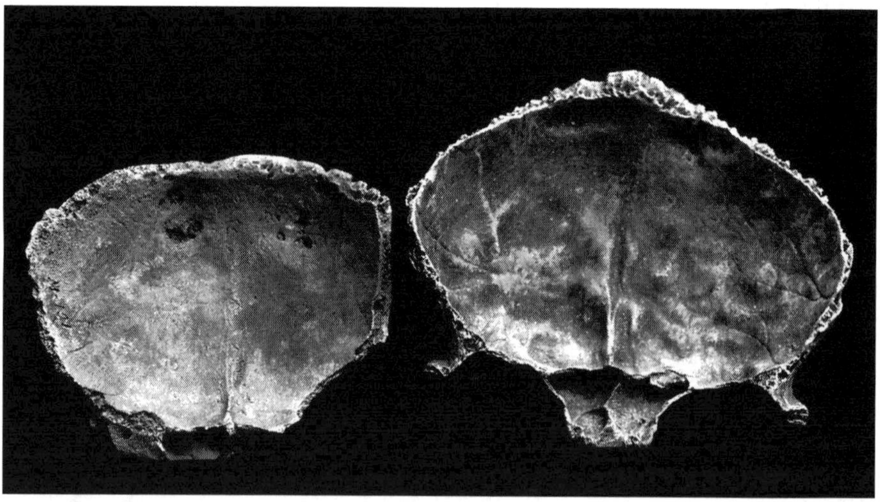

FIGURE 18.2. *Mechanical abrasion (polishing effect), color fainting, and patina formation on frontal bones from the Cenote Xlacah, Dzibilchaltún, Yucatán (photograph by author).*

FIGURE 18.3. *Mechanical erosion of bony surface from weathering process in skull fragment recovered at Chac II, Yucatán (photograph by author).*

depth, along with other associated karstic phenomena. The edaphological[6] and geologic floor properties vary with the presence of sediments and rocks, steepness, and underwater currents. Agents responsible for biotic degradation include aquatic flora—as well as microfauna, mesofauna, and macrofauna—the latter represented mainly by fish and crustaceans.

The careful assessment of natural postmortem conditions provides an important analytical tool in the evaluation of submerged skeletal assemblages. Their identification prevents misinterpretation of potential cultural processes, for some geological and biological processes tend to resemble human action. The taphonomic profile also permits identification of those decompositional traits that could not have originated in aquatic settings. Along this line, and knowing the complexity of mortuary treatment and funerary practices performed by the ancient Maya, vestiges of weathering (Figure 18.3) or marks left by terrestrial rodent gnawing would point toward protracted burial activities, indicating that the aquatic placement was preceded by a nonaqueous treatment or deposition.

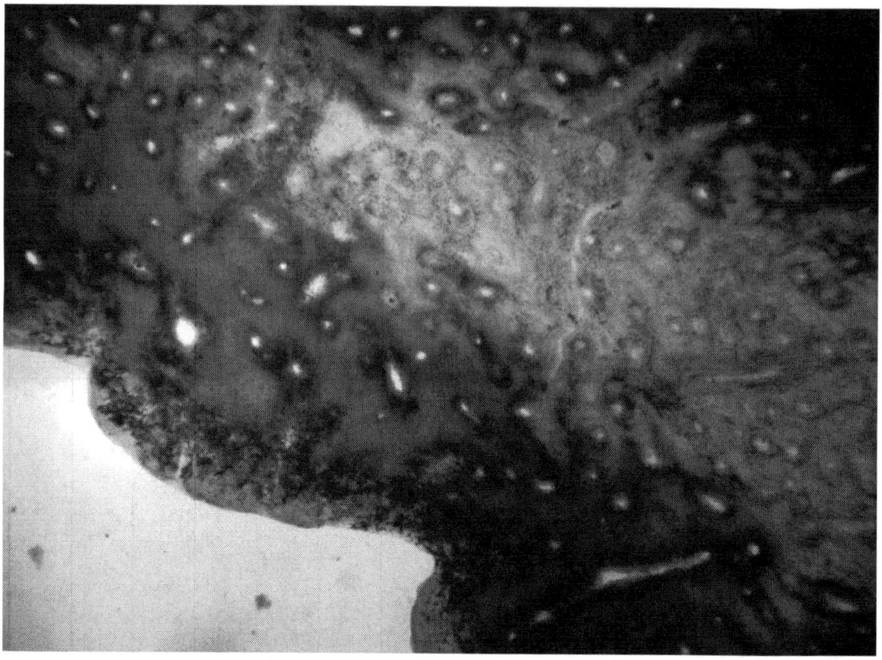

FIGURE 18.4. *Tibial midshaft section (× 20), showing natural osteon organization in core and diagenetic substitution in external portions, Cenote San José, Mayapán, Yucatán (photograph by author).*

Special consideration should also be given to natural events that influence the early stages of decomposition in water environments, as these could also have played a role during the ritual activities performed in conjunction with the deposition of human remains. Some phenomena may have been interpreted by religious practitioners during augury rituals, such as the body's emergence after initial drowning. At times, reemergence to the surface appears to have been prevented by tying weights to the corpse (Scholes and Adams 1938: see, for example, 118–119, 137).

Taphonomy is also relevant as a prospector tool. Opportunities for extracting DNA samples are reduced in seemingly well-preserved but partly mineralized human remains. Advanced fragmentation, chalky consistency, and surface erosion also appear to impose severe limits on stable isotope and trace element analysis (Carney Matheson 2001, Samuel Tejeda 2000, and Lori Wright 1998: personal communications). Contamination can alter the original histological or chemophysical composition, although it may not be macroscopically visible, therefore limiting the reliability of histomorpological, trace element, radiocarbon, or DNA analyses (Figure 18.4). Preliminary evaluations of bone constitution and diagenetic patterns by means of thin sections of different skeletal units, combined with substance identification, can facilitate the selection of the skeletal segments to be used and assist prospection of the types of analyses that are feasible (Garland 1989; Grupe and Dreses-Werringloer 1993; Piepenbrink 1984; Schultz 1994; White and Hannus 1983).

Cultural modifications to bone assemblages may have originated at the time of deposition or long afterward. The fact that subaquatic settings were not easily accessible protected their archaeological contents from desecration during colonial and early historic times, although the situation has changed with the advent of modern sport diving. Because of the high value of the archaeological remains, submerged archaeological materials, unfortunately, present an attractive target for modern looting. Aside from illegal depredations, careless excavation, documentation, recovery, sample taking, and curatorship can also introduce conditions that may mimic ancient secondary treatments and therefore should be considered in taphonomic evaluation and archaeological interpretation. The reconstruction of the circumstances and timing of the original aquatic depositions, such as the place of introduction into the *cenote* or the use of weights, poses another challenge to taphonomic research, along with the identification of some predepositional treatments (Tables 18.2, 18.3, 18.4).

As shown previously, an array of taphonomic processes combine to affect the analytical possibilities of submerged osseous deposits. Bone from *cenotes* is usually better preserved compared to remains recovered from surface sites in karstic areas. This yields a higher overall presence of anatomical segments with well-preserved bone surfaces. Conversely, factors like diagenetic substitution, disarticulation, and intermingling limit their analytical potential and constitute a challenge for both recovery and interpretation.

CASE STUDIES FROM CENOTE SAGRADO, CHICHÉN ITZÁ, AND CENOTE SAN JOSÉ, MAYAPÁN

These two case studies of ancient human remains recovered from *cenotes* are intended to illustrate the potential of osteological information to contribute to the

TABLE 18.2. Causal, extrinsic factors in the decomposition in aqueous environments

CULTURAL MODIFICATIONS
· Predepositional mortuary treatments (sacrifice, bleeding, deskinning, dismemberment, previous primary deposition)
· Circumstances of mortuary deposition (placement of weights, wrapping)
· Modern cultural modification (vandalism, looting, excavation)
NON-CULTURAL MODIFICATIONS
· Geological changes (pH, properties of the bottom sediments, currents, oxygenation, pressure)
· Climate (temperature, humidity, wind)
· Biological degradation
Fauna (micro-, meso-, macrofauna)
Vegetation (roots, algae)

TABLE 18.3. Applied taphonomic criteria I: Individual contexts

IDENTIFICATION OF POSTDEPOSITIONAL CONDITIONS (IN SITU)
· Identification of hydric and edaphologic patterns
· Taphonomic changes (surface, texture, integrity, disposal)
· Cultural alterations
DEFINITION OF MORTUARY SPACE (IN SITU)
· Delimitation of the area/stratigraphy
· Superficial, emerged, buried in sustrate
· Properties of the bottom (bank, steepness, position related to the mound)
ANATOMIC ARTICULATION (IN SITU)
· Primary, partial articulation, secondary
· Dynamics of dispersion of anatomic units
BONE SURFACE QUALITIES (LABORATORY)
· Previous deposition (differential conditions of degradation, cultural marks)
· Postdepositional (patina, cleansing, process of substitution)
PRESENCE OF ANATOMIC ELEMENTS (LABORATORY)
· Depositional or postdepositional (parts present, global assemblage)
BIOGRAPHIC INFORMATION (LABORATORY)
· Sex/age
· Pathologies, nutrition, stature, life conditions
· Filiation
· Biocultural practices
CHRONOLOGIC DETERMINATION (LABORATORY)
· Absolute dating
· Relative dating by presence of artifacts

TABLE 18.4. Applied taphonomic criteria II: Multiple and collective assemblages

DEPOSITIONAL SEQUENCE (IN SITU, LABORATORY)
· Simultaneous or subsequent deposition (stratigraphy, dating)
· Determination of minimum number of individuals and representation of anatomic parts (taphonomic principle of second order)
· Population patterns/skeletal assemblage
COMPARISON WITH LOCAL AND REGIONAL PATTERNS
· Regional presence/absence of traits
· Cultural context
HISTORICAL RECONSTRUCTION
· Cultural interpretation

interpretation of the utilization of *cenotes*. Analysis was conducted on skeletal samples recovered during archaeological explorations of the Cenote Sagrado, in Chichén Itzá,[7] and the Cenote San José, on the outskirts of Mayapán.[8] The collections, curated at INAH facilities in Mérida and Mexico City, were studied by the author between 1993 and 1999 as part of a broad regional skeletal study aimed at interpreting two pre-Hispanic biocultural practices: cranial modification and dental decoration (Tiesler 1998, 1999a, 1999b, 2001).

The analytical techniques were based on osteometry and macroscopic observation, supported by microscopy. In determining sex, commonly used parameters were employed (Buikstra and Ubelaker 1994). Age estimates for children were based on the degree of dental eruption and closure of the epiphyses. In estimating adult age, morphological modification of auricular, pubic, and costosternal surfaces, dental wear, degenerative changes, and degree of ectocranial suture obliteration were taken into account. A macroscopic assessment of orbital and cranial porotic hyperostosis was conducted to provide general indications of lifestyle and deprivation in the samples under study.

To evaluate the presence, degree, and type of cranial deformation, metric and nonmetric parameters were employed as they appear in Tiesler (1998, 1999b). The tables developed by Adolfo Dembo and José Imbelloni (1938), Fédéric Falkenburger (1938), Melvin Moss (1958), and Arturo Romano Pacheco (1965) were used in classifying forms and techniques. In studying dental decoration patterns, some aspects relevant to formal and technical classification were specified, complemented by review of information gleaned from other regional research (Romero Molina 1986; Tiesler 2001). Contextual information was limited to published references and reports on file, restricting direct insights on recovery strategies, taphonomic conditions, and the completeness of the skeletal sample.

Cenote Sagrado, Chichén Itzá

The skull collection from the *cenote* of Chichén Itzá consists of seventy-three mostly well-preserved complete specimens or large segments. The bony surfaces display a characteristic grayish tone and a smooth surface, with a few marks of mechanical attrition as a result of underwater bone movement. Most teeth recovered with skulls were multirooted molars, the rest having fallen from their sockets. Only scarce signs of weathering, root etching, or rodent marks were present, which might indicate that these were secondary burials.

Subadults predominate in the sample over individuals 15 years of age and older in a 2:1 ratio, with the former centering around late childhood and adolescence (i.e., 6–15 years of age) (Tiesler 1998, 1999b). Determining age in the adults solely from skulls is problematic and is not considered here in terms of numerical age ranges. Nevertheless, it is significant that four individuals clearly appeared to be of advanced age. The prevalence of males, who make up two-thirds of the specimens identified as to sex (twenty-seven to eighteen), is noticeable in the mature sample. The distribution by sex and age is consistent with the tendencies recorded by Earnest Hooton (1940), who reported on the remains of at least forty-two individuals recovered from the *cenote* by Edward H. Thompson in 1909. In that sample he identified eight (mostly) young females and thirteen males of all age ranges. Immature individuals (N = 21) cover all age ranges but center between 10–12 years and

4–6 years of age. Only one infant was assigned an age between 3–4 years, and the youngest specimen was 18 months old (Hooton 1940).

Additional light is shed on the biographic profile by the prevalence of nonspecific diseases of the skull caused by deprivation, testifying to periods of acute stress and chronically exposed lifestyle during childhood. More than half of the thirty assessable skulls showed porotic thickening of the vault and around 30 percent displayed pathological changes in the orbits, responses commonly resulting from iron-deficiency anemia, although other conditions (like Vitamin C and D deficiency or infectious disease) may produce similar responses (Larsen 1997; Schultz 1994, 2003). Although no intrasite comparison was possible for lack of comparative samples from Chichén Itzá, the prevalence of porotic hyperostosis in the *cenote* sample appears much elevated when compared to most other pre-Hispanic peninsular collections (see, for example, Cetina and Sierra 2003; Márquez Morfín et al. 1982; Tiesler 1998), although comparisons are problematic because of the varying methods used in recording the porotic lesions. In the literature, these lesions have been associated most often with environmental stress (as posed by tropical/subtropical settings), poor diets, and health hazards like parasitism and lack of sanitary conditions (Larsen 1997). The high prevalence of both conditions in Chichén's *cenote* population probably finds its origin in a composite of such stressors, combined with an unprotective social environment (or lack of "cultural buffering"). The high rates thus seem to identify the individuals from the *cenote* with the more marginal, "fringe" segments of society.

Results indicate that 93 percent of the observable crania were artificially modeled.[9] To this end, the infants' fronts and backs had been compressed in deforming cradleboards, which resulted in broad and high head shapes ("tabular erect" types, according to our classification). All degrees of artificial modification occur, ranging from slight occipital and frontal flattening to pronounced combined anterior-posterior compressions of the calvaria, which were noted in four cases. Two calvaria display superior "paralelepipedic" flattening in the vertex area of the crania (see Tiesler 1999b), leading to a cubic head shape. Other specimens show the effects of additional binding. Less than 6 percent of the artificially modified vaults display oblique forms, suggesting they may have been submitted to cephalic compression boards during early childhood. The diversity in shapes mirrors Hootons's comment that "the varieties of cranial deformation are so numerous that they are bewildering" (Hooton 1940: 273). Males and females were equally affected by the practice in terms of presence and type, and no sex-specific modifications were observed. All five unmodified crania were determined to be subadults of different age groups.

Comparisons with other available skeletal collections from Chichén Itzá were limited to seven skulls recovered from inside a construction filling of the Caracol, dated to the early Postclassic (Ruppert 1937; see Tiesler 1998). Only one of these specimens did not show artificial changes. The remaining six calvaria displayed shaping effected by cradleboards, ranging from slight occipital flattening on the back of the skull (two cases) to its pronounced anterior-posterior compression (one case). Although no conclusions on cultural norms or traditions can be drawn from the Caracol specimens for lack of adequate sample size, it is interesting that shaping techniques are exclusively related to cradleboarding here. Its diversity of head forms, which is relatively reduced, is encompassed in that of the *cenote* sample.

The distribution of intentional modeling by type, observed in the present study of the *cenote* skulls, corresponds to the relative frequencies of techniques documented in the region for the onset of the Postclassic period, which witnessed the abandonment of the use of head compression boards (Tiesler 1998, 1999b). Considering the long duration of use of the *cenote* as a ritual depository, securely documented by artifacts dated to the Terminal Classic until well after the Spanish contact (Coggins and Shane 1989: 33–41; Landa 1982; Scholes and Adams 1938), the evidence of oblique and mimetic head modifications common to the Classic period strengthens the idea that the *cenote* served as a ritual human depository during that period.

Cenote San José, Mayapán

The human remains available from Mayapán were recovered during recent explorations of a subterranean *cenote* located in the periphery of the walled center of the city, an important Postclassic regional center (Tiesler 1999a). Mayapán grew to power after the fall of Chichén Itzá and thrived for 200 years before suffering a similar fate. The collection consisted of bones of the skull, trunk, and extremities, constituting a small portion of the total assemblage, which was largely left in situ. The minimum number of represented individuals in the study sample was determined from the skull segments and femurs of the recovered material. The results indicate an anatomically robust sample of at least twenty-four individuals. The general state of preservation was good despite the postmortem fractures of some bones and the general loss of single-rooted teeth. The surface color of most fragments was homogeneously dark brownish, similar to that of the muddy soil of the bottom of the sinkhole. Contamination by substance replacement mainly affects the superficial bone layers, visible in a histomorphological midshaft section of a tibia (Figure 18.4). The organic osteon structure is displayed in the well-preserved inner portions of the compact bone. Like the assemblage from Chichén, the surface properties do not show evidence of deposition before immersion, for no signs of patina formation, bioerosion, weathering, root etching, or rodent marks were found.The age/sex profile in the skeletal sample was determined from the right hip bone and the skull. The calvaria indicate the presence of thirteen male or probably male individuals and seven female or probably female individuals.[10] Sex discrimination in the pelvis indicates six males and six females plus twelve undetermined individuals, pointing toward a more balanced ratio. Age distribution, determined from auricular surfaces and pubic symphysis, indicates an even distribution in all adult age classes. The three youngest specimens were ages 15–25 years. The age ranges are generally consistent with the results obtained from the skulls, although

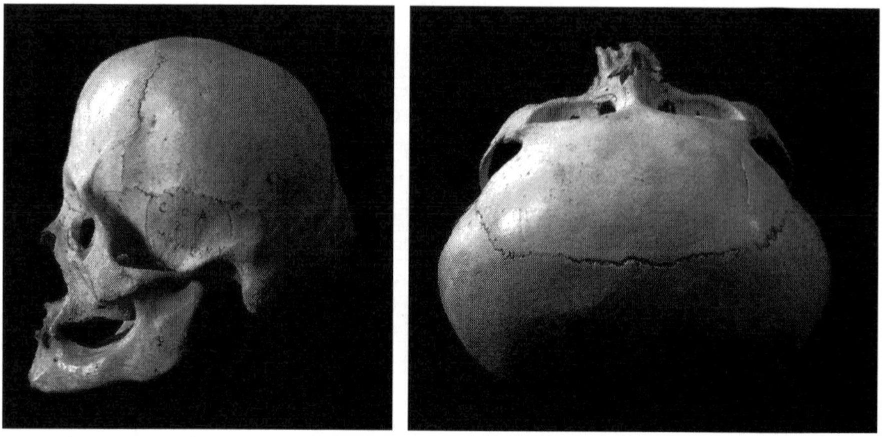

FIGURE 18.5. *a. Artificial head shape, affected by cradleboards (left lateral view, tabular erect shape). B. C-30-A, Mayapán, Yucatán (photograph by author). b. Same skull (vertical view, tabular erect shape). B. C-30-A, Mayapán, Yucatán (photograph by author).*

it cannot be ascertained if the diagnostic segments of hip bone and skull belong to the same individuals.

Nonspecific markers of deprivation, like those described for the Chichén Itzá sample, could be assessed in sixteen skulls. Only five skull vaults were exempt from porotic hyperostosis, pointing to an even higher prevalence of this affliction than in Chichén, indicative of the harsh living conditions of this mortuary population.

Additional biocultural information was recorded on body modifications. Whereas no data on dental decoration patterns were retrieved for lack of frontal teeth, artificial modeling was noted in eleven skull vaults. The remaining nine calvarias (42.9 percent) conserved their natural shape. The single technique employed was cradleboarding, which exhibits a homogeneous pattern showing slight occipital flattening. The pattern was compared to nine fairly preserved skulls recovered by the Carnegie Institution from deposits in the center of Mayapán (Fry 1956). Eight of the nine vaults show artificial modification in differing degrees, resulting from cradleboarding just as the sample from Cenote San José (Figure 18.5). Although the modeling modalities appear similar when the two samples are compared, the latter differed importantly in its high ratio of nonmodified individuals and the reduced expression of shaping when present. The discrepancy becomes significant when compared to the ratios of other Postclassic skeletal collections from Yucatán (Tiesler 1999b), all of which exhibit modification in over 90 percent of the individuals, including the collection from Chichén Itzá. The low occurrence in the deposit from San José, Mayapán, raises doubts about the antiquity of the *cenote*, which has not yet been conclusively dated (Eunice Uc 1999: personal communication).

FIGURE 18.6. *Gummatous treponemal lesions on adult male skull recovered from the Cenote San José, Mayapán, Yucatán (photograph by author).*

Its contemporaneity with Mayapán's rise during the second half of the Postclassic is further put into question by the presence of skeletal lesions, pathognomic for venereal syphilis, displayed by one of the unmodified skull vaults from the *cenote* (Figure 18.6). The lesions I am describing are exclusively found in veneral syphilis and have not been documented in other forms of treponemal disease like endemic syphilis or yaws. The skullcap is extensively covered by multiple small cavitating lesions and shows an advanced sclerotic response (*caries sicca*), diagnostic of tertiary syphilis (Aufderheide and Rodríguez-Martin 1998; Ortner and Putschar 1981; Schultz 2003). Minor gummatous lesions also affect its endocranium and facial portion. Although the presence of acquired syphilis before the Spanish contact is a topic of debate, the post-Columbian spread of this venereal disease throughout the New World is clearly documented by historical references and the colonial skeletal record. Its presence in this sample strengthens the possibility that the sinkhole was still employed as a mortuary depository after the onset of colonization.

A DISCUSSION OF PATTERNS OF *CENOTE* DISPOSAL

The specific age distribution patterns of the Cenote Sagrado assemblage, recorded in both the Thompson collection and the INAH collections, differ from a natural paleodemographic profile. Infant mortality in a normal burial population is expected to peak during the first year of life and drop in older age classes (Hoppa and Vaupel 2002). In the collection under study, specimens in their first infancy are almost completely missing, and older children and adolescents predominate. The excellent preservation of the calvaria lessens the possibility of an underrepresentation of the more fragile infant bones as a result of decay. Additional discrepancies are introduced by the strong male predominance in the sexed sample in both collections from Chichén's *cenote*. Although no definite pattern should be asserted because of the complex sequence of processes and multiple circumstances that led to the formation of the human bone assemblage in the Cenote Sagrado, our results are consistent with the documented use of the *cenote* for nonfunerary ritual purposes.

The osteological age profile mirrors the abundant colonial testimonies of sacrificed older children and youngsters of both sexes, who were thrown into the Cenote Sagrado alive or discarded there after being sacrificed (Scholes and Adams 1938). Interestingly, testimonies transcribed by Scholes and Adams (1938) refer to 85 percent of the sexed victims as male, pointing to a strong male predominance also in the ritual placements of Chichén's *cenote* (De Anda 2003). At the same time, historical assertions concerning the preference for casting young female victims into the Cenote Sagrado (Tozzer 1957) are called into question by the sex distribution of the skeletal population.

The sex and age distribution observed at San José, Mayapán, differs both from a natural paleodemographic profile and from the biographic profile of the individuals in Chichén's *cenote*. No skeletal elements of infants or small children were recovered from Cenote San José. The youngest individuals are well above ten years of age. Males seem overrepresented despite the discrepancies in the results obtained from different skeletal parameters in sex discrimination. Albeit that the present tendencies give no conclusive information on the use of the body of water as a human disposal place, the biographic profile suggests a different use from the Cenote Sagrado, with its high portions of subadults.

The present information does not permit us to ascertain the origins, occasions, and duration of use of Cenote San José as a resting place for the dead. Nevertheless, its hidden subterranean location on the periphery outside the walled epicenter argues against any public display in the fashion documented for the regional gatherings during pre-contact times at the *cenote* in Chichén's epicenter. This argument is further strengthened by a comparison of associated goods. The abundance, craftsmanship, and symbolic meaning of imported artifacts recovered from the Cenote Sagrado have no counterpart at Cenote San José.

The large numbers of apparently complete skeletons that characterize the burial population of both the San José and Chichén *cenotes* underscore the intentionality of their placement and distinguish them from the incidental and scarce presence recorded in Dzibilchaltún's Cenote Xlacah (Andrews IV and Andrews V 1980: 245) or the purely artifactual nature in the Cenote Azul in Chinkultik (Gallegos Ruiz 1976: 102). The general differences encountered between the two analyzed human assemblages in terms of age and sex distribution, lifestyle indicators, and biocultural practices underscore the variability in the use of *cenotes* as mortuary sites. This stresses the importance of considering individual and collective contexts in a wider regional and cultural setting. Naturally, more direct insights on posthumous body manipulation could have been gained had stratigraphic and detailed taphonomic data been taken into consideration. As mentioned, these had not been the original focus of my skeletal studies, and suitable detailed contextual data were not available for assessment.

CONCLUSION

In presenting osteotaphonomic applications for the study of human remains from *cenotes*, I have emphasized the importance of multidisciplinary research to enhance our understanding of the function of *cenotes* as mortuary depositories. I am confident that some of the uncertainties revolving around specific practices—such as funerary or extra-funerary activities that resulted in mortuary deposition, dating, and methods of human sacrifice—could be clarified. Guillermo De Anda's ongoing study of *cenote* bone assemblages is a recent example of how to expand our vision of ritual body processing among the Maya. Particularly, his recent documentation of vestiges of heat exposure and ancient cut marks that cover many of the bony surfaces from Chichén Itzá's Cenote Sagrado (De Anda 2004) should provide promising new insights into different posthumous body treatments. These likely included burning, skinning, and defleshing following sacrificial killings, with more specific patterns still to be investigated.

The different lines of evidence leave no doubts as to the fundamental importance of *cenotes* in ancient Maya ritual activity involving human sacrifice, whereas much of their varied depositional histories still awaits in-depth study. In this sense, this chapter hopes to raise new questions and challenges for forthcoming investigations related to the interpretation, recovery techniques, and laboratory analysis of human skeletal assemblages from *cenotes*. I conclude that only the combined reconstruction of entangled agencies that result in postmortem change, integrated into a broader scheme of interpretative multidisciplinary burial reconstruction, will offer a truly fruitful contribution to future *cenote* research. This requires the collaboration and exchange of ideas and data between archaeologists, physical anthropologists, engineers, historians, professional divers, and restoration specialists.

ACKNOWLEDGMENTS

The author wishes to thank James Brady (California State University, Los Angeles), Margaret Streeter (University of Missouri at Columbia), Iván Oliva and Patricia Quintana (CINVESTAV/Politécnico Nacional), and Carlos Evia Cervantes and Guillermo De Anda (Facultad de Ciencias Antropológicas, UADY) for their generous assistance, comments, or kind collaboration. Special thanks to Andrea Cucina (Facultad de Ciencias Antropológicas, UADY) and an anonymous reviewer for assistance in editing the manuscript. The study and photographic documentation of the human remains from Mayapán were conducted by the author on skeletal series retrieved by the Archaeological Project Cenote San José Mayapán directed by Eunice Uc and Carlos Peraza, INAH, and the Carnegie Institution of Washington, D.C. The remains from Dzibilchaltún and Chac, photographed by the author, were recovered by the Archaeological Projects of Dzibilchaltún (Middle American Research Institute, Tulane University) and of Chac, Yucatán (directed by Michael Smyth, financed by the National Geographic Society).

NOTES

1. This chapter is a much-expanded version of a paper presented in June 2002 during the First Congress of Underwater Archaeology and Speleology in Mérida, Mexico.

2. The term *cenote* is defined here simply as any underground body of water.

3. A mandible was the only human skeletal piece recovered among abundant other archaeological artifacts from the bottom of the Cenote Azul of Chinkultic in Chiapas (Gallegos Ruiz 1976: 102). In Dzibilchaltún, scarce human skeletal remains, pertaining to eight individuals of different ages, were produced during the underwater explorations of the Cenote Xlacah (Andrews IV and Andrews V 1980). The authors were not able to determine their chronological range and suggest that the *cenote* was not used for ritual sacrifice (Andrews IV and Andrews V 1980: 242–245).

4. The surface of the *cenote* was divided into four quadrants. Unfortunately, Piña Chan does not provide precise information on the distribution of the skulls among the sectors other than mentioning that skulls and pottery from later times were recovered from the western part.

5. According to Boyle's Law, depths of more than 20 m provide pressure to limit sufficiently the expansion of accumulating decomposition gas and prevent the body from floating (Guillermo De Anda 2002: personal communication).

6. The science that deals with the influence of soils on living things, particularly plants, including human's use of land for plant growth.

7. The collection was recovered during explorations conducted by INAH and directed by Román Piña Chan in the 1960s.

8. The material was recovered by INAH, directed by Carlos Peraza and Eunice Uc.

9. No insights could be gained on dental decoration patterns for lack of frontal teeth present.

10. Mandibles were not used for sexing.

REFERENCES CITED

Álvarez, Ticul

1976 *Restos óseos rescatados del cenote sagrado de Chichen Itzá, Yucatán.* Cuadernos de Trabajo, Departamento de Prehistoria, Instituto Nacional de Antropología e Historia, México.

Andrews, E. Wyllys, IV, and E. Wyllys Andrews V

1980 *Excavations at Dzibilchaltun, Yucatan, Mexico.* Middle American Research Institute, no. 48. Tulane University, New Orleans.

Aufderheide, Arthur C., and Conrado Rodríguez-Martin

1998 *The Cambridge Encyclopedia of Human Paleopathology.* Cambridge University Press, Cambridge.

Behrensmeyer, Anna K., and Andrew P. Hill

1980 *Fossils in the Making: Vertebrate Taphonomy and Paleoecology,* eds. Anna K. Behrensmeyer and Andrew P. Hill. Prehistoric Archeology and Ecology Series. University of Chicago Press, Chicago.

Binford, Lewis R.

1981 *Bones: Ancient Men and Modern Myths.* Academic Press, Orlando.

Boaz, Noel T., and Anna K. Behrensmeyer

1976 Hominid Taphonomy: Transport of Human Skeletal Parts in an Artificial Fluvial Enviroment. *American Journal of Physical Anthropology* 45:53–60.

Boddington, A., A. N. Garland, and R. C. Janaway

1987 Flesh, Bones, Dust and Society. In *Death, Decay and Reconstruction: Approaches to Archaeology and Forensic Science,* eds. A. Boddington, A. N. Garland, and R. C. Janaway, 3–9. Manchester University Press, Manchester.

Bonor Villarejo, Juan Luis

1989 *Las Cuevas Mayas: Simbolismo y Ritual.* Universidad Complutense de Madrid, Instituto de Cooperación Iberoamericana, Madrid.

Borhegyi, Stephan

1968 Archaeological Reconnaissance of Chinkultic, Chiapas, Mexico. In *Middle American Research Institute,* no. 26, 119–134. Tulane University, New Orleans.

Boulestin, Bruno

1999 *Approche Taphonomique des Restes Humains.* B.A.R. International Series 776, Archeopress, Oxford.

Brady, James E.

1989 An Investigation of Maya Ritual Cave Use With Special Reference to Naj Tunich, Peten, Guatemala. Ph.D. Dissertation. Department of Anthropology, University of California, Los Angeles.

1995 Harvest of Skulls & Bones. A 3,000-year-old Ossuary in Northeastern Honduras Yields Ritual Burials. *Archaeology* 48(3):36–40.

Buikstra, Jane E., and Douglas H. Ubelaker

1994 *Standards for Data Collections From Human Skeletal Remains.* Arkansas Archaeological Survey Research Series no. 44, Fayetteville, AR.

Cetina, Aleida, and Thelma Sierra

2003 Acercamiento a las condiciones de vida y nutrición de los antiguos habitantes de Xcambó, Yucatán. *Los Investigadores de la Cultura Maya* (Universidad Autónoma de Campeche, Campeche) 11:504–513.

Coggins, Clemency Chase

1992 *Artifacts From the Cenote of Sacrifice, Chichén Itzá, Yucatán,* ed. Clemency Chase Coggins. Peabody Museum of Archaeology and Ethnology, Harvard, Cambridge, MA.

Coggins, Clemency Chase, and Orrin C. Shane III
1989 *El Cenote de Sacrificios.* Trans. Jorge Ferreiro. Fondo de Cultura Económica, Mexico.

De Anda, Guillermo
2003 *Los cenotes y su reconocimiento, una aportación metodológica.* Tesis de Licenciatura en Ciencias Antropológicas, Facultad de Ciencias Antropológicas. Universidad Autónoma de Yucatán, Mérida.
2004 Análisis osteotafonómico de rasgos óseos sumergidos en *cenotes*: una visión desde el *cenote* sagrado de Chichén Itzá. Protocolo de Especialización en Antropología Esquelética, Facultad de Ciencias Antropológicas. Universidad Autónoma de Yucatán, Mérida.

De Anda, Guillermo, Vera Tiesler, and Pilar Zabala
2004 *Cenotes,* espacios sagrados y la practica de sacrificio humano en Yucatán. In *Los Investigadores de la Cultura Maya* 12, vol. 2, 376–386. Universidad Autónoma de Campeche, Campeche, Mexico.

Dembo, Adolfo, and José Imbelloni
1938 *Deformaciones Intencionales del Cuerpo Humano de Carácter Étnico.* Biblioteca Humanior, Buenos Aires.

Duday, Henry
1987 Contribution des observations ostéologiques à la chronologie interne des sépultures collectives. In *Anthropologie Physique et Archéologie. Méthodes d'Étude des Sépultures,* eds. Henry Duday and Claud Masset, 51–59. Éditions du CNRS, Paris.
1997 Antropología biológica "de campo," tafonomía y arqueología de la muerte. In *El Cuerpo Humano y su Tratamiento Mortuorio,* eds. Elsa Malvido, Grégory Pereira, and Vera Tiesler, 91–126. Colección Científica, Instituto Nacional de Antropología e Historia, Mexico.

Duday, Henry, Patrice Courtaud, Eric Crubezy, Pascal Sellier, and Anne-Marie Tillier
1990 L'anthropologie "de terrain": Reconnaissance et Interprétation des Gestes Funéraires. *Bulletins et Mémoires de la Société d'Anthropologie de Paris* 2(3–4):29–50.

Duday, Henry, and Pascal Sellier
1990 L'archéologie des Gestes Funéraires et la Taphonomie. *Les Nouvelles de l'Archéologie* 40:12–14.

Evia Cervantes, Carlos Augusto
2000 Rituales de Cavernas. *Por Esto!* January 30, 2000, Mérida.

Falkenburger, Fédéric
1938 Récherches anthropologiques sur la déformation artificielle du crâne. *Revista de Antropología de la Universidad de Tucumán* 1:1–70.

Folan, William J.
1968 *El cenote sagrado de Chichen Itzá.* Instituto Nacional de Antropología e Historia, Mexico.

Fry, Edward I.
1956 Skeletal Remains From Mayapán. In *Current Reports,* no. 38, 551–571. Carnegie Institution, Washington, D.C.

Gallegos Ruiz, Roberto
1976 *Chinkultic, una ciudad Maya y su culto a la lluvia.* Milwaukee Public Museum, Texto e Imagen, Mexico.

Garland, A. Neil
1989 Microscopical Analysis of Fossil Bone. *Applied Geochemistry* 4:215–229.

Gifford, Diane P.
1981 Taphonomy and Paleoecology: A Critical Review of Archaeology's Sister Disciplines. In *Advances in Archaeological Method and Theory,* Vol. 4, ed. Michael Schiffer, 365–438. Academic Press, San Diego.

Grupe, Gisela, and Ute Dreses-Werringloer
1993 Decomposition Phenomena in Thin Sections of Excavated Human Bone. In *Histology of Ancient Human Bone: Methods and Diagnosis,* eds. G. Grupe and A. N. Garland, 27–36. Springer, Stuttgart.

Haglund, William D., and Marcela H. Sorg
1997 *Forensic Taphonomy: The Postmortem Fate of Human Remains,* eds. William D. Haglund and Marcela H. Sorg. CRC Press, Boca Raton, FL.
2002a *Advances in Forensic Taphonomy: Method, Theory and Archaeological Perspectives.* CRC Press, Boca Raton, FL.
2002b Human Remains in Water Enviroments. In *Advances in Forensic Taphonomy: Method, Theory and Archaeological Perspectives*, eds. William D. Haglund and Marcella H. Sorg, 201–218. CRC Press, Boca Raton, FL.

Hooton, Earnest A.
1940 Skeletons From the *Cenote* of Sacrifice at Chichen Itzá. In *The Maya and Their Neighbors: Essays on Middle American Anthropology and Archaeology,* eds. C. L. Hay, R. L. Linton, S. K. Lothrop, H. Shapiro, and G. C. Vaillant, 272–280. Appleton-Century, New York.

Hoppa, Robert D., and James W. Vaupel
2002 *Paleodemography: Age Distribution From Skeletal Samples,* eds. Robert D. Hoppa and James W. Vaupel. Cambridge University, Cambridge.

Landa, Fray Diego de
1982 [~1566] *Relación de las Cosas de Yucatán.* Porrúa, Mexico.

Larsen, Clark Spencer
1997 *Bioarchaeology: Interpreting Behavior From the Human Skeleton.* Cambridge University, New York.

Leclerc, F.
1990 La Notion de Sépulture. *Bulletins et Mémoires de la Société d'Anthropologie de Paris* 2(3–4):13–38.

Márquez Morfín, Lourdes, María Elena Peraza, José Gamboa, and Teresa Miranda
1982 *Playa del Carmen: una población de la Costa Oriental en el Postclásico (un estudio osteológico).* Colección Científica, Instituto Nacional de Antropología e Historia, Mexico.

Martin, Ronald E.
2000 *Taphonomy: A Process Approach.* Cambridge Paleobiology Series No. 4. Cambridge University Press, Cambridge.

Micozzi, Marc S.

1991 *Postmortem Change in Human and Animal Remains: A Systematic Approach.* Charles C. Thomas, Springfield.

Moss, Melvin

1958 The Pathogenesis of Artificial Cranial Deformation. *American Journal of Physical Anthropology* 16(3):269–286.

Nájera, Martha Ilia

1987 *El Don de la Sangre en el Equilibrio Cósmico.* Centro de Estudios Mayas, Universidad Nacional Autónoma de México, Mexico.

Ortner, Donald J., and Walter G. Putschar

1981 *Identification of Pathological Conditions in Human Skeletal Remains.* Smithsonian Institution Press, Washington, D.C.

Piepenbrink, H.

1984 Beispiele biogener Dekompositionserscheinungen an Knochen unter längerer Liegezeit. *Anthropologischer Anzeiger* 42:241–251.

Piña Chan, Román

1970 *Informe Preliminar de la Reciente Exploración del Cenote Sagrado de Chichen Itzá.* Instituto Nacional de Antropología e Historia, no. 24, Mexico.

Proskouriakoff, Tatiana

1974 *Jades From the Cenote of Sacrifice, Chichen Itza, Yucatan.* Memoirs of the Peabody Museum of Archaeology and Ethnology, no. 10(1). Harvard University, Cambridge.

Rodríguez, William C., III

1997 Decomposition of Buried and Submerged Bodies. In *Forensic Taphonomy: The Postmortem Fate of Human Remains,* eds. William D. Haglund and Marcella H. Sorg, 459–467. CRC Press, Boca Raton, FL.

Romano Pacheco, Arturo

1965 *Estudio morfológico de la deformación craneana en Tamuín, S.L.P., y en la Isla del Idolo, Veracruz.* Serie de Investigaciones 10. Instituto Nacional de Antropología e Historia, Mexico.

Romero Molina, Javier

1986 *Catálogo de la Colección de Dientes Mutilados Prehispánicos IV Parte.* Colección Fuentes. Instituto Nacional de Antropología e Historia, Mexico.

Ruppert, Karl

1937 *The Caracol at Chichen Itza, Yucatan.* Carnegie Institution of Washington, Washington, D.C.

Ruz Lhuillier, Alberto

1991 *Costumbres funerarias de los antiguos Mayas.* Mexico City: Instituto de Investigaciones Filológicas. Centro de Estudios Mayas, Universidad Nacional Autónoma de México, Mexico.

Sánchez de Aguilar, Pedro

1937 [1639] *Informe contra idolorum cultores del obispado de Yucatán,* Third Edition. E. G. Triay e Hijas, Merida, Madrid.

Scholes, France V., and Eleanor Adams

1938 *Don Diego Quijada Alcalde Mayor de Yucatán (1561–1565).* Vol. 1, José Porrua, Mexico.

Schultz, Michael
1994 Ergebnisse mikroskopischer Untersuchungen an archäologischen Skelettfunden. Ein Beitrag zur Paläopathologie. In *Beiträge zur Archäozoologie und Prähistorischen Anthropologie,* compiled by Mostefa Kokabi and Joachim Wahl, 107–116. Forschungen und Berichte zur Vor- und Frühgeschichte in Baden-Württemberg 53, Stuttgart.
2003 Light Microscopic Analysis in Skeletal Paleopathology. In *Identification of Pathological Conditions in Human Skeletal Remains,* Second Edition, ed. Donald J. Ortner, 73–108. Academic Press, Amsterdam.

Sievert, April K.
1992 *Maya Ceremonial Specialization: Lithic Tools From the Sacred* Cenote *at Chichén Itzá, Yucatán.* Monographs in World Archaeology No. 12. Prehistory Press, Madison.

Tiesler, Vera
1998 *La costumbre de la deformación cefálica entre los antiguos Mayas: aspectos morfológicos y culturales.* Colección Científica/Instituto Nacional de Antropología e Historia, Mexico.
1999a Reporte del análisis de los restos humanos, recuperados como parte de las excavaciones en el cenote San José Mayapán, Yucatán. Instituto Nacional de Antropología e Historia, Mexico (report on file).
1999b Rasgos bioculturales entre los antiguos Mayas: aspectos arqueológicos y sociales. Ph.D. Dissertation. Department of Anthropology, Universidad Nacional Autónoma de México, Mexico.
2001 *Decoraciones dentales de los antiguos Mayas.* Ediciones Euroamericanas/INAH, Mexico.
2004 Maya Mortuary Treatments of the Elite: An Osteotaphonomic Perspective. In *Continuity and Change: Maya Religious Practices in Temporal Perspective: Fifth European Maya Conference,* University of Bonn, December 2000, eds. Daniel Graña Behrens, Nikolai Grube, Christian M. Prager, Frauke Sachse, Stefanie Teufel, and Elisaeth Wagner, 143–156. Anton Saurwein, Markt Schwaben, Germany.

Tozzer, Alfred M.
1957 *Chichen Itza and Its Cenote of Sacrifice.* Memoirs of the Peabody Museum of Archaeology and Ethnology, nos. 11–12. Harvard University, Cambridge.

Voorhies, M.
1969 Taphonomy and Population Dynamics of an Early Pliocene Vertebrae Fauna, Knox County, Nebraska. *Contributions to Geology* 1:1–69. University of Wyoming Press, Laramie.

White, E. M., and L. A. Hannus
1983 Chemical Weathering of Bone in Archaelogical Soils. *American Antiquity* 48:316–322.

Yarrow, H. C.
1881 *Further Contribution to the Study of the Mortuary Customs of the North American Indians.* Smithsonian Institution Press, Washington, D.C.

Chapter Nineteen

Maya Cave Archaeology

A New Look at Religion and Cosmology

by James E. Brady
Keith M. Prufer

One of the major accomplishments of cave archaeology has been to champion a new view of Maya religion and cosmology. This has been accomplished to no small degree by embracing the explicit use of ethnographic analogy. Ethnographers have long recognized the fundamental role caves, mountains, and springs play in social reproduction in communities across Mesoamerica, as well as the pervasiveness of religious specialists who engage indigenous deities in Maya social and political life and have long agreed that many types of religious expression have pre-Columbian antecedents (Green 1972; Holland 1964; Vogt 1964). Ethnohistoric sources indicated that caves were fundamental features in Maya religious organization at the dawn of Spanish colonialism. Although Maya archaeologists have generally been hesitant in their explicit acceptance of analogy as a method, they often acknowledge similarities between the ethnographic present and the archaeological past (Culbert 1988; Gossen and Leventhal 1993: 185–186; Sharer 1993: 91–92).

The use of analogy has been heavily criticized by Processualists who saw in its application the danger of "assuming what one is trying to discover" (Clark 1951: 52) and a throwback to the days of the Direct Historical Approach (Binford 1968; Deetz 1970). When one combined the Processualist bias against religion (discussed in the Introduction) with the reaction against ethnographic analogy, a particularly insidious situation developed for those investigating Maya religion. Because religion was relegated to a secondary position, archaeologists tended not to be well-informed on the vast anthropological literature on the subject. Disdaining the use of ethnographic analogy, archaeologists further cut themselves off from non-Western models, particularly those historically connected to the very civilization they are studying. What one sees being applied are very uninformed and inexplicit models of religion drawn primarily from personal experience. An amusing example of just how uninformed some of these models can be was provided by a reviewer of one of Brady's papers on pilgrimage. The unidentified reviewer states, "[T]he authors themselves dismiss pilgrimage as a cave function by their final reference to Garcia-Zambrano—who states a cave must be present at every site to legitimize both settlement and rulership. If this is true and every site has a cave then why would people need to make pilgrimages?" Clearly, this person knew nothing about pilgrimage or the "need" that drives people all over the world to make such journeys. If this questionable "logic" were applied to Europe, no one would "need" to make pilgrimages to the churches of Rome, Fatima, Lourdes, or Canterbury because each town already has its own church.

We feel Maya studies have too frequently applied Western models of religion to the ancient Maya. We do not want this to be taken as the type of general criticism that appears all too frequently in academic literature, but instead we wish to point to very specific Western biases that have been employed. The resulting misconceptions, as we shall show, have enormous implications for understanding the importance of caves in ancient Maya religion.

At the highest level, we note that Western assumptions about the structure of the cosmos have often been unconsciously adopted. To appreciate a Maya cosmology, we must go back in time to restructure our own notions of the cosmos. Even at the time of the Spanish conquest, Europe had not yet been exposed to the Copernican heliocentric view of the universe. Historians of Western science point out that a geocentric universe with the earth at the center is actually far more in accord with common sense than is the heliocentric view (Westfall 1977: 15–16). Cross-culturally, centrality carries deep cosmological implications, as Galileo was to discover to his chagrin in the seventeenth century. In the geocentric universe, the earth is not simply at the center but is also the largest object. We see this in the Maya belief system because celestial bodies set into the earth and rise out of it the next day (Duby and Blom 1969: 292; Villa Rojas 1945: 156). Size is always significant because it connotes power and importance. Thus, in Maya cosmology, the earth is the dominant feature at the center of the cosmos.

Adopting a geocentric view of the universe is only the first step in appreciating how fundamentally Maya cosmology differs from our own. As Westerners, we know that God is in heaven, and as we "look to heaven" there is no doubt about the direction of our gaze. This, however, has caused archaeologists to ignore the indigenous Amerindian focus on *Earth* as a sacred and animate entity. The difference in the Maya perspective is profound, as noted in one group: "[T]o the Kekchi [Q'eqchi'], there is only one deity with whom he must be vitally concerned: Cu:l Taq'a [*tzuultaqa'*], the 'Earth God.' While the Kekchi does acknowledge the existence of other deities, he nevertheless feels that their effect on earth-dwellers is marginal, if not nil" (Carlson and Eachus 1977: 38). Calixta Guiteras-Holmes (1961: 289) made a very similar observation for the Tzotzil: "Throughout the interviews his idea of a universal power, the source of both good and evil—that is, the earth, and in a broader sense the universe—is evident, although never expressed in so many words." The implications of *Earth* as the ultimate power are significant in appreciating the importance of landscape features in indigenous thought.

The name for the most important indigenous deity (such as *tzuultaqa'* in Q'eqchi') in most Maya languages translates as "hill-valley" (Tedlock 1992: 454). The term is not used exclusively to denote a deity but occurs in ordinary speech as well to refer to a geographical entity, the hill-valley. Even in this mundane sense, however, it is referring to *Earth* and so is laden with supernatural connotations (Schackt 1984: 18). In the Q'eqchi' area, all major hill-valleys are given names and personalities, which represents the personification and animation of landscape. These figures live in caves within named sacred mountains, which may be why the Maya word for cave often translates as "stone house."

Even here, one must be careful not to equate the cave as the house of the god with the Western concept of church. They are not just buildings or enclosed spaces. Caves are the most important part of a mountain. Edward Fischer (2001: 154) explains, "Caves, where one descends toward the *k'u'x* (heart or center) of a mountain, are especially hot places. This is due to their symbolic proximity to the powers unleashed by cosmic convergence at the *axis mundi*." In addition, Richard Wilson (1995: 53) points out that "[t]raditional Q'eqchi's say that the mountains are living (*yo'yo*). They have the quality of *wiinqilal*, or 'personhood,' a concept that applies only to mountains and people. Those with the quality of *wiinqilal* have a spirit (*xmuhel*)—an honor accorded only to people, maize, saints' images, and, sometimes, houses." Sergio Garza (2003), who also worked with the Q'eqchi', was repeatedly told that caves were "very alive." The air exchange that can be felt at the entrances to caves as a result of differences in atmospheric pressure is interpreted by the Maya as the cave breathing. Thus, caves must be understood as immense, living, sentient, sacred, and powerful to the Maya.

Geographer Erich Isaac (1962), in attempting to explain which types of societies practice large-scale religious landscape modification, notes that as ideal polar opposites, there are two very different justifications for human existence. One resides in a divine covenant, and the religion will continually refer back to the covenant. The Judeo-Christian tradition clearly falls in this category. The problem is that this tends to blind us to the tremendous importance of the act of creation for religions in the other category. Mircea Eliade (1959: 81), however, underscores the importance of the act of creation in noting that "[t]he paramount time of origins is the time of the cosmogony, the instant that saw the appearance of the most immediate of realities, the world. This . . . is the reason the cosmogony serves as the paradigmatic model for every creation, for every kind of doing." For noncovenant societies the act of creation becomes the model for religious landscape modification. As Isaac (1962: 12) says, "[T]he attempt will be made to reproduce the cosmic plan in the landscape with greater or lesser effect upon the land, depending on the elaborateness of reproduction attempted." Mesoamerican religions are clearly of this latter type, as can be seen in Angel García-Zambrano's (1994: 217–218) description of the ideal landscape for a new settlement:

> Essentially, Mesoamerican migrants searched for an environment with specific characteristics that comprised several symbolic levels. . . . Such a place had to recall the mythical moment when the earth was created: an aquatic universe framed by four mountains with a fifth elevation protruding in the middle of the water. The mountain at the core had to be dotted with caves and springs, and sometimes surrounded by smaller hills. A setting like this duplicated, and forever would freeze, the primordial scene when the waters and the sky separated and the earth sprouted upwards.

The ancient Maya fall into the category of cultures practicing large-scale landscape modification designed to model the moment of creation. Evon Vogt (1964: 194) suggested over forty years ago that Maya pyramids represented the sacred mountain, and hieroglyphic decipherments appear to confirm this. Since humans are widely seen as being born or created within the earth and then emerging onto the surface from a cave, local caves become the symbol of creation for their respective populations. Guiteras-Holmes (1952: 103) makes the connection explicitly for the Tzeltal, saying, "Each clan is composed of an indefinite number of lineages, whose members originated from or came out of four caves." William Holland (1963: 108–109) found a similar idea in Larraínzar.

In other cases this concern with creation is focused on the actual or mythological community founders. For Jakaltekos this is so important that one of the pillars of ethnic identity is one's claim of descent from the founding couple, the *Jich Mam* and *Jich Mi* (Casaverde 1974). This concern appears to be quite ancient. David Stuart suggests that the iconography of Stela 31 from El Peru provides Classic period evidence for the founding couple. He says:

> Perhaps the most interesting features of this hill spirit are the small people inside the eyes of the mountain. I am quite convinced from parallel imagery that one figure is always male and one figure always female. We have here, again visually represented, the idea of male/female ancestors within the mountain, corresponding to the *totil me'il* of Zinacanteco cosmology. These are the mother/father characters who define the ancestral spirits of that Tzotzil community. At El Peru they seem to be shown as the quintessential ancestors, living inside the mountain and peeking out from the eyes of the mountain spirit." (Stuart 1997: 16)

For Jakaltekos, as with the Classic period residents of El Peru, the couple lives in a cave within a hill, and Oliver LaFarge (1947: 128) concludes, "I suspect from these indications that the cave is the true center of the ceremonial."

Maya religion differs fundamentally from Christianity in gender as well. One of the "mysteries" of Catholic theology is the "Holy Trinity." Certainly, the mystery for the Maya is how one can have "God the Father" and "God the Son" without the third element being "God the Mother." As J.E.S. Thompson (1970: 204) says, "The notion of a single creator god is out of keeping with the prevalent Middle American concept of a pair of creators who populate the world by sexual intercourse." Nathaniel Tarn and Martin Prechtel (1986: 173) see this as basic to modern Maya thinking in noting, "[I]t would appear that Atiteco thought conceives of male and female as aspects of one original unit and that no unit can be other than both male and female. Certainly, nothing complete, nothing fully fulfilling its function in the world, can be other than this." Whereas the Q'eqchi' *tzuultaqa'* living in the sacred mountains can be either male or female, the vast majority are male. Both Q'eqchi' and Tzotzil informants have suggested that mountains are male and earth is female (Garza 2003; Guiteras-Holmes 1961: 203). This issue needs further investigation, but it appears that the female element may be the most powerful. Guiteras-Holmes (1961: 289) says, "The Earth is the mother of universal life. She is the most compelling power in the universe. She is the supreme power. All others seem to form part of her or have proceeded from her depths." This reinforces the points made previously as to why caves are considered so important in indigenous thought. They are associated with the female earth, particularly the generative aspects: the womb and the vagina (Brady 1988; Heyden 1991). Fertility is a focal concern of Maya religion, and caves are a central symbol of fertility.

For any agricultural society, fertility is an immediate and never-ending concern simply in relation to crops. The two most important elements in agricultural success are soil and rain. Soil is part of *Earth,* which we have discussed. Rain in Maya thinking is again strikingly different than Western concepts that see rain as an essentially celestial phenomenon. For the Maya, rain and clouds are formed within caves and then sent into the sky. As Vogt (1969: 387) observes, the Maya belief is completely reasonable:

> The *Ch'enetik* are also important as the sources of lightning bolts and clouds. I have had a number of interesting conversations in which I have attempted to convince Zinacantecos that Lightning does *not* come out of caves and go up into the sky and that clouds form in the air. One of these arguments took place in Paste?. As I stood on the rim with an informant, and we watched the clouds and lightning in a storm in the lowlands some thousands of feet below us. I finally had to concede that, given the empirical evidence available to Zinacantecos living in their highland Chiapas terrain, their explanation does make sense. For, as the clouds formed rapidly in the air and then poured up and over the highland ridges in much the same way that the fog comes in from the Pacific and pours over the coastal range in northern California, they did give the appearance of

> coming up from caves on the slopes of the Chiapas highlands. Furthermore, since we were standing some thousands of feet above a tropical storm that developed in the late afternoon, I had to concede that it was difficult to tell whether the lightning was triggered off in the air and then struck downward to the ground, or was coming from the ground and going into the air as the Zinacantecos believe. Given their premises and the evidence observable from day-to-day behavior of clouds and lightning, their beliefs were as understandable as mine.

If the powers controlling both soil fertility and rain reside in caves, it is easy to understand why caves are so crucial to agricultural rituals throughout the Maya area.

Without belaboring the point, we note that rain is not the only phenomenon that we perceive as celestially related but that the Maya see as terrestrially produced. For the Maya, rainbows are thought to enter the sky after emerging from caves and sinkholes. Unlike our own positive evaluation, the Maya envision rainbows as evil and as causing illness (Guiteras-Holmes 1961: 231, 288; Redfield and Villa Rojas 1962: 207). This example underscores the fact that important features like caves are powerful but have both positive and negative aspects. It has often been noted that the Maya do not tend to dichotomize good and evil as we do (Monaghan 2000). Clearly, Maya cosmology differs radically from our own, particularly in beliefs related to *Earth.* The importance of caves has gone unrecognized precisely because archaeologists have failed to appreciate their significance in indigenous cosmology.

Space does not allow us to present anything but the most minimal discussion of Maya beliefs in relation to caves. We chose to examine a number of aspects of Maya cosmology in which the basic premises are fundamentally different than those of our own belief system. The *Earth* is the greatest power in the universe. The primacy of the sacred *Earth* imbues landscape features such as caves and mountains with a power and importance that has no counterpart in Western religion. Caves are not simply places of worship; they are living beings with personhood and souls. The cave is the place of creation, and it controls resources, such as rain, on which human existence depends. Finally, because the *Earth* is fertile, it is sexual and it is also feminine, and caves epitomize this. Caves are powerful and also generally feared and thus are not used by people for nonritual purposes. Because of the disdain for religion and ethnography, archaeologists have failed to appreciate how profoundly Maya cosmology differs from our own. Lacking the indigenous perspective, they have not recognized the significance of recent cave discoveries.

THE MATERIALIZATION OF COSMOLOGY

The reformulation of our model of Maya cosmology was essential to cave archaeology because the new emphasis on the sacred *Earth* explained why landscape features should be so important. Almost from the beginning of cave studies, archaeologists have been confronted with physical evidence of this importance but time and again failed to recognize it because of preconceptions that such "natural places" could not be significant. At the beginning of the twentieth century, Eduard Seler (1901) discovered a cave containing large-scale architecture and massive stone sculpture at the site of Quen Santo. The name of the site is a straightforward combination of Maya and Spanish meaning Holy Cave. Through a torturous process, Seler convinced himself that the meaning was Holy Stone and that it referred to the entire plateau on which the site was located. This then allowed him to interpret the cave as merely a storeroom where the sculptures had been placed when the site was abandoned.

Even J. Eric Thompson appears not to have believed that caves were overly significant. He was clearly perplexed by "Las Casas' inference that caves and temples were partially interchangeable as scenes for religious rites" (J.E.S. Thompson 1959: 124). He pointed out that the sixteenth-century Yucatec use of the term *actun* to refer to both caves and stone buildings supported Las Casas but immediately offered the alternative explanation that the buildings might have fallen into ruin by that time and thus looked like artificial caves. One of Sergio Garza's (2005) Q'eqchi' Maya informants provides an eloquent answer to Thompson. He says, "For us, this cave is sacred and although other people say that church is a sacred place I know that this cave is important because this is the first temple of the world (*el primer templo del mundo*). My father and grandfather taught me this and all the elders and ancient ones have also taught us this. They say, and I know it, that many things began here. . . . Even the sun and the moon have come out of caves." The tremendous strides made by cave archaeology are directly traceable to the rise of cave specialists who recognize the theoretical importance of cave data and have applied those data in augmenting our understanding of these important features.

One of the most theoretically significant examples of the materialization of cosmology has been in recognizing caves as a central element in the validation of settlements based on the meanings described previously. The actual materialization takes the form of incorporating caves into important public architecture in site cores. J.E.S. Thompson (1959: 128) was aware of this phenomenon and remarked in his earlier synthesis that "[m]ention should be made of caverns beneath buildings, notably the High Priest's Grave at Chichen Itza, but discussion of them would vastly extend our subject." Thompson clearly appears to indicate that this was part of a larger pattern of utilization. Interestingly, rather than develop the theme in his revised version where space was available, he instead relegates it to "Other Uses" and once again mentions only the High Priest's Grave (J.E.S. Thompson 1975: xlii). We have concluded that Thompson simply was not prepared to accept the implications of such placements. Doris Heyden (1973, 1975, 1981) immediately grasped the importance of the cave beneath the Pyramid of the Sun and set out the reasons caves might have been used in this manner. Heyden was successful in making her point, as René Millon (1981: 235) summed up explicitly, "Nevertheless, the stubborn fact remains: the pyramid must be where it is and nowhere else because the cave below it was the most sacred of sacred places." Unfortunately, because Heyden was unfamiliar with the Maya literature, she did not recognize the Teotihuacan example as part of a basic Mesoamerican pattern.

With the advent of cave specialists who combed the archaeological literature for cave references, it became apparent that a pattern of cave appropriation could be discerned. Even at the time Thompson first wrote, examples of structures built over caves had been reported from Chichén Itzá (E. H. Thompson 1938), Tulum (Lothrop 1924: 109–110), Cozumel (Mason 1927: 278; Sanders 1955: 191–192), Pusilha (Joyce 1929; Joyce et al. 1928), and Polol (Lundell 1934: 177; also see Patton 1987), suggesting that the practice was widely occurring. A project mounted at Dos Pilas to test this idea found that architecture was constructed around caves far more frequently than ever imagined (Brady 1997). Since then, cave archaeologists have continued to find that the appropriation of caves was a common feature of Maya settlement (Brown 2005; Halperin, this volume; King and Shaw 2003; Prufer, this volume; Pugh 2001, this volume).

Because cave data have accumulated so rapidly, surface archaeologists who have not followed developments have been uncertain how to interpret these cases of cave/architecture relationships. Cave surveys (Bonor Villarejo 1988, 1989; Brady 1997; Peterson 2001; Prufer 2002; Reeder 1993; Reeder, Brady, and Webster 1998; Rissolo 2001; Scott 1992) have documented that caves exist in large numbers in most areas of the lowlands, including right within site boundaries. But as cave archaeologists proclaim that caves exist in large numbers, surface archaeologists wonder whether this implies that some of the relationships may simply be coincidental.

That issue was settled by another dramatic example of the materialization of cosmology. Cave archaeology discovered a series of artificial caves in the nonkarstic Maya Highlands that were associated with many important surface sites (Brady and Veni 1992). The discovery was dramatic simply because the construction of these subterranean tunnels, some of which are more than 100 m long, was often a major undertaking and indicated that these features must have been of great importance to the Maya. Second, they are often located under important real estate like central plazas and so, once again, must be important themselves. Third, many were aligned with surface architecture; therefore, clearly, the arrangement was deliberate. At La Lagunita, the tunnel starts at the stairway of one of the central pyramids and terminates in the middle of the central plaza (Ichon and Arnauld 1985). The best example in Mesoamerica is still the cave under the Pyramid of the Sun at Teotihuacan, which was discovered to be artificial in the 1990s (Manzanilla et al. 1994). The cave begins at the foot of the central stairway and ends near the center of the pyramid. This clearly demonstrates that the Maya were deliberately aligning surface architecture with caves and should lay to rest any doubts about the alignment with natural caves being coincidental. Finally, some artificial caves are elaborate enough that their religious and cosmological significance is clear. At Q'umarkaj (Utatlan), the artificial cave ending under the central plaza modeled the seven-chamber cave of emergence (Brady 1991). This cave has a counterpart in the Chicomoztoc complex constructed at the site of Acatzingo Viejo, Puebla (Aguilar et al. 2005).

Maya studies as a whole has had difficulty accepting the view that the validation of sites may lie in a landscape feature enshrined within the settlement, in part because it runs contrary to entrenched notions that place priority on ecological considerations. But how accurately do these ecological models reflect the people we study? Ethnographic analogy is powerful because it shows us what real people think and do and often underscores how different their view is from ours. Ann Scott (Scott and Little 2003) has recorded an interesting case that underscores the extent of the difference between archaeologists and the Maya. Scott accompanied a Kaqchikel shaman who was conducting a cave ceremony at Tikal. When they reached the "cave," it turned out to be an abandoned tunnel excavated by University of Pennsylvania archaeologists in the 1960s. In a single generation, the tunnel abandoned by archaeologists without a second thought had become a sacred cave for the Maya. Although amusing, such incidents are wake-up calls that should alert us to the fact that our "logical" Western models will not model what the Maya were doing. Archaeology's hostility to ethnographic analogy may lie in the fact that it consistently points out the naïveté of our thinking.

Finally, one of the hallmarks of cave archaeology has been its ability to address wider issues. This reflects the field's acceptance of a larger, more dynamic perspective of religion as an institution. This view encompasses political agendas and recognizes economic implications as regular elements of religion rather than intrusions of other societal subsystems into religion. This is nowhere better illustrated than with pilgrimage. The mass movement of people will have economic implications. At Naj Tunich, pilgrimage traffic generated specialized ceramic production in forms utilized primarily in the cave itself (Brady and Sears 2000). Shankari Patel (2004, this volume) shows that Cozumel Island's economy and infrastructure were totally structured around pilgrimage and that there is no validity to the model of the island as a port of trade. On a related theme, cave ritual has been shown to be economically significant in its own right (Brady, this volume).

Although archaeology as a whole generally accepted peasant use of caves based on continued modern Maya practice, early work showed that archaeological evidence suggested that elites also used some caves (Brady and Stone 1986). More recent articles have shown that elite utilization of caves is materialized within surface sites in the incorporation of speleothems in public architecture (Brady et al. 1997; Peterson, McAnany, and Cobb, this volume). Andrea Stone (1995) elaborated on the elite presence in caves by focusing on the role of scribes in cave art, an idea that appears to be gaining acceptance (Coe and Kerr 1997). In this volume, Stone presents a detailed argument for the close association of scribes with caves. Recently, efforts have also been made to detect the presence of other groups, especially religious specialists, who have been almost invisible in the archaeological record (Brady and Prufer 1999; Prufer 2002). The interest here is not just in reconstructing religion since, as Prufer (2002) notes, these individuals are frequently important sociopolitical actors.

In its short existence, cave archaeology has developed a number of distinctive approaches and produced a body of significant data that offer unique insights into the nature of ancient Maya society. Because of its newness and because its emerging literature tends to be widely scattered, most Mayanists tend to be unaware of the extent of the development of the subdiscipline. We hope this volume will help remedy the problem by bringing together in one place a sample of the exciting ongoing research.

REFERENCES CITED

Aguilar, Manuel, Miguel Medina Jaen, Tim M. Tucker, and James E. Brady

2005 Constructing Mythic Space: The Significance of a Chicomoztoc Complex at Acatzingo Viejo. In *In the Maw of the Earth Monster: Mesoamerican Ritual Cave Use,* eds. James E. Brady and Keith M. Prufer, 69–87. University of Texas Press, Austin.

Binford, Lewis R.

1968 Archeological Perspectives. In *New Perspectives in Archeology,* eds. Sally R. Binford and Luis R. Binford, 5–32. Aldine, Chicago.

Bonor Villarejo, Juan Luis

1988 Cuevas Mayas en Yucatán. *Historia* (Madrid) 16(151):152–160.

1989 Las cuevas de Oxkintok: informe preliminar. *Memorias del Segundo Coloquio Internacional de Mayistas,* 303–309. Universidad Nacional Autónoma de México, Mexico.

Brady, James E.

1988 The Sexual Connotation of Caves in Mesoamerican Ideology. *Mexicon* 10(3):51–55.

1991 Caves and Cosmovision at Utatlan. *California Anthropologist* 18(1):1–10.

1997 Settlement Configuration and Cosmology: The Role of Caves at Dos Pilas. *American Anthropologist* 99(3):602–618.

Brady, James E., and Keith Prufer

1999 Caves and Crystalmancy: Evidence for the Use of Crystals in Ancient Maya Religion. *Journal of Anthropological Research* 55:129–144.

Brady, James E., Ann Scott, Hector Neff, and Michael Glascock

1997 Speleothem Breakage, Movement, Removal and Caching: An Unreported Aspect of Ancient Maya Cave Modification. *Geoarchaeology* 12(6):725–750.

Brady, James E., and Erin Sears

2000 Cuevas, peregrinaciones y arqueología. *Los investigadores de la cultura Maya* 8, Tomo 2:219–227. Campeche, Mexico.

Brady, James E., and Andrea Stone

1986 Naj Tunich: Entrance to the Maya Underworld. *Archaeology* 39(6):18–25.

Brady, James E., and George Veni

1992 Man-Made and Pseudo-Karst Caves: The Implications of Sub-Surface Geologic Features Within Maya Centers. *Geoarchaeology* 7(2):149–167.

Brown, Clifford

2005 Caves, Karst, and Settlement at Mayapán, Yucatán. In *In the Maw of the Earth Monster: Mesoamerican Ritual Cave Use,* eds. James E. Brady and Keith M. Prufer, 373–401. University of Texas Press, Austin.

Carlson, Ruth, and Francis Eachus

1977 The Kekchi Spirit World. In *Cognitive Studies of Southern Mesoamerica,* eds. Helen L. Neuenswander and Dean E. Arnold, 36–65. Summer Institute of Linguistics Museum of Anthropology, Dallas.

Casaverde, Juvenil

1974 Jacaltec Social and Political Structure. Ph.D. Dissertation. Department of Anthropology, University of Rochester.

Clark, J. Graham

1951 Folk-Culture and the Study of European Prehistory. In *Aspects of Archaeology,* ed. W. F. Grimes, 49–65. Edwards Press, London.

Coe, Michael D., and Justin Kerr

1997 *The Art of the Maya Scribe.* Harry N. Abrams, New York.

Culbert, Patrick T.

1988 Political History and the Decipherment of Maya Glyphs. *Antiquity* 62:135–152.

Deetz, Jame F.

1970 Archeology as Social Science. *American Anthropological Association,* Bulletin 3 (3):115–125.

Duby, Gertrude, and Frans Blom

1969 The Lacandon. In *Handbook of Middle American Indians, Vol. 7: Ethnology,* ed. Evon Z. Vogt, 276–297. University of Texas Press, Austin.

Eliade, Mircea

1959 *The Sacred and the Profane: The Nature of Religion.* Trans. Willard R. Trask. Harcourt Brace Jovanovich, New York.

Fischer, Edward F.

2001 *Cultural Logics and Global Economies: Maya Identity in Thought and Practice.* University of Texas Press, Austin.

García-Zambrano, Angel J.

1994 Early Colonial Evidence of Pre-Columbian Rituals of Foundations. In *Seventh Palenque Round Table, 1989,* eds. Merle Greene Robertson and Virginia Field, 217–227. Pre-Columbian Art Research Institute, San Francisco.

Garza, Sergio

2003 An Ethnoarchaeological Approach to Maya Caves. Paper presented at the 68th Annual Meeting of the Society for American Archaeology, Milwaukee.

2005 Ethnographic Models of Cave-Community Relations. Paper presented at the 70th Annual Meeting of the Society for American Archaeology, Salt Lake City.

Gossen, Gary H., and Richard M. Leventhal

1993 The Topography of Ancient Maya Religious Pluralism: A Dialogue With the Present. In *Lowland Maya Civilization in the Eighth Century A.D.,* eds. Jeremy A. Sabloff and John S. Henderson, 185–218. Dumbarton Oaks Research Library and Collection, Washington, D.C.

Green, Ernestine L.
1972 Use of Analogy for Interpretation of Maya Prehistory. *Papers of the Kroeber Anthropological Society* 45–46:18–39.

Guiteras-Holmes, Calixta
1952 Social Organization. In *Heritage of Conquest: The Ethnology of Middle America,* ed. Sol Tax, 97–118. Free Press, Glencoe, IL.
1961 *Perils of the Soul: The World View of a Tzotzil Indian.* The Free Press, New York.

Heyden, Doris
1973 ¿Un chicomostoc en Teotihuacan? La cueva bajo la Pirámide del Sol. *Boletín del Instituto Nacional de Antropología e Historia,* Época II, No. 6:3–18.
1975 An Interpretation of the Cave Underneath the Pyramid of the Sun in Teotihuacan, Mexico. *American Antiquity* 40:131–147.
1981 Caves, Gods and Myths: World-View and Planning in Teotihuacan. In *Mesoamerican Sites and World-Views,* ed. Elizabeth P. Benson, 1–39. Dumbarton Oaks Research Library and Collection, Washington, D.C.
1991 La matriz de la tierra. In *Arqueoastronomía y etnoastronomía en Mesoamérica,* eds. Johanna Broda, Stanislaw Iwaniszewski, and Lucrecia Maupomé, 501–515. Universidad Nacional Autónoma de México, Mexico.

Holland, William R.
1963 *Medicina Maya en los altos de Chiapas: un estudio del cambio socio-cultural.* Instituto Nacional Indigenista, Mexico.
1964 Contemporary Tzotzil Cosmological Concepts as a Basis for Interpreting Prehistoric Maya Civilization. *American Antiquity* 29:301–306.

Ichon, Alain, and Marie Charlotte Arnauld
1985 *Le protoclassique á la Lagunita, El Quiché Guatemala.* Centre National de la Recherche Scientifique/R.C.P. 294 et 500, Institut d'Ethnologie, Paris. Piedra Santa, Guatemala.

Isaac, Erich
1962 The Act and the Covenant. *Landscape* 11:12–17.

Joyce, T. A.
1929 Report on the British Museum Expedition to British Honduras, 1929. *Journal of the Royal Anthropological Institute* 59:439–459.

Joyce, T. A., T. Gann, E. L. Gruning, and R.C.E. Long
1928 Report on the British Museum Expedition to British Honduras, 1928. *Journal of the Royal Anthropological Society* 58:323–349.

King, Eleanor M., and Leslie C. Shaw
2003 A Heterarchical Approach to Site Variability. In *Heterarchy, Political Economy, and the Ancient Maya,* eds. Vernon L. Scarborough, Fred Valdez Jr., and Nicholas Dunning, 64–76. University of Arizona Press, Tucson.

LaFarge, Oliver
1947 *Santa Eulalia: The Religion of a Cuchumatan Indian Town.* University of Chicago Press, Chicago.

Lothrop, Samuel Kirkland
1924 *Tulum: An Archaeological Study of the East Coast of Yucatan.* Publication No. 335. Carnegie Institution of Washington, Washington, D.C.

Lundell, Cyrus Longwork
1934 Ruins of Polol and Other Archaeological Discoveries in the Department of Peten, Guatemala. *Contributions to American Archaeology, No. 8,* Carnegie Institution of Washington, Washington, D.C.

Manzanilla, L., L. Barba, R. Chávez, A. Tejero, C. Cifuentes, and N. Peralta
1994 Caves and Geophysics: An Approximation to the Underworld of Teotihuacan, Mexico. *Archaeometry* 36:141–157.

Mason, Gregory
1927 *Silver Cities of Yucatan.* G. P. Putnam and Sons, New York.

Millon, René
1981 Teotihuacan: City, State, and Civilization. In *Supplement to the Handbook of Middle American Indians, Vol. 1: Archaeology,* ed. Jeremy A. Sabloff, 198–243. University of Texas Press, Austin.

Monaghan, John D.
2000 Theology and History in the Study of Mesoamerican Religion. In *Ethnology. Supplement to the Handbook of Middle American Indians.* Volume Six, ed. John Monaghan, 24–49. University of Texas Press, Austin.

Patel, Shankari
2004 Caves and Pilgrimage on Cozumel. M.A. Thesis. Department of Anthropology, California State University, Los Angeles.

Patton, James L.
1987 The Architecture and Sculpture of Polol, El Peten, Guatemala. M.A. Thesis. Department of Anthropology, San Francisco State University, San Francisco.

Peterson, Polly A.
2001 Shedding Light on Xibalba Through Cave Survey and Surface Collection. In *Sacred Landscape and Settlement in the Sibun River Valley: XARP 1999 Archaeological Survey and Excavation,* ed. Patricia A. McAnany, 41–64. Department of Archaeology, Boston University, Boston.

Prufer, Keith M.
2002 Cave, Communities, and Ritual Specialists: A Study of Sacred Space in the Maya Mountains of Southern Belize. Ph.D. Dissertation. Department of Anthropology, Southern Illinois University, Carbondale.

Pugh, Timothy W.
2001 Flood Reptiles, Serpent Temples, and the Quadripartite Universe: The *Imago Mundi* of Late Postclassic Mayapan. *Ancient Mesoamerica* 12:247–258.

Redfield, Robert, and Alfonso Villa Rojas
1962 *Chan Kom: A Maya Village.* University of Chicago Press, Chicago.

Reeder, Philip
1993 Speleological and Geoarchaeological Investigation of the Northern Vaca Plateau, Belize, Central America. Report presented to the Commissioner of Archaeology, Belmopan, Belize.

Reeder, Philip, James E. Brady, and James Webster
1998 Geoarchaeological Investigations on the Northern Vaca Plateau, Belize. *Mexicon* 20:37–41.

Rissolo, Dominique A.

2001 Ancient Maya Cave Use in the Yalahau Region, Northern Quintana Roo, Mexico. Ph.D. Dissertation. Department of Anthropology, University of California, Riverside.

Sanders, William T.

1955 An Archaeological Reconnaissance of Northern Quintana Roo. *Current Report* No. 24. Carnegie Institution of Washington, Washington, D.C.

Schackt, Jon

1984 The Tzuultak'a: Religious Lore and Cultural Processes Among the Kekchi. *Belizean Studies* 12(5):16–29.

Scott, Ann M.

1992 Cave Reconnaisance in the Copan Valley. Report presented to the Instituto Hondureño de Antropología e Historia, Copan.

Scott, Ann M., and Walter E. Little

2003 Contemporary Maya Beliefs and Cave Utilization: Implications for Archaeological Interpretations. Paper presented at the 68th Annual Meeting of the Society for American Archaeology, Milwaukee.

Seler, Eduard

1901 *Die Alten Ansiedlungen von Chaculá, im Distrikte Nentón des Departments Huehuetenango der Republik Guatemala.* Dietrich Reiner Verlag, Berlin.

Sharer, Robert J.

1993 Social Organization of the Late Classic Maya: Problems of Definition and Approaches. In *Lowland Maya Civilization in the Eighth Century A.D.* eds. Jeremy A. Sabloff and John S. Henderson, 91–110. Dumbarton Oaks Research Library and Collection, Washington, D.C.

Stone, Andrea J.

1995 *Images From the Underworld: Naj Tunich and the Tradition of Maya Cave Painting.* University of Texas Press, Austin.

Stuart, David

1997 The Hills Are Alive: Sacred Mountains in the Maya Cosmos. *Symbols,* Spring: 13–17. Harvard University, Cambridge.

Tarn, Nathaniel, and Martin Prechtel

1986 Constant Inconstancy: The Feminine Principal in Atiteco Mythology. In *Symbol and Meaning Beyond the Closed Community: Essays in Mesoamerican Ideas,* ed. Gary H. Gossen, 173–184. Institute of Mesoamerican Studies, Studies in Culture and Society, Vol. 1. State University of New York, Albany.

Tedlock, Barbara

1992 The Role of Dreams and Visionary Narratives in Mayan Cultural Survivals. *Ethnos* 20:453–476.

Thompson, Edward H.

1938 *The High Priest's Grave, Chichen Itza, Yucatan, Mexico.* Prepared for publication, with notes and introduction by J. Eric Thompson. Field Museum of Natural History, Anthropology Series 27, No. 1.

Thompson, J. Eric S.

1959 The Role of Caves in Maya Culture. *Mitteilungen aus dem Museum für Völkerkunde in Hamburg* 25:122–129.

1970 *Maya History and Religion.* University of Oklahoma Press, Norman.

1975 Introduction to the Reprint Edition. In *The Hill-Caves of Yucatan,* by Henry C. Mercer, vii–xliv. University of Oklahoma Press, Norman.

Villa Rojas, Alfonso

1945 *The Maya of East Central Quintana Roo.* Publication 599. Carnegie Institution of Washington, Washington, D.C.

Vogt, Evon Z.

1964 Ancient Maya and Comtemporary Tzotzil Cosmology: A Comment on Some Methodological Problems. *American Antiquity* 30:192–195.

1969 *Zinacantan: A Maya Community in the Highlands of Chiapas.* Harvard University Press, Cambridge.

Westfall, Richard S.

1977 *The Construction of Modern Science: Mechanisms and Mechanics.* Cambridge University Press, New York.

Wilson, Richard

1995 *Maya Resurgence in Guatemala: Q'eqchi' Experiences.* University of Oklahoma Press, Norman.

Index

Page numbers in italics indicate illustrations.